T0364815

Land Rover Freelander
Owners Workshop Manual

Martynn Randall

Models covered

(5636 - 256 - 2AZ1)

'Freelander 2' models (2WD and 4x4 versions) with 2.2 litre (2179cc) turbo-diesel engines

Does NOT cover petrol engine models

© Haynes Group Limited 2014

ABCDE
FGH

A book in the **Haynes Owners Workshop Manual Series**

ISBN **978 0 85733 636 1**

British Library Cataloguing in Publication Data
A catalogue record for this book is available from the British Library.

Printed in India

Haynes Group Limited
Sparkford, Yeovil, Somerset BA22 7JJ, England

Haynes North America, Inc
2801 Townsgate Road, Suite 340, Thousand Oaks, CA 91361

Disclaimer

Contents

Contents

REPAIRS AND OVERHAUL

Engine and Associated Systems

Transmission

Brakes and suspension

Body equipment

Wiring diagrams

REFERENCE

Index

The second generation of the popular Freelander model, was introduced in December 2006, with a choice of a 2.2 litre 4-cylinder turbo-diesel engine, or a 3.2 litre 6-cylinder petrol engine. The diesel engine was developed from a joint venture by the Ford motor company, and PSA – the French parent company of Peugeot and Citroen, whilst the petrol engine is of Volvo origin. Only available as a 5 door station wagon, at the model launch all models had permanent four wheel drive.

Although fashionably styled, the Freelander 2 has high ground clearance, power assisted steering, and fully independent suspension front and rear, making it a capable off-road performer, as well as exceeding current standards of on-road performance for this type of vehicle. Safety levels are further enhanced by features such as Terrain Reponse system, Traction control, ABS, triple front airbags, side airbags and head airbags, aswell as seatbelt pre-tensioners.

In September 2010, the range underwent a 'facelift', which involved changes to the internal and external appearance of the vehicle, and a revised version of the diesel engine introduced, featuring increased output with reduced emissions.

A two wheel drive version was added to the range in January 2011, where only the front wheels provide drive (FWD), appealing to owners who rarely venture away from paved roads.

This manual covers the following models:
a) 2.2 litre 4-cylinder diesel engines
b) Two-, and four-wheel drive models from 2006 to 2014
c) Manual and automatic transmissions
d) Does not cover petrol engines

Your Freelander 2 manual

The aim of this Manual is to help you get the best value from your vehicle. It can do so in several ways. It can help you decide what work must be done (even should you choose to get it done by a garage). It will also provide information on routine maintenance and servicing, and give a logical course of action and diagnosis when random faults occur. However, it is hoped that you will use the manual by tackling the work yourself. On simpler jobs it may even be quicker than booking the car into a garage and going there twice, to leave and collect it. Perhaps most important, a lot of money can be saved by avoiding the costs a garage must charge to cover its labour and overheads.

The manual has drawings and descriptions to show the function of the various components so that their layout can be understood. Tasks are described and photographed in a clear step-by-step sequence. The illustrations are numbered by the Section number and paragraph number to which they relate – if there is more than one illustration per paragraph, the sequence is denoted alphabetically.

References to the "left" or "right" of the vehicle are in the sense of a person in the driver's seat, facing forwards.

Acknowledgements

Thanks are due to Draper Tools, who provided some of the workshop tools, and to all those people at Sparkford who helped in the production of this manual.

This manual is not a direct reproduction of the vehicle manufacturer's data, and its publication should not be taken as implying any technical approval by the vehicle manufacturers or importers.

We take great pride in the accuracy of information given in this manual, but vehicle manufacturers make alterations and design changes during the production run of a particular vehicle of which they do not inform us. No liability can be accepted by the authors or publishers for loss, damage or injury caused by any errors in, or omissions from, the information given.

Project vehicles

The main vehicle used in the preparation of this manual, and which appears in many of the photographic sequences, was a 2007 Land Rover Freelander 2 with 2.2 Litre diesel engine and automatic transmission.

Land Rover Freelander 2

Working on your car can be dangerous. This page shows just some of the potential risks and hazards, with the aim of creating a safety-conscious attitude.

General hazards

Scalding

• Don't remove the radiator or expansion tank cap while the engine is hot.
• Engine oil, transmission fluid or power steering fluid may also be dangerously hot if the engine has recently been running.

Burning

• Beware of burns from the exhaust system and from any part of the engine. Brake discs and drums can also be extremely hot immediately after use.

Crushing

• When working under or near a raised vehicle, always supplement the jack with axle stands, or use drive-on ramps.
Never venture under a car which is only supported by a jack.
• Take care if loosening or tightening high-torque nuts when the vehicle is on stands. Initial loosening and final tightening should be done with the wheels on the ground.

Fire

• Fuel is highly flammable; fuel vapour is explosive.
• Don't let fuel spill onto a hot engine.
• Do not smoke or allow naked lights (including pilot lights) anywhere near a vehicle being worked on. Also beware of creating sparks (electrically or by use of tools).
• Fuel vapour is heavier than air, so don't work on the fuel system with the vehicle over an inspection pit.
• Another cause of fire is an electrical overload or short-circuit. Take care when repairing or modifying the vehicle wiring.
• Keep a fire extinguisher handy, of a type suitable for use on fuel and electrical fires.

Electric shock

• Ignition HT and Xenon headlight voltages can be dangerous, especially to people with heart problems or a pacemaker. Don't work on or near these systems with the engine running or the ignition switched on.

• Mains voltage is also dangerous. Make sure that any mains-operated equipment is correctly earthed. Mains power points should be protected by a residual current device (RCD) circuit breaker.

Fume or gas intoxication

• Exhaust fumes are poisonous; they can contain carbon monoxide, which is rapidly fatal if inhaled. Never run the engine in a confined space such as a garage with the doors shut.
• Fuel vapour is also poisonous, as are the vapours from some cleaning solvents and paint thinners.

Poisonous or irritant substances

• Avoid skin contact with battery acid and with any fuel, fluid or lubricant, especially antifreeze, brake hydraulic fluid and Diesel fuel. Don't syphon them by mouth. If such a substance is swallowed or gets into the eyes, seek medical advice.
• Prolonged contact with used engine oil can cause skin cancer. Wear gloves or use a barrier cream if necessary. Change out of oil-soaked clothes and do not keep oily rags in your pocket.
• Air conditioning refrigerant forms a poisonous gas if exposed to a naked flame (including a cigarette). It can also cause skin burns on contact.

Asbestos

• Asbestos dust can cause cancer if inhaled or swallowed. Asbestos may be found in gaskets and in brake and clutch linings. When dealing with such components it is safest to assume that they contain asbestos.

Special hazards

Hydrofluoric acid

• This extremely corrosive acid is formed when certain types of synthetic rubber, found in some O-rings, oil seals, fuel hoses etc, are exposed to temperatures above 4000C. The rubber changes into a charred or sticky substance containing the acid. *Once formed, the acid remains dangerous for years. If it gets onto the skin, it may be necessary to amputate the limb concerned.*
• When dealing with a vehicle which has suffered a fire, or with components salvaged from such a vehicle, wear protective gloves and discard them after use.

The battery

• Batteries contain sulphuric acid, which attacks clothing, eyes and skin. Take care when topping-up or carrying the battery.
• The hydrogen gas given off by the battery is highly explosive. Never cause a spark or allow a naked light nearby. Be careful when connecting and disconnecting battery chargers or jump leads.

Air bags

• Air bags can cause injury if they go off accidentally. Take care when removing the steering wheel and trim panels. Special storage instructions may apply.

Diesel injection equipment

• Diesel injection pumps supply fuel at very high pressure. Take care when working on the fuel injectors and fuel pipes.

⚠ *Warning: Never expose the hands, face or any other part of the body to injector spray; the fuel can penetrate the skin with potentially fatal results.*

Remember...

DO

• Do use eye protection when using power tools, and when working under the vehicle.

• Do wear gloves or use barrier cream to protect your hands when necessary.

• Do get someone to check periodically that all is well when working alone on the vehicle.

• Do keep loose clothing and long hair well out of the way of moving mechanical parts.

• Do remove rings, wristwatch etc, before working on the vehicle – especially the electrical system.

• Do ensure that any lifting or jacking equipment has a safe working load rating adequate for the job.

DON'T

• Don't attempt to lift a heavy component which may be beyond your capability – get assistance.

• Don't rush to finish a job, or take unverified short cuts.

• Don't use ill-fitting tools which may slip and cause injury.

• Don't leave tools or parts lying around where someone can trip over them. Mop up oil and fuel spills at once.

• Don't allow children or pets to play in or near a vehicle being worked on.

The following pages are intended to help in dealing with common roadside emergencies and breakdowns. You will find more detailed fault finding information at the back of the manual, and repair information in the main chapters.

If your car won't start and the starter motor doesn't turn

- ☐ If it's a model with automatic transmission, make sure the selector is in 'P' or 'N'.
- ☐ Open the bonnet, and make sure the battery terminals are clean and tight (unclip the battery cover for access).
- ☐ Switch on the headlights and try to start the engine. If the headlights go very dim when you're trying to start, the battery is probable flat. Get out of trouble by jump starting using a friends car.

If your car won't start even though the starter motor turns as normal

- ☐ Is there fuel in the tank?
- ☐ Is there moisture on electrical connections under the bonnet? Switch off the ignition, then wipe off any obvious dampness with a dry cloth. Spray a water-dispersant aerosol product (WD-40 or equivalent) on ignition and fuel system electrical connectors like those shown in the photos.

A Check the condition and security of the battery connections.

B Check the security of the fuel injection system components wiring plugs.

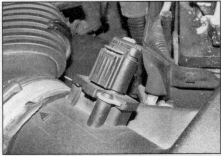

C Check the mass air flow sensor wiring plug.

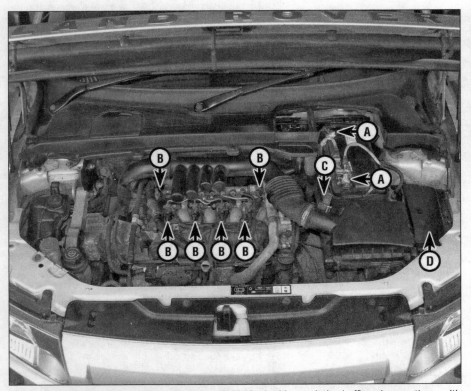

D Check the engine compartment fuses.

Check that electrical connections are secure (with the ignition switched off) and spray them with a water-dispersant spray like WD-40 if you suspect a problem due to damp.

Jump starting will get you out of trouble, but you must correct whatever made the battery go flat in the first place. There are three possibilities:

1 *The battery has been drained by repeated attempts to start, or by leaving the lights on.*

2 *The charging system is not working properly (alternator drivebelt slack or broken, alternator wiring fault or alternator itself faulty).*

3 *The battery itself is at fault (electrolyte low, or battery worn out).*

When jump-starting a car using a booster battery, observe the following precautions:

✓ Before connecting the booster battery, make sure that the ignition is switched off.

Caution: Remove the key in case the central locking engages when the jump leads are connected

✓ Ensure that all electrical equipment (lights, heater, wipers, etc) is switched off.

✓ Take note of any special precautions printed on the battery case.

✓ Make sure that the booster battery is the same voltage as the discharged one in the vehicle.

Jump starting

✓ f the battery is being jump-started from the battery in another vehicle, the two vehicles MUST NOT TOUCH each other.

✓ Make sure that the transmission is in neutral (or PARK, in the case of automatic transmission)

 Budget jump leads can be a false economy, as they often do not pass enough current to start large capacity or diesel engines. They can also get hot.

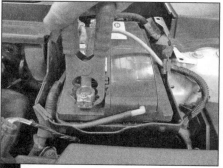

1 Connect one end of the red jump lead to the positive (+) terminal of the flat battery.

2 Connect the other end of the red lead to the positive (+) terminal of the booster battery.

3 Connect one end of the black jump lead to the negative (-) terminal of the booster battery.

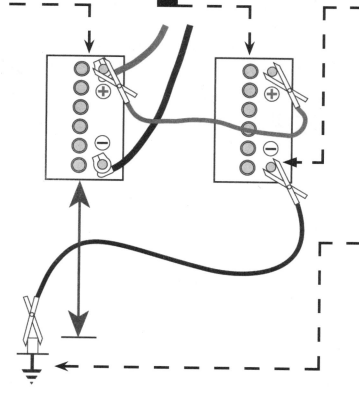

4 Connect the other end of the black jump lead to a bolt or bracket on the engine block, well away from the battery, on the vehicle to be started.

5 Make sure that the jump leads will not come into contact with the fan, drive-belts or other moving parts of the engine.

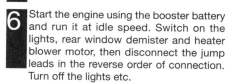

6 Start the engine using the booster battery and run it at idle speed. Switch on the lights, rear window demister and heater blower motor, then disconnect the jump leads in the reverse order of connection. Turn off the lights etc.

Identifying leaks

Puddles on the garage floor or drive, or obvious wetness under the bonnet or underneath the car, suggest a leak that needs investigating. It can sometimes be difficult to decide where the leak is coming from, especially if the engine bay is very dirty already. Leaking oil of fluid can also be blown rearwards by the passage of air under the car, giving a false impression of where the problem lies.

 Warning: *Most automotive oils and fluids are poisonous, Wash them off skin, and change out of contaminated clothing without delay.*

 The smell of a fluid leaking from the car may provide a clue to what's leaking. Some fluids are distinctly coloured. It may help to clean the car carefully and to park it over some clean paper overnight as an aid to locating the source of the leak. Remember that some leaks may only occur while the engine is running.

Sump oil

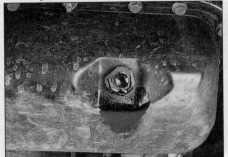

Engine oil may leak from the drain plug...

Oil from filter

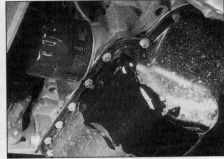

...or from the base of the oil filter.

Gearbox oil

Gearbox oil can leak from the seals at the inboard ends of the driveshafts.

Antifreeze

Leaking antifreeze often leaves a crystalline deposit like this.

Brake fluid

A leak occurring at a wheel is almost certainly brake fluid.

Power steering fluid

Power steering fluid may leak from the pipe connectors on the steering rack.

Towing

When all else fails, you may find yourself having to get a tow home – or of course you may be helping somebody else. Long-distance recovery should only be done by a garage or breakdown service. For shorter distances, DIY towing using another car is easy enough, but observe the following points:

☐ Use a proper tow-rope – they are not expensive. The vehicle being towed must display an ON TOW sign in its rear window.

☐ Always turn the ignition to the 'on' position when the vehicle is being towed, so that the steering lock is released, and that the direction indicator and brake lights will work.

☐ The front towing eyes are located under the front bumper. Rotate the fasteners anti-clockwise and remove the cover **(see illustration)**.

☐ The rear towing eye protrudes through the bumper cover **(see illustration)**.

☐ Before being towed, release the handbrake and make sure the transmission is in neutral.

☐ Land Rover insist that the vehicle should only be towed with all 4 wheels on the ground. If this is not possible, the vehicle should be lifted onto a recovery truck.

☐ Note that greater-than-usual pedal pressure will be required to operate the brakes, since the vacuum servo unit is only operational with the engine running, and no power assistance will be available for the steering.

☐ The driver of the car being towed must keep the tow-rope taut at all times to avoid snatching.

☐ Only drive at moderate speeds, and keep the distance towed to a minimum. Drive smoothly, and allow plenty of time for slowing down at junctions.

☐ Land Rover state that the vehicle should be towed at a speed of no more than 50 mph (80 kmh) for a distance of no more than 50 miles (80 km).

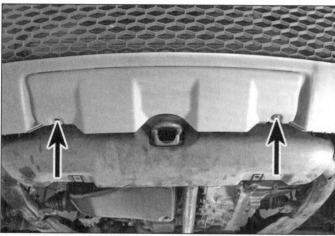

Rotate the fasteners anti-clockwise and remove the cover

Rear towing eye

Wheel changing

 Warning: Do not change a wheel in a situation where you risk being hit by another vehicle. On busy roads, try to stop in a lay-by or a gateway. Be wary of passing traffic while changing the wheel – it is easy to become distracted by the job in hand.

Preparation

☐ When a puncture occurs, stop as soon as it is safe to do so.

☐ Park on firm level ground, if possible, and well out of the way of other traffic. If jacking on a slope is unavoidable,

chock the wheel diagonally opposite the one to be removed on the downhill side, using the chock provided in the toolkit.

☐ Use hazard warning lights if necessary.

☐ Chock the wheel diagonally opposite the one being removed – a couple of large stones will do for this.

☐ If the ground is soft, use a flat piece of wood to spread the load under the jack.

Changing the wheel

1 The vehicle jack, toolkit and spare wheel are located under the luggage compartment floor panel. Lift the panel, pull it rearwards and remove it. Slacken the spare wheel locking ring, undo the retaining bolt and lift out the spare wheel ...

2 ... followed by the tool kit/jack.

3 Using the wheel brace supplied, slacken the roadwheel nuts half a turn each. The wheels may have special locking nuts – these are removed with a special tool, which should be provided with the wheelbrace (or it may be in the glovebox).

4 Position the jack head beneath the jacking point (indicated by a triangular mark) under the sill closest to the punctured wheel. Engage the jack head with the sill flange, then smoothly raise the vehicle undo the tyre is clear of the road surface.

5 Unscrew the wheel nuts, noting which way round they fit (tapered side inwards), and remove the wheel.

6 Fit the spare wheel, and screw on the nuts. Lightly tighten the nuts with the wheelbrace, then lower the vehicle to the ground. Securely tighten the wheel nuts. Note that the wheel nuts should be slackened and retightened to the specified torque at the earliest possible opportunity.

Caution: If a temporary 'space-saver' spare wheel is fitted, do not exceed 50 mph (80 kmh), and take particular care when cornering.

Finally . . .

☐ Remove the wheel chocks.

☐ Stow the punctured wheel and tools back in the luggage compartment, and secure them in position.

☐ Check the tyre pressure on the tyre just fitted. If it is low, or if you don't have a pressure gauge with you, drive slowly to the next garage and inflate the tyre to the correct pressure. In the case of the narrow 'space-saver' spare wheel this pressure is much higher than for a normal tyre.

☐ Have the punctured wheel repaired as soon as possible, or another puncture will leave you stranded.

Introduction

There are some very simple checks which need only take a few minutes to carry out, but which could save you a lot of inconvenience and expense.

These Weekly checks require no great skill or special tools, and the small amount of time they take to perform could prove to be very well spent, for example:

☐ Keeping an eye on tyre condition and pressures, will not only help to stop them wearing out prematurely, but could also save your life.

☐ Many breakdowns are caused by electrical problems. Battery-related faults are particularly common, and a quick check on a regular basis will often prevent the majority of these.

☐ If your car develops a brake fluid leak, the first time you might know about it is when your brakes don't work properly. Checking the level regularly will give advance warning of this kind of problem.

☐ If the oil or coolant levels run low, the cost of repairing any engine damage will be far greater than fixing the leak, for example.

Underbonnet check points

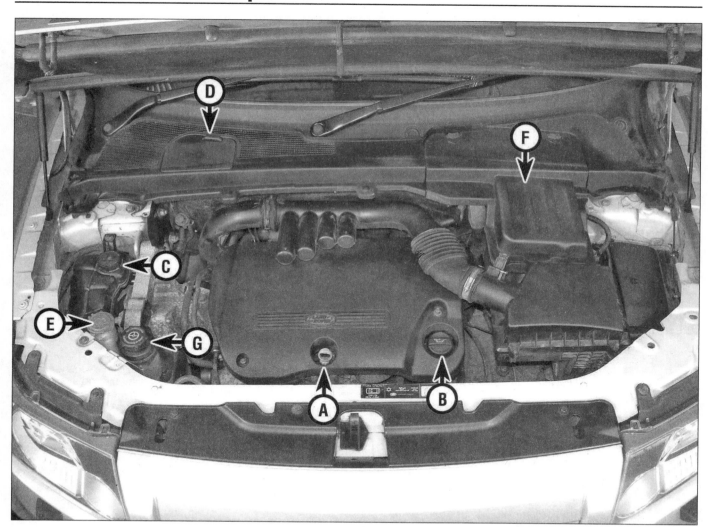

▲ **2.2 litre diesel Freelander 2**

A *Engine oil level dipstick*

B *Engine oil filler cap*

C *Coolant expansion tank*

D *Brake fluid reservoir (unclip the cover for access)*

E *Screen/headlight washer fluid reservoir*

F *Battery (unclip the cover for access)*

G *Power steering fluid reservoir*

Engine oil level

Before you start

✔ Make sure that your car is on level ground
✔ Check the oil level before the car is driven, or at least 5 minutes after the engine has been switched off.

 If the oil is checked immediately after driving the vehicle, some of the oil will remain in the upper engine components, resulting in an inaccurate reading on the dipstick!

The correct oil

Modern engines place great demands on their oil. It is very important that the correct oil for your car is used (See "*Lubricants and fluids*").

Car care

● If you have to add oil frequently, you should check whether you have any oil leaks. Place some clean paper under the car overnight, and check for stains in the morning. If there are no leaks, the engine may be burning oil (see "*Fault Finding*").

● Always maintain the level between the upper and lower dipstick marks. If the level is too low severe engine damage may occur. Oil seal failure may result if the engine is overfilled by adding too much oil.

● On all diesel models it is located on the right-hand front of the engine. It is brightly coloured for ease of location. See "*Underbonnet Check Points*" for the exact location of the dipstick.

1 Withdraw the dipstick. Using a clean rag or paper towel, wipe all the oil from the dipstick. Insert the clean dipstick into the tube as far as it will go, then withdraw it again.

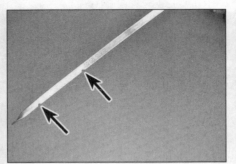

2 Note the oil level on the end of the dipstick, which should be between the upper MAX mark and the lower MIN mark. Approximately 1.5 litres of oil will raise the level from the lower mark to the upper mark.

3 Oil is added through the filler cap on top of the engine. Rotate the cap through a quarter-turn anti-clockwise and withdraw it. Top-up the level. A funnel may help to reduce spillage. Add the oil slowly, checking the level on the dipstick often. Do not overfill.

Coolant level

 Warning: DO NOT attempt to remove the expansion tank pressure cap when the engine is hot, as there is a very great risk of scalding. Do not leave open containers of coolant about, as it is poisonous.

Car care

● With a sealed-type cooling system, adding coolant should not be necessary on a regular basis. If frequent topping-up is required, it is likely there is a leak. Check the radiator, all hoses and joint faces for signs of staining or wetness, and rectify as necessary.

● It is important that antifreeze is used in the cooling system all year round, not just during the winter months. Don't top-up with water alone, as the antifreeze will become too diluted.

● The coolant level varies with the temperature of the engine. When the engine is cold, the coolant level should be on the MAX mark on the side of the expansion tank. When the engine is hot, the level will rise slightly.

1 If topping-up is necessary, wait until the engine is cold, then slowly unscrew the expansion tank filler cap anti-clockwise, to release any pressure in the system, and remove it.

2 Add a mixture of water and antifreeze through the expansion tank filler neck . ...

3 ... until the level is above the MIN mark, and below the MAX mark. Refit the cap, turning it clockwise as far as it will go until it is secure.

Brake/clutch fluid level

 Warning: Brake fluid can harm your eyes and damage painted surfaces, so use extreme caution when handling and pouring it.
Caution: Do not use fluid that has been standing open for some time, as it absorbs moisture from the air, which can cause a dangerous loss of braking effectiveness.
Note: *The fluid level in the reservoir will drop slightly as the brake pads wear down, but the fluid level must never be allowed to drop below the "MIN" mark.*

Before you start

✔ Make sure that your car is on level ground.

Safety first!

● If the reservoir requires repeated topping-up this is an indication of a fluid leak somewhere in the system, which should be investigated immediately.

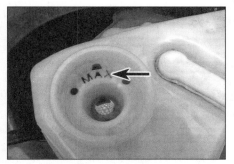

3 The MAX level is also indicated within the filler neck.

1 The brake master cylinder and fluid reservoir are mounted on the vacuum servo unit in the engine compartment on the right-hand side of the bulkhead. Unclip the cover for access.

4 On manual transmission models, the clutch master cylinder is supplied with fluid from the brake master cylinder reservoir. If topping-up is necessary, wipe the area around the filler cap with a clean rag before removing the cap. It's a good idea to inspect the reservoir. The fluid should be changed if dirt is visible.

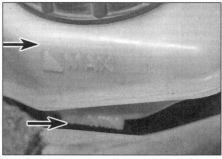

2 The MAX and MIN level marks are indicated on the side of the reservoir and the fluid level should be maintained between these marks at all times.

5 Place rags around the filler neck then carefully add fluid, avoiding spilling it on surrounding paintwork. Use only the specified hydraulic fluid; mixing different types of fluid can cause damage to the system and/ or a loss of braking effectiveness. After filling to the correct level, refit the cap securely. Wipe off any spilt fluid.

Power steering fluid level

Before you start

✔ Park the vehicle on level ground
✔ Set the steering wheel straight-ahead
✔ The engine should be cold and turned off

Safety first!

● The need for frequent topping-up indicates a leak, which should be investigated immediately.

Note: *For the check to be accurate, the steering must not be turned once the engine has been stopped.*

1 The reservoir is mounted at the right-hand side of the engine compartment.

2 Wipe clean the area around the filler cap, then unscrew it from the reservoir. The level should be between the marks on the reservoir.

3 If topping-up is necessary, use the specified type of fluid – do not overfill the reservoir. Take care not to introduce dirt into the system when topping-up. When the level is correct, securely refit the cap.

Screen/headlight washer fluid level

● Screenwash additives not only keep the windscreen clean during foul weather, they also prevent the washer system freezing in cold weather – which is when you are likely to need it most. Don't top up using plain water as the screenwash will become too diluted, and will freeze during cold weather.

 Warning: On no account use coolant antifreeze in the washer system – this could discolour or damage paintwork.

1 The reservoir for the windscreen and rear window, and headlight (where applicable) washer systems is located in the front right-hand corner of the engine compartment. If topping up is necessary, open the cap.

2 When topping-up the reservoir a screenwash additive should be added in the quantities recommended on the bottle.

Wiper blades

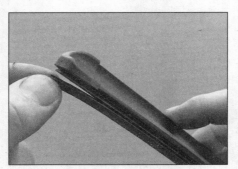

1 Check the condition of the wiper blades. If they are cracked or show any signs of deterioration, or if the glass swept area is smeared, renew them. For maximum clarity of vision, wiper blades should be renewed annually, as a matter of course.

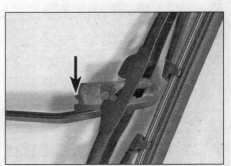

2 On rear wiper blades, pull the blade away from the screen, rotate it 90°, depress the clip and slide it from the arm.

Front wiper blades

Set the wipers in the 'Service position' by switching off the ignition, then within 3 seconds, pull the wiper switch down to the single wipe position, and hold it briefly.

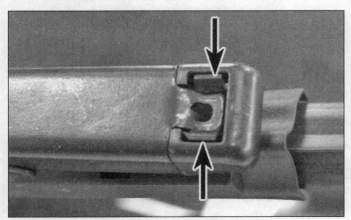

3 Depress the clips and pivot the blade away...

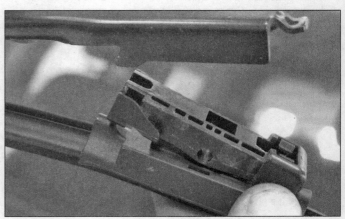

4 ... and slide it from the arm.

Battery

Caution: Before carrying out any work on the vehicle battery, read the precautions given in "Safety first" at the start of this manual.

✔ Make sure that the battery tray is in good condition, and that the clamp is tight.

Corrosion on the tray, retaining clamp and the battery itself can be removed with a solution of water and baking soda. Thoroughly rinse all cleaned areas with water. Any metal parts damaged by corrosion should be covered with a zinc-based primer, then painted.

✔ Periodically (approximately every three months), check the charge condition of the battery as described in Chapter 5A Section 3.
✔ If the battery is flat, and you need to jump start your vehicle, see Section 4.

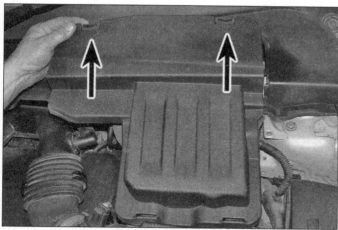

1 The battery is located on the rear left-hand side of the engine compartment. Unclip the cover for access. The exterior of the battery should be inspected periodically for damage such as a cracked case or cover.

2 Check the tightness of the battery cable clamps to ensure good electrical connections. You should not be able to move them. Also check each cable for cracks and frayed conductors.

HAYNES HINT

Battery corrosion can be kept to a minimum by applying a layer of petroleum jelly to the clamps and terminals after they are reconnected.

3 If corrosion (white, fluffy deposits) is evident, remove the cables from the battery terminals, clean them with a small wire brush, then refit them. Automotive stores sell a tool for cleaning the battery post...

4 ... as well as the battery cable clamps

Tyre condition and pressure

It is very important that tyres are in good condition, and at the correct pressure – having a tyre failure at any speed is highly dangerous. Tyre wear is influenced by driving style – harsh braking and acceleration, or fast cornering, will all produce more rapid tyre wear. As a general rule, the front tyres wear out faster the the rears. Interchanging the tyres from front to rear ("rotating" the tyres) may result in more even wear. However, if this is completely effective, you may have the expense of replacing all four tyres at once!

Remove any nails or stones embedded in the tread before they penetrate the tyre to cause deflation. If removal of a nail does reveal that the tyre has been punctured, refit the nail so that its point of penetration is marked. Then immediately change the wheel, and have the tyre repaired by a tyre dealer.

Regularly check the tyres for damage in the form of cuts or bulges, especially in the side walls. Periodically remove the wheels, and clean any dirt or mud from the inside and outside surfaces. Examine the wheel rims for signs of rusting, corrosion or other damage. Light alloy wheels are easily damaged by "kerbing" whilst parking; steel wheels may also become dented or buckled. A new wheel is very often the only way to overcome severe damage.

New tyres should be balanced when they are fitted, but it may become necessary to re-balance them as they ear, or if the balance weights fitted to the wheel rim should fall off. Unbalanced tyres will wear more quickly, as will the steering and suspension components. Wheel imbalance is normally signified by vibration, particularly at t certain speed (typically around 50 mph). If this vibration is felt only through the steering wheel, then it is likely that just the front wheels need balancing. If, however, the vibration is felt through the whole car, the rear wheels could be out of balance. Wheel balancing should be carried out by a tyre dealer or garage.

Caution: Land Rover state that if new tyres are to be fitted, ensure they are fitted to the rear axle only or both front and rear axles. New tyres should not be fitted to the front axle only.

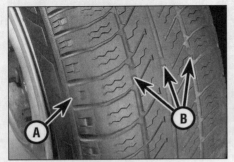

1 *Tread Depth - visual check*
The original tyres have tread wear safety bands (B), which will appear when the tread depth reaches approximately 1.6 mm. The band positions are indicated by a triangular mark on the tyre sidewall (A).

2 *Tread Depth - manual check*
Alternatively, tread wear can be monitored with a simple, inexpensive device known as a tread depth indicator gauge.

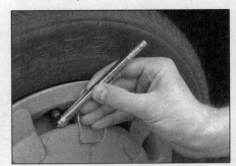

3 *Tyre Pressure Check*
Check the tyre pressures regularly with the tyres cold. Do not adjust the tyre pressures immediately after the vehicle has been used, or an inaccurate setting will result.

Tyre tread wear patterns

Shoulder Wear

Underinflation (wear on both sides)
Under-inflation will cause overheating of the tyre, because the tyre will flex too much, and the tread will not sit correctly on the road surface. This will cause a loss of grip and excessive wear, not to mention the danger of sudden tyre failure due to heat build-up.
Check and adjust pressures
Incorrect wheel camber (wear on one side)
Repair or renew suspension parts
Hard cornering
Reduce speed!

Centre Wear

Overinflation
Over-inflation will cause rapid wear of the centre part of the tyre tread, coupled with reduced grip, harsher ride, and the danger of shock damage occurring in the tyre casing.
Check and adjust pressures

If you sometimes have to inflate your car's tyres to the higher pressures specified for maximum load or sustained high speed, don't forget to reduce the pressures to normal afterwards.

Uneven Wear

Front tyres may wear unevenly as a result of wheel misalignment. Most tyre dealers and garages can check and adjust the wheel alignment (or "tracking") for a modest charge.
Incorrect camber or castor
Repair or renew suspension parts
Malfunctioning suspension
Repair or renew suspension parts
Unbalanced wheel
Balance tyres
Incorrect toe setting
Adjust front wheel alignment
Note: *The feathered edge of the tread which typifies toe wear is best checked by feel.*

Bulbs and fuses

✔ Check all external lights and the horn. Refer to the appropriate Sections of Chapter 12 for details if any of the circuits are found to be inoperative.

✔ Visually check all accessible wiring connectors, harnesses and retaining clips for security, and for signs of chafing or damage.

HAYNES HiNT *If you need to check your brake lights and indicators unaided, back up to a wall or garage door and operate the lights. The reflected light should show if they are working properly.*

1 If a single indicator light, brake light or headlight has failed, it is likely that a bulb has blown and will need to be replaced. Refer to Chapter 12 for details. If both brake lights have failed, it is possible that the stop-light switch operated by the brake pedal has failed. Refer to Chapter 9 Section 18 for details.

2 If more than one indicator light or headlight has failed, it is likely that either a fuse has blown or that there is a fault in the circuit (see Chapter 12 Section 2). The main fusebox is located behind the passengers glovebox. A further fusebox is located in the left-hand side of the engine compartment, with a further fusebox beneath the luggage compartment floor. To access the main fusebox, remove the glovebox as described in Chapter 11 Section 24.

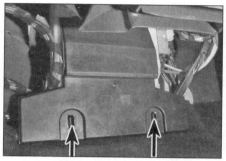

3 Release the clips to remove the main fusebox cover beneath the facia

4 The luggage compartment fusebox is beneath the floor panel

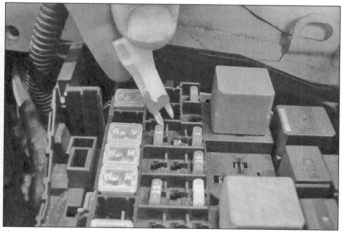

5 To replace a blown fuse, pull it out directly from the fusebox, using the tweezers clipped to the underside of the engine compartment fusebox lid. Fit a new fuse of the same rating, available from car accessory shops. It is important that you find the reason that the fuse blew (see 'Electrical fault finding' in Chapter 12 Section 2).

Lubricants and fluids

Engine oil:

Models without diesel particulate filter . . . . 5W/30 meeting Ford specification 913-B. Eg. Castrol Magnatec 5W/30 A1

Models with diesel particulate filter . . . . 5W/30 meeting Ford specification 934-B

Coolant . . . . Ethylene-glycol based antifreeze, containing no methanol with only Organic Acid Technology (OAT) corrosion inhibitors. Eg. Texaco XLC or Castrol SF

Transmission

Manual gearbox:
  Vehicles up to 2011 model year . . . . Castrol MTF 97309
  Vehicles from 2011 model year . . . . Castrol BOT 350 M3
Automatic gearbox:
  Vehicles up to 2011 model year . . . . Esso JWS3309
  Vehicles from 2011 model year . . . . Nippon AW-1
Transfer case . . . . Castrol BOT 118
Haldex coupling . . . . STAT OIL SL01-301
Final drive . . . . Castrol EPX

Brake/clutch fluid . . . . Hydraulic fluid to DOT 4 to ISO 4925 specification

Power steering fluid . . . . Pentosin CHF202

Tyre pressures

Pressures apply to original-equipment tyres, and may vary if any other make or type of tyre is fitted; check with the tyre manufacturer or supplier for correct pressures if necessary.

Vehicles up to 2013 model year

On vehicles up to 2013 model year, the tyre pressures are listed on a label attached to the drivers door pillar.

Vehicles 2013 model year-on

Note: *Pressures should be checked when the tyres are cold.*

Tyre size	Front	Rear
225/65 R17 H	2.3 bar (33 psi)	2.3 bar (33 psi)
235/65 R17 V	2.2 bar (32 psi)	2.2 bar (32 psi)
235/60 R18 V	2.2 bar (32 psi)	2.2 bar (32 psi)
235/55 R19 V	2.4 bar (35 psi)	2.4 bar (35 psi)
235/55 R19 H	2.4 bar (35 psi)	2.4 bar (35 psi)

Chapter 1
Routine maintenance and servicing

Contents

Degrees of difficulty

Easy, suitable for novice with little experience | **Fairly easy,** suitable for beginner with some experience | **Fairly difficult,** suitable for competent DIY mechanic | **Difficult,** suitable for experienced DIY mechanic | **Very difficult,** suitable for expert DIY or professional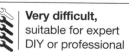

Lubricants and fluids............................... Refer to 'Weekly checks'

Capacities

Engine oil (with filter):
  All diesel engines .... 5.9 litres
  Difference between dipstick maximum and minimum marks....... 1.5 litres
Cooling system... 8.5 llitres
Fuel tank .... 68 litres
Manual transmission .... 1.9 litres
Automatic transmission (initial dry fill) .... 7.0 litres
Transfer case .... 0.75 litres
Final drive... 0.7 litres
Haldex coupling .... 0.65 litres

Cooling system

Protection at mixture of 50% antifreeze and 50% water............ –40°C

Braking system

Brake pad friction material minimum thickness (front and rear)....... 2.0 mm

Torque wrench settings

	Nm	lbf ft
Automatic transmission:		
Drain plug	47	35
Filler plug	39	29
Level plug	7	4
Cylinder block drain plug	23	17
Engine oil drain plug	20	15
Engine oil filter cover	25	18
Manual transmission		
Drain plug	30	22
Filler plug	35	26
Roadwheel nuts	133	98

1 Maintenance schedule

1 The maintenance intervals in this manual are provided with the assumption that you, not the dealer, will be carrying out the work. These are the minimum maintenance intervals recommended by us for cars driven daily. If you wish to keep your car in peak condition at all times, you may wish to perform some of these procedures more often. We encourage frequent maintenance, because it enhances the efficiency, performance and resale value of your car.

2 If the car is driven in dusty areas, used to tow a trailer, or driven frequently at slow speeds (idling in traffic) or on short journeys, more frequent maintenance intervals are recommended.

Every 250 miles or weekly
☐ Refer to 'Weekly checks'

Every 6000 miles or 6 months, whichever occurs first
☐ Renew the engine oil and filter (Section 4).

Note: *Frequent oil and filter changes are good for the engine. We recommend changing the oil at the mileage specified here, or at least twice a year if the mileage covered is less.*

Every 12 000 miles or 12 months, whichever occurs first
In addition to the item listed in the previous service, carry out the following:

☐ Check the battery and clean the terminals (Section 5).
☐ Check the auxiliary drivebelt (Section 6).
☐ Check the electrical system (Section 7).
☐ Check under the bonnet for fluid leaks and hose condition (Section 8).
☐ Check the condition of all engine compartment wiring (Section 9).
☐ Check the condition of the air conditioning components (Section 10).
☐ Check the seat belts (Section 11).
☐ Check the antifreeze concentration (Section 12).
☐ Check the steering, suspension and roadwheels (Section 13).
☐ Check the driveshaft rubber gaiters and CV joints (Section 14).
☐ Check the exhaust system (Section 15).
☐ Check the underbody, and all fuel/brake lines (Section 16).
☐ Check the braking system (Section 17).
☐ Check the doors and bonnet, and lubricated their hinges and locks (Section 18).
☐ Road test (Section 21).
☐ Renew the pollen filter (Section 19).
☐ Drain the fuel sedimentor (Section 20).
☐ Reset the service indicator (Section 22).

Every 24 months or 24 000 miles, whichever occurs first
☐ Remove the roadwheels, and apply anti-seize grease to the hubs (Section 23).
☐ Renew the air cleaner element (Section 24).
☐ Renew the fuel filter element (Section 25).

Every 3 years, regardless of mileage
☐ Renew the brake fluid (Section 26).

Every 6 years, regardless of mileage
☐ Replace all flexible brake hoses (Section 27).

Every 9 years, or 144 000 miles, whichever occurs first
☐ Renew the auxiliary drivebelt (Section 28). Vehicles from 2013 model year-on.
☐ Renew the timing belt, tensioner and idler pulley (Section 29). Vehicles from 2013 model year-on.

Note: *It is strongly recommended that the timing belt renewal interval is halved to 72 000 miles on vehicles which are subjected to intensive use, ie, mainly short journeys or a lot of stop-start driving. The actual belt renewal interval is therefore very much up to the individual owner, but bear in mind that severe engine damage will result if the belt breaks.*

Every 10 years, or 150 000 miles, whichever occurs first
☐ Renew the auxiliary drivebelt (Section 28). Vehicles upto 2013 model year.
☐ Renew the timing belt, tensioner and idler pulley (Section 29). Vehicles upto 2013 model year.

Note: *It is strongly recommended that the timing belt renewal interval is halved to 75 000 miles on vehicles which are subjected to intensive use, ie, mainly short journeys or a lot of stop-start driving. The actual belt renewal interval is therefore very much up to the individual owner, but bear in mind that severe engine damage will result if the belt breaks.*

☐ Renew the manual transmission oil (Section 30).
☐ Renew the automatic transmission oil (Section 31).
☐ Check the transfer case oil – 4x4 models only (Section 32).
☐ Renew the rear final drive oil – 4x4 models only (Section 33).

Every 10 years, regardless of mileage
☐ Renew the coolant (Section 34).

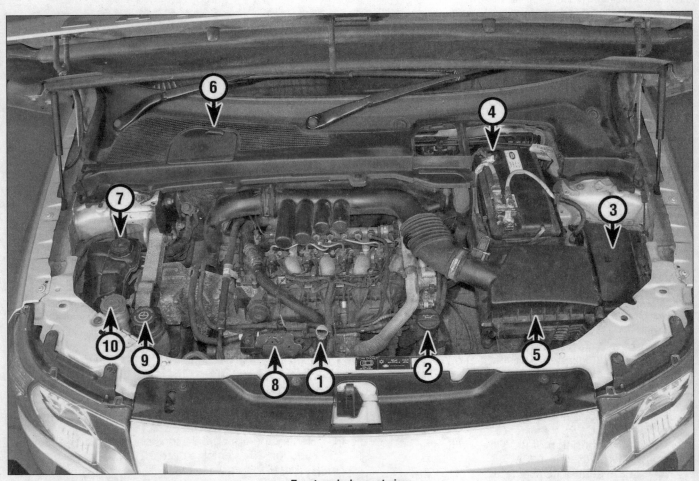

Front underbonnet view

1 Engine oil level dipstick
2 Engine oil filler cap
3 Engine compartment fuse/relay box
4 Battery negative terminal clamp

5 Air filter cover
6 Brake fluid reservoir cover
7 Coolant expansion tank cap
8 Fuel filter

9 Power steering fluid reservoir
10 Windscreen/headlamp washer fluid
   reservoir

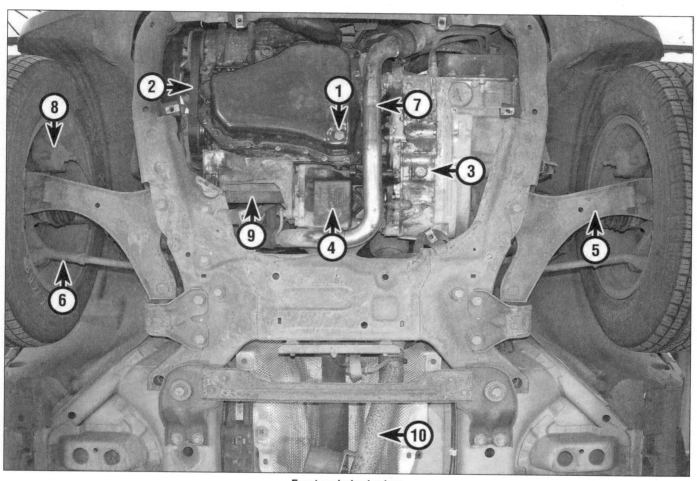

Front underbody view

1 Engine oil drain plug
2 Auxiliary drivebelt
3 Transmission drain/level plug (Automatic transmission shown)
4 Transfer case
5 Lower control arm
6 Track rod end
7 Turbocharger-to-intercooler pipe
8 Brake caliper
9 Right-hand driveshaft
10 Front exhaust pipe

Rear underbody view

1 Haldex coupling
2 Final drive filler plug
3 Rear anti-roll bar

4 Rear transverse link
5 Front transverse link
6 Trailing arm

7 Driveshaft
8 Fuel tank
9 Handbrake cable

2 General information

1 This Chapter is designed to help the home mechanic maintain his/her car for safety, economy, long life and peak performance.

2 The Chapter contains a master maintenance schedule, followed by Sections dealing specifically with each task in the schedule. Visual checks, adjustments, component renewal and other helpful items are included. Refer to the accompanying illustrations of the engine compartment and the underside of the car for the locations of the various components.

3 Servicing your car in accordance with the mileage/time maintenance schedule and the following Sections will provide a planned maintenance programme, which should result in a long and reliable service life. This is a comprehensive plan, so maintaining some items but not others at the specified service intervals, will not produce the same results.

4 As you service your car, you will discover that many of the procedures can – and should – be grouped together, because of the particular procedure being performed, or because of the proximity of two otherwise-unrelated components to one another. For example, if the car is raised for any reason, the exhaust can be inspected at the same time as the suspension and steering components.

5 The first step in this maintenance programme is to prepare yourself before the actual work begins. Read through all the Sections relevant to the work to be carried out, then make a list and gather all the parts and tools required. If a problem is encountered, seek advice from a parts specialist, or a dealer service department.

3 Regular maintenance

1 If, from the time the car is new, the routine maintenance schedule is followed closely, and frequent checks are made of fluid levels and high-wear items, as suggested throughout this manual, the engine will be kept in relatively good running condition, and the need for additional work will be minimised.

2 It is possible that there will be times when the engine is running poorly due to the lack of regular maintenance. This is even more likely if a used car, which has not received regular and frequent maintenance checks, is purchased. In such cases, additional work may need to be carried out, outside of the regular maintenance intervals.

3 If engine wear is suspected, a compression test (refer to Chapter 2A Section 2) will provide valuable information regarding the overall performance of the main internal components. Such a test can be used as a basis to decide on the extent of the work to be carried out. If, for example, a compression test indicates serious internal engine wear, conventional maintenance as described in this Chapter will not greatly improve the performance of the engine, and may prove a waste of time and money, unless extensive overhaul work is carried out first.

4 The following series of operations are those most often required to improve the performance of a generally poor-running engine:

Primary operations

a) Clean, inspect and test the battery (see 'Weekly checks' and Section 5).
b) Check all the engine-related fluids (refer to 'Weekly checks').
c) Check the condition and tension of the auxiliary drivebelt (Section 6).
d) Check the condition of all hoses, and check for fluid leaks (Section 8).
e) Renew the fuel filter (Section 25).

f) Check the glow plugs (Chapter 5B Section 2).
g) Check the condition of the air filter, and renew if necessary (Section 24).

5 If the above operations do not prove fully effective, carry out the following secondary operations:

Secondary operations

6 All items listed under Primary operations, plus the following:
a) Check the charging system (Chapter 5A Section 5).
b) Check the fuel system (Chapter 4A Section 9).

4 Engine oil and filter renewal

Note: A new engine oil drain plug sealing washer will be required.

1 Frequent oil changes are the most important preventive maintenance the DIY home mechanic can give the engine, because ageing oil becomes diluted and contaminated, which leads to premature engine wear.

2 Before starting this procedure, gather together all the necessary tools and materials. Also make sure that you have plenty of clean rags and newspapers handy, to mop-up any spills. Ideally, the engine oil should be warm, as it will drain more easily and more built-up sludge will be removed with it. Take care not to touch the exhaust or any other hot parts of the engine when working under the car. To avoid any possibility of scalding and to protect yourself from possible skin irritants and other harmful contaminants in used engine oils, it is advisable to wear gloves when carrying out this work.

3 Raise the front of the vehicle and support it securely on axle stands (see 'Vehicle jacking and support').

4 Release the 6 fasteners and remove the engine undershield (see illustration).

5 Place a drain tray under the engine, unscrew the oil filter plastic cover from the oil filter housing, then remove and discard the

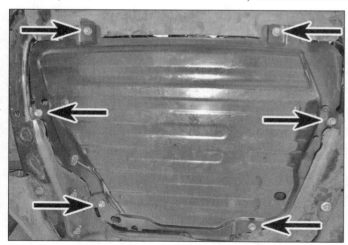

4.4 Engine undershield fasteners

4.5a The oil filter cover is located at the front of the engine (radiator removed for clarity)

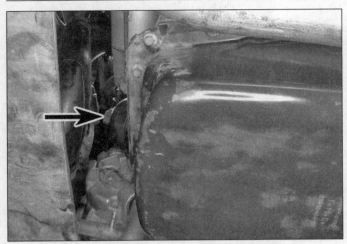

4.5b Oil filter cover viewed from underneath

4.5c Remove the cover complete with filter element

4.7a Unscrew the engine oil drain plug

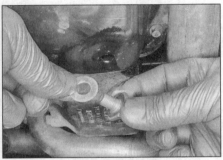

4.7b Renew the drain plug sealing washer

sealing washer. Clean the area around the drain plug opening, and fit the new plug. Tighten the plug to the specified torque.

10 Fit the new O-ring seal onto the filter cover and lubricate it with a little engine oil **(see illustration)**.

11 Locate the new paper element on the cover **(see illustration)**, then screw the assembly into the filter housing and tighten it to the specified torque.

12 Refit the engine undershield, remove the old oil and all tools from under the car, then lower the car to the ground.

13 Remove the dipstick, then unscrew the oil filler cap from the cylinder head cover. Fill the engine, using the correct grade and type of oil (see 'Weekly checks'). An oil can spout or funnel may help to reduce spillage. Pour in half the specified quantity of oil first, then wait a few minutes for the oil to run to the sump. Continue adding oil a small quantity at a time until the level is up to the lower mark on the dipstick. Refit the filler cap.

paper element **(see illustrations)**. Discard the cover O-ring seal – a new one should be supplied with the new filter element. Be prepared for fluid spillage

6 Clean the filter housing and cover.

7 Unscrew the engine oil drain plug (located at the lowest point of the sump) about half a turn. Position the draining container under the

drain plug, then remove the plug completely. Note that the plug sealing ring must be renewed **(see illustrations)**.

8 Allow some time for the oil to drain, noting that it may be necessary to reposition the container as the oil flow slows to a trickle.

9 After all the oil has drained, wipe off the drain plug with a clean rag, and fit a new

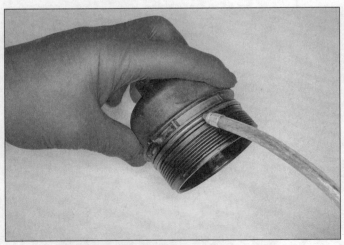

4.10 Renew the cover O-ring seal, and lubricate it

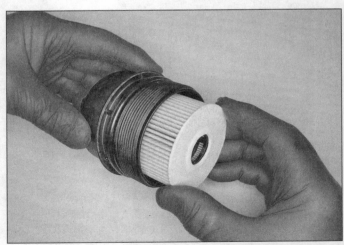

4.11 Insert the new oil filter element into the cover

14 Start the engine and run it for a few minutes; check for leaks. Note that there may be a delay of a few seconds before the oil pressure warning light goes out when the engine is first started, as the oil circulates through the engine oil galleries and the new oil filter before the pressure builds-up.

15 Switch off the engine, and wait a few minutes for the oil to settle in the sump once more. With the new oil circulated and the filter completely full, recheck the level on the dipstick, and add more oil as necessary.

16 Dispose of the used engine oil safely, with reference to *General Repair Procedures*.

5 Battery maintenance and charging

⚠️ *Warning: Certain precautions must be followed when checking and servicing the battery. Hydrogen gas, which is highly flammable, is always present in the battery cells, so keep lighted tobacco and all other open flames and sparks away from the battery. The electrolyte inside the battery is actually dilute sulphuric acid, which will cause injury if splashed on your skin or in your eyes. It will also ruin clothes and painted surfaces. When disconnecting the battery, always detach the negative (earth) lead first and connect it last.*

Note: *Before disconnecting the battery, refer to Battery disconnection in Chapter 5A Section 4.*

General

1 A routine preventive maintenance programme for the battery in your car is the only way to ensure quick and reliable starts. For general maintenance, refer to *'Weekly checks'* at the start of this manual. Also at the front of the manual is information on jump starting. For details of removing and installing the battery, refer to Chapter 5A Section 4.

Battery electrolyte level

2 On models not equipped with a sealed or 'maintenance-free' battery, check the electrolyte level of all six battery cells.

3 The level must be approximately 10 mm above the plates; this may be shown by maximum and minimum level lines marked on the battery's casing.

4 If the level is low, use a coin or screwdriver to release the filler/vent cap, and add distilled water. Do not overfill – this can actually render the battery useless. To improve access to the centre caps, it may be helpful to remove the battery hold-down clamp.

5 Install and securely retighten the cap, then wipe up any spillage.

Caution: Overfilling the cells may cause electrolyte to spill over during periods of heavy charging, causing corrosion or damage.

Charging

⚠️ *Warning: When batteries are being charged, hydrogen gas, which is very explosive and flammable, is produced. Do not smoke, or allow open flames, near a charging or a recently-charged battery. If the battery is being charged indoors, ensure this is done in a well-ventilated area. Wear eye protection when near the battery during charging. Also, make sure the charger is unplugged before connecting or disconnecting the battery from the charger.*

6 Slow-rate charging is the best way to restore a battery that's discharged to the point where it will not start the engine. It's also a good way to maintain the battery charge in a car that's only driven a few miles between starts. Maintaining the battery charge is particularly important in winter, when the battery must work harder to start the engine, and electrical accessories that drain the battery are in greater use.

7 Check the battery case for any instructions regarding charging the battery. Some maintenance-free batteries may require a particularly low charge rate or other special conditions, if they are not to be damaged.

8 It's best to use a one- or two-amp battery charger (sometimes called a 'trickle' charger), or a 'Smart/intelligent' charger. They are the safest, and put the least strain on the battery. For a faster charge, you can use a higher-amperage charger, but don't use one rated more than 1/10th the amp/hour rating of the battery (ie, no more than 5 amps, typically). Rapid boost charges that claim to restore the power of the battery in one to two hours are hardest on the battery, and can damage batteries not in good condition. This type of charging should only be used in emergency situations.

9 The average time necessary to charge a battery should be listed in the instructions that come with the charger. As a general rule, a trickle charger will charge a battery in 12 to 16 hours.

6 Auxiliary drivebelt check

General

1 The auxiliary drivebelt is of flat, multi-ribbed type, and is located on the right-hand end of the engine. It drives the alternator, power steering pump, and air conditioning compressor from the engine's crankshaft pulley.

2 The good condition and proper tension of the auxiliary drivebelt is critical to the operation of the engine. It must, therefore, be regularly inspected.

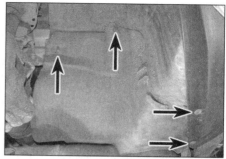

6.4 Undo the fasteners and remove the lower section of the liner

Check

3 Slacken the right-hand front roadwheel nuts, raise the front of the vehicle, and support it securely on axle stands (see *'Vehicle jacking and support'*). Remove the roadwheel.

4 Undo the fasteners and remove the lower section of the wheelarch liner to access the belt **(see illustration)**.

5 Using an inspection light or a small electric torch, and rotating the engine with a spanner applied to the crankshaft pulley bolt, check the whole length of the drivebelt for cracks, separation of the rubber, and torn or worn ribs. Also check for fraying and glazing, which gives the drivebelt a shiny appearance.

6 Both sides of the drivebelt should be inspected, which means you will have to twist the drivebelt to check the underside. Use your fingers to feel the drivebelt where you can't see it. If you are in any doubt as to the condition of the drivebelt, renew it as described in Section 28.

Tension

7 The auxiliary drivebelt is tensioned by an automatic tensioner; regular checks are not required, and manual 'adjustment' is not possible.

8 If you suspect that a drivebelt is slipping and/or running slack, or that the tensioner is otherwise faulty, it and/or an idler pulley must be renewed.

7 Electrical system check

1 If you suspect that a drivebelt is slipping and/or running slack, or that the tensioner is otherwise faulty, it must be renewed.

2 Check for satisfactory operation of the instrument panel, its illumination and warning lights, the switches and their function lights.

3 Check the horns for satisfactory operation.

4 Check all other electrical equipment for satisfactory operation.

5 If a fault is suspected, proceed as described in Chapter 12 Section 2.

8 Underbonnet check for fluid leaks and hose condition

1 Visually inspect the engine joint faces, gaskets and seals for any signs of water or oil leaks. Pay particular attention to the areas around the cylinder head cover, cylinder head, oil filter and sump joint faces. Bear in mind that, over a period of time, some very slight seepage from these areas is to be expected – what you are really looking for is any indication of a serious leak. Should a leak be found, renew the offending gasket or oil seal by referring to the appropriate Chapters in this manual
2 Also check the security and condition of all the engine-related pipes and hoses, and all braking system pipes and hoses and fuel lines. Ensure that all cable ties or securing clips are in place, and in good condition. Clips which are broken or missing can lead to chafing of the hoses, pipes or wiring, which could cause more serious problems in the future.
3 Carefully check the radiator hoses and heater hoses along their entire length. Renew any hose which is cracked, swollen or deteriorated. Cracks will show up better if the hose is squeezed. Pay close attention to the hose clips that secure the hoses to the cooling system components. Hose clips can pinch and puncture hoses, resulting in cooling system leaks. If the crimped-type hose clips are used, it may be a good idea to update them with Jubilee clips.
4 Inspect all the cooling system components (hoses, joint faces, etc) for leaks
5 Where any problems are found on system components, renew the component or gasket with reference to Chapter 3.
6 With the car raised, inspect the fuel tank and filler neck for punctures, cracks and other damage. The connection between the filler neck and tank is especially critical. Sometimes a rubber filler neck or connecting hose will leak due to loose retaining clamps or deteriorated rubber.
7 Carefully check all rubber hoses and metal

A leak in the cooling system will usually show up as white-or antifreeze coloured deposits on the area adjoining the leak.

fuel lines leading away from the fuel tank. Check for loose connections, deteriorated hoses, crimped lines, and other damage. Pay particular attention to the vent pipes and hoses, which often loop up around the filler neck and can become blocked or crimped. Follow the lines to the front of the car, carefully inspecting them all the way. Renew damaged sections as necessary. Similarly, whilst the car is raised, take the opportunity to inspect all underbody brake fluid pipes and hoses.
8 From within the engine compartment, check the security of all fuel, vacuum and brake hose attachments and pipe unions, and inspect all hoses for kinks, chafing and deterioration.
9 Check the condition of the power steering and, where applicable, the automatic transmission fluid pipes and hoses.

9 Engine compartment wiring check

1 With the car parked on level ground, apply the handbrake firmly and open the bonnet. Using an inspection light or a small electric torch, check all visible wiring within and beneath the engine compartment.
2 What you are looking for is wiring that is obviously damaged by chafing against sharp edges, or against moving suspension/transmission components and/or the auxiliary drivebelt, by being trapped or crushed between carelessly-refitted components, or melted by being forced into contact with the hot engine castings, coolant pipes, etc. In almost all cases, damage of this sort is caused in the first instance by incorrect routing on reassembly after previous work has been carried out.
3 Depending on the extent of the problem, damaged wiring may be repaired by rejoining the break or splicing-in a new length of wire, using solder to ensure a good connection, and remaking the insulation with adhesive insulating tape or heat-shrink tubing, as appropriate. If the damage is extensive, given the implications for the car's future reliability, the best long-term answer may well be to renew that entire section of the loom, however expensive this may appear.
4 When the actual damage has been repaired, ensure that the wiring loom is rerouted correctly, so that it is clear of other components, and not stretched or kinked, and is secured out of harm's way using the plastic clips, guides and ties provided.
5 Check all electrical connectors, ensuring that they are clean, securely fastened, and that each is locked by its plastic tabs or wire clip, as appropriate. If any connector shows external signs of corrosion (accumulations of white or green deposits, or streaks of 'rust'), or if any is thought to be dirty, it must be unplugged and cleaned using electrical contact cleaner. If the connector pins are severely corroded, the connector must be

renewed; note that this may mean the renewal of that entire section of the loom – see your local Land Rover dealer for details.
6 If the cleaner completely removes the corrosion to leave the connector in a satisfactory condition, it would be wise to pack the connector with a suitable material which will exclude dirt and moisture, preventing the corrosion from occurring again; a Land Rover dealer may be able to recommend a suitable product.
7 Check the condition of the battery connections – remake the connections or renew the leads if a fault is found (see Chapter 5A Section 4). Use the same techniques to ensure that all earth points in the engine compartment provide good electrical contact through clean, metal-to-metal joints, and that all are securely fastened.

10 Air conditioning system check

1 The following maintenance checks will ensure that the air conditioner operates at peak efficiency:
a) *Check the auxiliary drivebelt (see Section 6).*
b) *Check the system hoses for damage or leaks.*
c) *Inspect the condenser fins for leaves, insects and other debris. Use a clean paint brush to clean the condenser. The condenser is mounted in front of the radiator.*
d) *Check that the drain tube from the evaporator housing is clear – the hose is located under the drivers side of the facia, and connects the housing to the engine compartment bulkhead. Note that it is normal to have clear fluid (water) dripping from this while the system is in operation, to the extent that quite a large puddle can be left under the car when it is parked.*
2 It's a good idea to operate the system for about 30 minutes at least once a month, particularly during the winter. Long term non-use can cause hardening, and subsequent failure, of the seals.
3 Because of the complexity of the air conditioning system and the special equipment necessary to service it, in-depth fault diagnosis and repairs are not included in this manual.
4 The most common cause of poor cooling is simply a low system refrigerant charge. If a noticeable drop in cool air output occurs, the following quick check will help you determine if the refrigerant level is low.
5 Warm the engine up to normal operating temperature.
6 Place the air conditioning temperature selector at the coldest setting, and put the blower at the highest setting. Open the doors – to make sure the air conditioning system doesn't cycle off as soon as it cools the passenger compartment

7 With the compressor engaged – the clutch will make an audible click, and the centre of the clutch will rotate – feel the inlet and outlet pipes at the compressor. One side should be cold, and one hot. If there's no perceptible difference between the two pipes, there's something wrong with the compressor or the system. It might be a low charge – it might be something else. Take the car to a dealer service department or an automotive air conditioning specialist.

11 Seat belt check

1 Check the seat belts for satisfactory operation and condition. Inspect the webbing for fraying and cuts. Check that they retract smoothly and without binding into their reels.
2 Check that the seat belt mounting bolts are tight, and if necessary tighten them to the specified torque wrench setting (Chapter 11 Specifications).

12 Antifreeze concentration check

1 The cooling system should be filled with the recommended antifreeze and corrosion protection fluid. Over a period of time, the concentration of fluid may be reduced due to topping-up (this can be avoided by topping-up with the correct antifreeze mixture) or fluid loss. If loss of coolant has been evident, it is important to make the necessary repair before adding fresh fluid. The exact mixture of antifreeze-to-water which you should use depends on the relative weather conditions. The mixture should contain at least 40% antifreeze, but not more than 70%. Consult the mixture ratio chart on the antifreeze container before adding coolant. Use

antifreeze which meets the car manufacturer's specifications.
2 With the engine cold, carefully remove the cap from the expansion tank. If the engine is not completely cold, place a cloth rag over the cap before removing it, and remove it slowly to allow any pressure to escape.
3 Antifreeze checkers are available from car accessory shops **(see illustration)**. Draw some coolant from the expansion tank and observe how many plastic balls are floating in the checker. Usually, 2 or 3 balls must be floating for the correct concentration of antifreeze, but follow the manufacturer's instructions.
4 If the concentration is incorrect, it will be necessary to either withdraw some coolant and add antifreeze, or alternatively drain the old coolant and add fresh coolant of the correct concentration.

13 Steering, suspension and roadwheel check

Front suspension and steering

1 Raise the front of the vehicle and support it securely on axle stands (see 'Vehicle jacking and support').
2 Visually inspect the balljoint dust covers and the steering rack-and-pinion gaiters for splits, chafing or deterioration **(see illustration)**. Any wear of these components will cause loss of lubricant, together with dirt and water entry, resulting in rapid deterioration of the balljoints or steering gear.
3 Check the power steering fluid hoses for chafing or deterioration, and the pipe and hose unions for fluid leaks. Also check for signs of fluid leakage under pressure from the steering gear rubber gaiters, which would indicate failed fluid seals within the steering gear.
4 Grasp the roadwheel at the 12 o'clock and

12.3 Check the concentration of the anti-freeze mixture

6 o'clock positions, and try to rock it **(see illustration)**. Very slight free play may be felt, but if the movement is appreciable, further investigation is necessary to determine the source. Continue rocking the wheel while an assistant depresses the footbrake. If the movement is now eliminated or significantly reduced, it is likely that the hub bearings are at fault. If the free play is still evident with the footbrake depressed, then there is wear in the suspension joints or mountings.
5 Now grasp the wheel at the 9 o'clock and 3 o'clock positions, and try to rock it as before. Any movement felt now may again be caused by wear in the hub bearings or the steering track rod balljoints. If the outer balljoint is worn, the visual movement will be obvious. If the inner joint is suspect, it can be felt by placing a hand over the rack-and-pinion rubber gaiter and gripping the track rod. If the wheel is now rocked, movement will be felt at the inner joint if wear has taken place.
6 Using a large screwdriver or flat bar, check for wear in the suspension mounting bushes by levering between the relevant suspension component and its attachment point. Some movement is to be expected, as the mountings are made of rubber, but excessive wear should be obvious. Also check the

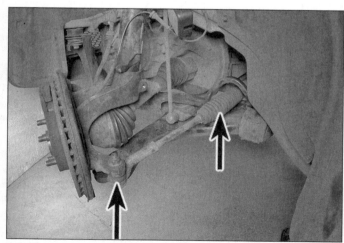
13.2 Check the condition of the balljoint dust covers and steering rack gaiters

13.4 Check for wear in the hub bearings by grasping the wheel and trying to rock it

condition of any visible rubber bushes, looking for splits, cracks or contamination of the rubber.

7 With the car standing on its wheels, have an assistant turn the steering wheel back-and-forth, about an eighth of a turn each way. There should be very little, if any, lost movement between the steering wheel and roadwheels. If this is not the case, closely observe the joints and mountings previously described. In addition, check the steering column universal joints for wear, and also check the rack-and-pinion steering gear itself.

Rear suspension

8 Chock the front wheels, then jack up the rear of the vehicle and support securely on axle stands (see 'Vehicle jacking and support').
9 Working as described previously for the front suspension, check the rear hub bearings, the suspension bushes and the strut or shock absorber mountings (as applicable) for wear.

Shock absorber

10 Check for any signs of fluid leakage around the shock absorber body, or from the rubber gaiter around the piston rod. Should any fluid be noticed, the shock absorber is defective internally, and should be renewed. **Note:** *Shock absorbers should always be renewed in pairs on the same axle.*
11 The efficiency of the shock absorber may be checked by bouncing the car at each corner. Generally speaking, the body will return to its normal position and stop after being depressed. If it rises and returns on a rebound, the shock absorber is probably suspect. Also examine the shock absorber upper and lower mountings for any signs of wear.

Roadwheels

12 Periodically remove the roadwheels, and clean any dirt or mud from the inside and outside surfaces. Examine the wheel rims for signs of rusting, corrosion or other damage. Light alloy wheels are easily damaged by 'kerbing' whilst parking, and similarly, steel wheels may become dented or buckled. Specialist firms do exist who will repair alloy wheels, but sometimes renewal of the wheel is the only course of remedial action possible.
13 The balance of each wheel and tyre assembly should be maintained, not only to avoid excessive tyre wear, but also to avoid wear in the steering and suspension components. Wheel imbalance is normally signified by vibration through the car's bodyshell, although in many cases it is particularly noticeable through the steering wheel. Conversely, it should be noted that wear or damage in suspension or steering components may cause excessive tyre wear. Out-of-round or out-of-true tyres, damaged wheels and wheel bearing wear/maladjustment also fall into this category. Balancing will not usually cure vibration caused by such wear.
14 Wheel balancing may be carried out with the wheel either on or off the car. If balanced on the car, ensure that the wheel-to-hub relationship is marked in some way prior to subsequent wheel removal, so that it may be refitted in its original position.
15 At this time, also check the spare wheel for damage.

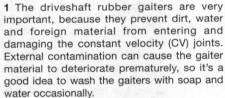

14 Driveshaft rubber gaiter and CV joint check

1 The driveshaft rubber gaiters are very important, because they prevent dirt, water and foreign material from entering and damaging the constant velocity (CV) joints. External contamination can cause the gaiter material to deteriorate prematurely, so it's a good idea to wash the gaiters with soap and water occasionally.
2 With the car raised and securely supported on axle stands, turn the steering onto full-lock, then slowly rotate each front wheel in turn. Inspect the condition of the outer constant velocity (CV) joint rubber gaiters, squeezing the gaiters to open out the folds **(see illustration)**. Check for signs of cracking, splits, or deterioration of the rubber, which may allow the escape of grease, and lead to the ingress of water and grit into the joint. Also check the security and condition of the retaining clips. Repeat these checks on the inner CV joints, and rear driveshafts. If any damage or deterioration is found, the gaiters should be renewed as described in Chapter 8 Section 3.
3 At the same time, check the general condition of the outer CV joints themselves, by first holding the driveshaft and attempting to rotate the wheels. Repeat this check on the inner joints, by holding the inner joint yoke and attempting to rotate the driveshaft.
4 Any appreciable movement in the CV joint indicates wear in the joint, wear in the driveshaft splines, or a loose driveshaft retaining bolt.

15 Exhaust system check

1 With the engine cold, check the complete exhaust system, from its starting point at the engine to the end of the tailpipe. If necessary, raise the front and rear of the car and support it on axle stands (see 'Vehicle jacking and support'). Remove any engine undershields as necessary for full access to the exhaust system.
2 Check the exhaust pipes and connections for evidence of leaks, severe corrosion, and damage. Make sure that all brackets and mountings are in good condition and that all relevant nuts and bolts are tight. Leakage at any of the joints or in other parts of the system will usually show up as a black sooty stain in the vicinity of the leak.
3 Rattles and other noises can often be traced to the exhaust system, especially the brackets and rubber mountings **(see illustration)**. Don't overlook loose exhaust

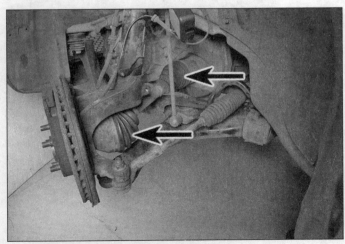

14.2 Check the condition of the inner and outer driveshaft gaiters

15.3 Check the condition of the exhaust system rubber mountings

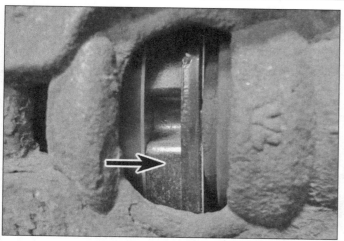

17.2 Check the thickness of the friction material

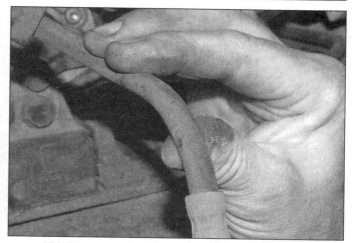

17.7 Check the brake hoses for cracks, cuts or splits

heat shields either, or the possibility that the internal baffles in a silencer box may be the source of a rattle. Try to move the pipes and silencers. If the components are able to come into contact with the body or suspension parts, secure the system with new mountings. Otherwise, separate the joints (if possible) and twist the pipes as necessary to provide additional clearance.

16 Underbody and fuel/brake line check

1 With the car raised and supported on axle stands (see *'Vehicle jacking and support'*), thoroughly inspect the underbody and wheel arches for signs of damage and corrosion. In particular, examine the bottom of the side sills, and any concealed areas where mud can collect. Also check the inside edges at the base of all doors.

2 Where corrosion and rust is evident, press and tap firmly on the panel with a screwdriver, and check for any serious corrosion which would necessitate repairs.

3 If the panel is not seriously corroded, clean away the rust, and apply a new coating of underseal. Refer to Chapter 11 for more details of body repairs.

4 At the same time, inspect the PVC-coated lower body panels for stone damage and general condition.

5 Inspect all of the fuel and brake lines on the underbody for damage, rust, corrosion and leakage. Particularly check the rear brake pipes where they pass over the fuel tank. Also make sure that the pipes are correctly supported in their clips. Where applicable, check the PVC coating on the lines for damage.

17 Braking system check

Front brakes

1 Apply the handbrake, then jack up the front of the car and support it on axle stands (see *'Vehicle jacking and support'*). For better access to the brake calipers, remove the wheels.

2 Look through the inspection window in the caliper, and check that the thickness of the friction lining material on each of the pads is not less than the recommended minimum thickness given in the Specifications **(see illustration)**.

3 If it is difficult to determine the exact thickness of the pad linings, or if you are at all concerned about the condition of the pads, then remove them from the calipers for further inspection (refer to Chapter 9 Section 4).

4 Check the caliper on the other side in the same way.

5 If any one of the brake pads has worn down to, or below, the specified limit, all four pads at that end of the car must be renewed as a set.

6 Check both front brake discs with reference to Chapter 9 Section 6.

7 Before refitting the wheels, check all brake lines and flexible hoses with reference to Chapter 9 Section 3. In particular, check the flexible hoses in the vicinity of the calipers, where they are subjected to most movement. Bend them between the fingers and check that this does not reveal previously-hidden cracks, cuts or splits **(see illustration)**.

8 On completion, refit the wheels and lower the car to the ground. Tighten the wheel nuts to the specified torque.

Rear brakes

9 Chock the front wheels, then jack up the rear of the car and support on axle stands (see *'Vehicle jacking and support'*). Remove the rear wheels.

10 The procedure for checking the rear brakes is much the same as described in paragraphs 1 to 8 above.

Handbrake

11 With the car on a slight slope, firmly apply the handbrake lever, and check that it holds the car stationary, then release the lever and check that there is no resistance to movement of the car. If necessary, the handbrake should be adjusted as described in Chapter 9 Section 14.

18 Door and bonnet check and lubrication

1 Check that the doors, bonnet and tailgate/boot lid close securely. Check that the bonnet safety catch operates correctly. Check the operation of the door check straps.

2 Lubricate the hinges, door check straps, the striker plates and the bonnet catch sparingly with a little oil or grease.

19 Pollen filter renewal

1 Remove the passenger's glovebox as described in Chapter 11 Section 24.

2 Release the 3 retaining clips, and remove

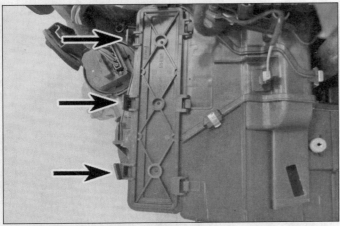

19.2 Release the clips at the front edge and open the cover

19.3a Slide the pollen filter from place

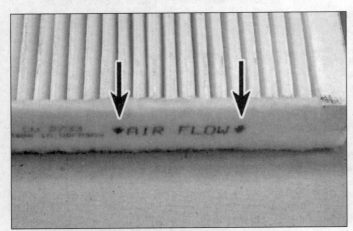

19.3b The arrows indicate air flow (front to back)

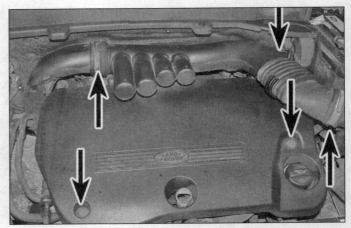

20.1 Release the clamps, disconnect the hoses, undo the fasteners and remove the engine top cover

the filter cover from the heater housing **(see illustration)**.

3 Slide the pollen filter from place **(see illustrations)**. Note its orientation.

4 Refitting is a reversal of removal.

20 Fuel sedimetor draining

1 The fuel filter is located in a mounting bracket at the front of the engine compartment. Release the air duct and breather hose clamps, then undo the fasteners and remove the plastic cover from the top of the engine **(see illustration)**.

2 Position a container under the filter location to collect any escaping water/fuel.

3 Slacken the drain screw on the top of the filter assembly, and allow any water in the filter to flow out into the container **(see illustration)**. When the flow of water stops, and only fuel emerges, close the drain screw securely.

4 Refit the filter cover and tighten the nuts securely.

5 Withdraw the container and wipe up any spilt fuel.

6 Switch on the 'ignition', and leave it on for a few seconds to refill the filter before starting the engine. If difficulty is experienced starting the engine, refer to Chapter 4A Section 6.

21 Road test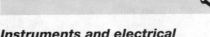

Instruments and electrical equipment

1 Check the operation of all instruments and electrical equipment.

2 Make sure that all instruments read correctly, and switch on all electrical equipment in turn, to check that it functions properly.

Steering and suspension

3 Check for any abnormalities in the steering, suspension, handling or road 'feel'.

4 Drive the car, and check that there are no unusual vibrations or noises.

5 Check that the steering feels positive, with no excessive 'sloppiness', or roughness, and check for any suspension noises when cornering and driving over bumps.

Drivetrain

6 Check the performance of the engine, clutch, transmission and driveshafts.

7 Listen for any unusual noises from the engine, clutch and transmission.

20.3 Slacken the drain screw

8 Make sure that the engine runs smoothly when idling, and that there is no hesitation when accelerating.

9 Check that, where applicable, the clutch action is smooth and progressive, that the drive is taken up smoothly, and that the pedal travel is not excessive. Also listen for any noises when the clutch pedal is depressed.

10 Check that all gears can be engaged smoothly without noise, and that the gear lever action is smooth and not abnormally vague or 'notchy'.

11 On automatic transmission models, make sure that all gearchanges occur smoothly, without snatching, and without an increase in engine speed between changes. Check that all of the gear positions can be selected with the car at rest.

12 Listen for a metallic clicking sound from the front of the car, as the car is driven slowly in a circle with the steering on full-lock. Carry out this check in both directions. If a clicking noise is heard, this indicates wear in a driveshaft joint (see Chapter 8 Section 4).

Braking system

13 Make sure that the car does not pull to one side when braking, and that the wheels do not lock when braking hard.

14 Check that there is no vibration through the steering when braking.

15 Check that the handbrake operates correctly, without excessive movement of the lever, and that it holds the car stationary on a slope.

16 Test the operation of the brake servo unit as follows. Depress the footbrake four or five times to exhaust the vacuum, then start the engine. As the engine starts, there should be a noticeable 'give' in the brake pedal as vacuum builds-up. Allow the engine to run for at least two minutes, and then switch it off. If the brake pedal is now depressed again, it should be possible to detect a hiss from the servo as the pedal is depressed. After about four or five applications, no further hissing should be heard, and the pedal should feel considerably harder

22 Reset the service indicator

Note: *If the time or distance is outside the service parameters of the vehicle, a manual reset of the service indicator may not be possible.*

Note: *If the vehicle has travelled less than 20% of the mileage to the next service interval, it may only be reset using Land Rover diagnostic equipment (or equivalent).*

1 Insert the key into the ignition slot. Do not start the engine, or press the brake or clutch pedal.

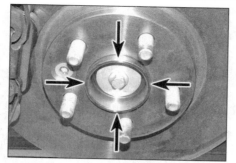

23.3 Apply anti-seize grease to the wheel hub spigots

Vehicles up to 2012 model year

2 Press and hold the trip reset button.

3 Press and hold the start/stop button to turn the ignition on, then within 10 seconds, release the trip button.

4 If the manual reset mode has been entered, 'dIst' or 'DATE will be displayed in the odometer.

5 To reset the 'dIst' light, press the trip reset button for at least 5 seconds, within 10 seconds of entering the reset mode. The display will show 'RESET' or 'END' if the reset was successful.

6 To reset the 'DATE' light, press the trip reset button for at least 5 seconds, within 10 seconds of entering the reset mode. The display will show 'RESET' followed by 'END'.

Vehicles 2012 to 2013

7 Set the ignition to the 'on' position, but don't start the engine.

8 Press the 'OK' button on the right side of the steering wheel controls to access the Instrument cluster Main Menu.

9 Operate the directional buttons to select the Service menu.

10 Again, operate the directional buttons to select the last option on the Menu.

11 Press and hold the trip button.

12 Press and hold the 'down' directional button.

13 Hold both buttons for 10 seconds to reset the Service indicator.

14 Turn the ignition off, then back on again to check the Service indicator has been reset. If necessary, repeat the resetting procedure.

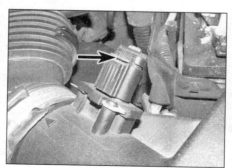

24.1 Slide up the locking clip, and disconnect the mass air flow sensor wiring plug

Vehicles 2014-on

15 Ensure any diagnostic equipment is not plugged into the diagnostic socket.

16 Switch the ignition ON.

17 Open the bonnet and the driver's door.

18 Press and hold the brake and throttle pedals fully depressed for 1 minute.

19 Release the pedals and switch the ignition OFF.

20 Switch the ignition ON and check the service message has been extinguished. If not, repeat the procedure.

23 Roadwheels anti-seize grease

1 Slacken the roadwheel nuts, raise the front and rear of the vehicle and support it securely on axle stands (see *'Vehicle jacking and support'*). Remove the roadwheels.

2 Check the condition of the wheel hub spigots, and where necessary remove any dirt/rust etc.

3 Apply a little anti-seize grease to the wheel hub spigots. Land Rover specify their grease (part no. RYL 105020), but any good quality anti-seize grease should suffice **(see illustration)**.

4 Take this opportunity to examine the wheels/tyres for signs of damage etc.

5 Refit the roadwheels, but do not fully tighten the retaining nuts yet.

6 Lower the vehicle to the ground, and tighten the roadwheel nuts as indicated in the Specifications at the beginning of this Chapter.

24 Air filter element renewal

1 Disconnect the wiring plug from the mass air flow meter **(see illustration)**.

2 Slacken the clamp and pull the air outlet duct from the air filter cover.

3 Undo the 4 retaining screws, and lift away the filter cover **(see illustration)**.

24.3 Air filter cover retaining screws

24.4 Note how the air filter element is fitted

25.3 Fuel filter cover screws

4 Lift the air filter element from the housing, noting its orientation **(see illustration)**.
5 Remove any debris, and wipe clean the housing.
6 Fit the new filter using a reversal of removal.

25 Fuel filter renewal

Note: *Before carrying out the following procedure, read carefully the precautions given in Chapter 4A Section 1.*
1 Release the air duct and breather hose clamps, then undo the fasteners and remove the plastic cover from the top of the engine **(see illustration 20.1)**.
2 Disconnect the wiring plug from the top of the filter.
3 Undo the 4 retaining nuts, and remove the filter cover **(see illustration)**.
4 Note the location of the supply and return hoses on the filter, then place some cloth rags beneath it to catch any spilled fuel.

5 Disconnect the quick-release fittings from the filter and position them to one side **(see illustration)**. Be prepared for some loss of fuel. Depending on type, the fittings either release by squeezing the plastic tabs together, or by carefully prising out/depressing the coloured plastic section.
Caution: Plug/seal the pipe openings to prevent contamination. Absolute cleanliness is essential.
6 Undo the 3 retaining screws from the top of the filter and remove it from the mounting bracket **(see illustration)**. The fuel filter is supplied as a single renewable unit, and cannot be dismantled.
7 Though not essential, it may help the engine to restart with less effort if the filter can be filled with fresh fuel prior to fitting. Take care not to introduce dirt into the new filter, and avoid spilling fuel over the engine or bodywork.
8 Insert the new filter in the mounting bracket with its stubs in the previously-noted positions, then reconnect the hoses. Make

sure that the quick-release fittings have engaged securely – on the type where the plastic section is prised out, reconnect the fitting, then press the section home until flush to secure.
9 Refit the retaining screws, and tighten them securely.
10 The remainder of refitting is a reversal of removal. Bleed the fuel system as described in Chapter 4A Section 6.

26 Brake fluid renewal

The procedure is similar to that for the bleeding of the hydraulic system as described in Chapter 9, except that the brake fluid reservoir should be emptied by syphoning, and allowance should be made for the old fluid to be removed from the circuit when bleeding a section of the circuit.
Caution: Do not allow the fluid level to drop below the bottom of the reservoir.

25.5 Depress the release buttons and disconnect the hoses from the filter

25.6 Fuel filter retaining screws

28.5 Rotate the tensioner pulley bolt clockwise

28.6 Auxiliary drivebelt routing

27 Flexible brake hose renewal

1 Due to the gradual deterioration of the rubber flexible brake hoses, Land Rover recommended that they are replaced every 6 years, regardless of mileage.
2 Replacement of the hoses is described in Chapter 9 Section 3.

28 Auxiliary drivebelt renewal

1 Disconnect the battery negative lead as described in Chapter 5A Section 4.
2 Slacken the right-hand front roadwheel nuts, raise the front of the vehicle, and support it securely on axle stands (see *Vehicle jacking and support*). Remove the roadwheel.
3 Undo the fasteners and remove the lower section of the wheelarch liner to access the belt (see illustration 6.4).
4 If the existing drivebelt is to be refitted, mark it, or note the maker's markings on its flat surface, so that it can be installed the same way round.
5 Using a suitable spanner, rotate the tensioner pulley clockwise to release its pressure on the drivebelt, and slip the belt from the idler pulley adjacent to the tensioner (see illustration).
6 Slip the drivebelt off the pulleys, noting how it is routed (see illustration).
7 Refitting is a reversal of removal, ensuring the belt ribs are correctly located in the various pulley grooves.

29 Timing belt, tensioner and idler pulley renewal

Refer to Chapter 2A Section 6.

30 Manual transmission oil renewal

Renewal of the manual transmission oil is described in Chapter 7A Section 2.

31 Automatic transmission oil renewal

Renewal of the automatic transmission oil is described in Chapter 7B Section 4.

32 Transfer case oil level check

Refer to Chapter 7C Section 2.

33 Final drive oil renewal

Refer to Chapter 8 Section 7.

34 Coolant renewal

 Warning: Refer to Chapter 3 Section 1 and observe the warnings given. In particular, never remove the expansion tank filler cap when the engine is running, or has just been switched off, as the cooling system will be hot, and the consequent escaping steam and scalding coolant

could cause serious injury. If the engine is hot, the electric cooling fan may start rotating even if the engine is not running, so be careful to keep hands, hair and loose clothing well clear when working in the engine compartment.

Cooling system draining

 Warning: Wait until the engine is cold before starting this procedure.

1 Slacken the right-hand front roadwheel nuts, raise the front of the vehicle and support it securely on axle stands (see *Vehicle jacking and support*). Remove the roadwheel.
2 Set the heater controls to the maximum temperature position.
3 Unscrew the coolant expansion tank cap.
4 Disconnect the battery negative lead as described in Chapter 5A Section 4.
5 Undo the fasteners and remove the engine undershield (see illustration 4.4).
6 Position a container under the radiator, then attach a rubber/plastic hose to the outlet on the drain tap located at the left-hand end of the radiator (see illustration).
7 Open the radiator drain tap and allow the coolant to drain into the container.
8 Reposition the container under the rear of the engine undo the cylinder block drain plug,

34.6 Attach a hose to the drain tap outlet

34.8 To drain the cylinder block, unscrew the Allen plug at the base of the coolant pump

located at the base of the coolant pump, and allow the coolant to drain **(see illustration)**.
9 When the coolant has finished draining, tighten the radiator tap securely, then tighten the cylinder block drain plug to the specified torque.
10 Remove the container from under the vehicle.
11 Refit the engine undershield, lower the vehicle to the ground, and tighten the roadwheel nuts to the specified torque.
12 Reconnect the battery negative lead as described in Chapter 5A Section 4.

Cooling system flushing

13 If coolant renewal has been neglected, or if the antifreeze mixture has become diluted, then in time, the cooling system may gradually lose efficiency, as the coolant passages become restricted due to rust, scale deposits, and other sediment. The cooling system efficiency can be restored by flushing the system clean.
14 The radiator should be flushed independently of the engine, to avoid unnecessary contamination.

Radiator flushing

15 Disconnect the top and bottom hoses and any other relevant hoses from the radiator, with reference to Chapter 3 Section 2.
16 Insert a garden hose into the radiator top inlet. Direct a flow of clean water through the radiator, and continue flushing until clean water emerges from the radiator bottom outlet.
17 If after a reasonable period, the water still does not run clear, the radiator can be flushed with a good proprietary cleaning agent. It is important that the manufacturer's instructions are followed carefully. If the contamination is particularly bad, remove the radiator, insert the hose in the radiator bottom outlet, and reverse-flush the radiator.

Engine flushing

18 Remove the thermostat as described in Chapter 3 Section 4 then, if the radiator top hose has been disconnected from the engine, temporarily reconnect the hose.
19 With the top and bottom hoses disconnected from the radiator, insert a garden hose into the radiator top hose. Direct a clean flow of water through the engine, and continue flushing until clean water emerges from the radiator bottom hose.
20 On completion of flushing, refit the thermostat and reconnect the hoses with reference to Chapter 3.

Antifreeze mixture

21 If the correct specification antifreeze is used, Land Rover state that the coolant only needs to be renewed every 10 years. The coolant must be renewed to provide the correct degree of protection. **Note:** *The specified anti-freeze is of the Organic Acid Technology (OAT) type, and must not be mixed with any other type of antifreeze.*
22 If the antifreeze used is to Land Rover's specification, the levels of protection it provides are indicated in the Specifications Section of this Chapter. To give the recommended standard mixture ratio for this antifreeze, 50% (by volume) of antifreeze must be mixed with 50% of clean, soft water.
23 Before adding antifreeze, the cooling system should be completely drained, preferably flushed, and all hoses checked for condition and security. Fresh antifreeze will rapidly find any weaknesses in the system.
24 After filling with antifreeze, a label should be attached to the expansion tank, stating the type and concentration of antifreeze used, and the date installed. Any subsequent topping-up should be made with the same type and concentration of antifreeze.

Cooling system filling

25 Before attempting to fill the cooling system, make sure that all hoses and clips are in good condition, and that the clips are tight. Note that an antifreeze mixture must be used all year round, to prevent corrosion of the engine components.
26 Slowly fill the system until the coolant level reaches the MAX mark on the side of the coolant expansion tank.
27 Refit the expansion tank cap, start the engine, and hold it at 2000 rpm until warm air begins to be expelled from the heater ducts.
28 Stop the engine and allow it to cool.
29 Top the coolant expansion tank up to the MAX mark, then refit the cap.
30 Allow the engine to idle for 2 minutes.

Monitor the coolant temperature gauge – if the engine starts to over-heat, turn the engine off immediately, and allow the engine to cool.
31 Raise the engine speed to 3000 rpm until the cooling fan operates, then turn off the engine and allow it to cool completely.
32 Remove the expansion tank cap and fill the system to the MAX mark.

Airlocks

33 If, after draining and refilling the system, symptoms of overheating are found which did not occur previously, then the fault is almost certainly due to trapped air at some point in the system, causing an airlock and restricting the flow of coolant; usually, the air is trapped because the system was refilled too quickly.
34 If an airlock is suspected, first try gently squeezing all visible coolant hoses. A coolant hose which is full of air feels quite different to one full of coolant, when squeezed. After refilling the system, most airlocks will clear once the system has cooled, and been topped-up.
35 While the engine is running at operating temperature, switch on the heater and heater fan, and check for heat output. Provided there is sufficient coolant in the system, any lack of heat output could be due to an airlock in the system.
36 Airlocks can have more serious effects than simply reducing heater output – a severe airlock could reduce coolant flow around the engine. Check that the radiator top hose is hot when the engine is at operating temperature – a top hose which stays cold could be the result of an airlock (or a non-opening thermostat).
37 If the problem persists, stop the engine and allow it to cool down completely, before unscrewing the expansion tank filler cap or loosening the hose clips and squeezing the hoses to bleed out the trapped air. In the worst case, the system will have to be at least partially drained (this time, the coolant can be saved for re-use) and flushed to clear the problem.

Pressure cap check

38 Clean the pressure cap (expansion tank), and inspect the seal inside the cap for damage or deterioration. If there is any sign of damage or deterioration to the seal, fit a new pressure cap. If the cap is old, it is worth considering fitting a new one for peace of mind – they are not expensive. If the pressure cap fails, excess pressure will be allowed into the system, which may result in the failure of hoses, the radiator, or the heater matrix.

Chapter 2 Part A
Engine in-car repair procedures

Contents

Degrees of difficulty

| **Easy,** suitable for novice with little experience | 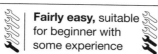 | **Fairly easy,** suitable for beginner with some experience | | **Fairly difficult,** suitable for competent DIY mechanic | | **Difficult,** suitable for experienced DIY mechanic | | **Very difficult,** suitable for expert DIY or professional | |

Specifications

General

Engine type	Four-cylinder in-line, double overhead camshaft, 16-valve, liquid-cooled, turbocharged
Engine code:	
2006 – 2010	DW12BTED4
2010-on	DW12C
Bore	85.0 mm
Stroke	96.0 mm
Capacity	2179 cc
Firing order	1-3-4-2 (No. 1 at the transmission end)
Direction of crankshaft rotation	Clockwise (seen from the right-hand side of the vehicle)
Compression ratio:	
DW12BTED4	16.6:1
DW12C	15.9:1
Output:	
Power:	
DW12BTED4	118 kW @ 4000 rpm
DW12C	110 or 140 kW @ 4000 rpm
Torque:	
DW12BTED4	400 Nm @ 2000 rpm
DW12C	420 Nm @ 2000 rpm
Idle speed:	
Manual transmission	750 ± 30 rpm
Automatic transmission	795 ± 30 rpm
Maximum engine speed	5000 rpm

Camshafts
Endfloat . . . .   0.15 to 0.33 mm

Lubrication system
Minimum system pressure:
  1750 rpm . . . .   1.6 bar
  4000 rpm . . . .   3.1 bar

Torque wrench settings

	Nm	lbf ft
Air conditioning compressor bolts	25	17
Alternator mounting bracket	18	13
Camshaft cover bolts	10	7
Camshaft sprocket bolts*:		
Stage 1	20	15
Stage 2	Angle-tighten a further 60°	
Crankshaft pulley bolt*:		
Stage 1	70	52
Stage 2	Angle-tighten a further 82°	
Cylinder head bolts*:		
Stage 1	20	15
Stage 2	60	44
Stage 3	Angle-tighten a further 220°	
Dipstick tube	10	7
Engine/transmission mountings:		
Left-hand mounting:		
Mounting bracket-to-body:		
M12*	80	59
M8	25	17
Mounting-to-transmission bracket	175	130
Bracket-to-transmission bolts	85	63
Right-hand mounting:		
Mounting bracket-to-engine bracket bolts (M12)	80	59
Mounting bracket-to-mounting bolt (M14)	175	130
Mounting-to-body	80	59
Upper tie rod bolts	110	81
Lower engine tie rod and bracket bolts:		
M10	45	33
M12	50	37
Upper engine tie rod mounting bolts	100	74
Flywheel/driveplate bolts*:		
Stage 1	33	25
Stage 2	Angle-tighten a further 34°	
Oil cooler bolts	10	7
Oil filter housing bolts	20	15
Oil pressure sensor	32	24
Oil pump bolts:		
Stage 1	7	5
Stage 2	9	6
Oil seperator	10	7
Oil temperature sensor	27	20
Sump drain plug	20	15
Sump extension bolts:		
To transmission	47	34
To engine:		
Stage 1	10	7
Stage 2	16	12
Sump pan bolts	9	6
Timing belt tensioner nut	25	18
Timing chain tensioner bolts	7	5

Do not re-use

1 General information

How to use this Chapter

1 This Part of the Chapter describes those repair procedures that can reasonably be carried out on the engine whilst it remains in the vehicle. If the engine has been removed from the vehicle and is being dismantled as described in Part B of this Chapter, any preliminary dismantling procedures can be ignored.

2 Note that whilst it may be possible physically to overhaul items such as the piston/connecting rod assemblies with the engine in the vehicle, such tasks are not usually carried out as separate operations and usually require the execution of several additional procedures (not to mention the cleaning of components and of oilways). For this reason, all such tasks are classed as major overhaul procedures and are described in Chapter 2B.

Engine description

3 The 2.2 litre diesel engine is the result of a joint development between Ford and PSA (Peugeot/Citroen), and is a four-cylinder, double overhead camshaft, 16-valve, in-line unit, mounted transversely at the front of the vehicle with the clutch and transmission on the left-hand end.

4 The cast-iron cylinder block is of the dry-liner type. The crankshaft is supported within the cylinder block on five shell-type main bearings. Thrustwashers are integral with the No.2 main bearing shells to control crankshaft endfloat.

5 The cylinder head is of the double overhead camshaft, 16-valve design – two intake and two exhaust valves per cylinder. The valves are operated by one intake camshaft and one exhaust camshaft, via rocker fingers. One end of each finger acts upon the valve stem, whilst the other end pivots on a support pillar. Valve clearances are maintained automatically by hydraulic compensation elements incorporated within the support pillars.

6 The connecting rods rotate on horizontally-split bearing shells at their big-ends. The pistons are attached to the connecting rods by gudgeon pins which are secured in position with circlips. The aluminium alloy pistons are fitted with three piston rings, comprising two compression rings and an oil control ring.

7 The intake and exhaust valves are each closed by coil springs and operate in guides pressed into the cylinder head. Valve guides cannot be replaced.

8 A timing belt, driven by the crankshaft, drives the coolant pump and exhaust camshaft. A Simplex chain from the exhaust camshaft then drives the intake camshaft. The high-pressure fuel pump is fitted to the left-hand end of the cylinder head, and is driven by the exhaust camshaft, whilst a vacuum pump is driven from the left-hand end of the intake camshaft.

9 Lubrication is by means of an eccentric-rotor type pump driven by the crankshaft via a Simplex chain. The pump draws oil through a strainer located in the sump, and then forces it through an externally-mounted full-flow paper element type oil filter into galleries in the cylinder block/crankcase, from where it is distributed to the crankshaft (main bearings), timing chain (sprayed by a jet), and camshaft. The big-end bearings are supplied with oil via internal drillings in the crankshaft, while the camshaft bearings and the followers receive a pressurised supply via drillings in the cylinder head. The camshaft lobes and valves are lubricated by oil splash, as are all other engine components. An oil cooler (integral with the oil filter housing) is fitted to keep the oil temperature stable under arduous operating conditions.

Repair operations possible with the engine in the car

10 The following work can be carried out with the engine in the vehicle:

a) Compression pressure – testing.
b) Camshaft cover – removal and refitting.
c) Crankshaft pulley – removal and refitting.
d) Camshaft oil seals – renewal.
e) Camshaft and rocker arms – removal, inspection and refitting.
f) Cylinder head – removal and refitting.
g) Cylinder head and pistons* – decarbonising.
h) Sump – removal and refitting.
i) Oil pump – removal and refitting.
j) Oil filter housing/cooler – removal and refitting.
k) Crankshaft oil seals – renewal.
l) Engine/transmission mountings – inspection and renewal.
m) Flywheel/driveplate – removal, inspection and refitting.
n) Timing belt – removal and refitting.

Note:* Although in theory it is possible to remove these components with the engine in place, for reasons of access and cleanliness, it is recommended that the engine is removal.

2 Compression test – description and interpretation

Compression test

Note: A compression tester specifically designed for diesel engines must be used for this test.

1 When engine performance is down, or if misfiring occurs which cannot be attributed to the fuel system, a compression test can provide diagnostic clues as to the engine's condition. If the test is performed regularly, it can give warning of trouble before any other symptoms become apparent.

2 A compression tester specifically intended for diesel engines must be used, because of the higher pressures involved. The tester is connected to an adaptor which screws into the glow plug hole. It is unlikely to be worthwhile buying such a tester for occasional use, but it may be possible to borrow or hire one – if not, have the test performed by a garage.

3 Unless specific instructions to the contrary are supplied with the tester, observe the following points:

a) The battery must be in a good state of charge, the air filter must be clean, and the engine should be at normal operating temperature.
b) All the glow plugs should be removed before starting the test, as described in Chapter 5B Section 3.

4 There is no need to hold the accelerator pedal down during the test, because the diesel engine air intake is not throttled.

5 Crank the engine on the starter motor; after one or two revolutions, the compression pressure should build up to a maximum figure, and then stabilise. Record the highest reading obtained.

6 Repeat the test on the remaining cylinders, recording the pressure in each.

7 All cylinders should produce very similar pressures; a difference of more than 10% between any two cylinders indicates a fault. Note that the compression should build up quickly in a healthy engine; low compression on the first stroke, followed by gradually-increasing pressure on successive strokes, indicates worn piston rings. A low compression reading on the first stroke, which does not build up during successive strokes, indicates leaking valves or a blown head gasket (a cracked head could also be the cause). Deposits on the undersides of the valve heads can also cause low compression. Note: The cause of poor compression is less easy to establish on a diesel engine than on a petrol one. The effect of introducing oil into the cylinders ('wet' testing) is not conclusive, because there is a risk that the oil will sit in the swirl chamber or in the recess on the piston crown instead of passing to the rings.

8 Although Land Rover do not specify exact compression pressures, as a guide, any cylinder pressure of below 20 bar can be considered as less than healthy. Refer to a Land Rover dealer or other specialist if in doubt as to whether a particular pressure reading is acceptable.

9 On completion of the test, refit the glow plugs as described in Chapter 5B Section 3.

Leakdown test

10 A leakdown test measures the rate at which compressed air fed into the cylinder is lost. It is an alternative to a compression test, and in many ways it is better, since the escaping air provides easy identification of where pressure loss is occurring (piston rings, valves or head gasket).

11 The equipment needed for leakdown testing is unlikely to be available to the home mechanic. If poor compression is suspected, have the test performed by a suitably-equipped garage

3 Engine assembly/valve timing settings – general information and usage

Note: *Land Rover tool No. 303-1270 or suitable home-made equivalent will be required to lock the crankshaft in position, and access to Land Rover tool No. 303-1277 or home-made equivalent is required to position the exhaust camshaft. Note that it may be possible to obtain equivalent tools from AST tools (ASTtools.co.uk).*

1 The flywheel is equipped with an indent, which aligns with a hole in the engine block when Nos.1 and 4 pistons are at TDC (top dead centre). In this position, if No.1 piston is at TDC on its compression stroke, it must

be possible to fit a Land Rover special tool (No. 303-1270) or home-made equivalent, through a hole in the timing belt cover, into corresponding holes in the exhaust camshaft sprocket and cylinder head.

2 Disconnect the battery negative lead as described in Chapter 5A Section 4.

3 Slacken the right-hand front road wheel nuts, firmly apply the handbrake then jack up the front of the vehicle and support it securely on axle stands (see 'Vehicle jacking and support'). Remove the front right-hand road wheel.

4 Undo the retaining screws/clips and remove the engine undertray, and right-hand wheel arch splash shield **(see illustration)**.

5 Remove the starter motor as described in Chapter 5A Section 9.

6 Undo the retaining bolt and remove the plastic cover from the lower part of the starter motor aperture **(see illustration)**.

7 Pull out the blanking plug from the timing belt cover, then using a socket and extension bar on the crankshaft pulley centre bolt, turn the crankshaft clockwise (viewed from the right-hand end of the engine) until Land Rover tool No. 303 1277 (or after-market equivalent) can be inserted, aligning the slot in the exhaust camshaft sprocket with the corresponding hole in the cylinder head **(see illustrations)**. In the absence of the Land Rover tool, use an 8.0 mm drill bit or rod.
Note: *Do not turn the engine anti-clockwise.*

8 In this position, it should be possible to insert Land Rover tool No. 303-1270 (or equivalent) through the hole in the cylinder block (below the starter motor aperture) into the corresponding indent in the flywheel/driveshaft. In the absence of this tool, use an 8.0 mm drill bit or rod **(see illustrations)**. The engine timing is now set.
Caution: On automatic transmission models, there is more than one hole in the back of the driveplate. However, only one hole will allow the tool/drill bit/rod to be fully inserted.

4 Camshaft cover – removal and refitting

Removal

1 Disconnect the battery negative lead (refer to Chapter 5A Section 4).

2 Remove the air cleaner assembly as described in Chapter 4A Section 2.

3 Raise the front of the vehicle and support it securely on axle stands (see 'Vehicle jacking and support').

4 Remove the exhaust camshaft seal as described in Section 13.

5 With reference to Chapter 4A, remove the fuel rail, fuel injectors, high pressure fuel pump and intake manifold.

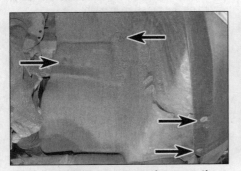

3.4 Undo the fasteners and remove the splash shield

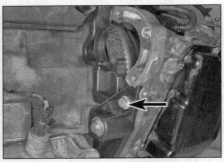

3.6 Starter motor aperture cover bolt

3.7a Prise the blanking plug from the timing cover

3.7b Insert an 8.0 mm drill bit through the slot in the camshaft sprocket into the hole in the cylinder head

3.8a Insert the timing pin/drill bit into the hole in the cylinder block...

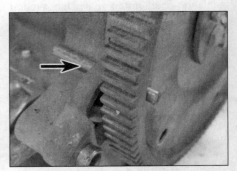

3.8b...into the corresponding hole in the flywheel/driveplate

4.6a Depress the release button and disconnect the breather hose at the left-hand end of the camshaft cover...

4.6b...and the hoses at the right-hand end

6 Note their fitted positions, then disconnect the various hoses from the camshaft cover **(see illustrations)**.

7 Remove the camshaft position sensor as described in Chapter 4A Section 12.

8 Undo the retaining bolts and remove the oil separator from the camshaft cover **(see illustrations)**. Discard the seals – new ones must be fitted.

9 Remove the bolts securing the oil filler cap to the vacuum pump **(see illustration)**.

10 Remove the vacuum pump as described in Chapter 9 Section 19.

11 Remove the EGR cooler as described in Chapter 4B Section 2.

12 Remove the crankshaft timing tool, and rotate the crankshaft backwards (anti-clockwise) through 90°. This positions all the pistons half way down their bores, to prevent accidental valve-to-piston contact.

13 Pull the timing chain tensioner service pin upwards (retracting the tensioner piston), then rotate it clockwise to lock it in place **(see illustration)**.

14 Working in a diagonal pattern, evenly slacken and remove the 27 bolts securing

4.8a Oil separator retaining bolts

4.8b Renew the oil separator seals

4.9 Oil filler cap retaining bolts

4.13 Pull the service pin upwards, and rotate it clockwise to lock it

4.14 Undo the retaining bolts and remove the camshaft cover

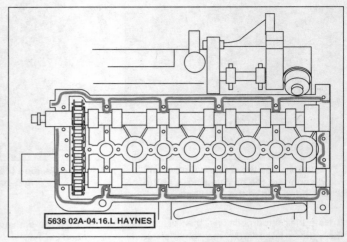

4.16 Apply a continuous bead of sealant to the areas shown

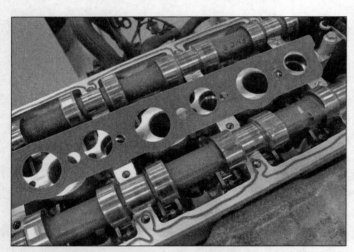

4.18a Position the new gasket between the camshafts

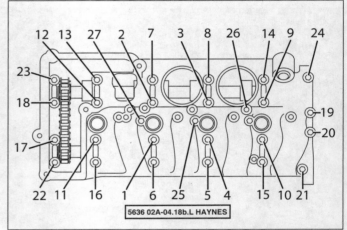

4.18b Camshaft cover bolt tightening sequence

the camshaft cover to the cylinder head (see illustration).

15 Remove the cover and discard its gasket.

Refitting

16 Ensure the mating surfaces are clean, then apply a continuous bead of sealant (Loctite No. 518) to the mating surface of the cylinder head (see illustration).

17 Temporarily refit the exhaust camshaft sprocket, then rotate the camshaft clockwise and re-insert the camshaft timing pin.

18 Lubricate the camshaft bearing surfaces with clean engine oil, then refit the camshaft cover, with a new gasket, and tighten the retaining bolts gradually and evenly in sequence to the specified torque (see illustrations).

Caution: If the camshaft cover bolts are carelessly tightened, the bearing caps might break. If the caps are broken then the complete cylinder head assembly must be renewed; the cover/caps are matched to the head and are not available separately

19 Rotate the chain tensioner service pin anti-clockwise and release it.

20 Carefully rotate the crankshaft 90° clockwise and re-insert the crankshaft timing pin.

21 Remove the camshaft sprocket and timing pin.

22 The remainder of refitting is a reversal of removal, noting the following points:
a) Renew all gaskets/seals.
b) Tighten all fasteners to their specified torque where given.
c) Check for fuel/oil leaks before venturing out onto the road.

5 Crankshaft pulley – removal and refitting

Removal

1 Disconnect the battery negative lead as described in Chapter 5A Section 4.

2 Firmly apply the handbrake then slacken the right-hand front road wheel nuts. Jack up the front of the vehicle and support it securely on axle stands (see 'Vehicle jacking and support'). Unscrew the bolts and remove the right-hand front road wheel.

3 Remove the starter motor as described in Chapter 5A Section 9.

4 Remove the auxiliary drivebelt as described in Chapter 1 Section 28.

5 Fit the crankshaft and camshaft timing tools as described in Section 3.

6 To prevent the crankshaft from rotating whist the retaining bolt is slackened, use Land Rover tool No. 303-1272 or equivalent. This tool bolts to the starter motor aperture, and engages with the teeth on the outer edge of the flywheel/driveplate (see illustration). **Note:** *Do not be tempted to use just the crankshaft timing tool to prevent rotation – damage may result.*

7 With the crankshaft firmly locked, undo the crankshaft pulley retaining bolt, and recover

5.6 Flywheel/driveplate locking tool

5.7 Remove the retaining bolt and washer

6.2 Carefully extract the sensor ring from the end of the crankshaft

the washer **(see illustration)**. Note that a new bolt must be fitted upon reassembly.

8 Withdrawn the pulley from the end of the crankshaft.

Refitting

9 Fit the pulley to the crankshaft and screw in the new retaining bolt with the washer fitted.

10 Lock the crankshaft by the method used on removal, and tighten the pulley retaining bolt to the specified Stage 1 torque setting then angle-tighten the bolt through the specified Stage 2, using a socket and extension bar. It is recommended that an angle-measuring gauge is used during the final stages of the tightening, to ensure accuracy. If a gauge is not available, use paint to make alignment marks between the bolt

head and pulley prior to tightening; the marks can then be used to check that the bolt has been rotated through the correct angle.

11 The remainder of refitting is a reversal of removal.

---

6 Timing belt, tensioner and idler pulleys – removal and refitting

Removal

1 Disconnect the battery negative lead as described in Chapter 5A Section 4.

2 Remove the crankshaft pulley as described in Section 5, then extract the crankshaft position sensor ring from the end of the

crankshaft **(see illustration)**. On some models, the sensor ring is withdrawn using two 6 mm bolts, and the threaded holes in the ring.

3 Release the clamps securing the air and breather hoses to the ducting on the top of the engine, then undo the 3 fasteners remove the engine top cover **(see illustration)**.

4 Release the clamp, undo the bolt, then manoeuvre the turbocharger air intake pipe upwards from the engine compartment **(see illustrations)**.

5 Unclip the wiring harness from the rear of the upper timing belt cover.

6 Release the catch and unclip the fuel hoses from the timing belt cover **(see illustration)**.

7 Undo the retaining bolts and remove the upper timing belt cover **(see illustration)**.

6.3 Release the clamps, disconnect the hoses, undo the fasteners and remove the engine top cover

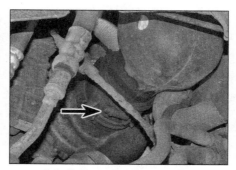

6.4a Release the clamp at the turbocharger...

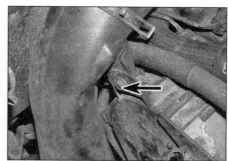

6.4b...undo the bolt...

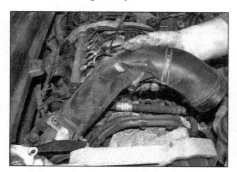

6.4c...and remove the air intake pipe

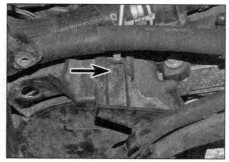

6.6 Release the fuel hose bracket retaining clip

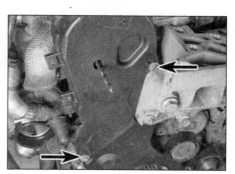

6.7 Upper timing belt cover retaining bolts

6.8 Crankshaft position sensor retaining bolt

6.9 Lower timing belt cover retaining bolts

6.10 Insert an Allen key into the hole

8 Working underneath the vehicle, disconnect the wiring plug, undo the retaining bolt and remove the crankshaft position sensor (see illustration).
9 Undo the 3 retaining bolts and remove the lower timing belt cover (see illustration).
10 Insert an Allen key into the hole, then slacken the tensioner retaining nut, and slowly release the tension (see illustration).
11 Slide the belt from the pulleys. Note that the belt must not be re-used.
12 If required, undo the retaining nut/bolt and remove the tensioner and idler pulleys (see illustration). **Note:** *The crankshaft and camshafts must not be rotated with the belt removed.*

Refitting

13 Check the condition of the tensioner and idler pulleys. If there is any doubt as to their condition, renew them.
14 Rotate the coolant pump sprocket, checking for any roughness/play. Check for any signs of leaking from the pump. If in any doubt as to its condition, renew it.
15 Ensure that the camshaft sprocket and crankshaft timing tools are still in place (see Section 3), and that the crankshaft key is centred within the key way (see illustration).
16 Ensure the belt sprockets are clean, then fit the new belt, starting with the camshaft sprocket, followed by the idler pulley,

crankshaft sprocket, coolant pump sprocket, then the tensioner pulley. Keep the belt taut between the camshaft and crankshaft sprockets, so all the belt slack is at the tensioner pulley.
17 Slacken the tensioner retaining nut, insert an Allen key into the hole in the tensioner hub, and rotate the hub anti-clockwise until the pointer arm is in the position shown (see illustration). Tighten the tensioner nut to the specified torque.
18 Refit the crankshaft position sensor signal ring, and the crankshaft pulley, then insert the old pulley bolt and tighten it to 70 Nm.
19 Remove the crankshaft locking tool (Section 5) and the camshaft/crankshaft timing tools (Section 3), then rotate the crankshaft 10 complete revolutions and refit the camshaft/crankshaft timing tools.
20 Refit the crankshaft locking tool (Section 5), and slacken the crankshaft pulley bolt.
21 Insert the Allen key into the hole in the tensioner hub, then slacken the tensioner retaining nut, and rotate the hub clockwise until the pointer aligns with the notch in the pointer arm backplate (see illustration). **Note:** *If the pointer arm is to the right-hand side of the backplate (ie. the belt is too slack), repeat the tensioning procedure from Paragraph 17 onwards.*
22 With the pointer aligned correctly, tighten the tensioner nut to the specified torque.
23 Tighten the crankshaft pulley bolt to 70 Nm (still using the old bolt).
24 Remove the camshaft/crankshaft timing/locking tools, and rotate the crankshaft 2 complete revolutions, and check that the tensioner pointer arm is still aligned with the notch on the backplate. If not, repeat the tensioning procedure.
25 Refit the camshaft/crankshaft timing/locking tools, undo the retaining bolt, and remove the crankshaft pulley and position sensor signal ring (using the two 6 mm bolts).
26 The remainder of refitting is a reversal of removal, noting the following points:
a) *Renew the crankshaft pulley bolt.*
b) *Tighten all fasteners to their specified torque where given.*
c) *Reconnect the battery negative lead as described in Chapter 5A Section 4.*

6.12 Timing belt tensioner nut and idler pulley bolt

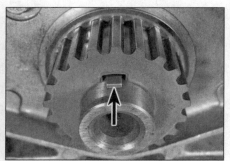

6.15 Ensure the key is centred within the key way

6.17 Rotate the hub anti-clockwise until the pointer arm is almost at the 6 o'clock position

6.21 The pointer arm must align with the notch in the backplate

7.2 Timing chain tensioner retaining bolts

7.4 Lift each rocker arm and tappet assembly from the cylinder head

7.8a Each camshaft sprocket has an arrow mark which must align with the marked/coloured link in the chain

7 Camshafts, rocker arms and hydraulic tappets – removal, inspection and refitting

Removal

1 Remove the camshaft cover as described in Section 4.

2 Undo the 3 bolts securing the timing chain tensioner to the cylinder head **(see illustration)**.

3 Carefully lift the camshafts, timing chain and tensioner from place.

4 Lift the rocker arms and hydraulic tappets from the cylinder head and place them in sixteen small, clean plastic containers – label them for identification. Alternatively, divide a larger container into compartments. Withdraw each hydraulic tappet in turn, invert it to prevent oil loss and place it in its respective container, which should then be filled with clean engine oil **(see illustration)**.

Caution: Do not interchange the tappets, and do not allow the tappets to lose oil, as they will take a long time to refill with oil on restarting the engine, which could result in incorrect valve clearances. Absolute cleanliness is essential at all times when handling the tappets.

Inspection

5 Examine the camshaft bearing surfaces and cam lobes for signs of wear ridges and scoring. Renew the camshaft if any of these conditions are apparent. Examine the condition of the bearing surfaces both on the camshaft journals and in the cylinder head. If the head bearing surfaces are worn excessively, the cylinder head will need to be renewed.

6 Examine the rocker bearing surfaces which contact the camshaft lobes for wear ridges and scoring. If the engine's valve clearances have sounded noisy, particularly if the noise persists after initial start-up from cold, then there is reason to suspect a faulty tappet. If any tappet is thought to be faulty or is visibly worn it should be renewed.

Refitting

7 Where removed, lubricate the tappets and rocker arms with clean engine oil and carefully insert each one into its original location in the cylinder head.

8 To facilitate correct camshaft timing, the timing chain has 2 links marked/coloured which must align with the arrows on the front face of each camshaft sprocket (arrows uppermost) **(see illustrations)**. Position the chain around the sprockets with the marks/links aligned and fit the tensioner between the chain runs.

9 Lubricate the lower bearing surfaces in the cylinder head with clean engine oil, and carefully lower the camshafts/chain/tensioner assembly into place **(see illustration)**.

10 Insert the tensioner retaining bolts and tighten them to the specified torque.

11 The remainder of refitting is a reversal of removal.

8 Cylinder head – removal and refitting

Removal

1 Remove the camshafts, rocker arms and tappets as described in Section 7.

2 Drain the cooling system, as described in Chapter 1 Section 34.

3 Remove the exhaust manifold as described in Chapter 4A Section 18.

4 Remove the thermostat as described in Chapter 3 Section 4.

5 Position a workshop jack under the sump to support the engine. Use a block of wood to prevent damage to the sump.

6 Remove the right-hand engine mounting as described in Section 15.

7 Undo the bolts securing the engine mounting support bracket to the cylinder head **(see illustration)**.

7.8b With the camshafts correctly located in the chain, there must be 5 links between the sprocket arrows/coloured links

7.9 Lower the camshaft/chain and tensioner assembly into place

8.7 Support bracket-to-cylinder head bolts

8.8 Inner timing belt cover retaining bolts

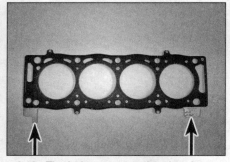

8.19a The holes representing the piston protrusion may be at each end of the gasket...

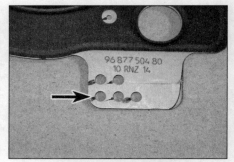

8.19b...the forwardmost holes at the flywheel/driveplate end (3 holes in this instance)...

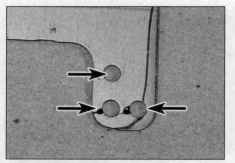

8.19c...and/or all the holes at the timing chain end (3 holes in this instance)

8.22 Measure the piston protrusion with a DTI gauge

8 Undo the 3 retaining bolts and remove the timing belt inner cover (see illustration).

9 Release the clamp and disconnect the coolant hose from the left-hand front of the cylinder head.

10 Unclip the wiring harness, and disconnect the wiring plugs from the glow plugs.

11 Working in the reverse of the tightening sequence (see illustration 8.29), progressively slacken the cylinder head bolts by a third of a turn at a time until all bolts can be unscrewed by hand. Withdraw and discard the bolts, new ones must be fitted.

12 With the help of an assistant, lift the cylinder head from the cylinder block. If necessary, tap the cylinder head gently with a soft-faced mallet to free it from the block, but do not lever at the mating faces.

13 When the joint is broken, lift the cylinder head away then remove the gasket. Note the fitted positions of the two locating dowels, and remove them for safe-keeping if they are loose. Keep the gasket for identification purposes (see paragraph 19).

Caution: Do not lay the head on its lower mating surface; support the head on wooden blocks, ensuring each block only contacts the head mating surface not the glow plugs. The glow plugs protrude out the bottom of the head and they will be damaged if the head is placed directly onto a bench.

14 If the cylinder head is to be dismantled, refer to the relevant Sections of Chapter 2B.

Preparation for refitting

15 The mating faces of the cylinder head and block must be perfectly clean before refitting the head. Use a scraper to remove all traces of gasket and carbon, and also clean the tops of the pistons. Take particular care with the aluminium surfaces, as the soft metal is damaged easily. Also, make sure that debris is not allowed to enter the oil and water channels – this is particularly important for the oil circuit, as carbon could block the oil supply to the camshaft or crankshaft bearings. Using adhesive tape and paper, seal the water, oil and bolt holes in the cylinder block. To prevent carbon entering the gap between the pistons and bores, smear a little grease in the gap. After cleaning the piston, rotate the crankshaft so that the piston moves down the bore, then wipe out the grease and carbon with a cloth rag. Clean the piston crowns in the same way.

16 Check the block and head for nicks, deep scratches and other damage. If slight, they may be removed carefully with a file. More serious damage may require a new cylinder head. Consult a Land Rover dealer or specialist.

17 If warpage of the cylinder head gasket surface is suspected, use a straight-edge to check it for distortion. Refer to Chapter 2B Section 7.

18 Ensure that the cylinder head bolt holes in the crankcase are clean and free of oil. Syringe or soak up any oil left in the bolt holes. This is most important in order that the correct bolt tightening torque can be applied and to prevent the possibility of the block being cracked by hydraulic pressure when the bolts are tightened.

19 On this engine, the cylinder head to piston clearance is controlled by fitting different thickness head gaskets. The piston protrusion is represented by the number of holes in the gasket at the front edge (see illustrations).

Holes in gasket	Largest piston protrusion
One hole	0.55 to 0.60 mm
Two holes	0.61 to 0.65 mm
Three holes	0.66 to 0.70 mm
Four holes	0.71 to 0.75 mm

20 Select the replacement gasket which has the same thickness/number of holes as the original, unless new piston and connecting rod assemblies have been fitted. In that case, the correct thickness of gasket required is selected by measuring the piston protrusions as follows.

21 Remove the timing pin from the flywheel and mount a dial test indicator securely on the block so that its pointer can be easily pivoted between the piston crown and block mating surface.

22 Ensure the piston is at exactly TDC then zero the dial test indicator on the gasket surface of the cylinder block. Carefully move the indicator over No.1 piston, taking measurements in line with the gudgeon pin axis, measure the protrusion on both the left-hand and right-hand side of the piston (see illustration). Repeat this procedure on No.4 piston.

23 Rotate the crankshaft half-a-turn to bring Nos.2 and 3 pistons to TDC. Ensure the crankshaft is accurately positioned then measure the protrusions of Nos.2 and 3 pistons, taking two measurements for each piston. Once both pistons have been measured, rotate the crankshaft through half-a-turn to bring Nos.1 and 4 pistons back to TDC and lock the crankshaft in position again.

24 Use the table in paragraph 19 to select the appropriate gasket.

Refitting

25 Wipe clean the mating faces of the head and

8.25 Ensure the locating dowels are in position

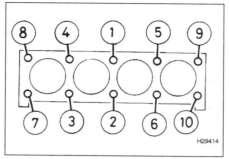

8.29 Cylinder head bolt tightening sequence

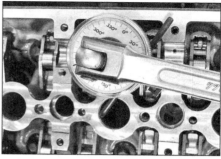

8.31 Using an angle-measuring gauge

block and ensure that the two locating dowels are in position at each end of the cylinder block/crankcase surface **(see illustration)**.

26 Fit the new gasket to the cylinder block, ensuring that it fits correctly over the locating dowels.

27 With the help of an assistant, carefully refit the cylinder head, locating it on the dowels.

28 Carefully enter the new bolts into the cylinder head screw them in, by hand only, until finger-tight.

Caution: Do not drop the bolts into their holes.

29 Working progressively and in the sequence shown, first tighten all the cylinder head bolts to the Stage 1 torque setting **(see illustration)**.

30 Again, in sequence, tighten the bolts to the Stage 2 torque setting.

31 Now angle-tighten the bolts in sequence 220° (Stage 3), using an angle-measuring gauge **(see illustration)**.

32 The remainder of refitting is a reversal of removal, noting the following points:

a) Tighten all fasteners to their specified torque where given.

b) Fill the cooling system as described in Chapter 1 Section 34.

c) Reconnect the battery negative lead as described in Chapter 5A Section 4.

---

9 Sump – removal and refitting

Sump pan

Removal

1 Apply the handbrake, then jack up the front of the vehicle and support it securely on axle stands (see 'Vehicle jacking and support'). Remove the retaining screws and fasteners and remove the undercover from beneath the engine and transmission.

2 Drain the engine oil and remove the oil filter as described in Chapter 1 Section 4. Refit the sump plug with a new washer and tighten the plug to the specified torque.

3 Undo the bolts securing the intercooler air duct beneath the sump **(see illustration)**.

4 Undo the bolts and remove the sump sound insulation panel (where fitted).

5 Unscrew the sump pan retaining bolts.

6 Break the sump pan joint by striking the plate with the palm of the hand, then lower the plate away from the sump. Be prepared for fluid spillage.

Refitting

7 Ensure the pan and extension mating surfaces are clean and dry, apply a bead of sealant (Three bond TB1215 or equivalent) to the sump pan mating surface.

8 Refit the pan and evenly tighten the bolts to the specified torque.

9 The remainder of refitting is a reversal of removal.

Sump extension

Removal

10 Remove the sump pan as described previously in this Section.

11 Release the clamps securing the air and breather hoses to the ducting on the top of the engine, then undo the 2 retaining

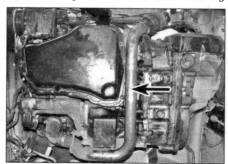

9.3 Intercooler air duct

9.17 Dipstick guide tube upper bolt...

bolts and remove the engine top cover **(see illustration 6.3)**.

12 Remove the alternator as described in Chapter 5A Section 6.

13 Undo the retaining bolt and remove the auxiliary drivebelt tensioner **(see illustration)**.

14 Remove the bolt securing the lower tie rod to the engine bracket **(see illustration 15.21)**.

15 Undo the 3 mounting bolts and position the air conditioning compressor away from the engine. There's no need to disconnect the refrigerant pipes.

16 The alternator mounting bracket it secured by 9 bolts. Slacken the upper 6 bolts, and remove the lower 3 bolts.

17 Undo the 2 retaining bolts and pull the engine oil level dipstick guide tube from the sump **(see illustration)**. Discard and renew the O-ring seal.

18 Disconnect the engine oil temperature sensor wiring plug, then release the clamp and disconnect the breather hose from the sump **(see illustration)**.

9.13 Auxiliary drivebelt tensioner Torx bolt

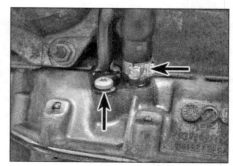

9.18...lower bolt, and breather hose clamp

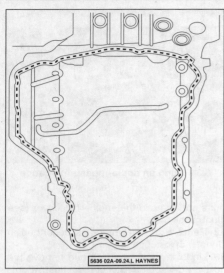

9.24 Apply sealant to the areas shown

19 Remove the 4 bolts securing the sump extension to the transmission bellhousing.
20 Progressively slacken and remove the 20 bolts securing the sump extension to the base of the cylinder block.
21 Break the joint by striking the sump extension with the palm of the hand, then lower it away from the engine.
22 While the sump is removed, take the opportunity to check the oil pump pick-up/strainer for signs of clogging or splitting.

Refitting

23 Clean all traces of sealant from the mating surfaces of the cylinder block and sump extension, then use a clean rag to wipe out the sump and the engine interior.
24 Apply a 3 mm bead of suitable sealant (Loctite 518 or equivalent) to the sump extension mating surface in the areas shown **(see illustration)**.
25 Refit the sump extension retaining bolts, and tighten the bolts finger-tight only.
26 Fit the bolts securing the sump extension to the transmission bellhousing. In order to align the rear sump flange with the gearbox, lightly tighten the bolts, then slacken them.

If the sump extension is being refitted to the engine with the gearbox removed, use a straight edge to ensure that the sump extension casting is flush with the end of the engine block.
27 Tighten the sump extension-to-engine block bolts, and then the sump extension-to-transmission bolts to the specified torque.
28 The remainder of refitting is a reversal of removal.

10 Balance shafts and housing – general information

General information

1 On these engines, a housing with twin-counter rotating balance shafts is fitted to the base of the cylinder block. The function of the assembly is to counteract the vibration caused by the crankshaft rotating, and the pistons etc. The shafts linked by helical gears integral with the shafts, and the front shaft is driven by a matched helical gear integral with the crankshaft. Backlash between the gears is controlled by shims located between the housing and the engine block.
2 Due to the fine tolerances used during manufacture and the special tools required during assembly, removal and refitting of the balance shaft housing is considered beyond the scope of this manual. Land Rover insist that the assembly must not be dismantled.

11 Oil pump – removal and refitting

Removal

1 Remove the sump pan as described in Section 9.
2 Undo the retaining bolts and remove the pump, noting the fitted position of the bolts. Disengage the sprocket from the chain as the pump is withdrawn **(see illustration)**. **Note:**

No information concerning the inspection or dismantling of the pump is available from Land Rover. If faulty, the pump should be renewed.

Refitting

3 Ensure the mating surfaces of the oil pump and cylinder block are clean and dry.
4 Position the oil pump, engaging the sprocket with the chain, and tighten the retaining bolts to the specified torque. Note that the shouldered-bolt is fitted at the front, upper location on the pump.
5 Refit the sump main casting as described in Section 9.

12 Oil cooler – removal and refitting

Removal

1 Remove the air conditioning compressor with reference to Chapter 3 Section 11.
2 Drain the engine coolant, engine oil, and remove the oil filter as described in Chapter 1 Section 4.
3 With reference to Chapter 4A Section 12, remove the throttle body.
4 Disconnect the engine oil pressure sensor wiring plug **(see illustration 16.3)**.
5 Disconnect the hoses from the cooler, and unclip the wiring harness **(see illustration)**.
6 Undo the 4 retaining nuts and remove the oil cooler and filter housing **(see illustration)**. Discard and renew the seal. Be prepared for fluid spillage.
7 If required, undo the bolts and detach the oil cooler from the oil filter housing. Discard and renew the seal.

Refitting

8 Ensure the mating surfaces of the oil cooler and oil filter housing are clean and dry, and with a new seal, fit the cooler to the housing. Tighten the bolts to the specified torque.
9 Refit the oil filter housing with a new seal and tighten the bolts to the specified torque.
10 The remainder of refitting is a reversal of removal.

11.2 Disengage the sprocket from the chain as the pump is withdrawn

12.5 Cooler hose clamps

12.6 Oil filter housing retaining nuts

13 Oil seals – renewal

Crankshaft right-hand (timing belt end) seal

1 Remove the timing belt as described in Section 6.

2 Slide the crankshaft sprocket from place and recover the key **(see illustrations)**.

3 Very carefully punch or drill two small holes opposite each other in the oil seal. Screw a self-tapping screw into each and pull on the screws with pliers to extract the seal **(see illustrations)**.

Caution: Great care must be taken to avoid damage to the crankshaft

4 Clean the seal housing and polish off any burrs or raised edges which may have caused the seal to fail in the first place.

5 Drive the new seal into position on the end of the shaft, pressing squarely into position until it is flush with the housing, using a suitable tubular drift, such as a socket, which bears only on the hard outer edge of the seal. Take great care not to damage the seal lips during fitting and ensure that the seal lips face inwards. Do not apply any lubricant to the seal.

6 Refit the keys to the crankshaft, followed by the sprocket.

7 Refit the timing belt as described in Section 6.

Crankshaft left-hand (flywheel/driveplate end) oil seal

8 Remove the flywheel or driveplate as described in Section 14.

9 Very carefully punch or drill two small holes opposite each other in the oil seal. Screw a self-tapping screw into each and pull on the screws with pliers to extract the seal **(see illustration 13.3a and 13.3b)**.

10 Clean the seal housing and polish off any burrs or raised edges which may have caused the seal to fail.

11 Land Rover use a special tool (No 303-1271) to fit the new seal into the housing. One part of the tool fits over the end of the crankshaft to guide the seal, whilst the other part draws the seal into place.

12 Press the seal evenly into the housing, until its outer flange is flush with the housing lip. Do not lubricate the seal.

13 Refit the flywheel/driveplate as described in Section 14.

Camshaft oil seal

14 Remove the timing belt as described in Section 6.

15 Slacken the camshaft sprocket retaining bolt and remove it, along with its washer. To prevent the camshaft rotating as the bolt is slackened, a sprocket-holding tool will be

13.2a Slide the sprocket from the crankshaft...

13.3a Drill a hole in the hard, outer shell of the oil seal...

Fabricate a holding tool from 2 lengths of steel strip bolted together, with a bolt/nut at each end.

13.2b...and recover the key

13.3b...insert a self-tapping screw, and pull the seal out

required. In the absence of the special Land Rover tool, an acceptable substitute can be fabricated as follows. Use two lengths of steel strip (one long, the other short), and three nuts and bolts; one nut and bolt forms the pivot of a forked tool, with the remaining two nuts and bolts at the tips of the 'forks' to engage with the sprocket spokes **(see Tool Tip)**. Discard the bolt – a new one must be fitted.

Caution: Do not attempt to use just the sprocket locking pin to prevent the sprocket from rotating whilst the bolt is slackened.

16 Very carefully punch or drill two small holes opposite each other in the oil seal. Screw a self-tapping screw into each and pull on the screws with pliers to extract the seal **(see illustration 13.3a and 13.3b)**.

Caution: Great care must be taken to avoid damage to the camshaft.

17 Clean the seal housing and polish off any burrs or raised edges which may have caused the seal to fail in the first place.

18 Drive the new seal into position on the end of the shaft, pressing squarely into position until it is flush with the housing, using a suitable tubular drift, such as a socket, which bears only on the hard outer edge of the seal **(see illustration)**. Take great care not to damage the seal lips during fitting and ensure that the seal lips face inwards. Do not apply any lubricant to the seal.

19 Refit the sprocket, and tighten the new bolt and washer to the specified torque. Hold the sprocket using the same method employed on removal.

20 Refit the timing belt as described in Section 6.

13.18 Use a suitable tubular drift to install the new seal

14 Flywheel/driveplate – removal, inspection and refitting

Flywheel

Removal

Note: *New flywheel retaining bolts must be used on refitting.*

1 Remove the clutch assembly as described in Chapter 6 Section 6.

2 Prevent the flywheel from turning by locking the ring gear teeth with a similar arrangement to that shown **(see illustration)**. Alternatively, bolt a strap between the flywheel and the cylinder block/crankcase.

3 Slacken and remove the retaining bolts and remove the flywheel, noting its locating dowel. Do not drop it, as it is very heavy. Discard the bolts, they must be renewed whenever they are disturbed.

Inspection

4 If the flywheel-to-clutch mating surface is deeply scored, cracked or otherwise damaged, then the flywheel must be renewed, unless it is possible to have it surface ground. Seek the advice of a Land Rover dealer or engine reconditioning specialist.

5 If the ring gear is badly worn or has missing teeth, then it must be renewed. This job is best left to a Land Rover dealer or engine reconditioning specialist.

Refitting

6 Clean the mating surfaces of the flywheel and crankshaft and remove all traces of locking compound from the crankshaft threaded holes.

7 Fit the flywheel to the crankshaft, engaging it with the crankshaft locating dowel, and fit the new retaining bolts. Note:If the new bolts are not supplied pre-coated with locking compound, apply a few drops prior to fitting the bolts.

8 Lock the flywheel using the method employed on dismantling then, working in a diagonal sequence, tighten all the retaining bolts to the specified torque setting.

9 Refit the clutch assembly as described in Chapter 6 Section 6.

Driveplate

Removal

Note: *New driveplate retaining bolts must be used on refitting.*

10 Remove the automatic transmission and torque converter as described in Chapter 7B Section 5.

11 Prevent the driveplate from turning by locking the ring gear teeth with a similar arrangement to that shown **(see illustration 13.2)**. Alternatively, bolt a strap between the driveplate and the cylinder block/crankcase.

12 Slacken and remove the retaining bolts and remove the driveplate, noting its locating

14.2 Homemade flywheel locking tool

dowel **(see illustration)**. Discard the bolts, they must be renewed whenever they are disturbed.

Inspection

13 If the ring gear is badly worn or has missing teeth, then it must be renewed. This job is best left to a Land Rover dealer or engine reconditioning specialist.

Refitting

14 Clean the mating surfaces of the driveplate and crankshaft and remove all traces of locking compound from the crankshaft threaded holes.

15 Fit the driveplate to the crankshaft, engaging it with the crankshaft locating dowel, and fit the new retaining bolts. **Note:** *If the new bolts are not supplied pre-coated with locking compound, apply a few drops prior to fitting the bolts.*

16 Lock the driveplate using the method employed on dismantling then, working in a diagonal sequence, tighten all the retaining bolts to the specified torque setting.

17 Refit the torque converter and automatic transmission as described in Chapter 7B Section 5.

15 Engine/transmission mountings – inspection and renewal

Inspection

1 If improved access is required, firmly apply the handbrake, raise the front of the vehicle and support it securely on axle stands (see *Vehicle jacking and support*). If necessary, undo the retaining screws and fasteners and remove the undercover from beneath the engine/transmission unit.

2 Check the mounting rubber to see if it is cracked, hardened or separated from the metal at any point. Renew the mounting if any such damage or deterioration is evident.

3 Check that all mounting fasteners are securely tightened. Use a torque wrench to check, if possible.

4 Using a large screwdriver or a pry bar, check for wear in the mountings by carefully

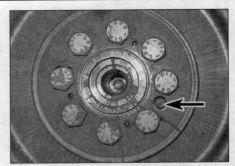

14.12 Locating dowel position

levering against it to check for free play. Where this is not possible, enlist the aid of an assistant to move the engine/gearbox unit back and forth or from side to side while you watch the mountings. While some free play is to be expected even from new components, excessive wear should be obvious. If excessive free play is found, check first that the fasteners are correctly secured, then renew any worn components as described below.

Renewal

Left-hand mounting

5 Firmly apply the handbrake, raise the front of the vehicle and support it securely on axle stands (see *Vehicle jacking and Support*). Undo the retaining screws and fasteners and remove the undercover from beneath the engine/transmission unit.

6 With reference to Chapter 4A Section 2, remove the air cleaner and intake ducts.

7 Remove the battery tray, as described in Chapter 5A Section 4.

8 Position a jack under the transmission with a block of wood between the jack head and casing, and take the weight if the engine and transmission.

9 Undo the nuts/bolts and remove the bracket above the engine mounting **(see illustration)**. On automatic transmission models, unclip the breather pipe from the mounting. Renew the nuts.

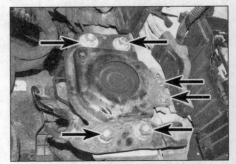

15.9 Undo the nuts/bolts and remove the bracket

15.10 Left-hand mounting retaining bolts

15.15a Right-hand engine mounting bracket bolts

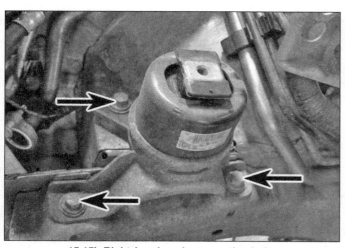

15.15b Right-hand engine mounting bolts

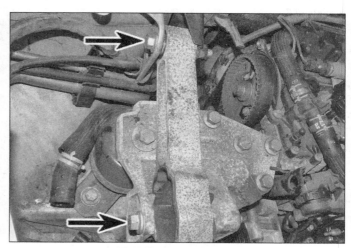

15.18 Upper tie rod bolts

10 Undo the bolts and remove the mounting **(see illustration)**.

11 Refitting is a reversal of removal.

Right-hand mounting

12 Raise the front of the vehicle and support it securely on axle stands (see *Vehicle Jacking and Support*'). Undo the retaining screws and fasteners and remove the undercover from beneath the engine/transmission unit.

13 Release the clamps securing the air and breather hoses to the ducting on the top of the engine, then undo the 2 retaining bolts and remove the engine top cover **(see illustration 6.3)**.

14 Remove the upper engine tie rod as described in this Section, then position a jack under the engine with a block of wood between the jack head and the casing. Take the weight of the engine.

15 Unclip the fuel pipes, then undo the bolts

and remove the right-hand engine mounting bracket, followed by the mounting **(see illustrations)**.

16 Refitting is a reversal of removal.

Upper engine tie rod

17 Undo the retaining bolt, slide the coolant expansion tank upwards, and position it to one side. There's no need to disconnect the hose.

18 Slacken and remove the retaining bolts and remove the tie rod **(see illustration)**.

19 Refitting is a reversal of removal.

Lower engine tie rod

20 Raise the front of the vehicle and support it securely on axle stands (see *Vehicle Jacking and Support*'). Undo the retaining screws and fasteners and remove the undercover from beneath the engine/transmission unit.

21 Undo the tie rod front through-bolt, and the 2 bolts securing the mounting bracket to

the subframe **(see illustration)**. Manoeuvre the assembly from place.

22 If required, remove the remaining through-bolt and detach the tie-rod from the mounting bracket.

23 Refitting is a reversal of removal.

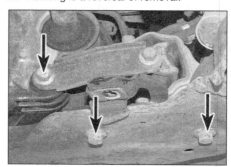

15.21 Lower tie rod through-bolt and mounting bracket bolts

16 Engine oil pressure and temperature sensors – renewal

Oil pressure sensor

1 Raise the front of the vehicle and support it securely on axle stands (see '*Vehicle Jacking and Support*'). Undo the retaining screws and fasteners and remove the undercover from beneath the engine/transmission unit.
2 Undo the fasteners and remove the panel and bashplate beneath the radiator.
3 Disconnect the wiring plug, then unscrew the sensor from the filter housing **(see illustration)**. Renew the sealing washer. Be prepared for fluid spillage.
4 Refitting is a reversal of removal, noting the following points:
a) *Renew the sensor sealing washer.*
b) *Tighten the sensor to the specified torque.*

16.3 Disconnect the oil pressure sensor wiring plug

c) *Check the engine oil level as described in 'Weekly checks'.*

Oil temperature sensor

5 Remove the starter motor as described in Chapter 5A Section 9.
6 Disconnect the wiring plug, and unscrew the sensor from the housing **(see illustration)**.

16.6 Disconnect the oil temperature sensor wiring plug

Renew the sealing washer. Be prepared for fluid spillage.
7 Refitting is a reversal of removal, noting the following points:
a) *Renew the sensor sealing washer.*
b) *Tighten the sensor to the specified torque.*
c) *Check the engine oil level as described in 'Weekly checks'.*

Chapter 2 Part B
General engine removal and overhaul procedures

Contents

Degrees of difficulty

Easy, suitable for novice with little experience	Fairly easy, suitable for beginner with some experience	Fairly difficult, suitable for competent DIY mechanic	Difficult, suitable for experienced DIY mechanic	Very difficult, suitable for expert DIY or professional

Specifications

Note: *At the time of writing, some specifications for certain engines were not available. Where the relevant specifications are not given here, refer to your Land Rover dealer for further information.*

Cylinder head
Maximum gasket face distortion . . . .   0.03 mm
No machining of the cylinder head permitted

Valves

	Intake	Exhaust
Valve stem diameter: All engines	5.978 ± 0.009 mm	5.968 ± 0.009 mm

Balance shafts
Endfloat . . . .   0.03 to 0.20 mm
Backlash clearance between shafts. . . . .   0.01 to 0.70 mm
Backlash clearance between driver shaft and crankshaft gear . . . . . .   0.01 to 0.26 mm

Crankshaft
Endfloat . . . .   0.07 to 0.32 mm

1 General information

1 Included in this Part of Chapter 2 are details of removing the engine/transmission from the car and general overhaul procedures for the cylinder head. At the time of writing, no information or specifications concerning the crankshaft, connecting rods, pistons or pistons rings were available.
2 The information given ranges from advice concerning preparation for an overhaul and the purchase of parts, to detailed step-by-step procedures covering removal, inspection, renovation and refitting of engine internal components.
3 Apart from torque wrench settings, which are given at the beginning of Part A (as applicable), all specifications available relating to engine overhaul are at the beginning of this Part of Chapter 2.

2 Engine overhaul – general information

1 It is not always easy to determine when, or if, an engine should be completely overhauled, as a number of factors must be considered.
2 High mileage is not necessarily an indication that an overhaul is needed, while low mileage does not preclude the need for an overhaul. Frequency of servicing is probably the most important consideration. An engine which has had regular and frequent oil and filter changes, as well as other required maintenance, should give many thousands of miles of reliable service. Conversely, a neglected engine may require an overhaul very early in its life.
3 Excessive oil consumption is an indication that piston rings, valve seals and/or valve guides are in need of attention. Make sure that oil leaks are not responsible before deciding that the rings and/or guides are worn. Perform a compression test, as described in Part A of this Chapter, to determine the likely cause of the problem.
4 Check the oil pressure with a gauge fitted in place of the oil pressure switch, and compare it with that specified. If it is extremely low, the main and big-end bearings, and/or the oil pump, are probably worn out.
5 Loss of power, rough running, knocking or metallic engine noises, excessive valve gear noise, and high fuel consumption may also point to the need for an overhaul, especially if they are all present at the same time. If a complete service does not cure the situation, major mechanical work is the only solution.
Note: *Critical cooling system components such as the hoses, thermostat and coolant pump should be renewed when an engine is overhauled. The radiator should be checked carefully, to ensure that it is not clogged or leaking. Also, it is a good idea to renew the oil pump whenever the engine is overhauled.*

6 Before beginning the engine overhaul, read through the entire procedure, to familiarise yourself with the scope and requirements of the job. Overhauling an engine is not difficult if you follow carefully all of the instructions, have the necessary tools and equipment, and pay close attention to all specifications. It can, however, be time-consuming. Plan on the car being off the road for a minimum of two weeks, especially if parts must be taken to an engineering works for repair or reconditioning. Check on the availability of parts and make sure that any necessary special tools and equipment are obtained in advance. Most work can be done with typical hand tools, although a number of precision measuring tools are required for inspecting parts to determine if they must be renewed. Often the engineering works will handle the inspection of parts and offer advice concerning reconditioning and renewal.
7 At the time of writing, no information or specifications concerning the crankshaft, connecting rods, pistons or pistons rings were available. Consequently, before attempting to dismantle these components, consult a Land Rover dealer or specialist. It may be the case that fitting a reconditioned 'short' engine is the most viable option.
8 As a final note, to ensure maximum life and minimum trouble from a reconditioned engine, everything must be assembled with care, in a spotlessly-clean environment.

3 Engine/transmission removal – methods and precautions

1 If you have decided that the engine must be removed for overhaul or major repair work, several preliminary steps should be taken.
2 Engine/transmission removal is extremely complicated and involved on these vehicles. It must be stated, that unless the vehicle can be positioned on a ramp, or raised and supported on axle stands over an inspection pit, it will be very difficult to carry out the work involved.
3 Cleaning the engine compartment and engine/transmission before beginning the removal procedure will help keep tools clean and organised.
4 An engine hoist may also be necessary. Make sure the equipment is rated in excess of the combined weight of the engine and transmission. Safety is of primary importance, considering the potential hazards involved in removing the engine/transmission from the car.
5 The help of an assistant is essential. Apart from the safety aspects involved, there are many instances when one person cannot simultaneously perform all of the operations required during engine/transmission removal.
6 Plan the operation ahead of time. Before starting work, arrange for the hire of or obtain all of the tools and equipment you will need. Some of the equipment necessary to perform engine/transmission removal and installation

safely (in addition to an engine hoist) is as follows: a heavy duty trolley jack, complete sets of spanners and sockets as described in the rear of this manual, wooden blocks, and plenty of rags and cleaning solvent for mopping-up spilled oil, coolant and fuel. If the hoist must be hired, make sure that you arrange for it in advance, and perform all of the operations possible without it beforehand. This will save you money and time.
7 Plan for the car to be out of use for quite a while. An engineering machine shop or engine reconditioning specialist will be required to perform some of the work which cannot be accomplished without special equipment. These places often have a busy schedule, so it would be a good idea to consult them before removing the engine, in order to accurately estimate the amount of time required to rebuild or repair components that may need work.
8 During the engine/transmission removal procedure, it is advisable to make notes of the locations of all brackets, cable ties, earthing points, etc, as well as how the wiring harnesses, hoses and electrical connections are attached and routed around the engine and engine compartment. An effective way of doing this is to take a series of photographs of the various components before they are disconnected or removed; the resulting photographs will prove invaluable when the engine/transmission is refitted.
9 Always be extremely careful when removing and refitting the engine/transmission. Serious injury can result from careless actions. Plan ahead and take your time, and a job of this nature, although major, can be accomplished successfully.
10 On all Freelander models, the engine must be removed complete with the transmission as an assembly. There is insufficient clearance in the engine compartment to remove the engine leaving the transmission in the vehicle. The assembly is removed by raising the front of the vehicle, and lowering the assembly from the engine compartment.
Note: *Such is the complexity of the power unit arrangement on these vehicles, and the variations that may be encountered according to model and optional equipment fitted, that the following should be regarded as a guide to the work involved, rather than a step-by-step procedure. Where differences are encountered, or additional component disconnection or removal is necessary, make notes of the work involved as an aid to refitting.*

4 Engine and transmission – removal, separation and refitting

Removal

1 On models with air conditioning, have the refrigerant system evacuated by a suitably equipped specialist.

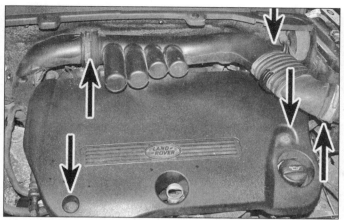

4.3 Release the clamps, disconnect the hoses, undo the bolts and remove the engine top cover

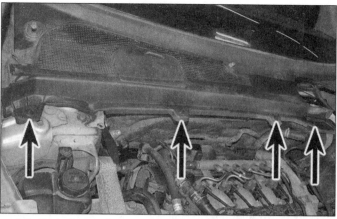

4.5a Undo the centre screws, prise out the plastic expansion rivets at the front edge...

2 To improve access remove the bonnet as described in Chapter 11 Section 8.

3 Release the clamps securing the air and breather hoses to the ducting on the top of the engine, then undo the 3 retaining bolts and remove the engine top cover **(see illustration)**.

4 Remove the front wiper arms as described in Chapter 12 Section 13.

5 Remove the 5 fasteners and pull the scuttle trim panel upwards from the base of the windscreen **(see illustrations)**.

6 Remove the battery and battery tray as described in Chapter 5A Section 4.

7 With reference to Chapter 4A Section 2, remove the air cleaner assembly.

8 Drain the cooling system as described in Chapter 1 Section 34.

9 Remove the catalytic converter as described in Chapter 4B Section 2.

10 Working underneath, undo the front through-bolt and remove the bolts securing the engine lower rear tie-rod mounting bracket to the subframe **(see illustration)**. Manoeuvre the subframe assembly from place.

4.5b ...and pull the scuttle trim panel upwards from the base of the windscreen

11 Remove the front subframe as described in Chapter 10 Section 8.

12 Disconnect the wiring plugs from the engine management ECM, and release the wiring harness from the bulkhead grommet **(see illustration)**.

13 Release the clips and disconnect the hoses from the vacuum pump and thermostat housing at the left-hand end of the cylinder head.

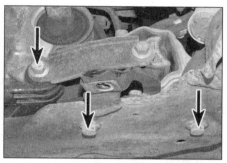

4.10 Lower rear tie-rod front through bolt and mounting bracket bolts

14 Disconnect the gearchange/selector cable(s) from the transmission as described in Chapter 7A Section 3 or Chapter 7B Section 3.

15 Remove both front driveshafts as described in Chapter 8 Section 2.

16 Disconnect the cooling fan control unit wiring plug **(see illustration)**.

17 Release the clamp, undo the retaining bolt

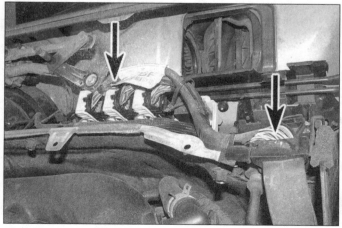

4.12 Disconnect the ECM wiring plugs, and release the grommet

4.16 Fan control unit wiring plug

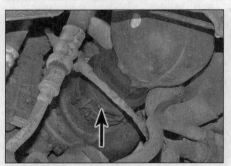

4.17a Working through the wheel arch aperture, release the intake duct clamp

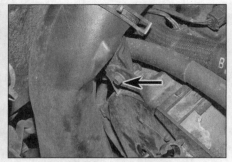

4.17b Undo the retaining bolt...

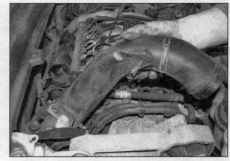

4.17c...and remove the turbocharger air intake duct

and manoeuvre the turbocharger air intake duct from place **(see illustrations)**.

18 Syphon as much fluid as possible from the power steering reservoir, then release the clamps and disconnect the lower end of the fluid supply hose. Be prepared for fluid spillage. Plug the openings to prevent contamination.

19 Undo the retaining bolts and disconnect the power steering high-pressure pipe from the pump. Discard the seal, a new one must be fitted. Plug the openings to prevent contamination.

20 Undo the retaining bolts and disconnect the refrigerant pipes from the condenser and the connection at the right-hand inner wing **(see illustration)**. Discard the seals, new ones

must be fitted. Plug the openings to prevent contamination.

21 Prise out the wire clip a little, and pull the upper and lower coolant hoses from the radiator.

22 Disconnect the fuel supply and return hoses from the filter assembly, and unclip them from the timing belt cover **(see illustration)**. Be prepared for fuel spillage. Plug the openings to prevent contamination.

23 Undo the retaining bolts, and remove the intercooler air inlet pipe assembly **(see illustration)**.

24 Slacken the clamp and disconnect the air outlet hose from the right-hand end of the intercooler.

25 Remove the cover, undo the retaining nut,

disconnect the wiring plugs, the release the clips and slide the fuse/relay box upwards from place **(see illustrations)**.

26 At the left-hand side of the engine compartment, undo the bolts, disconnect the 4 earth connections and the battery positive lead.

27 Undo the retaining bolt, lift the coolant expansion tank a little, then disconnect the coolant hoses and the level sensor wiring plug. Remove the tank.

28 On 4WD models, remove the 6 bolts and 3 reinforcement plates, then disconnect the front of the propeller shaft from the transfer case – refer to Chapter 8 if necessary.

29 Prise out the clips a little, and pull the heater coolant hoses from the engine

4.20 Undo the nut and disconnect the refrigerant pipe at the right-hand inner wing

4.22 Depress the release buttons, and disconnect the supply and return hoses from the filter

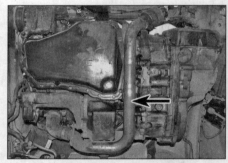

4.23 Remove the intercooler air pipe from under the engine

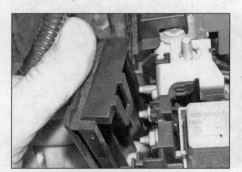

4.25a Remove the cover...

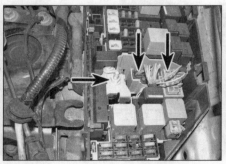

4.25b...undo the nut, disconnect the wiring plugs...

4.25c...and slide the front section of the fuse/relay box up from place

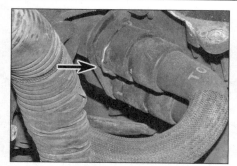

4.29a Prise out the wire clips a little...

4.29b...and disconnect the heater coolant hoses

4.31 Attach a hoist to the engine lifting eyes

compartment bulkhead **(see illustrations)**. Be prepared for fluid spillage. Plug the openings to prevent contamination.

30 On manual transmission models, prise out the clip a little and pull the fluid pipe from the clutch slave cylinder connection on the transmission housing.

31 Raise the front of the vehicle sufficiently high enough to be able to remove the engine/transmission assembly from underneath it. Position a workshop trolley jack under the engine/transmission, or attach an engine lifting hoist **(see illustration)**. Take the weight of the engine.

32 Refer to Chapter 2A Section 15 and remove the left-hand engine/transmission mounting.

33 Undo the bolts and remove the right-hand engine mounting tie-rod and bracket.

34 Make a final check that any components which would prevent the removal of the engine/transmission from the car have been removed or disconnected. Ensure that components such as the gearchange selector cables are secured so that they cannot be damaged on removal.

35 Carefully lower the assembly to the ground, making sure it clears the surrounding engine compartment components.

Separation

36 With the engine/transmission assembly removed, support the assembly on suitable blocks of wood on a workbench (or failing that, on a clean area of the workshop floor).

37 Undo the retaining bolts, and remove the flywheel cover plate from the starter motor aperture.

38 Slacken and remove the retaining bolts, and remove the starter motor from the transmission.

39 On automatic transmission models, working through the starter motor aperture, undo the 6 bolts spaced at 60° intervals securing the driveplate to the torque converter. Use a socket on the crankshaft to rotate the driveplate to access the bolts. Note that new bolts must be fitted.

40 On all models, ensure that both engine and transmission are adequately supported, then slacken and remove the remaining bolts

securing the transmission housing to the engine. Note the correct fitted positions of each bolt (and the relevant brackets) as they are removed, to use as a reference on refitting.

41 Carefully withdraw the transmission from the engine, ensuring that the weight of the manual transmission is not allowed to hang on the input shaft while it is engaged with the clutch friction disc.

42 If they are loose, remove the locating dowels from the engine or transmission, and keep them in a safe place.

Refitting

43 If the engine and transmission have not been separated, perform the operations described below from paragraph 53 onwards.

44 On manual transmission models, Land Rover insist that no lubricant is applied to the transmission input shaft splines prior to refitting.

Automatic transmission models

45 Prior to reconnection it is necessary to make a simple tool to align the torque converter with the driveplate as the transmission is refitted. To make the tool, obtain a bolt of the same size as the torque converter retaining bolts, but long enough to extend through the access hole in the cylinder block when the transmission is refitted.

46 Cut the head off the bolt and cut a slot (to enable it to be unscrewed) in the plain end. Check that the tool will slide easily through the torque converter retaining bolt hole in the driveplate.

47 Turn the engine crankshaft so that one of the torque converter retaining bolt holes in the driveplate, is aligned with the access hole in the cylinder block. Screw the alignment tool (finger-tight only) into one of the retaining bolt holes in the torque converter. Turn the torque converter so that the alignment tool is in approximately the correct position, relative to the cylinder block access hole. As the transmission is refitted, the alignment tool will pass through the retaining bolt hole in the driveplate and through the access hole. It can then be unscrewed with a screwdriver and the first torque converter retaining bolt fitted in its place.

All models

48 Ensure that the engine/transmission locating dowels are correctly positioned prior to installation.

49 Carefully offer the transmission to the engine, until the locating dowels are engaged.

50 Refit the transmission housing-to-engine bolts, ensuring that all the necessary brackets are correctly positioned, and tighten them securely.

51 On automatic transmission models, bear in mind the following points:
a) Guide the transmission into position ensuring that the alignment tool passes through the driveplate and access hole.
b) Remove the bolt used to retain the torque converter in place, just before the transmission engages with the engine.
c) Once the transmission is bolted to the engine, remove the alignment tool and fit the first torque converter retaining bolt.
d) Turn the crankshaft as necessary and fit the remaining bolts.

52 The remainder of the refitting procedure is a direct reversal of the removal sequence, with reference to the relevant chapters and noting the following points:
a) Ensure that the wiring loom is correctly routed and retained by all the relevant retaining clips; all connectors should be correctly and securely reconnected.
b) Prior to refitting the driveshafts to the transmission, renew the driveshaft oil seals as described in Chapter 7A Section 5.
c) Ensure that all coolant hoses are correctly reconnected, and securely retained by their retaining clips.
d) Refill the engine and transmission with the correct quantity and type of lubricant, as described in Chapter 1.
e) Refill the cooling system as described in Chapter 1 Section 34.
f) Bleed the power steering system as described in Chapter 10 Section 22.
g) Have the air conditioning system recharged (where applicable) by a suitably equipped specialist.

5 Engine overhaul – dismantling sequence

1 It is much easier to dismantle and work on the engine if it is mounted on a portable engine stand. These stands can often be hired from a tool hire shop. Before the engine is mounted on a stand, the flywheel/driveplate should be removed, so that the stand bolts can be tightened into the end of the cylinder block/crankcase.

2 If a stand is not available, it is possible to dismantle the engine with it blocked up on a sturdy workbench, or on the floor. Be extra-careful not to tip or drop the engine when working without a stand.

3 If you are going to obtain a reconditioned engine, all the external components must be removed first, to be transferred to the new engine (just as they will if you are doing a complete engine overhaul yourself). These components include the following:

a) *Engine wiring harness and support brackets.*
b) *Alternator, power steering pump and air conditioning compressor mounting brackets (as applicable).*
c) *Coolant inlet and outlet housings*
d) *Dipstick guide tube.*
e) *Fuel system components*
f) *All electrical switches and sensors.*
g) *Inlet, exhaust manifolds and turbocharger.*
h) *Oil filter and oil cooler.*
i) *Flywheel/driveplate.*

Note: *When removing the external components from the engine, pay close attention to details that may be helpful or important during refitting. Note the fitted position of gaskets, seals, spacers, pins, washers, bolts, and other small items.*

4 If you are obtaining a 'short' engine (which consists of the engine cylinder block/crank-case, crankshaft, pistons and connecting rods all assembled), then the cylinder head, sump, oil pump, and timing belt will have to be removed also.

5 If you are planning a complete overhaul, bear in mind that Land Rover provide no information (procedures, torque wrench setting, tolerances, etc.) concerning the crankshaft, connecting rods, pistons and piston rings. We recommend you consult a Land Rover dealer or specialist before attempting to dismantle these parts.

6 Before beginning the dismantling and overhaul procedures, make sure that you have all of the correct tools necessary. See *'Tools and working facilities'* for further information

6 Cylinder head – dismantling

Note: *New and reconditioned cylinder heads are available from the manufacturer, and from engine overhaul specialists. Be aware that some specialist tools are required for the dismantling and inspection procedures, and new components may not be readily available. It may therefore be more practical and economical for the home mechanic to purchase a reconditioned head, rather than dismantle, inspect and recondition the original head.*

1 Remove the cylinder head as described in Chapter 2A Section 8.

2 If not already done, remove the intake and exhaust manifolds with reference to Chapter 4A Section 18. Remove any remaining brackets or housings as required.

3 If not already done, remove the glow plugs as described in Chapter 5B Section 3.

4 Using a valve spring compressor, compress each valve spring in turn until the split collets can be removed. Release the compressor, and lift off the spring retainer and spring. Using a pair of pliers, carefully extract the valve stem oil seal from the top of the guide. The valve stem oil seal also forms the spring seat and is deeply recessed in the cylinder head. It is also a tight fit on the valve guide making it difficult to remove with pliers or a conventional valve stem oil seal removal tool. It can be easily removed, however, using a self-locking nut of suitable diameter screwed onto the end of a bolt and locked with a second nut. Push the nut down onto the top of the seal; the locking portion of the nut will grip the seal allowing it to be withdrawn from the top of the valve guide. Access to the valves is limited, and it may be necessary to make up an adaptor out of metal tube – cut out a 'window' so that the valve collets can be removed **(see illustrations)**.

5 If, when the valve spring compressor is screwed down, the spring retainer refuses to free and expose the split collets, gently tap the top of the tool, directly over the retainer, with a light hammer. This will free the retainer.

6 Withdraw the valve from the combustion chamber. Remove the valve stem oil seal and seat from the top of the guide.

7 It is essential that each valve is stored together with its collets, retainer, spring, and spring seat. The valves should also be kept in their correct sequence, unless they are so badly worn that they are to be renewed. If they are going to be kept and used again, place each valve assembly in a labelled polythene bag or similar small container **(see illustration)**. Note that No 1 valve is nearest to the transmission (flywheel/driveplate) end of the engine.

7 Cylinder head and valves – cleaning and inspection

1 Thorough cleaning of the cylinder head and valve components, followed by a detailed inspection, will enable you to decide how much valve service work must be carried out during the engine overhaul. Note: If the engine has been severely overheated, it is best to assume that the cylinder head is warped – check carefully for signs of this.

Cleaning

2 Carefully scrape away all traces of old gasket material from the cylinder head.

3 Scrape away the carbon from the combustion chambers and ports, then wash the cylinder head thoroughly with paraffin or a suitable solvent.

4 Scrape off any heavy carbon deposits that may have formed on the valves, then use a power-operated wire brush to remove deposits from the valve heads and stems.

Inspection

Note: *Be sure to perform all the following inspection procedures before concluding that the services of a machine shop or engine*

6.4a Compress the valve spring and remove the collets

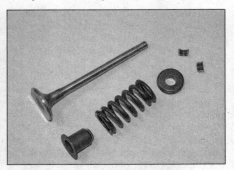
6.4b Followed by the retainer, spring, valve, and stem seal/spring seat

6.7 Store the valve components in a labelled bag

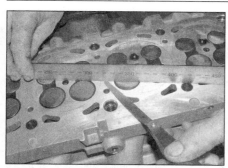

7.5 Check for cylinder head gasket face distortion

7.10 Measure the valve stem diameter with a micrometer

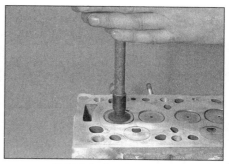

7.13 Grinding-in a valve

overhaul specialist are required. Make a list of all items that require attention.

Cylinder head

5 Inspect the head very carefully for cracks, evidence of coolant leakage, and other damage. If cracks are found, a new cylinder head should be obtained. Use a straight-edge and feeler blade to check that the cylinder head gasket surface is not distorted **(see illustration)**. If it is, it may be possible to have it machined, provided that the cylinder head height is not significantly reduced.

6 Examine the valve seats in each of the combustion chambers. If they are severely pitted, cracked, or burned, they will need to be renewed or recut by an engine overhaul specialist. If they are only slightly pitted, this can be removed by grinding-in the valve heads and seats using fine valve-grinding compound, as described below. If in any doubt, have the cylinder head inspected by an engine overhaul specialist.

7 Check the valve guides for wear by inserting the relevant valve, and checking for side-to-side motion of the valve. A very small amount of movement is acceptable. If the movement seems excessive, remove the valve. Measure the valve stem diameter (see below), and renew the valve if it is worn. If the valve stem is not worn, the wear must be in the valve guide, and the guide must be renewed. The renewal of valve guides is best carried out by a Land Rover dealer or engine overhaul specialist, who will have the necessary tools available. Where no valve stem diameter is specified, seek the advice of a Land Rover dealer on the best course of action.

8 If renewing the valve guides, the valve seats should be recut or reground only after the guides have been fitted.

Valves

9 Examine the head of each valve for pitting, burning, cracks, and general wear. Check the valve stem for scoring and wear ridges. Rotate the valve, and check for any obvious indication that it is bent. Look for pits or excessive wear on the tip of each valve stem. Renew any valve that shows any such signs of wear or damage.

10 If the valve appears satisfactory at this

stage, measure the valve stem diameter at several points using a micrometer **(see illustration)**. Any significant difference in the readings obtained indicates wear of the valve stem. Should any of these conditions be apparent, the valve must be renewed.

11 If the valves are in satisfactory condition, they should be ground (lapped) into their respective seats, to ensure a smooth, gas-tight seal. If the seat is only lightly pitted, or if it has been recut, fine grinding compound only should be used to produce the required finish. Coarse valve-grinding compound should not be used, unless a seat is badly burned or deeply pitted. If this is the case, the cylinder head and valves should be inspected by an expert, to decide whether seat recutting, or even the renewal of the valve or seat insert (where possible) is required.

12 Valve grinding is carried out as follows. Place the cylinder head upside-down on a bench.

13 Smear a trace of (the appropriate grade of) valve-grinding compound on the seat face, and press a suction grinding tool onto the valve head **(see illustration)**. With a semi-rotary action, grind the valve head to its seat, lifting the valve occasionally to redistribute the grinding compound. A light spring placed under the valve head will greatly ease this operation.

14 If coarse grinding compound is being used, work only until a dull, matt even surface is produced on both the valve seat and the valve, then wipe off the used compound, and repeat the process with fine compound. When

a smooth unbroken ring of light grey matt finish is produced on both the valve and seat, the grinding operation is complete. Do not grind-in the valves any further than absolutely necessary, or the seat will be prematurely sunk into the cylinder head.

15 When all the valves have been ground-in, carefully wash off all traces of grinding compound using paraffin or a suitable solvent, before reassembling the cylinder head.

Valve components

16 Examine the valve springs for signs of damage and discoloration. No minimum free length is specified by Land Rover, so the only way of judging valve spring wear is by comparison with a new component.

17 Stand each spring on a flat surface, and check it for squareness. If any of the springs are damaged, distorted or have lost their tension, obtain a complete new set of springs. It is normal to renew the valve springs as a matter of course if a major overhaul is being carried out.

18 Renew the valve stem oil seals/lower seats regardless of their apparent condition.

8 Cylinder head – reassembly

1 Working on the first valve assembly, dip the new valve stem oil seal/lower seat in fresh engine oil. Locate the seal on the valve guide and press the seal firmly onto the guide using a suitable socket **(see illustrations)**.

8.1a Position the seal/seat over the valve guide...

8.1b...and press it into place using a deep socket

8.4 Use a little grease to hold the collets in place

2 Lubricate the stem of the first valve, and insert it in the guide.

3 Locate the valve spring on top of its seat, then refit the spring retainer. As the spring is symmetrical, the spring can be fitted either way up.

4 Compress the valve spring, and locate the split collets in the recess in the valve stem **(see illustration)**. Release the compressor, then repeat the procedure on the remaining valves. Ensure that each valve is inserted into its original location. If new valves are being fitted, insert them into the locations to which they have been ground. Use a little dab of grease to hold the collets in position on the valve stem while the spring compressor is released.

5 With all the valves installed, support the cylinder head and, using a hammer and interposed block of wood, tap the end of each valve stem to settle the components.

6 Refit any remaining components using the reverse of the removal sequence and with new seals or gaskets as necessary.

7 The cylinder head can then be refitted as described in Chapter 2A Section 8.

9 Crankshaft, main bearings, connecting rods and pistons – general information

Although the design of the cylinder block components appear to be conventional, no information concerning the dismantling, reassembly, torque wrench settings or tolerances of these components is provided by Land Rover. Consequently, we can only advise that, should these items require attention, seek advice from a Land Rover dealer or specialist before attempting any dismantling procedures.

10 Engine – initial start-up after overhaul

1 With the engine refitted in the vehicle, double-check the engine oil and coolant levels. Make a final check that everything has been reconnected, and that there are no tools or rags left in the engine compartment.

2 Remove the fuel pump relay/fuse – see Chapter 12 Section 3.

3 Turn the engine on the starter until the oil pressure warning light goes out. Refit the fuel pump fuse/relay.

4 Prime the fuel system (refer to Chapter 4A Section 6). Although the system is self-priming, it will help if the ignition is switched on and off several times before attempting to start the engine in order to purge air from the system.

5 Fully depress the accelerator pedal, turn the ignition key to position II, and wait for the preheating warning light to go out.

6 Start the engine, noting that this may take a little longer than usual, due to the fuel system components having been disturbed.

7 While the engine is idling, check for fuel, water and oil leaks. Don't be alarmed if there are some odd smells and smoke from parts getting hot and burning off oil deposits.

8 Assuming all is well, keep the engine idling until hot water is felt circulating through the top hose, then switch off the engine.

9 After a few minutes, recheck the oil and coolant levels as described in '*Weekly Checks*', and top-up as necessary.

10 Note that there is no need to retighten the cylinder head bolts once the engine has first run after reassembly.

11 If a reconditioned engine has been fitted, the engine must be treated as new, and run-in for the first 500 miles (800 km). Do not operate the engine at full-throttle, or allow it to labour at low engine speeds in any gear. It is recommended that the oil and filter be changed at the end of this period.

Chapter 3
Cooling, heating and ventilation systems

Contents

Degrees of difficulty

Easy, suitable for novice with little experience	Fairly easy, suitable for beginner with some experience	Fairly difficult, suitable for competent DIY mechanic	Difficult, suitable for experienced DIY mechanic	Very difficult, suitable for expert DIY or professional

Specifications

System
Type .... Pressurised, pump-assisted with front mounted radiator and ECM controlled cooling fan

Thermostat
Type .... Wax

Operating temperatures

	Starts to open	Fully open
All engines	83° C	91° C

Expansion tank
Cap pressure .... 1.45 bar

Air conditioning system
Refrigerant R134a
Refrigerant charge quantity .... 730 ± 10g
Lubricating oil... WSH-M1C321-B

Torque wrench settings

	Nm	lbf ft
Coolant manifold-to-thermostat housing pipe....................	8	5
Coolant pump bolts...	17	13
Cylinder block sealing plug	42	31
Thermostat housing bolts...................................	8	5
Compressor mounting bolts.................................	25	19
Compressor refrigerant pipe connections	24	18
Condenser refrigerant pipe connections	10	7
Condenser mounting bolts..................................	10	7
Pressor sensor	8	5

1 General information and precautions

General information

1 The cooling system is of pressurised type, comprising a front-mounted radiator, a coolant expansion tank, twin electric cooling fans mounted on the rear of the radiator, a thermostat and a centrifugal coolant pump. The cooling fan is controlled by the engine management electronic control module. The thermostat is located on the right-hand end of the engine, and is driven by the timing belt.

2 The system functions as follows. With the engine cold, the thermostat is closed and circulation is restricted to the cylinder block, cylinder head and heater matrix; there is no circulation through the radiator. When the coolant reaches a predetermined temperature, the thermostat opens and the coolant is allowed to flow freely through the top hose to the radiator. As the coolant circulates through the radiator, it is cooled by the inrush of air when the vehicle is in forward motion. Airflow is supplemented by the action of the electric cooling fans when necessary. Upon reaching the bottom of the radiator, the coolant is now cooled and the cycle is repeated.

3 With the engine at normal operating temperature, the coolant expands and some of it is displaced into the expansion tank. This coolant collects in the tank and is returned to the radiator when the system cools.

4 The operation of the fans is controlled by the engine management electronic control module, which receives engine temperature data from the engine coolant temperature sensor. At a predetermined temperature, the ECM signals the cooling fan module which operates the cooling fans.

5 Some cold-climate models are equipped with an auxiliary electric heating element, and/or an FBH (fuel-burning heater) to shorten the passenger cabin heater warm-up period. The electrically powered element located in the heater box behind the facia, whilst the fuel-burning heater is located behind the front right-hand wheelarch liner, and burns a small amount of diesel to quickly warm up the coolant flowing through the heater circuit. A small electrically powered pump, located alongside the fuel tank, supplies the diesel to the heater from the fuel tank.

Precautions

Cooling system

6 Do not attempt to remove the expansion tank filler cap or to disturb any part of the cooling system with the engine hot, as there is a risk of scalding. If the expansion tank filler cap must be removed before the engine and radiator have fully cooled down (even though this is not recommended) the pressure in the cooling system must first be released. Cover the cap with a thick layer of cloth, to avoid scalding, and slowly unscrew the filler cap until a hissing sound can be heard. When the hissing has stopped, showing that the pressure is released, slowly unscrew the filler cap until it can be removed. If more hissing sounds are heard, wait until they have stopped before unscrewing the cap completely. At all times keep well away from the filler opening.

7 Do not allow antifreeze to come in contact with your skin or painted surfaces of the vehicle. Rinse off spills immediately with plenty of water. Never leave antifreeze lying around; it is fatal if ingested.

8 If the engine is hot, the electric cooling fan may start rotating even if the engine is not running, so be careful to keep hands, hair and loose clothing well clear when working in the engine compartment.

Air conditioning system

9 On models equipped with an air conditioning system, it is necessary to observe special precautions whenever dealing with any part of the system, its associated components and any items which necessitate disconnection of the system. If for any reason the system must be disconnected, entrust this task to your Land Rover dealer or a refrigeration engineer.

10 Refrigerant must not be allowed to come in contact with a naked flame, otherwise a poisonous gas will be created. Do not allow the fluid to come in contact with the skin or eyes.

2 Cooling system hoses – disconnection and renewal

Warning: Never work on the cooling system when it is hot. Release any pressure from the system by loosening the expansion tank cap, having first covered it with a cloth to avoid any possibility of scalding.

1 If inspection of the cooling system reveals a faulty hose, then it must be renewed as follows.

2 First drain the cooling system (see Chapter 1 Section 34). If the coolant is not due for renewal, it may be re-used if collected in a clean container.

3 To disconnect the hoses, use a screwdriver to slacken the clips then move them along the hose clear of the outlet. Carefully work the hose off its outlets. Note that some hoses are secured using a spring type clip, where the two ends of the clip must be squeezed together to release, and some hoses are secured using a 'quick-release' system. To release these hoses, prise out the retaining clip a little until it is felt to come to a stop, then pull the hose from the connection **(see illustrations)**.

Caution: Do not attempt to disconnect any part of the system when still hot.

4 Note that the radiator hose outlets are fragile. Do not use excessive force when attempting to remove the hoses. If a hose proves stubborn, try to release it by rotating it on its outlets before attempting to work it off.

> **HAYNES HiNT** *If all else fails, cut the hose with a sharp knife then slit it so that it can be peeled off in two pieces. While expensive, this is preferable to buying a new radiator.*

5 When refitting a hose, first slide the clips onto the hose then work the hose onto its outlets. If the hose is stiff, use washing-up liquid as a lubricant.

6 Work each hose end fully onto its outlet, check that the hose is settled correctly and is properly routed, then slide each clip along the hose until it is behind the outlet flared end before tightening it securely. Spring type clips must have the ends squeezed together, and the clip positioned over the outlet flared end, then released. 'Quick-release' clips are simply pushed over the outlet until they are heard, or felt, to click into place.

7 Refill the system with coolant (see Chapter 1 Section 34).

8 Check carefully for leaks as soon as possible after disturbing any part of the cooling system.

2.3a Using a special tool to squeeze together the ends of a spring-type clip

2.3b Prise out the retaining clip a little, and pull the hose from the connection

3.5a Disconnect the right-hand radiator hose...

3.5b...the left-hand hose...

3.5c...then squeeze together the clips and disconnect the hose from the expansion tank

3 Radiator and expansion tank – removal, inspection and refitting

Radiator

Removal

1 Drain the cooling system as described in Chapter 1 Section 34.

2 Remove the cooling fans assembly as described in Section 6.

3 Remove the intercooler as described in Chapter 4A Section 17.

4 Undo the retaining bolt and slide the air conditioning condenser upwards from the lugs (see illustrations 11.14a and 11.14b). Position the condenser to one side. Support the condenser to prevent damage to the refrigerant pipes. Note that there is no need to disconnect the pipes.

5 Release the clips and disconnect the various hoses from the radiator (see illustrations).

6 On automatic transmission models, disconnect the upper coolant hose from the transmission cooler-to-the radiator, then undo the retaining bolt and position the cooler to one side (see illustration).

7 Undo the 2 retaining bolts at the top of the radiator, remove the brackets, and manoeuvre it upwards from place (see illustrations).

8 Recover the rubber mountings at the base of the radiator, and renew if necessary.

Inspection

9 If the radiator was removed because of clogging (causing overheating) then try reverse flushing using a garden hose or, in severe cases, use a radiator cleanser strictly in accordance with the manufacturer's instructions.

10 Use a soft brush and an air line or garden hose to clear the radiator matrix of leaves, insects etc.

11 Major leaks or extensive damage should be repaired by a specialist, or the radiator should be renewed or exchanged for a reconditioned unit.

12 Examine the mounting rubbers for signs of damage or deterioration and renew if necessary.

Refitting

13 Refitting is a reversal of removal, but tighten all nuts and bolts to the specified torque where given in the Specifications. On completion, refill the cooling system as described in Chapter 1 Section 34.

Expansion tank

Removal

14 With the engine cold, unscrew and remove the filler cap from the expansion tank.

15 Place a suitable container near the expansion tank to collect the drained coolant.

16 Undo the retaining bolt and lift the expansion tank from place (see illustration).

17 Squeeze together the clips and

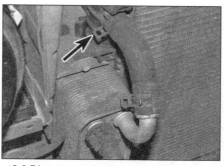

3.6 Disconnect the transmission cooler upper hose

3.7a Undo the retaining bolt...

3.7b...remove the bracket each side...

3.7c...and manoeuvre the radiator from place

3.16 Coolant expansion tank retaining bolt

3.18 Disconnect the hose from the base of the expansion tank

disconnect the small diameter hose from the tank.

18 Lift the tank, disconnect the level sensor wiring plug, release the clamp and disconnect the hose from the base of the tank **(see illustration)**.

Inspection

19 Empty any remaining coolant from the tank and flush it with fresh water to clean it. If the tank is leaking it must be renewed.

20 The expansion tank cap should be cleaned and checked whenever it is removed. Check that its sealing surfaces and threads are clean and undamaged.

21 The cap's performance can only be checked by using a cap pressure-tester (cooling system tester) with a suitable adaptor. On applying pressure, the cap's pressure relief valve should hold until the specified pressure

is reached, at which point the valve should open.

22 If there is any doubt about the cap's performance, then it must be renewed. Ensure that the replacement is of the correct type and rating.

Refitting

23 Refitting is a reversal of removal, but tighten the expansion tank mounting securely and top up the cooling system with reference to 'Weekly checks'.

---

4 Thermostat – removal, testing and refitting

Removal

1 Disconnect the battery negative (earth) lead (see Chapter 5A Section 4).

2 Drain the cooling system (see Chapter 1 Section 34).

3 Release the clamps, disconnect the air duct hoses and breather hose, then undo the retaining bolts and pull the plastic cover on the top of the engine upwards from place **(see illustrations)**.

4 Remove the air cleaner assembly as described in Chapter 4A Section 2.

5 The thermostat housing is located at the left-hand end of the cylinder head. Release the clamps and disconnect the 2 large diameter hoses from the front of the thermostat housing.

6 Squeeze together the sides of the clip and disconnect the small diameter hose from the top of the thermostat housing **(see illustration)**.

7 Unclip the hose, undo the 2 nuts and remove the support bracket from the thermostat housing/vacuum pump **(see illustration)**.

8 Prise out the wire clip a little, and disconnect the large diameter hose from the left-hand side of the thermostat housing.

9 Undo the 2 nuts, and 2 bolts, then unscrew the thermostat housing mounting studs **(see illustration)**.

10 Undo the bolt securing the hose to the rear of the thermostat housing, disconnect the sensor wiring plug, and manoeuvre the housing from place **(see illustration)**. Renew the thermostat housing seal.

11 If required, slide out the clip and pull the coolant temperature sensor from the housing. Note that no further dismantling of the housing is recommended. If the thermostat is faulty, the complete housing must be replaced.

Testing

12 If the thermostat remains in the open position at room temperature, then it is faulty and the complete housing assembly must be renewed.

13 To test it fully, suspend the (closed) thermostat housing on a length of string in a container of cold water, with a thermometer beside it.

14 Heat the water and check the temperature at which the thermostat begins to open.

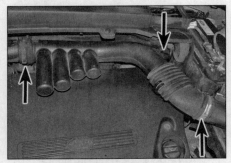

4.3a Release the air duct clamps and disconnect the breather hose

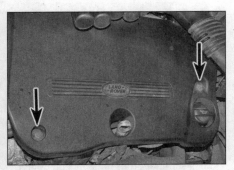

4.3b Undo the bolts and remove the plastic cover from the top of the engine

4.6 Squeeze together the clips and pull the hose from the top of the housing

4.7 Undo the nuts and remove the support bracket

4.9 Undo the nuts and bolts, then unscrew the mounting studs

4.10 Undo the bolt securing the hose at the rear of the housing

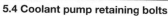

5.4 Coolant pump retaining bolts

6.3 Disconnect the fan control module wiring plug

Compare this value with that specified. Continue to heat the water until the thermostat is fully open. Allow the thermostat to cool down and check that it closes fully.

15 If the thermostat does not open and close as described, if it sticks in either position, or if it does not open at the specified temperature, then it must be renewed.

Refitting

16 Refitting is a reversal of removal, but note the following additional points:
a) Clean all mating surfaces thoroughly before reassembly.
b) Renew the thermostat housing seal regardless of condition.
c) Renew the hose O-ring seals if they show signs of deterioration.
d) Tighten all bolts to their specified torque wrench settings (where given).
e) Ensure the coolant hose clips are positioned so that they do not foul any other component, then tighten them securely.
f) Refill the cooling system (see Chapter 1 Section 34).

5 Coolant pump – removal and refitting

Removal

1 Coolant pump failure is usually indicated by coolant leaking from the gland behind the pump bearing, or by rough and noisy operation, usually accompanied by excessive pump spindle play. If the pump shows any of these symptoms then it must be renewed as follows.
2 Drain the cooling system (see Chapter 1 Section 34).
3 Remove the timing belt as described in Chapter 2A Section 6.
4 Undo the 7 retaining bolts and withdraw the coolant pump from the cylinder block **(see**

illustration). Recover the gasket – a new one must be fitted.

Refitting

5 Refitting is a reversal of removal, but note the following additional points:
a) Clean all mating surfaces thoroughly before reassembly.
b) Renew all seals and gaskets, and smear O-rings with a little rubber grease to aid seating.
c) Tighten all bolts to their specified torque wrench settings (where given).
d) Ensure the coolant hose clips are positioned so that they do not foul any other component, then tighten them securely.
e) Refill the cooling system as described in Chapter 1 Section 34.

6 Electric cooling fan assembly – removal and refitting

Removal

Note: Fault investigation and diagnosis is only possible using dedicated test equipment, which can interrogate the engine management ECM for any stored faults. Consult your Land Rover dealer or specialist.

1 Disconnect the battery negative (earth) lead (see Chapter 5A Section 4).
2 Unclip the coolant hose above the fan assembly.
3 Disconnect the wiring plug from the coolant fan control module, and unclip the wiring harness **(see illustration)**.
4 Unclip the hose running along the top of the fan shroud, and tie the refrigerant pipes to one side.
5 Release the 4 retaining clips (2 each side) and slide the cooling fan assembly upwards from place **(see illustration)**. Have an assistant hold the refrigerant pipes away to improve access.

Refitting

6 Refitting is a reversal of removal, but on completion refill the cooling system as described in Chapter 1 Section 34.

7 Cooling system sensors/ control unit – testing, removal and refitting

Engine coolant temperature sensor (ECT)

Testing

1 The engine coolant temperature sensor monitors the temperature of the coolant as it leaves the engine. The sensor is a 'thermistor', i.e. the resistance of the sensor changes as the temperature changes. The signal from the sensor is used by the engine management ECM (electronic control module) to regulate fuel injection quantity and timing, glow plugs, cooling fan operation, and the temperature gauge in the instrument cluster. Should the sensor fail, the ECM will adopt a pre-determined substitute value, and illuminate the MIL (malfunction indicator lamp) on the instrument cluster. No specific test values are available for the sensor. Consequently, testing is limited to inspecting the wiring

6.5 Release the clips each side, and slide the fan assembly upwards from place

7.6 Disconnect the hose from the left-hand end of the thermostat housing

7.7 Prise out the clip and pull the sensor from the housing

and connectors to the sensor. Further investigation can only be carried out by the use of dedicated test equipment. Consult your Land Rover dealer or fuel injection specialist. Testing by any other means could result in ECM damage.

Removal

2 Disconnect the battery negative lead (see Chapter 5A Section 4).
3 Drain the cooling system as described in Chapter 1 Section 34.
4 Remove the air cleaner assembly as described in Chapter 4A Section 2.
5 Release the clamps, disconnect the air duct hoses and breather hose, then undo the retaining bolts and pull the plastic cover on the top of the engine upwards from place **(see illustrations 4.3a and 4.3b)**.
6 Prise out the wire clip a little, and disconnect the large diameter coolant hose from the left-hand end of the thermostat housing **(see illustration)**.
7 Remove the clip and pull the coolant temperature sensor from the thermostat housing **(see illustration)**. Renew the O-ring seal. Disconnect the wiring plug as the sensor is withdrawn.

Refitting

8 Refitting is a reversal of removal, but renew the sensor O-ring seal. Top up the cooling system with reference to Chapter 1 Section 34.

Radiator cooling fan control module

Removal

9 Disconnect the battery negative lead (see Chapter 5A Section 4).
10 Disconnect the wiring plugs from the control unit, located at the upper edge of the cooling fan shroud **(see illustration 6.3)**.
11 Undo the retaining bolt and manoeuvre the control unit from position.

Refitting

12 Refitting is a reversal of removal.

Coolant level sensor

Removal

13 The sensor is fitted into the base of the

coolant expansion tank. Undo the retaining bolt and invert the expansion tank **(see illustration 3.16)**.
14 Disconnect the sensor wiring plug, and detach the sensor from the base of the tank **(see illustration 3.18)**.

Refitting

15 Refitting is a reversal of removal. Top up the cooling system as described in *'Weekly checks'*.

8 Heating and ventilation system – general information

1 The heating/ventilation system consists of a blower motor (housed in the heater distribution box in the centre of the facia), face level vents in the centre and at each end of the facia, and air ducts to the front and rear footwells.
2 The control unit is located in the centre of the facia, and the controls operate flap valves to deflect and mix the air flowing through the various parts of the heating/ventilation system. The flap valves are contained in the air distribution housing, which acts as a central distribution unit, passing air to the various ducts and vents.
3 Cold air enters the system through the grille at the rear of the engine compartment. If required, the airflow is boosted by the blower fan, and then flows through the various ducts, according to the settings of the controls. Stale

air is expelled through ducts at the rear of the vehicle. If warm air is required, the cold air is passed over the heater matrix, which is heated by the engine coolant.
4 A recirculation switch enables the outside air supply to be closed off, while the air inside the vehicle is recirculated. This can be useful to prevent unpleasant odours entering from outside the vehicle, but should only be used briefly, as the recirculated air inside the vehicle will soon become stale.
5 On models sold in cold climates, an optional fuel-burning heater is available to supplement the main heater. This uses fuel from the main fuel tank, only operates whilst the engine is running and the ambient temperature is less than 5°C. Also available for diesel models in cold climates, is an electrical heating element fitted into the heater unit assembly, to supplement the heater matrix.

9 Heating and ventilation system components – removal and refitting

Heater matrix

Removal

1 Drain the cooling system as described in Chapter 1 Section 34, or alternatively clamp the heater hoses at the bulkhead in the engine compartment using purpose-made hose clamps.
2 Disconnect the battery negative lead as described in Chapter 5A Section 4.
3 Remove the gear change/selector lever assembly as described in Chapter 7A Section 4 or Chapter 7B Section 2.
4 Remove the footwell side kick panel, and drivers side lower facia panel as described in Chapter 11 Section 24.
5 Undo the 2 retaining screws and remove the plastic cover over the matrix pipes on the right-hand side of the heater housing **(see illustration)**.
6 Slide out the clips and detach the coolant pipes from the matrix **(see illustration)**. Be prepared for coolant spillage – place rags to absorb the spillage prior to disconnect the pipes.

9.5 Matrix pipe cover screws

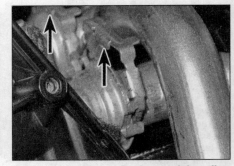

9.6 Slide out the matrix pipe retaining clips

9.7 Unclip the air ducts

9.9 Remove the yaw rate sensor from the cabin floor

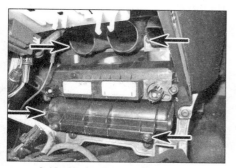

9.10a Undo the cover screws...

9.10b...manoeuvre the cover rearwards...

9.10c...and lift out the matrix

7 Unclip and remove the rear air ducts from in front of the centre console **(see illustration)**.

8 Disconnect the wiring plugs, undo the 2 screws and slide the auxiliary electrical element (where fitted) from the housing **(see illustration 9.36)**.

9 Disconnect the wiring plug, undo the nuts and remove the yaw rate sensor **(see illustration)**.

10 Undo the 4 screws/nuts, remove the cover and slide the matrix from the heater housing **(see illustrations)**.

Refitting

11 Refitting is a reverse of the removal procedure, but tighten all nuts and bolts securely and on completion refill the cooling system as described in Chapter 1 Section 34.

Heater blower motor

Removal

12 Set the controls for air recirculation.

13 Remove the facia/heater housing assembly as described in Chapter 11 Section 26.

14 On manual transmission models, remove the clutch pedal assembly as described in Chapter 6 Section 2.

15 Working under the right-hand side of the facia, disconnect the wiring plug from the blower motor **(see illustration)**.

16 Disconnect the wiring plug, unclip the harness, then remove the 3 retaining screws and manoeuvre the recirculation blend door housing from the heater housing **(see illustrations)**.

9.15 Disconnect the blower motor wiring plug

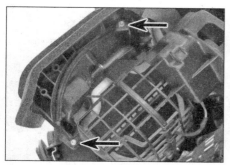

9.16a Remove the screws on the top of the blend door housing...

9.16b...and the screw behind the housing...

9.16c...then detach the blend door housing from the blower housing

9.17a Depress the locking tab...

9.17b...then reach through, rotate the motor anti-clockwise, and manoeuvre it through the blend door housing aperture

9.21 Heater blower motor resistor

17 Release the locking tab, rotate the blower motor anti-clockwise (top to the front) a little and withdraw it from the heater housing (see illustrations).

Refitting

18 Refitting is a reversal of removal.

Heater blower motor resistor

Removal

19 Remove the panel (where fitted) beneath the passengers side of the facia.
20 Undo the screw, and unclip the passengers side footwell kick panel from the centre console.
21 Rotate the resistor anti-clockwise a little,

and pull it from the housing (see illustration). Disconnect the wiring plug as the resistor is withdrawn.

Refitting

22 Refitting is a reversal of removal.

Air recirculation servo motor

23 In order to remove the various servo motors attached to the heater/air conditioning housing, remove the complete facia/heater housing as described in Chapter 11 Section 26.
24 Disconnect the wiring plug, remove the retaining screws, and release any operating linkage as the relevant servo motor is removed.

Heater control panel

Removal

25 Unclip the rubber mat from the central storage compartment and oddment tray in the facia (see illustration).
26 Carefully prise up and remove the facia central speaker trim panel (see illustration).
27 Undo the 6 retaining screws, and carefully pull the facia central panel rewards to release the clips (see illustrations). Disconnect any wiring plugs as the panel is withdrawn.
28 Undo the 4 screws and pull the control panel rearwards (see illustration). Disconnect the wiring plug as the panel is withdrawn.

Refitting

29 Refitting is a reversal of removal, but position the cables to their original settings.

Heater blower motor control switch

30 It would appear at the time of writing, the switch is only available as a complete assembly with the control panel. Consult your Land Rover dealer or specialist.

Auxiliary electrical heating element

Removal

31 Disconnect the battery negative lead as described in Chapter 5A Section 4.
32 Remove the gear change/selector lever

9.25 Unclip the rubber mat

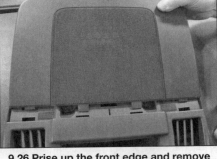

9.26 Prise up the front edge and remove the speaker grille

9.27a Undo the 6 screws...

9.27b...and pull the centre panel rearwards

9.28 Heater control panel retaining screws

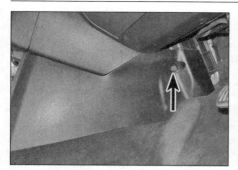

9.33 Undo the screw and remove the footwell panel each side

9.35a Pull the large connectors from the terminals, and disconnect the small wiring plug

9.35b Undo the retaining screws...

assembly as described in Chapter 7A Section 4 or Chapter 7B Section 2.

33 Remove the passengers and drivers side footwell side kick panel **(see illustration)**.

34 Remove the plastic cover, then unclip the rear air ducts from in front of the centre console **(see illustration 9.7)**.

35 Disconnect the wiring plugs, undo the 2 retaining screws and slide the element rearwards from the heater housing **(see illustrations)**.

Refitting

36 Refitting is a reversal of removal.

Outside temperature sensor

Removal

37 Fold the passengers side door mirror outwards, and unclip the sensor cover from the inside edge of the mirror housing. Disconnect the wiring plug as the cover is withdrawn.

38 Unclip the sensor from the cover.

Refitting

39 Refitting is a reversal of removal.

Air quality sensor

Removal

40 Remove the passengers side glovebox as described in Chapter 11 Section 24.

41 Disconnect the wiring plug, rotate the sensor anti-clockwise a little, and pull it from the recirculation blend door housing.

Refitting

42 Refitting is a reversal of removal.

10 Air conditioning system – general information and precautions

General information

1 An air conditioning system is available as an option on all models. The system enables the temperature of incoming air to be lowered, and it also dehumidifies the air, which makes for rapid demisting and increased comfort.

2 The cooling side of the system works in

the same way as a domestic refrigerator. Refrigerant gas is drawn into a belt-driven compressor, and passes into a condenser mounted on the front of the radiator, where it loses heat and becomes liquid. The liquid passes through an expansion valve to an evaporator, where it changes from liquid under high pressure to gas under low pressure. This change is accompanied by a drop in temperature, which cools the evaporator. The refrigerant returns to the compressor, and the cycle begins again.

3 Air blown through the evaporator passes to the air distribution unit and then into the passenger compartment.

4 The heating side of the system works in the same way as on models without air conditioning.

5 The system is electronically-controlled. Any problems with the system should be referred to a Land Rover dealer or automotive air conditioning specialist.

Precautions

6 With an air conditioning system, it is necessary to observe special precautions whenever dealing with any part of the system, or its associated components. If for any reason the system must be disconnected, entrust this task to your Land Rover dealer or a refrigeration engineer. Refrigerant circuit service ports are located at the rear of the engine compartment **(see illustration)**.

⚠️ *Warning: The refrigeration circuit contains a liquid refrigerant which is potentially dangerous, and should only be handled by qualified persons. If it is splashed onto the skin, it can cause frostbite. It is not itself poisonous, but in the presence of a naked flame (including a cigarette), it forms a poisonous gas. Uncontrolled discharging of the refrigerant is dangerous, and potentially damaging to the environment. For all these reasons, it is dangerous to disconnect any part of the system without specialised knowledge and equipment. Note that Land Rover recommend the receiver/drier is renewed every time the air conditioning system is opened.*

7 Do not operate the air conditioning system

9.35c...and slide the element from place

if it is known to be short of refrigerant, as this may damage the compressor.

11 Air conditioning system components – removal and refitting

Compressor

Removal

1 Have the air conditioning system evacuated by a Land Rover dealer or suitable equipped specialist.

2 Disconnect the battery negative (earth) lead (see Chapter 5A Section 4).

3 Apply the handbrake, then jack up the front of the vehicle and support it on axle stands

10.6 Refrigerant circuit service ports

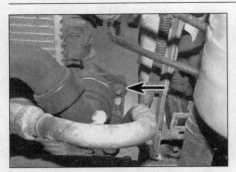

11.13a Undo the bolt at the right-hand rear of the condensor

11.13b Slide the condenser upwards from the lugs

(see 'Vehicle jacking and support'). Undo the retaining screws and remove the engine undershield.

4 Remove auxiliary drivebelt as described in Chapter 1 Section 28.

5 Disconnect the wiring plug from the compressor located in the right-hand corner of the engine compartment.

6 Unscrew the bolts and detach the air conditioning pipe unions from the compressor. Tape over or plug the refrigerant apertures. Remove the seals and discard. New ones must be fitted on refitting.

7 Remove the engine lower rear tie-rod front through-bolt, and tilt the engine rearwards a little. Use a suitable block of wood to wedge the engine in place.

8 Support the compressor, then unscrew and remove the 3 mounting bolts and lower the unit from under the engine compartment.

Refitting

9 Refitting is a reversal of removal, but renew the receiver/drier and tighten all bolts to the specified torque. Before fitting the new seals, smear a little refrigerant oil on each side. On completion, have the air conditioning system recharged by a refrigeration specialist or suitably-equipped Land Rover dealer.

Condenser

Removal

10 Have the air conditioning system evacuated by a Land Rover dealer or suitable equipped specialist.

11 Remove the intercooler as described in Chapter 4A Section 17.

12 Unscrew the bolts and detach the air conditioning pipes from the condenser. Tape over or plug the refrigerant apertures. Remove the seals and discard. New ones must be fitted on refitting.

13 Undo the retaining bolt, and slide the condenser upwards from the locating lugs **(see illustrations)**.

Refitting

14 Refitting is a reversal of removal, tighten all bolts to the specified torque. Before fitting the new seals, smear a little refrigerant oil on them. On completion, have the air conditioning system recharged by a refrigeration specialist or suitably-equipped Land Rover dealer.

Evaporator

Removal

15 Have the air conditioning system evacuated by a Land Rover dealer or suitable equipped specialist.

16 Remove the facia/heater housing assembly as described in Chapter 11 Section 26.

17 Remove the clamp, release the clips and remove the upper and lower plastic casing around the refrigerant pipes **(see illustration)**. Recover the foam insulation around the pipes.

18 Using a sharp knife, cut through the evaporator cover on the side of the housing, following the recessed line in the cover **(see illustration)**.

19 Remove the cover and slide the evaporator from the housing.

Refitting

20 Obtain an evaporator service kit from a Land Rover dealer or parts specialist. This kit includes the necessary foam seals, refrigerant pipes, asphalt tape, expansion valve and evaporator 'service door'.

21 Apply the new foam seals to the evaporator in the same positions as on the original.

22 Slide the new evaporator into the housing.

23 Using a sharp knife, cut 2 slots in the new service door to match the profile of the heater housing.

24 Fit the service door, then secure it with the screws and clips provided in the service kit.

25 Guide the new pipes through the engine compartment bulkhead, until 20 mm remains visible, then fit the pipe retaining plate.

26 Using the new seals provided, connect the refrigerant pipes to the evaporator, and tighten the retaining bolts securely.

27 The remainder of refitting is a reversal of removal. Before fitting the new seals, smear a little refrigerant oil on each side. On completion, have the air conditioning system recharged by a refrigeration specialist or suitably-equipped Land Rover dealer.

Receiver/drier

28 The receiver/drier is integral with the condenser. Removal of the condenser is described earlier in this Section.

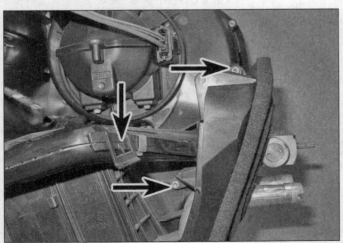

11.17 Undo the screws, remove the clamp, then unclip the plastic casing

11.18 Cut through the evaporator cover with a sharp knife

11.32 Undo the centre screws, and prise out the plastic expansion rivets along the front edge of the scuttle trim panel

11.33 Undo the refrigerant pipe retaining nut

11.34 Undo the Allen bolts and remove the expansion valve

Expansion valve

Removal

29 Have the air conditioning system evacuated by a Land Rover dealer or suitable equipped specialist.

30 Release the clamps, disconnect the air duct hoses and breather hose, then undo the retaining bolts and pull the plastic cover on the top of the engine upwards from place **(see illustrations 4.3a and 4.3b)**.

31 Remove the wiper arms as described in Chapter 12 Section 13.

32 Remove the fasteners, and pull the scuttle trim panel upwards from the base of the windscreen **(see illustration)**.

33 Undo the nut securing the air conditioning pipes to the valve on the engine compartment bulkhead **(see illustration)**. Discard the O-ring seals, new ones must be fitted.

34 Undo the 2 retaining bolts and remove the expansion valve **(see illustration)**. Discard the O-ring seals, new ones must be fitted.

Refitting

35 Refitting is a reversal of removal.

Evaporator temperature sensor

36 Remove the passengers and drivers side footwell side kick panel.

37 Disconnect the wiring plug, and pull the sensor from the evaporator housing **(see illustration)**.

38 Refitting is a reversal of removal

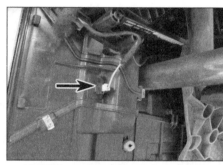
11.37 Evaporator temperature sensor

Chapter 4 Part A
Fuel and exhaust systems

Contents

Degrees of difficulty

Easy, suitable for novice with little experience | **Fairly easy,** suitable for beginner with some experience | **Fairly difficult,** suitable for competent DIY mechanic | **Difficult,** suitable for experienced DIY mechanic | **Very difficult,** suitable for expert DIY or professional

Specifications

System type . . . . Direct injection common rail with Bosch high-pressure delivery pump and Electronic Diesel Control

Fuel pump pressure:
At idle speed. . . . . 1.33 bar
Full load . . . . 2.67 bar
Fuel injection pump pressure. . . . . upto 1600 bar
Turbocharger boost pressure:
2000 rpm . . . . 1.1 bar
3000 rpm . . . . 1.2 bar

Torque wrench settings	Nm	lbf ft
Camshaft position sensor	8	6
Catalytic converter:		
DW12BTED4 engine	25	18
DW12C engine	10	7
Crankshaft position sensor	8	6
EGR valve-to manifold screws	10	7
Exhaust gas temperature sensor	30	22
Exhaust manifold-to-cylinder head:		
DW12BTED4 engine	25	18
DW12C engine	20	15
Exhaust catalytic converter/particulate filter-to-tail pipe	10	7
Fuel injector clamp bolts:		
Stage 1	5	4
Stage 2	Angle-tighten a further 130°	
Fuel pipe union nuts*:		
Stage 1	22	16
Stage 2	25	18
Fuel injection pump	22	16
Fuel rail retaining bolts	22	16
Fuel tank cradle-to-body bolts*	25	18

Torque wrench settings (continued)

	Nm	lbf ft
Intake air temperature sensor...............................	10	7
Intake manifold.......................................	10	7
Manifold absolute pressure sensor (MAP)	10	7
Particulate filter temperature sensor	35	26
Oxygen sensor...	45	33
Throttle body screws	9	7
Turbocharger-to-exhaust manifold bolts/nuts*..................	24	18
Turbocharger coolant manifold bolts:		
M6	10	7
M12	29	21
Turbocharger oil feed banjo bolt:		
Manual transmission:		
Upto engine number 10DZ584056158.....................	24	18
From engine number 10DZ584056159.....................	17	13
Automatic transmission:		
Upto engine number 10DZ594055666.....................	24	18
From engine number 10DZ594055667.....................	17	13
Turbocharger oil return..................................	10	7

Do not re-use

1 General information and precautions

General information

1 The operation of the fuel injection system is described in more detail in Section 5.

2 Fuel is drawn from a tank under the rear of the vehicle, through the pipework, and through fuel filter/water separator/heater by a lift-pump incorporated into the high-pressure injection pump. The high-pressure injection pump is driven by the left-hand end of the exhaust camshaft, and supplies very high pressure fuel to the common fuel rail, which is connected to each individual injector. The injectors are operated by solenoids controlled by the ECM, based on information supplied by various sensors. The multi-hole piezo injectors are capable of upto 6 individual injections per stroke. The engine ECM also controls the pre-heating side of the system – refer to Chapter 5B for more details.

3 The EDC (electronic diesel control) system fitted, incorporates a 'drive by wire' system, where the traditional accelerator cable is replaced by an accelerator pedal position sensor. The position and rate-of-change of the accelerator pedal is reported by the position sensor to the ECM, which then adjusts the fuel injectors to deliver the required amount of fuel, and optimum combustion efficiency.

4 Fuel level in the tank is determined by 2 level sensors – on each side of the saddle tank. The right-hand side sensor is fitted to in the in-tank pump module. This pump is purely responsible for drawing fuel from each side of the tank and filling the fuel delivery pot. Which provides a reservoir for the lift pump (in the high-pressure pump) to draw from.

5 The exhaust system incorporates a turbocharger, EGR and on some models, a diesel particulate filter. Further detail of the emission control systems can be found in Chapter 4B.

Precautions

6 When working on diesel fuel system components, scrupulous cleanliness must be observed, and care must be taken not to introduce any foreign matter into fuel lines or components.

7 After carrying out any work involving disconnection of fuel lines, it is advisable to check the connections for leaks; pressurise the system by cranking the engine several times.

8 Electronic control units are very sensitive components, and certain precautions must be taken to avoid damage to these units as follows.

9 When carrying out welding operations on the vehicle using electric welding equipment, the battery and alternator should be disconnected.

10 Although the underbonnet-mounted modules will tolerate normal underbonnet conditions, they can be adversely affected by excess heat or moisture. If using welding equipment or pressure-washing equipment in the vicinity of an electronic module, take care not to direct heat, or jets of water or steam, at the module. If this cannot be avoided, remove the module from the vehicle, and protect its wiring plug with a plastic bag.

11 Before disconnecting any wiring, or removing components, always ensure that the ignition is switched off.

12 Do not attempt to improvise ECM fault diagnosis procedures using a test lamp or multi-meter, as irreparable damage could be caused to the module.

13 After working on fuel injection/engine management system components, ensure that all wiring is correctly reconnected before reconnecting the battery or switching on the ignition.

2 Air cleaner assembly – removal and refitting

Removal

1 Disconnect the mass airflow sensor wiring plug **(see illustration)**. The mass airflow sensor is located on the top of the air cleaner outlet pipe.

2 Release the clamp and disconnect the air outlet pipe from the air cleaner upper cover **(see illustration)**.

2.1 Release the clip and disconnect the mass air flow sensor wiring plug

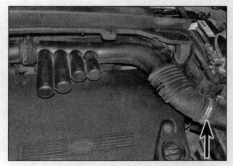

2.2 Slacken the air outlet pipe clamp

3 Undo the 4 screws, lift up the cover and remove the air cleaner element **(see illustration)**.

4 Release the clip, and lift the air cleaner housing from place. Disconnect the air inlet pipe as the housing is withdrawn **(see illustration)**.

Refitting

5 Refitting is a reversal of removal.

3 Fuel tank – removal and refitting

Note: *Before removing the fuel tank, all fuel must be drained from the tank. Since a drain plug is not provided, it is therefore preferable to carry out the removal operation when the fuel tank is nearly empty. The remaining fuel can then be siphoned or hand-pumped from the tank.*

Removal

1 Disconnect the battery negative terminal (see Chapter 5A Section 4).

2 Raise the vehicle and support it securely on axle stands (see *'Vehicle jacking and support'*).

3 Prise up the coin tray from the rear of the

2.3 Air cleaner cover screws

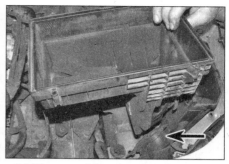

2.4 Disconnect the air outlet pipe as the cleaner housing is removed

centre console, then slacken the adjusting nut and detach the handbrake cables from the compensator bracket **(see illustrations)**.

4 Fold the right-hand rear seat cushion forwards, lift the carpet flap, and prise the grommet from the floor above the tank **(see illustration)**.

5 Working through the grommet aperture, disconnect the wiring plug, then squeeze together the sides of the collar and disconnect the breather hose from the tank **(see illustration)**.

6 On models with a fuel-burning heater, disconnect the fuel supply pipe from the tank through the aperture.

7 Remove the exhaust system as described in Section 19.

8 On 4WD models, remove the propeller shaft as described in Chapter 8 Section 5.

9 Undo the bolts and remove the reinforcement bracket each side of the transmission tunnel at the front of the tank.

10 Undo the bolt securing the fuel filler pipe to the rear crossmember.

11 Slacken the clamp and disconnect the fuel filler pipe from the tank **(see illustration)**.

12 Unclip the handbrake cables from the fuel tank cradle **(see illustration)**.

13 Undo the nut, remove the fuel pipe cover from the front of the tank, then prise out the

3.3a Prise up the rear coin tray

3.3b Slacken the adjusting nut and disconnect the handbrake cables

3.4 Prise the plastic grommet from the floor

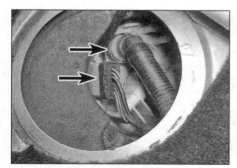

3.5 Disconnect the wiring plug and the breather hose (arrowed)

3.11 Slacken the fuel filler pipe clamp (arrowed)

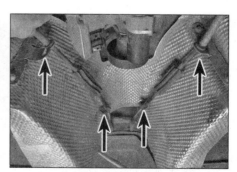

3.12 Release the handbrake cables from the clips (arrowed)

3.13a Undo the nut (arrowed), and fold down the cover

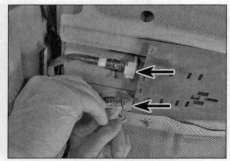

3.13b Prise out the clips (arrowed) and disconnect the fuel pipes

3.15a Undo the bolts (arrowed) at the front of the tank cradle...

3.15b...and the ones at the rear (arrowed)

locking clips and disconnect the fuel supply and return pipes (see illustrations).

14 Support the fuel tank with a transmission jack or similar, placing a piece of wood on the jack head to prevent damage.

15 Undo the 4 retaining bolts, and lower the tank from place (see illustrations). The help of an assistant is advisable. Note that new retaining bolts will be required.

16 Separate the tank from the cradle, and recover the heat shields.

17 If the tank is contaminated with sediment or water, swill the tank out with clean fuel. The tank is injection-moulded from a synthetic material – if seriously damaged, it should be renewed. However, in certain cases, it may be possible to have small leaks or minor damage repaired. Seek the advice of a specialist before attempting to repair the fuel tank.

Refitting

18 Refitting is the reverse of the removal procedure, noting the following points:
a) When lifting the tank back into position, take care to ensure that none of the hoses or the fuel gauge sender unit wiring become trapped between the tank and vehicle body.
b) Adjust the handbrake as described in Chapter 9 Section 14.
c) Refit the cradle, and tighten the new bolts to the specified torque.
d) Ensure all pipes and hoses are correctly routed and all hoses unions are securely joined.

e) On completion, refill the tank with a small amount of fuel, and check for signs of leakage prior to taking the vehicle out on the road.

4 Accelerator pedal – removal and refitting

Removal

1 Working underneath the drivers side facia, unscrew the 3 nuts securing the pedal assembly to the vehicle bulkhead (see illustration).

2 Disconnect the sensor wiring plug as the assembly is withdrawn.

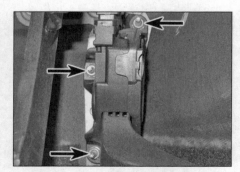

4.1 Accelerator pedal assembly retaining nuts

3 It would appear that the sensor is only available as a complete unit with the pedal assembly.

Refitting

4 Refitting is a reversal of removal. Tighten the retaining nuts to their specified torque.

5 Fuel injection system – general information

1 The system is under the overall control of the Electronic Diesel Control (EDC) system, which also controls the pre-heating system (see Chapter 5B).

2 Fuel is supplied from the rear-mounted fuel tank, via an electrically powered lift pump, and fuel filter, to the fuel injection pump. The fuel injection pump supplies fuel under high pressure to the common fuel rail. The fuel rail provides a reservoir of fuel under pressure ready for the injectors to deliver direct to the combustion chamber. The individual fuel injectors incorporate solenoids, which when operated, allow the high pressure fuel to be injected. The solenoids are controlled by the ECM. The fuel injection pump purely provides high pressure fuel. The timing and duration of the injection is controlled by the ECM based, on the information received from the various sensors. In order to increase combustion efficiency and reduce combustion noise (diesel 'knock'), a small amount of fuel is injected before the main injection takes place – this is known as Pre- or Pilot-injection.

3 Additionally, the control module activates the pre-heating system, and the exhaust gas recirculation (EGR) system (see Chapter 5B).

4 The system uses the following sensors:
a) Crankshaft sensor – informs the ECM of the crankshaft speed and position.
b) Coolant temperature sensor – informs the ECM of engine temperature.
c) Mass airflow/intake temperature sensor – informs the ECM of the mass and temperature of air entering the intake tract.
d) Wheel speed sensor – informs the ECM of the vehicle speed.
e) Accelerator pedal position sensor – informs the ECM of throttle position, and the rate of throttle opening/closing.
f) Fuel high-pressure sensor – informs the ECM of the pressure of the fuel in the common rail.
g) Manifold absolute pressure sensor – informs the ECM of the pressure in the intake manifold.
h) Fuel temperature sensor – informs the ECM of the fuel supply temperature.
i) Camshaft position sensor – informs the ECM of the camshaft position so that the engine firing sequence can be established.
j) Stop-light switch – informs the ECM when the brakes are being applied.

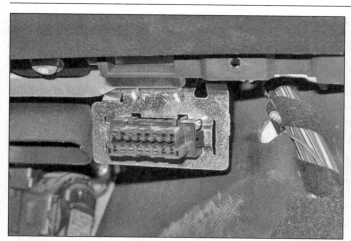

5.9 The 16-pin diagnostic connector is located under the drivers side of the facia

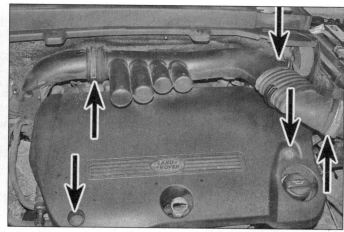

6.2 Release the clamps, disconnect the hoses, undo the bolts and remove the engine top cover

k) *Exhaust gas temperature sensor – informs the ECM of the temperature of the exhaust gases.*

l) *Exhaust gas temperature sensor – informs the ECM of the temperature of the exhaust gases.*

5 On all models, a 'drive-by-wire' throttle control system is used. Instead of a traditional throttle cable, an accelerator pedal position sensor informs the ECM of the pedal position and rate of change.

6 The signals from the various sensors are processed by the ECM, and the optimum fuel quantity and injection timing settings are selected for the prevailing engine operating conditions.

7 A catalytic converter and an exhaust gas recirculation (EGR), and on some models, a diesel particulate filter system is fitted, to reduce harmful exhaust gas emissions. Details of this and other emissions control system equipment are given in Chapter 4B.

8 If there is an abnormality in any of the readings obtained from any sensor, the ECM enters its back-up mode. In this event, the ECM ignores the abnormal sensor signal, and assumes a pre-programmed value which will allow the engine to continue running (albeit at reduced efficiency). If the ECM enters this back-up mode, the warning light on the instrument panel will come on, and the relevant fault code will be stored in the ECM memory.

9 If the warning light comes on, the vehicle should be taken to a Land Rover dealer or specialist at the earliest opportunity. A complete test of the Electronic Diesel Control (EDC) system can then be carried out, using a special electronic test unit which is simply plugged into the system's diagnostic connector **(see illustration)**. The connector is located behind the driver's side of the facia; to gain access to the connector unclip the storage pocket and reach in through the facia aperture.

6 Fuel system – priming and bleeding

1 After disturbing the fuel system, it will be necessary to prime and bleed the system as follows.

2 Release the air duct and breather hose clamps, then undo the fasteners and remove the plastic cover from the top of the engine **(see illustration)**.

3 Disconnect the fuel supply pipe from the fuel filter, and connect a hand-held pump (Land Rover tool no. 310-163 or equivalent) between the pipe and the filter **(see illustration)**. If using the Land Rover tool, ensure the arrow on the tool is pointing towards the fuel filter.

4 Operate the hand held pump until resistance is felt.

5 Depress the accelerator pedal to the floor then start the engine as normal (this may take longer than usual, especially if the fuel system has been allowed to run dry – operate the starter in ten second bursts with 5 seconds rest in between each operation). Run the engine at a fast idle speed for a minute or so to purge any remaining trapped air from the fuel lines. After this time the engine should idle smoothly at a constant speed.

6 If the engine idles roughly, then there is still

6.3 Connect a hand-held pump between the fuel supply pipe and the filter

some air trapped in the fuel system. Increase the engine speed again for another minute or so then recheck the idle speed. Repeat this procedure as necessary until the engine is idling smoothly.

7 Fuel level sensors – removal and refitting

Removal

1 Remove the tank-mounted fuel pump as described in Section 8.

Right-hand sensor

2 Remove the fuel pump unit as described in Section 8.

3 Disconnect the wiring plug, and unclip the sensor from the side of the pump unit.

Left-hand sensor

4 Remove the fuel pump unit as described in Section 8.

5 Grasp the white plastic framework, then slide it to the right and downwards, disengaging the lugs from the slots in the mounting bracket **(see illustration)**. Manoeuvre the sensor assembly from the tank.

Refitting

6 Refitting is a reversal of removal.

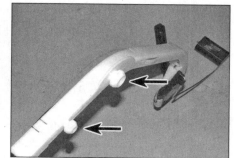

7.5 Slide the framework sideways to disengage the lugs

8.2a Squeeze together the clips, disconnect the fuel pipes...

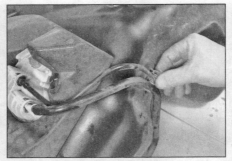

8.2b ...and unclip them from the tank

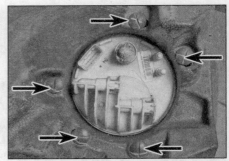

8.3 Undo the fasteners and remove the pad

8 Fuel pump unit – removal and refitting

Removal

1 Remove the fuel tank as described in Section 3.

2 Squeeze together the clips, disconnect the fuel pipes and unclip them from the side of the tank **(see illustrations)**.

3 Undo the 5 fasteners, and remove the pad around the pump module locking ring **(see illustration)**.

4 Clean the area around the pump module, then make alignment marks between the locking ring and the tank, and unscrew the locking ring from the tank **(see illustration)**. Note that the locking ring will be extremely tight – use Land Rover tool no. 310-123 or equivalent.

5 Carefully lift the pump module cover a little from the tank. Discard the sealing ring between the cover and tank – a new one must be fitted.

6 Disconnect the breather hose from the underside of the module cover **(see illustration)**.

7 Disconnect the fuel hoses and wiring plug from the left-hand sensor **(see illustrations)**.

8 Rotate the pump module anti-clockwise a little, and carefully manoeuvre it from the tank **(see illustration)**. Take care not to damage the level sensor float arm.

Refitting

9 Refitting is a reversal of removal, using a new module cover sealing ring **(see illustration)**. Note that Land Rover specify a tank locking ring torque of 200 Nm. Whilst this setting may be difficult to achieve without using the Land Rover special tool, needless to say, the locking ring must be tightened securely, at least aligning the previously made marks

8.4 In the absence of the correct tool, carefully slacken the locking ring with a soft-metal punch

8.6 Squeeze together the side of the collar, and disconnect the breather hose

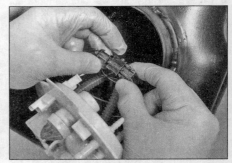

8.7a Disconnect the left-hand sensor wiring plug

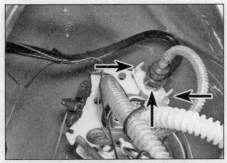

8.7b Squeeze together the clips and disconnect the fuel hoses

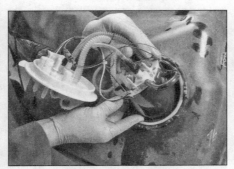

8.8 Manoeuvre the pump module from the tank, taking care not to damage the float arm

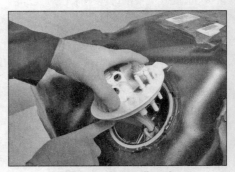

8.9 Renew the sealing ring

10.3 Depress the button and disconnect the breather hose

10.4 Remove the pipe from the EGR cooler to the intake manifold

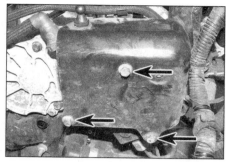

10.5 Undo the bolts and remove the bracket/cover

9 Fuel injection system – testing and adjustment

Testing

1 If a fault appears in the fuel injection system, first ensure that all the system wiring connectors are securely connected and free from corrosion. Ensure that the fault is not due to poor maintenance; ie, check that the air cleaner filter element is clean, that the cylinder compression pressures are correct (see Chapter 2A Section 2), and that the engine breather hoses are clear and undamaged (see Chapter 4B).
2 If the engine will not start, check the condition of the glow plugs (see Chapter 5B).
3 If these checks fail to reveal the cause of the problem, the vehicle should be taken to a Land Rover dealer or specialist for testing using special electronic equipment which is plugged into the diagnostic connector (see Section 5). The tester should locate the fault quickly and simply, avoiding the need to test all the system components individually, which is time-consuming, and also carries a risk of damaging the ECM.

Adjustment

4 The engine idle speed, and maximum speed are all controlled by the ECM. Whilst in theory it is possible to check the settings, if they are found to be in need of adjustment, the car will have to be taken to a suitably-equipped Land Rover dealer or specialist. They will have access to the necessary diagnostic equipment required to test and (where possible) adjust the settings.

10 Fuel injection pump – removal and refitting

Caution: Be careful not to allow dirt into the injection pump or injector pipes during this procedure.

Removal

1 Disconnect the battery negative lead (see Chapter 5A Section 4).
2 Release the air duct and breather hose clamps, then undo the fasteners and remove the plastic cover from the top of the engine **(see illustration 6.2)**.
3 Depress the release button and disconnect the breather hose from the cylinder head cover **(see illustration)**.
4 Undo the nuts, remove the retaining bolt, and remove the EGR pipe from the EGR cooler to the intake manifold **(see illustration)**. Plug the openings to prevent contamination.
5 Unclip the hoses and the wiring harness, then undo the 3 retaining bolts and remove the engine cover mounting bracket from the left-hand end of the cylinder head **(see illustration)**.
6 Disconnect the vacuum hose from the top of the vacuum pump.
7 Disconnect the fuel supply and return hoses from the high-pressure fuel pump **(see illustration)**. Plug the openings to prevent contamination.
8 Clean the area around the high-pressure fuel pipe from the pump to the fuel rail, then undo the unions, and remove the retaining bolt. Use a second spanner to prevent the union port from rotating whilst the union is slackened. Discard the pipe, a new one must be fitted.
9 Disconnect the wiring plug from the pump.
10 Undo the 3 nuts, and remove the pump. Ensure the pump drive remains captive as the

pump is withdrawn **(see illustration)**. Renew the pump seal.

Refitting

11 Manoeuvre the new high-pressure fuel pipe between the pump and fuel rail into place.
12 Ensure that the mating surfaces of the pump and engine are clean and dry, and fit the new pump gasket.
13 Position the fuel pump, and tighten the mounting nuts to the specified torque.
14 Attach the high-pressure fuel pipe unions to the pump and fuel rail, then tighten the unions in two stages to the specified torque. Once the unions are tightened, refit the pipe retaining bolt and tighten it securely.
15 The remainder of refitting is a reversal of removal, noting the following points:
a) Tighten all fasteners to their specified torque where given.
b) Bleed the fuel system as described in Section 6.

11 Fuel injectors – removal and refitting

Caution: Be very careful not to allow dirt into the injection pump or injector pipes during this procedure.

Removal

1 Disconnect the battery negative lead, as described in Chapter 5A Section 4.

10.7 Depress the release buttons and disconnect the fuel hoses

10.10 Fuel pump retaining nuts

11.4 Prise up the clip and pull the return pipe upwards

11.5 Undo the unions and remove the injector pipes

11.7a Undo the retaining bolt...

11.7b...and remove the clamp

11.8a Pull injector upwards from the cylinder head

11.8b Store the injectors upright, and label them so they can be refitted to their original locations

2 Release the air duct and breather hose clamps, then undo the fasteners and remove the plastic cover from the top of the engine (see illustration 6.2).

3 Use a vacuum cleaner to remove any dirt/debris from the area around the injectors/fuel pipes. Absolute cleanliness is essential.

4 Prise up the locking clip and pull up the return pipe from each injector (see illustration). Plug the openings to prevent contamination.

5 Slacken the pipe unions and remove the relevant injector pipe (see illustration). Discard the pipes, new ones must be fitted. Plug the common rail and injector openings to prevent contamination.

6 Disconnect the wiring plugs from the injectors.

7 Unscrew the retaining bolt, and remove the

injector clamp (see illustrations). Note the position of the clamp peg.

8 Pull the injector upwards from place. Note the position of the plastic alignment sleeve. The injectors must be stored vertically, and capped immediately after removal to prevent the fuel from draining (see illustrations). Discard the sealing washers – new ones must be fitted. Note the fitted locations of the injectors – if refitted, it must be to their original locations.

Refitting

9 Ensure that the injectors and seats in cylinder head are clean and dry.

10 If new injectors are being fitted, make a note of the 10-digit identification number on the top each injector. This code will be needed to configure the engine management ECM

11 Fit new sealing washers to the injectors,

and refit them with the clamps (see illustration). Tighten the clamp bolts to the specified torque.

12 Fit the new high-pressure fuel pipes and tighten the unions to the specified torque.

13 Check the condition of the return hose connection seals on each injector, and renew if necessary.

14 Reconnect the fuel return hoses and wiring plugs to the injectors.

15 Reconnect the battery and bleed the fuel system as described in Section 6.

16 Refit the engine top cover.

12 Electronic Diesel Control (EDC) system components – removal and refitting

1 Disconnect the battery negative lead, as described in Chapter 5A Section 4, then wait at least 5 minutes for any residual electrical energy to dissipate.

Crankshaft sensor

2 Slacken the right-hand front roadwheel bolts, raise the front of the vehicle and support it securely on axle stands (see 'Vehicle jacking and support'). Remove the roadwheel.

3 Remove the fasteners and remove the wheelarch lower splashshield.

4 Disconnect the wiring connector from the sensor.

5 Slacken and remove the retaining bolt and carefully remove the sensor from the engine (see illustration).

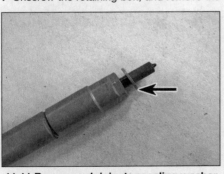

11.11 Renew each injector sealing washer

12.5 Crankshaft position sensor retaining bolt

12.12 Intake air temperature retaining screw

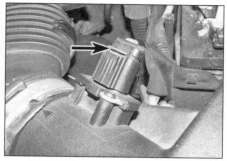

12.14 Slide out the locking clip and disconnect the mass air flow sensor wiring plug

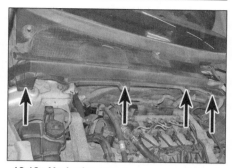

12.18a Undo the centre screws, prise out the plastic expansion rivets at the front edge...

6 Refitting is the reverse of removal, tightening the retaining bolt to the specified torque.

Coolant temperature sensor

7 Removal of the sensor is described in Chapter 3 Section 7.

Accelerator pedal position sensor

8 The sensor is integral with the accelerator pedal assembly – see Section 4.

Intake air temperature sensor

9 Release the air duct and breather hose clamps, then undo the fasteners and remove the plastic cover from the top of the engine **(see illustration 6.2)**.
10 Unclip the coolant hose from the oil level dipstick guide tube, then undo the bolt securing the guide tube bracket.
11 Disconnect the wiring plug from the sensor.
12 Slacken and remove the retaining screw, and withdraw the sensor **(see illustration)**. Renew the seal.
13 Refitting is a reversal of removal.

Mass airflow sensor

14 The mass airflow sensor is located in the air outlet duct from the air cleaner assembly. Disconnect the wiring plug from the sensor **(see illustration)**.
15 Undo the 2 retaining screws and detach the sensor from the air duct.
16 Refitting is a reversal of removal.

Stop-light switch

17 The engine control module receives a signal from the stop-light switch which indicates when the brakes are being applied. Stop-light switch removal and refitting details can be found in Chapter 9 Section 18.

Engine electronic control module (ECM)

Note: *If a new ECM is to be fitted, it must be configured using Land Rover diagnostic equipment. Entrust this task to a Land Rover dealer or suitably equipped specialist.*
18 Remove the wiper arms as described in Chapter 12, then remove the 5 fasteners and

12.18b...then pull the scuttle trim panel upwards from the base of the windscreen

pull the scuttle trim panel upwards from the base of the windscreen **(see illustrations)**.
19 Slide the ECM upwards from place, then pivot over the locking catches and disconnect the wiring plugs from the ECM **(see illustration)**.
20 If required, undo the 4 retaining bolts and detach the ECM from the bracket.
21 Refitting is the reverse of removal. **Note:** *On models with a diesel particulate filter, Land Rover insist that the engine oil and filter must be renewed.*

Fuel temperature sensor

22 The fuel temperature sensor is located in the fuel supply hose from the filter assembly to the high-pressure pump. Disconnect the wiring plug, and release the end of the

12.19 Depress the clip and pivot over the locking catch

fuel hose from the filter and pump **(see illustration)**. Note that the sensor is integral with the hose. Plug the openings to prevent contamination.
23 Refitting is a reversal of removal.

Manifold absolute pressure sensor

24 The MAP sensor is located at the front of the engine. Disconnect the wiring plug **(see illustration)**.
25 Undo the retaining bolt, and remove the sensor.
26 Ensure that the mating surfaces of the sensor and manifold are clean and dry. With a new seal, refit the sensor to the manifold, and tighten the securing bolt to the specified torque. Reconnect the wiring plug.

12.22 Fuel temperature sensor wiring plug

12.24 MAP sensor wiring plug

12.29 Release the clamp and disconnect the breather hose

12.30 Camshaft position sensor retaining bolt

12.32 Position a 7.5 mm drill bit between the sensor the the head cover

Camshaft position sensor

27 Release the air duct and breather hose clamps, then undo the fasteners and remove the plastic cover from the top of the engine (see illustration 6.2).
28 Remove the timing belt cover, as described in Chapter 2A Section 6.
29 Release the clamps and remove the breather hose from the right-hand end of the engine (see illustration).
30 Disconnect the wiring plug, undo the retaining bolt and remove the sensor (see illustration).
31 If a new sensor is being fitted, insert it into the locating hole until the sensor tip rests against one of the 3 webs of the camshaft belt sprocket. Tighten the retaining bolt securely.
32 If a used sensor is being refitted, insert it into the locating hole, and use a 7.5 mm drill bit between the edge of the sensor and the cylinder head cover (see illustration). Tighten the retaining bolt securely.
33 The remainder of refitting is a reversal of removal.

Exhaust gas temperature sensor

34 Release the air duct and breather hose clamps, then undo the fasteners and remove the plastic cover from the top of the engine (see illustration 6.2).
35 Disconnect the wiring plug, and unclip the sensor's wiring harness.
36 Unscrew the sensor from the manifold using a split-type socket. Plug the openings to prevent contamination.
37 Apply a little high-temperature anti-seize

grease to the threads and refit the sensor to the manifold. Tighten the sensor to the specified torque, and reconnect the wiring plug.
38 Refit the engine top cover.

13 Common fuel rail – removal and refitting

Removal

1 Disconnect the battery negative lead as described in Chapter 5A Section 4.
2 Release the air duct and breather hose clamps, then undo the fasteners and remove the plastic cover from the top of the engine (see illustration 6.2).
3 Clean the area around the high-pressure fuel pipes between the common fuel rail and the injectors.
4 Slacken the union nuts, and remove the high-pressure fuel pipes between the fuel rail and the injectors (see illustration 11.5). Plug the openings to prevent contamination. Discard the pipes, new ones must be fitted.
5 Disconnect the fuel return hose from the fuel rail (see illustration).
6 Squeeze together the side of the collar and disconnect the breather hose from the cylinder head cover (see illustration 10.3).
7 Undo the nuts, remove the retaining bolt, and remove the EGR pipe from the EGR cooler to the intake manifold (see illustration 10.4). Plug the openings to prevent contamination.

8 Unclip the hoses and the wiring harness, then undo the 3 retaining bolts and remove the engine cover mounting bracket from the left-hand end of the cylinder head (see illustration 10.5).
9 Clean the area around the high-pressure fuel pipe from the pump to the fuel rail, then undo the unions, and remove the retaining bolt. Use a second spanner to prevent the union port from rotating whilst the union is slackened. Discard the pipe, a new one must be fitted.
10 Disconnect the wiring plugs, undo the 2 retaining bolts and remove the fuel rail (see illustration).

Refitting

11 Refitting is a reversal of removal, noting the following points:
a) Renew all high-pressure fuel pipes.
b) Connect both end of the high-pressure pipes before tightening the union nuts.
c) Tighten all fasteners to their specified torque where given.
d) Bleed the fuel system as described in Section 6.

14 Turbocharger – description and precautions

Description

1 A turbocharger is fitted to all Freelander diesel engines. It increases engine efficiency by raising the pressure in the intake manifold above atmospheric pressure. Instead of the air simply being sucked into the cylinders, it is forced in. Additional fuel is supplied by the injection pump in proportion to the increased air intake.
2 Energy for the operation of the turbocharger comes from the exhaust gas. The gas flows through a specially-shaped housing (the turbine housing) and in so doing, spins the turbine wheel. The turbine wheel is attached to a shaft, at the end of which is another vaned wheel known as the compressor wheel. The compressor wheel spins in its own housing and compresses the inducted air on the way to the intake manifold.
3 The compressed air passes through an

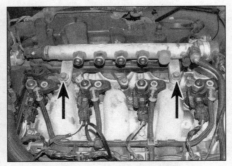

13.5 Depress the release button and disconnect the fuel return hose

13.10 Fuel rail retaining bolts

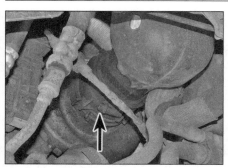

15.4a Release the clamp...

15.4b...undo the bolt...

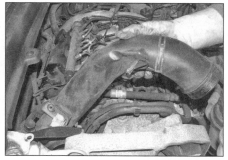

15.4c...and manoeuvre the air inlet duct upwards

intercooler. This is an air-to-air heat exchanger, mounted with the radiator at the front of the vehicle. The purpose of the intercooler is to remove from the inducted air some of the heat gained in being compressed. Because cooler air is denser, removal of this heat further increases engine efficiency.

4 The turbocharger has 6 adjustable guide vanes controlling the flow of exhaust gas into the turbine. The vanes are swivelled by the Rotary Electronic Actuator (REA), controlled by the engine management ECM (see Section 12). At lower engine speeds, the vanes close together, giving a smaller exhaust gas entry port, and therefore higher gas speed, which increases boost pressure at low engine speed. At high engine speed, the vanes are turned to give a larger exhaust gas entry port, and therefore lower gas speed, effectively maintaining a reasonably constant boost pressure over the engine rev range. This is known as a Variable Nozzle Turbocharger (VNT).

5 The turbo shaft is pressure-lubricated by an oil feed pipe from the main oil gallery. The shaft 'floats' on a cushion of oil. A drain pipe returns the oil to the sump.

6 On all DW12C engines, the engine coolant is circulated around the turbocharger housing, to control the operating temperature.

Precautions

7 The turbocharger operates at extremely high speeds and temperatures. Certain precautions must be observed to avoid premature failure of the turbo or injury to the operator.

8 Do not operate the turbo with any parts exposed. Foreign objects falling onto the rotating vanes could cause excessive damage and (if ejected) personal injury.

9 Do not race the engine immediately after start-up, especially if it is cold. Give the oil a few seconds to circulate.

10 Allow the engine to idle for several minutes before switching off after a high-speed run.

11 Observe the recommended intervals for oil and filter changing, and use a reputable oil of the specified quality (see 'Lubricants and fluids'). Neglect of oil changing, or use of inferior oil, can cause carbon formation on the turbo shaft and subsequent failure.

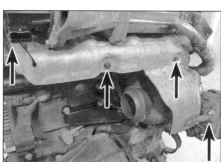

15.8 Turbocharger/manifold heatshield retaining bolts/nuts

15 Turbocharger – removal and refitting

Removal

1 Disconnect the battery negative lead, as described in Chapter 5A Section 4.

2 Raise the front of the vehicle and support it securely on axle stands (see 'Vehicle jacking and support').

3 Remove the catalytic converter as described in Section 19.

4 Release the clamps, undo the retaining bolt and remove the turbocharger air inlet duct (see illustrations).

5 Release the air duct and breather hose clamps, then undo the fasteners and remove the plastic cover from the top of the engine (see illustration 6.2).

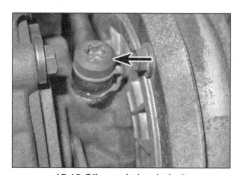

15.10 Oil supply banjo bolt

15.9 Oil return pipe bolts

6 Remove the exhaust gas temperature sensor as described in Section 12.

7 Remove the EGR cooler as described in Chapter 4B.

8 Undo the 4 retaining bolts/nuts and remove the turbocharger/manifold heat shield (see illustration).

9 Undo the 2 bolts securing the oil return pipe to the base of the turbocharger (see illustration). Discard the gasket. Be prepared for fluid spillage.

10 Undo the oil supply banjo bolt at the top of the turbocharger (see illustration). Discard the sealing washers, new ones must be fitted.

11 Undo the 4 retaining bolts and remove the turbocharger support bracket (see illustration).

DW12BTED4 engines

12 Disconnect the wiring plug, undo the 3 retaining bolts, and manoeuvre the

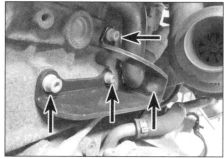

15.11 Turbocharger support bracket bolts

15.12 Turbocharger retaining bolts

turbocharger from place **(see illustration)**. Discard the bolts and the gasket, new ones must be fitted.

DW12C engines (water-cooled turbocharger)

13 Release the clamp and disconnect the coolant hose **(see illustration)**.
14 Undo the banjo bolt securing the coolant pipe to the cylinder block **(see illustration)**. Discard the sealing washers.
15 Disconnect the wiring plug from the vane position actuator on the turbocharger.
16 Support the turbocharger, then undo the 3 bolts/nuts securing it to the exhaust manifold. Lower the turbocharger a little, and discard the gasket. Also discard the nuts/bolt – new ones will be required.
17 Pull the turbocharger away from the cylinder block a little, undo the 2 bolts, and

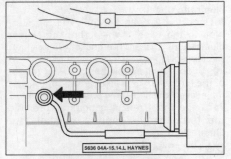

15.14 Coolant pipe banjo bolt

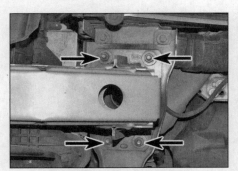

17.2 Undo the bumper reinforcement bars each side

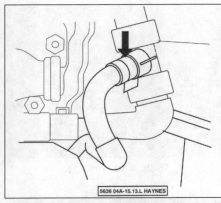

15.13 Release the clamp and disconnect the turbocharger coolant hose

detach the coolant manifold from the rear face **(see illustration)**. Renew the gasket.

Refitting

18 Refitting is a reversal of removal, noting the following points:
a) *Ensure all mating surfaces are clean and dry.*
b) *Renew all O-ring seals and gaskets.*
c) *Tighten all fasteners to their specified torque where given.*
d) *Prior to starting the engine, remove the fuel pump relay as described in Chapter 12 Section 3, and operate the starter until the oil pressure warning light extinguishes.*
e) *Replace the relay, start the engine and check for leaks.*

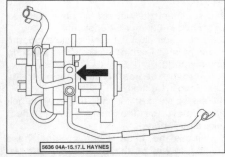

15.17 Detach the coolant pipe manifold from the turbocharger

17.3 Release the clip each side, and slide the baffle upwards

16 Turbocharger – examination and overhaul

1 With the turbocharger removed, inspect the housing for cracks or other visible damage.
2 Spin the turbine or the compressor wheel to verify that the shaft is intact and to feel for excessive shake or roughness. Some play is normal since in use the shaft is 'floating' on a film of oil. Check that the wheel vanes are undamaged.
3 The wastegate and actuator are integral with the turbocharger, and cannot be checked or renewed separately. Consult a Land Rover dealer or other specialist if it is thought that the wastegate may be faulty.
4 If the exhaust or induction passages are oil-contaminated, the turbo shaft oil seals have probably failed (On the induction side, this will also have contaminated the intercooler, where applicable, which if necessary should be flushed with a suitable solvent).
5 No DIY repair of the turbo is possible. A new unit may be available on an exchange basis.

17 Intercooler – removal and refitting

Removal

1 With reference to Chapter 11 Section 6, remove the front bumper.
2 Undo the nuts and remove the front bumper reinforcement bar **(see illustration)**. Undo the retaining bolt and detach the horn assembly from the rear of the bar, and unclip the wiring harness as it's withdrawn.
3 Release the clips, then remove the plastic radiator baffles **(see illustration)**.
4 Slacken the retaining clips, and disconnect the intercooler intake and outlet hoses **(see illustration)**.

17.4 Slacken the hose clip each side

5 Unscrew the 2 retaining bolts, and lift the intercooler from place **(see illustration)**.

Refitting

6 Refitting is a reversal of removal.

18 Manifolds – removal and refitting

Intake manifold

Removal

1 Disconnect the battery negative lead, as described in Chapter 5A Section 4.
2 Raise the front of the vehicle and support it securely on axle stands (see 'Vehicle jacking and support').
3 Remove the fuel filter assembly as described in Chapter 1 Section 25.
4 Squeeze together the side of the collar and disconnect the breather hose from the cylinder head cover **(see illustration 10.3)**.
5 Undo the nuts, remove the retaining bolt, and remove the EGR pipe from the EGR cooler to the intake manifold **(see illustration 10.4)**. Plug the openings to prevent contamination.
6 Unclip the hoses and the wiring harness, then undo the 3 retaining bolts and remove the engine cover mounting bracket from the left-hand end of the cylinder head **(see illustration 10.5)**.
7 Disconnect the wiring plugs from the injectors and the common fuel rail, then undo the 2 bolts securing the wiring harness support bracket **(see illustration)**.

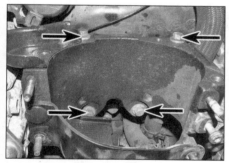

18.10a Undo the bolts and remove the filter bracket...

18.15 Renew the intake manifold seals

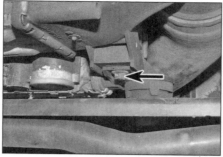

17.5 Remove the bolt each side on the underside of the intercooler

8 Disconnect the fuel return hose from the junction above the intake manifold. Plug the openings to prevent contamination.
9 Slacken the clamp and disconnect the breather pipe at the right-hand end of the engine **(see illustration 12.29)**.
10 Undo the bolts securing the engine oil level dipstick guide tube to the filter bracket, then unto the 4 bolts and remove the filter bracket, followed by the mounting **(see illustrations)**.
11 Disconnect the wiring plugs from the throttle body.
12 Slacken the clamp and disconnect the air hose from the throttle body.
13 Note their fitted positions, and disconnect any remaining wiring plugs/vacuum hoses from the manifold, then release the wiring harness and fuel return pipes from the manifold.
14 Undo the 8 retaining bolts and manoeuvre

18.10b...followed by the mounting

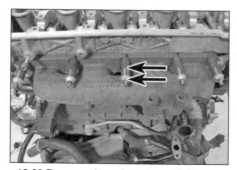

18.20 Remove the exhaust manifold nuts and sleeves

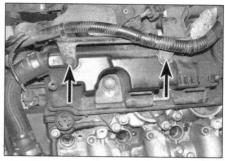

18.7 Wiring harness support bracket bolts

the intake manifold from place. Discard the seals, new ones must be fitted.

Refitting

15 Ensure the manifold and cylinder head mating surfaces are clean and dry, and position new seals on the intake manifold **(see illustration)**.
16 Refit the manifold to the cylinder head, and evenly tighten the bolts and nuts to the specified torque.
17 The remainder of refitting is a reversal of removal.

Exhaust manifold

Removal

18 Remove the turbocharger as described in Section 15.
19 Undo the nut securing the lower section of the exhaust manifold heat shield.
20 Undo the 9 retaining nuts, then remove the sleeves, followed by the exhaust manifold **(see illustration)**. Discard the retaining nuts and gasket, new ones must be fitted.

Refitting

21 Examine all the manifold studs for signs of damage and corrosion; remove all traces of corrosion, and repair or renew any damaged studs.
22 Ensure the mating surfaces of the exhaust manifold and cylinder head are clean and dry. Position the new gasket, and refit the exhaust manifold to the cylinder head **(see illustration)**. Tighten the nuts evenly and progressively to the specified torque.

18.22 Renew the gasket between the exhaust manifold and cylinder head

23 The remainder of refitting is a reversal of removal, noting the following points:

a) Tighten all fasteners to their specified torque where given.

b) Check, and if necessary, top-up the engine oil level as described in 'Weekly checks'.

c) Before restarting the engine, remove the fuel pump relay (see Chapter 12 Section 3) then turn the engine over on the starter until the oil pressure warning light goes out; this will allow oil to be circulated around the turbocharger bearings before the engine is started. Refit the relay and start the engine as normal.

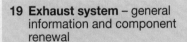

19 Exhaust system – general information and component renewal

General information

1 The exhaust system consists of two or three sections: the catalytic converter, the particulate filter (where fitted), the tailpipe and main silencer box.

2 The tailpipe is a sleeve fit over the end of the catalytic converter or particulate filter (as applicable), whilst the catalytic converter is secured to the turbocharger using a clamp. Where applicable, the particulate filter and catalytic converter are joined by a flanged joint, secured by nuts, and the system is suspended throughout its entire length by rubber mountings.

Removal

3 Each exhaust section can be removed individually, or alternatively, the complete system can be removed as a unit. Even if only one part of the system needs attention, it can sometimes be easier to remove the whole system and separate the sections on the bench.

4 To remove the system or part of the system, first jack up the front or rear of the car and support it securely on axle stands (see 'Vehicle jacking and support'). Alternatively, position the car over an inspection pit or on car ramps.

19.10 Catalytic converter-to-turbocharger clamp nut

Catalytic converter

5 Release the air duct and breather hose clamps, then undo the fasteners and remove the plastic cover from the top of the engine **(see illustration 6.2)**.

6 Undo the fasteners and remove the engine undershield.

7 Working at the rear of the engine, disconnect the oxygen sensor and temperature sensor (where fitted) wiring plugs.

8 Remove the particulate filter (where fitted) as described in this Section.

9 On models without a particulate filter, slacken the clamp securing the catalytic converter to the rear pipe.

10 Working at the front, undo the nut and release the clamp securing the catalytic converter to the turbocharger **(see illustration)**.

11 Release the catalytic converter the mounting rubbers, and manoeuvre it from place. Discard the turbo gasket, a new one must be fitted.

Particulate filter

12 Undo the fasteners and remove the engine undershield.

13 Note their fitted positions, release the clamps and disconnect the rubber hoses from the pressure take-off pipes on the particulate filter **(see illustration)**. Plug the openings to prevent contamination.

14 Trace the wiring back from the temperature sensor on the filter, then disconnect the wiring plug.

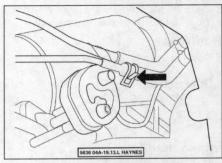

19.13 Disconnect the hoses from the pressure take-off pipes

15 Undo the nuts securing the particulate filter to the catalytic converter. Discard the nuts, new ones must be fitted.

16 Slacken the clamp bolt and separate the tail pipe from the particulate filter.

17 Free the particulate filter from its mounting rubbers then detach the pipe from the flange joints and remove it from underneath the vehicle. Recover the gasket from the front joint and discard it.

Tailpipe

18 Slacken clamp bolt securing the tailpipe joint to the catalytic converter or particulate filter as applicable.

19 Free the tailpipe from its mounting rubbers and remove it along with its gasket.

Refitting

20 Each section is refitted by reversing the removal sequence, noting the following points:

a) Ensure that all traces of corrosion have been removed from the flanges and renew all gaskets.

b) Inspect the rubber mountings for signs of damage or deterioration, and renew as necessary.

c) Prior to tightening the exhaust system fasteners to the specified torque, ensure that all rubber mountings are correctly located, and that there is adequate clearance between the exhaust system and vehicle underbody.

Chapter 4 Part B
Emission control systems

Contents

Degrees of difficulty

Easy, suitable for novice with little experience		Fairly easy, suitable for beginner with some experience		Fairly difficult, suitable for competent DIY mechanic		Difficult, suitable for experienced DIY mechanic		Very difficult, suitable for expert DIY or professional	

Specifications

Torque wrench settings	Nm	lbf ft
Crankcase vent oil separator-to-cylinder block:		
M6	10	7
M8	25	18
Exhaust gas recirculation (EGR) cooler bolts	10	7
Exhaust gas recirculation (EGR) valve:		
Nuts	10	7
Screws	6	4

1 General information

1 All diesel engine models are also designed to meet strict emission requirements. All models are fitted with a crankcase emission control system, a catalytic converter, an exhaust gas recirculation (EGR) system, and on some models, a particulate filter, to keep exhaust emissions down to a minimum.

2 The emission control systems function as follows.

Crankcase emission control

3 To reduce the emission of unburned hydrocarbons from the crankcase into the atmosphere, the engine is sealed and the blow-by gases and oil vapour are drawn from inside the crankcase, through a wire mesh oil separator, into the intake tract to be burned by the engine during normal combustion. Crankcase gasses are drawn via Positive Crankcase Ventilation (PCV) valve. The valve closes progressively as the engine speed increases, so limiting the maximum depression in the crankcase.

Exhaust emission control

4 To minimise the level of exhaust pollutants released into the atmosphere, a catalytic converter is fitted in the exhaust system of all models, and on some, a diesel particulate filter.

5 The catalytic converter consists of a canister containing a fine mesh impregnated with a catalyst material, over which the hot exhaust gases pass. The catalyst speeds up the oxidation of harmful carbon monoxide, unburned hydrocarbons and soot, effectively reducing the quantity of harmful products released into the atmosphere via the exhaust gases.

Particulate filter

6 This device is designed to trap carbon particulates produced by the combustion process. The particle filter is fitted downstream of the catalytic converter. In order to prevent the filter blocking, pressure and temperature sensors are fitted to the filter. Under the normal, high-speed driving conditions, the soot particles are burnt off in the filter by the high temperature of the exhaust gases. However, where the driving conditions are such that the exhaust gases are not sufficiently high, the engine management system injects fuel into the cylinders after the point of combustion. These are called post-injections, and raise the temperature of the exhaust gases, causing the soot particles in the filter to be burnt off.

Exhaust gas recirculation (EGR) system

7 This system is designed to recirculate small quantities of exhaust gas into the intake tract, and therefore into the combustion process. This process reduces the level of unburnt hydrocarbons present in the exhaust gas before it reaches the catalytic converter. The system is controlled by the engine management system ECM, using the information from its various sensors, via the EGR valve which is fitted to the metal pipe connecting the intake and exhaust manifolds. On some models, the exhaust gasses are cooled prior to entering the intake manifold by passing through a cooler mounted on the side of the EGR valve. Engine coolant circulates through the cooler.

2 Engine emission control systems – testing and component renewal

Crankcase emission control

Testing

1 The components of this system require no attention other than to check that the hose(s) are clear and undamaged at regular intervals. If the system is thought to be faulty, renew the crankcase pressure limiting valve as follows.

PCV – renewal

2 Renewal of the valve is described within the camshaft cover procedure, described in Chapter 2A Section 4.

Crankcase oil separator

3 Remove the intake manifold as described in Chapter 4A Section 18.

4 Release the clamps and disconnect the breather hoses from the oil separator. The separator is located at the left-hand front face of the cylinder block.

5 Undo the nuts, release the clips and remove the support bracket from the separator **(see illustration)**.

6 Refitting is a reversal of removal.

Exhaust emission control

Testing

7 The performance of the catalytic converter or diesel particulate filter can be checked only by using Land Rover diagnostic equipment (or equivalent). Entrust this task to a dealer or suitable equipped specialist.

8 Before assuming that the catalytic converter/particulate filter is faulty, it is worth checking whether the problem is not due to a faulty injector(s). Refer to your Land Rover dealer for further information.

Catalytic converter and particulate filter – renewal

9 Refer to Chapter 4A Section 19 for removal and refitting details.

Exhaust gas recirculation (EGR) system

Testing

10 Comprehensive testing of the system can only be carried out using specialist electronic equipment which is connected to the injection system diagnostic wiring connector (see Chapter 4A Section 5).

Exhaust gas recirculation (EGR) cooler – renewal

11 Remove the wiper arms as described in Chapter 12 Section 13.

12 Remove the fasteners, and pull the scuttle trim panel upwards from the base of the windscreen.

13 Release the air duct and breather hose clamps, then undo the fasteners and remove the plastic cover from the top of the engine **(see illustration)**.

14 At the rear of the cylinder head, disconnect the oxygen sensor wiring plug.

15 Using a split-type socket, unscrew the oxygen sensor from the catalytic converter **(see illustration)**.

2.5 Remove the support bracket from the oil separator

2.13 Release the clamps, disconnect the hoses, undo the fasteners and remove the engine top cover

2.15 Unscrew the oxygen sensor

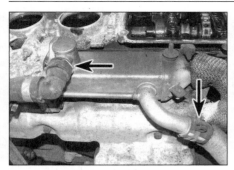

2.18 EGR cooler hose clamps

2.19 Remove the EGR pipe from the left-hand end of the engine

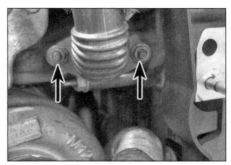

2.22 EGR pipe-to-exhaust manifold retaining nuts

16 Unclip the hose at the rear of the cylinder head, undo the bolts/nut and remove the hose bracket from the cylinder head cover.
17 Apply clamps to the coolant hoses to, and from the EGR cooler to minimise coolant loss.
18 Release the clamps and disconnect the coolant hoses from the EGR cooler **(see illustration)**.
19 Undo the retaining bolts/nuts and remove the EGR pipe from the left-hand end of the engine **(see illustration)**. Discard the gaskets.
20 Undo the retaining bolts and manoeuvre the exhaust manifold/turbocharger upper heat shield from place.
21 Disconnect the wiring plug from the EGR valve actuator.
22 Release the clamp, undo the nuts and remove the EGR pipe from the exhaust manifold to the EGR cooler **(see illustration)**. Discard the clamp and the nuts, new ones must be fitted.
23 Undo the retaining bolts and manoeuvre the EGR cooler from place.
24 If required, undo the 4 retaining screws, and detach the EGR cooler from the EGR valve **(see illustration)**. Renew the gasket.

25 Refitting is a reversal of removal. Top up the coolant level as described in Chapter 1.

Exhaust gas recirculation (EGR) valve – renewal

26 Remove the EGR cooler as described previously in this Section.
27 Undo the 4 retaining screws, and detach the EGR valve from the cooler **(see illustration 2.24)**. Renew the gasket.
28 Refitting is a reversal of removal, using a new gasket and tightening the valve retaining bolts to the specified torque.

3 Catalytic converter – general information and precautions

1 The catalytic converter is a reliable and simple device which needs no maintenance in itself, but there are some facts of which an owner should be aware if the converter is to function properly for its full service life.
a) *DO NOT use fuel or engine oil additives – these may contain substances harmful to the catalytic converter.*

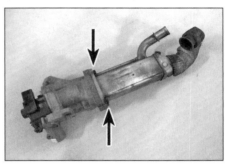

2.24 Undo the screws and detach the EGR valve from the cooler

b) *DO NOT continue to use the car if the engine burns oil to the extent of leaving a visible trail of blue smoke.*
c) *Remember that the catalytic converter operates at very high temperatures. DO NOT, therefore, park the car in dry undergrowth, over long grass or piles of dead leaves after a long run.*
d) *Remember that the catalytic converter is FRAGILE - do not strike it with tools during servicing work.*

Notes

Chapter 5 Part A
Starting and Charging systems

Contents

Degrees of difficulty

Easy, suitable for novice with little experience	Fairly easy, suitable for beginner with some experience	Fairly difficult, suitable for competent DIY mechanic	Difficult, suitable for experienced DIY mechanic	Very difficult, suitable for expert DIY or professional

Specifications

System type .... 12-volt, negative earth
Starter .... Bosch/Denso 2.0 kW
Alternator .... Bosch 90 to 180 A @ 25°C
Battery charge condition:
  Poor .... 12.5 volts
  Normal .... 12.6 volts
  Good .... 12.7 volts

Torque wrench settings	Nm	lbf ft
Alternator fixings	48	35
Alternator drive belt:		
Tensioner bolt	45	33
Idler pulley	48	35
Starter motor bolt	40	30

1 General information and precautions

General information

1 The engine electrical system consists mainly of the charging and starting systems. Because of their engine-related functions, these components are covered separately from the body electrical devices such as the lights, instruments, etc (which are covered in Chapter 12. Refer to Chapter 5B for information on the pre-heating system.

2 The electrical system is of the 12-volt negative earth type.

3 The battery is of the low maintenance or 'maintenance-free' (sealed for life) type and is charged by the alternator, which is belt-driven from the crankshaft pulley.

4 The starter motor is of the pre-engaged type incorporating an integral solenoid. On starting, the solenoid moves the drive pinion into engagement with the flywheel ring gear before the starter motor is energised. Once the engine has started, a one-way clutch prevents the motor armature being driven by the engine until the pinion disengages from the flywheel.

5 Vehicles from 2010 model year, can be equipped with a Stop/Start system, designed to reduce fuel consumption and emissions. These vehicles have uprated starter motors, alternators, dual mass flywheels, and AGM (Absorbent Glass Mat) batteries.

Precautions

6 Further details of the various systems are given in the relevant Sections of this Chapter. While some repair procedures are given, the usual course of action is to renew the component concerned. The owner whose interest extends beyond mere component renewal should obtain a copy of the *'Automotive Electrical & Electronic Systems Manual'*, available from the publishers of this manual.

7 It is necessary to take extra care when working on the electrical system to avoid damage to semi-conductor devices (diodes and transistors), and to avoid the risk of personal injury. In addition to the precautions given in 'Safety first!' at the beginning of this manual, observe the following when working on the system:

8 Always remove rings, watches, etc before working on the electrical system. Even with the battery disconnected, capacitive discharge could occur if a component's live terminal is earthed through a metal object. This could cause a shock or nasty burn.

9 Do not reverse the battery connections. Components such as the alternator, electronic control units, or any other components having semi-conductor circuitry could be irreparably damaged.

10 If the engine is being started using jump leads and a slave battery, connect the batteries positive-to-positive and negative-to-negative (see 'Jump starting'). This also applies when connecting a battery charger.

11 Never disconnect the battery terminals, the alternator, any electrical wiring or any test instruments when the engine is running.

12 Do not allow the engine to turn the alternator when the alternator is not connected.

13 Never 'test' for alternator output by 'flashing' the output lead to earth.

14 Never use an ohmmeter of the type incorporating a hand-cranked generator for circuit or continuity testing.

15 Always ensure that the battery negative lead is disconnected when working on the electrical system.

16 Before using electric-arc welding equipment on the car, disconnect the battery, alternator and components such as the fuel injection/ignition electronic control unit to protect them from the risk of damage.

17 The audio unit fitted as standard equipment by Land Rover is equipped with a built-in security code to deter thieves. If the power source to the unit is cut, the anti-theft system will activate. Even if the power source is immediately reconnected, the audio unit will not function until the correct security code has been entered. Therefore, if you do not know the correct security code for the audio unit do not disconnect the battery negative terminal of the battery or remove the audio unit from the vehicle.

2 Electrical fault finding – general information

1 Refer to Chapter 12 Section 2.

3 Battery – testing and charging

Standard and low maintenance battery – testing

1 If the vehicle covers a small annual mileage, it is worthwhile checking the specific gravity of the electrolyte every three months to determine the state of charge of the battery. Use a hydrometer to make the check and compare the results with the following table. Note that the specific gravity readings assume an electrolyte temperature of 15°C (60°F); for every 10°C (18°F) below 15°C (60°F) subtract 0.007. For every 10°C (18°F) above 15°C (60°F) add 0.007.

Ambient temperature	Above 25°C (77°F)	Below 25°C (77°F)
Fully charged	1.210 to 1.230	1.270 to 1.290
70% charged	1.17 to 1.190	1.230 to 1.250
Discharged	1.050 to 1.070	1.110 to 1.130

2 If the battery condition is suspect, first check the specific gravity of electrolyte in each cell. A variation of 0.040 or more between any cells indicates loss of electrolyte or deterioration of the internal plates.

3 If the specific gravity variation is 0.040 or more, the battery should be renewed. If the cell variation is satisfactory but the battery is discharged, it should be charged as described later in this Section.

Maintenance-free battery – testing

4 In cases where a 'sealed for life' maintenance-free battery is fitted, topping-up and testing of the electrolyte in each cell is not possible. The condition of the battery can therefore only be tested using a battery condition indicator or a voltmeter.

5 Models may be fitted with a 'Delco' type maintenance-free battery, with a built-in charge condition indicator. The indicator is located in the top of the battery casing, and indicates the condition of the battery from its colour. If the indicator shows green, then the battery is in a good state of charge. If the indicator turns darker, eventually to black, then the battery requires charging, as described later in this Section. If the indicator shows clear/yellow, then the electrolyte level in the battery is too low to allow further use, and the battery should be renewed. Do not attempt to charge, load or jump start a battery when the indicator shows clear/yellow.

6 If testing the battery using a voltmeter, connect the voltmeter across the battery and compare the result with those given in the Specifications under 'charge condition'. The test is only accurate if the battery has not been subjected to any kind of charge for the previous six hours. If this is not the case, switch on the headlights for 30 seconds, then wait four to five minutes before testing the battery after switching off the headlights. All other electrical circuits must be switched off, so check that the doors and tailgate are fully shut when making the test.

7 If the voltage reading is less than 12.2 volts, then the battery is discharged, whilst a reading of 12.2 to 12.4 volts indicates a partially discharged condition.

8 If the battery is to be charged, remove it from the vehicle (Section 4 and charge it as described later in this Section.

Standard and low maintenance battery – charging

Note: *The following is intended as a guide only. Always refer to the manufacturer's recommendations (often printed on a label attached to the battery) before charging a battery.*

9 Charge the battery at a rate of 3.5 to 4 amps and continue to charge the battery at this rate until no further rise in specific gravity is noted over a four hour period.

10 Alternatively, a trickle charger charging at the rate of 1.5 amps can safely be used overnight.

11 Specially rapid 'boost' charges which are claimed to restore the power of the battery in 1 to 2 hours are not recommended, as they can cause serious damage to the battery plates through overheating.

12 While charging the battery, note that the temperature of the electrolyte should never exceed 37.8°C (100°F).

Maintenance-free battery – charging

Note: *The following is intended as a guide only. Always refer to the manufacturer's recommendations (often printed on a label attached to the battery) before charging a battery.*

13 This battery type takes considerably longer to fully recharge than the standard type, the time taken being dependent on the extent of discharge, but it can take anything up to three days.

14 A constant voltage type charger is required, to be set, when connected, to 13.9 to 14.9 volts with a charger current below 25 amps. Using this method, the battery should be usable within three hours, giving a voltage reading of 12.5 volts, but this is for a partially discharged battery and, as mentioned, full charging can take considerably longer.

15 If the battery is to be charged from a fully discharged state (condition reading less than 12.2 volts), have it recharged by your Land Rover dealer or local automotive electrician, as the charge rate is higher and constant supervision during charging is necessary. Note: Do not charge AGM batteries above 14.8 volts, or the battery may be damaged.

4	Battery and battery tray – disconnection, removal and refitting	

Battery

Disconnection

1 Ensure that all electrical consumers are switched off, all windows are closed, and the alarm is disarmed. Remove the remote control from the vehicle, and wait at least 2 minutes for the electrical systems to 'power down'.

2 Unclip the cover, slacken the clamp nut

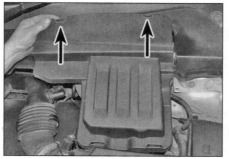

4.2a Release the clips and remove the battery cover

and disconnect the clamp from the battery negative (earth) terminal **(see illustrations)**.

3 Lift the insulation cover (where fitted) and disconnect the positive terminal lead in the same way **(see illustration)**.

Removal

4 Disconnect the battery as described previously in this Section.

5 Unscrew the bolt and remove the battery retaining clamp then lift the battery out of the engine compartment **(see illustration)**. Disconnect the vent pipe as the battery is withdrawn.

Refitting

6 Refitting is a reversal of removal, but smear petroleum jelly on the terminals when reconnecting the leads, and always reconnect the positive lead first, and the negative lead last.

7 After reconnection, the electric windows, and sunroof may need to be reset as follows:

Windows

a) *Close the electric window fully.*
b) *Release the switch, then lift it to the close position, and hold it there for 2 seconds.*
c) *Release the switch, then push it to the open position, and hold it there for 2 seconds.*
d) *Lift and release the switch to operate the one-touch function.*
e) *Repeat this procedure on each window.*

Sunroof

a) *Switch on the ignition, press the front of the sunroof switch, and hold it for 20 seconds.*

4.2b Slacken the nut and disconnect the negative (earth) terminal

b) *After 20 seconds the sunroof will begin to move.*
c) *Keep the front of the switch pressed until the sunroof has fully opened, then closed.*
d) *Once the open/close cycle has completed, and the sunroof has stopped moving, release the switch.*

Note: *Vehicles with the Stop/Start system are fitted with a Battery Monitoring System (BMS) module. This module calculates and communicates the battery status to the vehicle's ECM. If a new battery is fitted, the BMS module reset procedure must be carried out, using Land Rover diagnostic equipment (or equivalent). Entrust this task to a Land Rover dealer or suitably equipped specialist.*

Battery tray

Removal

8 Remove the battery as described previously in this Section.

9 Undo the 4 retaining bolts, and lift the battery tray from place **(see illustration)**.

Refitting

10 Refitting is a reversal of removal.

5	Charging system – testing	

1 Refer to the warnings given in Section 1 of this Chapter before starting work.

2 If the ignition warning light fails to illuminate when the ignition is switched on, first check

4.3 Slacken the positive terminal clamp nut

4.5 Battery retaining clamp bolt and vent pipe

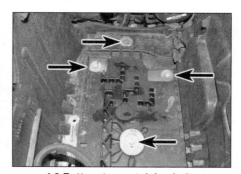

4.9 Battery tray retaining bolts

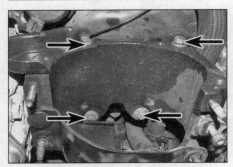

6.5 Fuel filter bracket retaining bolts

6.7 Disconnect the wiring from the alternator

the alternator wiring connections for security. If the light still fails to illuminate, check the continuity of the warning light feed wire from the alternator to the instrument. If all is satisfactory, the alternator maybe at fault and should be renewed or taken to an auto-electrician for testing and repair. Bear in mind that the Freelander is equipped with a sophisticated self-diagnosis system, and any fault detected by the system will generate a fault code. This code will be stored by the CJB (Central Junction Box). Use Land Rover diagnostic equipment (or equivalent) to interrogate the CJB, read the code, and investigate the fault recorded.

3 If the ignition warning light illuminates when the engine is running, stop the engine and check that the drivebelt is correctly tensioned (see Chapter 1 Section 6) and that the alternator connections are secure. If all is so far satisfactory, have the alternator checked by an auto-electrician for testing and repair.

4 If the alternator output is suspect even though the warning light functions correctly, the regulated voltage may be checked as follows.

5 Connect a voltmeter across the battery terminals and start the engine.

6 Increase the engine speed until the voltmeter reading remains steady; the reading should be approximately 12 to 13 volts, and no more than 14 volts.

7 Switch on as many electrical accessories (eg, the headlights, heated rear window and heater blower) as possible, and check that the alternator maintains the regulated voltage at around 13 to 14 volts.

8 If the regulated voltage is not as stated, the fault may be due to worn brushes, weak brush springs, a faulty voltage regulator, a faulty diode, a severed phase winding or worn or damaged slip rings. The alternator should be renewed or taken to an auto-electrician for testing and repair.

6 Alternator – removal and refitting

Removal

1 Firmly apply the handbrake then jack up the front of the vehicle and support it securely on axle stands (see *'Vehicle Jacking and Support'*). Undo the retaining bolts/clips and remove the undershield from beneath the engine/transmission unit.

2 Disconnect the battery negative lead as described in Section 4.

3 With reference to Chapter 1, remove the fuel filter and auxiliary drivebelt.

4 Unclip the coolant hose at the upper edge of the radiator.

5 Undo the bolt securing the engine oil level dipstick to the fuel filter bracket, then undo the 4 bolts and remove the filter bracket **(see illustration)**.

6 Undo the retaining bolts, and move the power steering pump, and reservoir to one side.

7 Disconnect the wiring from the alternator **(see illustration)**.

8 Prise off the plastic cap, undo the bolt and remove the auxiliary drivebelt idler pulley **(see illustration)**.

9 Undo the lower retaining bolt, and manoeuvre the alternator upwards from place **(see illustration)**.

Refitting

10 Refitting is the reverse of removal tightening all mounting bolts to their specified torque settings (where given). Ensure the drivebelt is correctly refitted and tensioned as described in Chapter 1 Section 6.

7 Alternator – testing and overhaul

1 If the alternator is thought to be suspect, it should be removed from the vehicle and taken to an auto-electrician for testing. Most auto-electricians will be able to supply and fit brushes at a reasonable cost. However, check on the cost of repairs before proceeding as it may prove more economical to obtain a new or exchange alternator.

8 Starting system – testing

Note: *Refer to the precautions given in 'Safety first!' and Section 1 of this Chapter before starting work.*

1 If the starter motor fails to operate when the ignition key is turned to the appropriate position, the following possible causes may be to blame:

a) *The battery is faulty.*

b) *The electrical connections between the switch, solenoid, battery and starter motor are somewhere failing to pass the necessary current from the battery through the starter to earth.*

c) *The solenoid is faulty.*

d) *The starter motor is mechanically or electrically defective.*

2 To check the battery, switch on the headlights. If they dim after a few seconds, this indicates that the battery is discharged – recharge (see Section 3) or renew the battery. If the headlights glow brightly, operate the ignition switch and observe the lights. If they dim, then this indicates that current is reaching the starter motor, therefore the fault must lie in the starter motor. If the lights continue to glow brightly (and no clicking sound can be heard from the starter motor solenoid), this indicates that there is a fault in the circuit or solenoid – see following paragraphs. If the starter motor turns slowly when operated, but the battery is in good condition, then this indicates that either the starter motor is faulty, or there is considerable resistance somewhere in the circuit.

3 If a fault in the circuit is suspected,

6.8 Prise off the cap and undo the pulley retaining bolt

6.9 Alternator retaining bolts

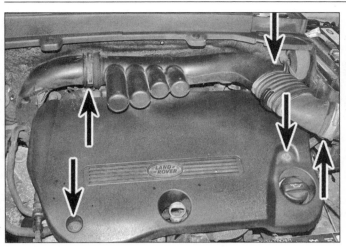

9.2 Release the clamps, disconnect the hoses, undo the fasteners and remove the engine top cover

9.5 Prise off the plastic cap, undo the nuts and disconnect the starter motor wiring connections

disconnect the battery leads (including the earth connection to the body), the starter/ solenoid wiring and the engine/ transmission earth strap. Thoroughly clean the connections, and reconnect the leads and wiring, then use a voltmeter or test lamp to check that full battery voltage is available at the battery positive lead connection to the solenoid, and that the earth is sound. Smear petroleum jelly around the battery terminals to prevent corrosion – corroded connections are amongst the most frequent causes of electrical system faults.

4 If the battery and all connections are in good condition, check the circuit by disconnecting the wire from the solenoid blade terminal. Connect a voltmeter or test lamp between the wire end and a good earth (such as the battery negative terminal), and check that the wire is live when the ignition switch is turned to the `start' position. If it is, then the circuit is sound – if not the circuit wiring can be checked as described in Chapter 12 Section 2.

5 The solenoid contacts can be checked by connecting a voltmeter or test lamp between

the battery positive feed connection on the starter side of the solenoid, and earth. When the ignition switch is turned to the 'start' position, there should be a reading or lighted bulb, as applicable. If there is no reading or lighted bulb, the solenoid is faulty and should be renewed.

6 If the circuit and solenoid are proved sound, the fault may lie in the starter motor. In this event, it may be possible to have the starter motor overhauled by a specialist, but check on the cost of spares before proceeding, as it may prove more economical to obtain a new or exchange motor.

9 Starter motor – removal and refitting

Removal

1 Disconnect the battery negative lead as described in Section 4.

2 Release the air duct and breather hose clamps, then undo the fasteners and remove

the plastic cover from the top of the engine **(see illustration)**.

3 Remove the air cleaner assembly as described in Chapter 4A Section 2.

4 Undo the retaining bolt securing the wiring harness at the left-hand end of the starter motor. This is to access the starter motor mounting bolts.

5 Disconnect the wiring from the starter motor **(see illustration)**.

6 Undo the 3 retaining bolts and manoeuvre the starter motor upwards from place **(see illustrations)**.

Refitting

7 Refitting is a reversal of removal tightening the mounting bolts to the specified torque. Ensure all wiring is correctly routed and its retaining nuts are securely tightened.

10 Starter motor – testing and overhaul

1 If the starter motor is thought to be suspect, it should be removed from the vehicle and taken to an auto-electrician for testing. Most auto-electricians will be able to supply and fit brushes at a reasonable cost. However, check on the cost of repairs before proceeding as it may prove more economical to obtain a new or exchange motor.

11 Start control unit – removal and refitting

1 Removal and refitting of the start control unit is described in Chapter 12 Section 4.

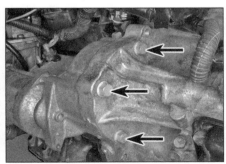

9.6a Undo the starter motor retaining bolts..

9.6b...and manoeuvre the starter motor from place

Notes

Chapter 5 Part B
Pre-heating system

Contents

Degrees of difficulty

Easy, suitable for novice with little experience	Fairly easy, suitable for beginner with some experience	Fairly difficult, suitable for competent DIY mechanic	Difficult, suitable for experienced DIY mechanic	Very difficult, suitable for expert DIY or professional 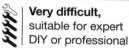

Specifications

Torque wrench setting	Nm	lbf ft
Glow plugs	10	7

1 General information

1 To assist cold starting, diesel engine models are fitted with a pre-heating system, which comprises control module/relay, and four glow plugs. The system is controlled by the Electronic Diesel Control (EDC) system, using information provided by the coolant temperature sensor (see Chapter 4A).
2 The glow plugs are miniature electric heating elements, encapsulated in a metal case with a probe at one end, and an electrical connection at the other. The combustion chambers have a glow plug threaded into it. When the glow plug is energised, it heats up rapidly causing the temperature of the air charge drawn into each of the combustion chambers to rise. Each glow plug probe is positioned directly in line with the incoming spray of fuel from the injector. Hence the fuel passing over the glow plug probe is also heated, allowing its optimum combustion temperature to be achieved more readily.
3 The duration of the pre-heating period is governed by the Electronic Diesel Control (EDC) system control module (ECM), using information provided by the coolant temperature sensor (see Chapter 4A). The ECM alters the pre-heating time (the length

for which the glow plugs are supplied with current) to suit the prevailing conditions.
4 A warning light informs the driver that pre-heating is taking place. The lamp extinguishes when sufficient pre-heating has taken place to allow the engine to be started, but power will still be supplied to the glow plugs for a further period until the engine is started. If no attempt is made to start the engine, the power supply to the glow plugs is switched off to prevent battery drain and glow plug burn-out. Power supply to the glow plugs is controlled by relays within the battery junction box on vehicles upto 2011 model year, and by a control module on vehicles after this date.

2 Pre-heating system – testing

1 Full testing of the system can only be carried out using specialist diagnostic equipment which is connected to the engine management system diagnostic wiring connector (see Chapter 4A Section 5). If the pre-heating system is thought to be faulty, some preliminary checks of the glow plug operation may be made as described in the following paragraphs.
2 Connect a voltmeter or 12-volt test lamp between the glow plug supply cable, and a good earth point on the engine.

Caution: Make sure that the live connection is kept well clear of the engine and bodywork.
3 Have an assistant activate the pre-heating system by turning the ignition key to the second position, and check that battery voltage is applied to the glow plug electrical connection. Note: The supply voltage will be less than battery voltage initially, but will rise and settle as the glow plug heats up. It will then drop to zero when the pre-heating period ends and the safety cut-out operates.
4 If no supply voltage can be detected at the glow plug, then the glow plug relay or the supply cable may be faulty.
5 To locate a faulty glow plug, first operate the pre-heating system to allow the glow plugs to reach working temperature, then disconnect the battery negative cable and position it away from the battery terminal.
6 Refer to Section 3, and remove the supply cable from No 2 glow plug terminal. Measure the electrical resistance between the glow plug terminal and the engine earth. A reading of anything more than a few Ohms indicates that the glow plug is defective. New plugs have a resistance of approximately 1.2 ohms.
7 As a final check, remove the glow plugs and inspect them visually, as described in Section 3.
8 If no problems are found, take the vehicle to a Land Rover dealer or suitably equipped specialist for testing using the appropriate diagnostic equipment.

3.3 The wiring plugs simply pull from the glow plugs

3.4 Unscrew the glow plugs from the cylinder head

3 Glow plugs – removal, inspection and refitting

Removal

1 Disconnect the battery negative lead as described in Chapter 5A Section 4.
2 With reference to Chapter 4A Section 18, remove the intake manifold.
3 Disconnect the wiring plugs from the glow plugs **(see illustration)**.
4 Clean the area around the glow plugs to prevent contamination, then using a deep socket, unscrew and remove them **(see illustration)**.

Inspection

5 Inspect the glow plugs for signs of damage. Burnt or eroded glow plug tips can be caused by a bad injector spray pattern. Have the

injectors checked if this sort of damage is found.
6 If the glow plugs are in good condition, check them electrically, as described in Section 2.
7 The glow plugs can be energised by applying 12 volts to them to verify that they heat up evenly and in the required time. Observe the following precautions:
a) Support the glow plug by clamping it carefully in a vice or self-locking pliers. Remember it will be red hot.
b) Make sure that the power supply or test lead incorporates a fuse or overload trip to protect against damage from a short-circuit.
c) After testing, allow the glow plug to cool for several minutes before attempting to handle it.
8 A glow plug in good condition will start to glow red at the tip after drawing current for 5 seconds or so. Any plug which takes much longer to start glowing, or which starts

glowing in the middle instead of at the tip, is probably defective.

Refitting

9 Thoroughly clean the glow plugs, and the glow plug seating areas in the cylinder head.
10 Apply a smear of anti-seize compound to the glow plug threads, then refit the glow plug and tighten it to the specified torque.
11 Reconnect the wiring to the glow plug.
12 Refit the intake manifold as described in Chapter 4A Section 18.

4 Glow plug control module – removal and refitting

Note: *The glow plug control module is only fitted to vehicle from 2011 model year*

Removal

1 Disconnect the battery negative lead as described in Chapter 5A Section 4.
2 Remove the front wiper arms as described in Chapter 12 Section 13.
3 Release the fasteners, and pull the scuttle trim panel upwards from the base of the windscreen **(see illustrations)**.
4 The glow plug control module is located to the right-hand side of the engine management ECM. Slide out the locking element and disconnect the wiring plug from the control unit.
5 Undo the retaining bolt and remove the control module.

Refitting

6 Refitting is a reversal of removal.

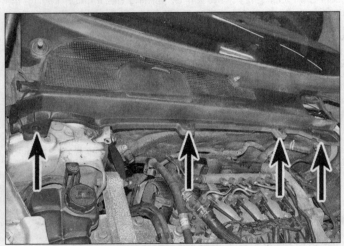

4.3a Undo the centre screws, prise out the plastic expansion rivets from the front edge...

4.3b...then pull the scuttle trim panel upwards from the base of the windscreen

Chapter 6
Clutch

Contents

Degrees of difficulty

Easy, suitable for novice with little experience	Fairly easy, suitable for beginner with some experience	Fairly difficult, suitable for competent DIY mechanic	Difficult, suitable for experienced DIY mechanic	Very difficult, suitable for expert DIY or professional

Specifications

Type	Self-adjusting, single dry plate with diaphragm spring, hydraulically-operated
Friction plate diameter	250 mm
Friction material-to-rivet head depth:	
New (approximate)	1.2 mm
Service limit	0.2 mm
Pressure plate	
Maximum diaphragm spring finger height difference	1.0 mm
Maximum warpage of machined surface	0.18 mm

Torque wrench settings	Nm	lbf ft
Pressure plate retaining bolts*:		
Vehicles upto 2011 model year	23	17
Vehicles from 2011 model year	29	21
Slave cylinder mounting bolt	11	8
Steering column pinch bolt*	25	18

*Do not re-use

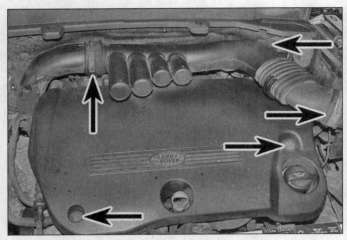

2.2 Release the clamps, undo the bolts, disconnect the breather hose and remove the engine cover

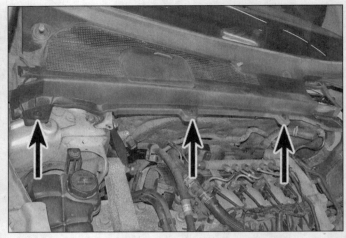

2.4a Undo the centre screws, prise out the plastic expansion rivets...

1 General information

1 The clutch consists of a friction plate, a pressure plate assembly, a release bearing and the release mechanism; all of these components are contained in the large cast-aluminium alloy bellhousing, sandwiched between the engine and the transmission. The clutch release mechanism is hydraulically operated.

2 The friction plate is fitted between the engine flywheel and the clutch pressure plate, and is allowed to slide on the transmission input shaft splines.

3 The pressure plate assembly is bolted to the engine flywheel. When the engine is running, drive is transmitted from the crankshaft, via the flywheel, to the friction plate (these components being clamped securely together by the pressure plate assembly) and from the friction plate to the transmission input shaft.

4 To interrupt the drive, the spring pressure must be relaxed. Depressing the pedal pushes on the master cylinder pushrod. The hydraulic pressure generated causes the centrally

mounted slave cylinder/release bearing to act against the pressure plate fingers. This causes the springs to deform and releases the clamping force on the pressure plate. The hydraulic clutch is self-adjusting and requires no manual adjustment.

2 Clutch pedal – removal and refitting

Removal

1 Disconnect the battery negative lead as described in Chapter 5A Section 4.

2 Release the clamps, disconnect the air duct hoses and breather hose, then undo the retaining bolts and pull the plastic cover on the top of the engine upwards from place (see illustration).

3 Remove the wiper arms as described in Chapter 12 Section 13.

4 Remove the fasteners, and pull the scuttle trim panel upwards from the base of the windscreen (see illustrations).

5 Squeeze together the sides of the clamp and disconnect the breather hose from the oil separator on the top of the engine.

2.4b...and pull the scuttle trim panel upwards from the base of the windscreen

6 Slacken the clamp, release the fastener and remove the turbocharger air inlet pipe (see illustrations).

7 Undo the bolts/nuts and remove the bulkhead secondary panel from the rear of the engine compartment.

8 Squeeze together the sides of the collar and disconnect the fluid supply pipe from the clutch master cylinder at the engine compartment bulkhead, then prise out the clip a little, and disconnect the fluid pressure pipe

2.6a Slacken the clamp...

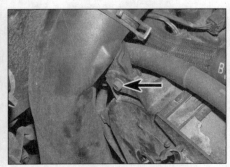

2.6b...undo the bolt...

2.6c...and remove the air inlet pipe

from the master cylinder **(see illustration)**. Be prepared for fluid spillage. Plug the openings to prevent contamination.

9 Disconnect the wiring plug (where applicable) from the clutch master cylinder at the engine compartment bulkhead.

10 Remove the drivers side lower air bag as described in Chapter 12 Section 20.

11 Undo the pinch bolt and slide the lower steering column universal joint upwards from the steering rack pinion **(see illustration)**. Discard the bolt, a new one must be fitted.

12 Release the fasteners and remove the drivers side footwell air duct.

13 Disconnect the wiring plug, then rotate the clutch position sensor anti-clockwise 45° and withdraw it from the bracket.

14 Unclip the wiring harness, and undo the 3 nuts securing the clutch pedal bracket to the bulkhead **(see illustration)**. Manoeuvre the pedal and bracket assembly from under the facia.

15 Squeeze together the retaining tabs and pull the master cylinder push rod pin from the pedal. Discard the pin, a new one must be fitted.

16 Rotate the collar 45° anti-clockwise and detach the master cylinder from the pedal assembly **(see illustration)**. No further dismantling is recommended. If it is worn or damaged the complete assembly must be renewed; no individual components are available.

Refitting

17 Refitting is a reversal of removal, noting the following points:

a) *Tighten all fasteners to their specified torque where given.*

b) *Renew the steering column pinch bolt.*

c) *Renew the master cylinder pushrod pivot pin.*

d) *Bleed the clutch hydraulic system as described in Section 5.*

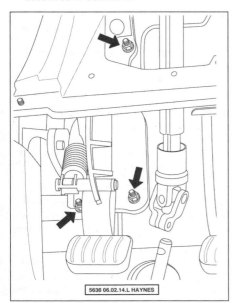

2.14 Pedal bracket retaining nuts

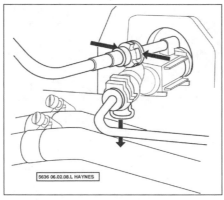

2.8 Squeeze the sides of the collar, disconnect the fluid pipe, then prise out the clip and disconnect the pressure pipe

3 Clutch master cylinder – removal and refitting

Removal of the clutch master cylinder is described within the clutch pedal removal procedure, as described in Section 2.

4 Clutch slave cylinder – removal and refitting

Removal

1 With reference to Chapter 7A Section 7, remove the gearbox.

2 Clean the area around the pipe, then prise out the wire retaining clip a little, and slide the fluid pipe away from the slave cylinder/release bearing approximately 20 mm.

3 Undo the retaining bolt and slide the slave cylinder/release bearing from the input shaft **(see illustration)**.

4 Check that the release bearing contact surface rotates smoothly and easily, with no sign of noise or roughness. Also check that the surface itself is smooth and unworn, with

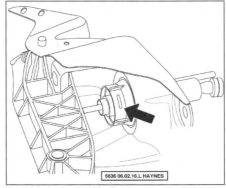

2.16 Rotate the master cylinder 45° anti-clockwise

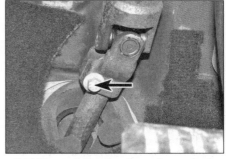

2.11 Remove the steering column pinch bolt

no signs of cracks, pitting or scoring. If there is any doubt about its condition, the bearing must be renewed along with the slave cylinder.

Refitting

5 Refitting is a reversal of removal.

5 Clutch hydraulic system – bleeding

⚠️ *Warning: Hydraulic fluid is poisonous; thoroughly wash off spills from the bare skin without delay. Seek immediate medical advice if any fluid is swallowed or gets into the eyes. Certain types of fluid are inflammable and may ignite when brought into contact with hot components. Hydraulic fluid is also an effective paint stripper. If spillage occurs onto painted bodywork or fittings, it should be washed off immediately, using copious quantities of cold water. It is also hygroscopic (i.e. it can absorb moisture from the air) which then renders it useless. Old fluid may have suffered contamination, and should never by re-used.*

1 If any part of the hydraulic system is dismantled, or if air has accidentally entered the system, the system will need to be bled. The presence of air is characterised by the pedal having a spongy feel and it results in difficulty in changing gear.

2 During the bleeding procedure, add only clean, unused hydraulic fluid of the

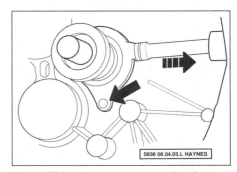

4.3 Slide the fluid pipe from the slave cylinder and undo the retaining bolt

recommended type; never re-use fluid that has already been bled from the system. Ensure that sufficient fluid is available before starting work. The help of an assistant will be required.

3 Check that the slave cylinder bleed screw is closed. Remove the dust cap, and clean any dirt from around the bleed screw located at the front/top of the transmission.

4 Fill the brake master cylinder fluid reservoir to the MAX mark, and attach a clear plastic tube to the bleed screw on the fluid junction on the transmission. Immerse the free end of the tube into a jar of clean brake fluid.

5 Have and assistant depress the clutch pedal as the bleed screw is opened 2 complete turns.

6 When the pedal is fully depressed, close the bleed screw, then allow the pedal to return.

7 Check the level of fluid in the reservoir, and top up if necessary.

8 Check the operation of the clutch pedal, and if air is still suspected of being in the hydraulic system, repeat the bleeding procedure described in Paragraphs 5 to 7.

9 If the clutch operation is satisfactory, disconnect the tube.

10 Wash off any spilt fluid, check once more that the bleed screw is tightened securely, and refit the dust cap.

11 Check the hydraulic fluid level in the reservoir, and top-up if necessary (see 'Weekly checks').

12 Discard any hydraulic fluid that has been bled from the system; it will not be fit for re-use.

13 Check the feel of the clutch pedal. If it feels at all spongy, air must still be present in the system, and further bleeding is required. Failure to bleed satisfactorily after a procedure may be due to worn master or slave cylinder seals.

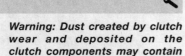

6 Clutch assembly – removal, inspection and refitting

⚠️ **Warning: Dust created by clutch wear and deposited on the clutch components may contain asbestos, which is a health hazard. DO NOT blow it out with compressed air, or inhale any of it. DO NOT use petrol or petroleum-based solvents to clean off the dust. Brake system cleaner or methylated spirit should be used to flush the dust into a suitable receptacle. After the clutch components are wiped clean with rags, dispose of the contaminated rags and cleaner in a sealed, marked container.**

Removal

1 Unless the complete engine/transmission unit is to be removed from the car and separated for major overhaul (see Chapter 2B), the clutch can be reached by removing the gearbox as described in Chapter 7A Section 7.

6.3 Undo the clutch pressure plate bolts

2 Before disturbing the clutch, use chalk or a marker pen to mark the relationship of the pressure plate assembly to the flywheel.

3 Working in a diagonal sequence, slacken the pressure plate bolts by half a turn at a time, until spring pressure is released and the bolts can be unscrewed by hand **(see illustration)**. Discard the bolts, new ones must be fitted.

4 Prise the pressure plate assembly off its locating dowels, and collect the friction plate, noting which way round the friction plate is fitted.

Inspection

Note: *Due to the amount of work necessary to remove and refit clutch components, it is usually considered good practice to renew the clutch friction plate, pressure plate assembly and release bearing as a matched set, even if only one of these is actually worn enough to require renewal. It is also worth considering the renewal of the clutch components on a preventive basis if the engine and/or transmission have been removed for some other reason.*

5 Remove the clutch assembly.

6 When cleaning clutch components, read first the warning at the beginning of this Section; remove dust using a clean, dry cloth, and working in a well-ventilated atmosphere.

7 Check the friction plate facings for signs of wear, damage or oil contamination. If the friction material is cracked, burnt, scored or damaged, or if it is contaminated with oil or grease (shown by shiny black patches), the friction plate must be renewed. No dimensions are given by Land Rover for friction plate wear. If in any doubt at all, renew the plate.

8 If the friction material is still serviceable, check that the centre boss splines are unworn, and that all the rivets are tight. If any wear or damage is found, the friction plate must be renewed.

9 If the friction material is fouled with oil, this must be due to an oil leak from the crankshaft left-hand oil seal, from the sump-to-cylinder block joint, or from the transmission input shaft. Renew the seal or repair the joint, as appropriate, as described in Chapter 2A Section 13 or Chapter 7A, before installing the new friction plate.

10 Check the pressure plate assembly for obvious signs of wear or damage; shake it to check for loose rivets or worn or damaged fulcrum rings, and check that the drive straps securing the pressure plate to the cover do not show signs (such as a deep yellow or blue discoloration) of overheating. Check the diaphragm spring fingers for signs of wear or damage and check that the height of each finger above the pressure plate machined face. If the finger height exceeds the specified service limit or the diaphragm spring is worn or damaged, or if its pressure is in any way suspect, the pressure plate assembly should be renewed.

11 Examine the machined bearing surfaces of the pressure plate and of the flywheel; they should be clean, completely flat, and free from scratches or scoring. If either is discoloured from excessive heat, or shows signs of cracks, it should be renewed – although minor damage of this nature can sometimes be polished away using emery paper. Using a straight edge and feeler blades check the pressure plate surface for warpage at several points around its diameter, if the warpage exceeds the specified limit the plate must be renewed.

12 Check that the release bearing contact surface rotates smoothly and easily, with no sign of noise or roughness. Also check that the surface itself is smooth and unworn, with no signs of cracks, pitting or scoring. If there is any doubt about its condition, the bearing must be renewed.

Refitting

13 On reassembly, ensure that the friction surfaces of the flywheel and pressure plate are completely clean, smooth, and free from oil or grease. Use solvent to remove any protective grease from new components.

14 New pressure plates are supplied with the self-adjusting mechanism preset, however, if the original pressure plate is to be refitted, the self-adjustment mechanism must be reset as follows.

15 A large diameter bolt (M14 at least) long enough to pass through the pressure plate, a matching nut, and several large diameter washers, will be needed for this procedure. Mount the bolt head in the jaws of a sturdy vice, with one large washer fitted.

16 Offer the plate over the bolts, friction plate surface facing down, and locate it centrally over the bolt and washer – the washer should bear on the centre hub.

17 Fit several further large washers over the bolt, so that they bear on the ends of the spring fingers, then add the nut and tighten by hand to locate the washers.

18 The purpose of the procedure is to turn the plate's internal adjuster disc so that the 3 small coil springs visible on the plate's outer surface are fully compressed. Tighten the nut just fitted until the adjuster disc is free to turn. Using a pair of thin-nosed or circlip pliers in one of the 3 windows on the top surface,

6.18a Tighten the nut until the adjuster nut is free to turn

6.18b Rotate the adjuster disc anti-clockwise until the springs are fully compressed

6.20a The friction plate should be marked to indicate which side faces the transmission or flywheel

6.20b Fit the friction plate with the spring hub assembly facing away from the flywheel

open the jaws of the pliers to turn the adjuster disc anti-clockwise, so that the springs are fully compressed **(see illustrations)**.

19 Hold the pliers in this position, and then unscrew the centre nut. Once the nut is released, the adjuster disc will be gripped in position, and the pliers can be removed. Take the pressure plate from the vice, and it's ready to fit.

20 Fit the friction plate so that its spring hub assembly faces away from the flywheel; there may also be a marking showing which way round the plate is to be refitted. On genuine Land Rover clutches the friction plate should be fitted with the 'Transmission side' or 'Flywheel side' marking facing away from the flywheel **(see illustrations)**.

21 Refit the pressure plate assembly, aligning the marks made on dismantling (if the original pressure plate is re-used), and locating the pressure plate on its locating dowels. Fit the new pressure plate bolts, but tighten them

only finger-tight, so that the friction plate can still be moved.

22 The friction plate must now be centralised, so that when the transmission is refitted, its input shaft will pass through the splines at the centre of the friction plate.

23 Centralisation can be achieved by passing a screwdriver or other long bar through the friction plate and into the hole in the crankshaft; the friction plate can then be moved around until it is centred on the crankshaft hole. Alternatively, a clutch-aligning tool can be used to eliminate the guesswork; these can be obtained from most accessory shops **(see illustration)**. A home-made aligning tool can be fabricated from a length of metal rod or wooden dowel which fits closely inside the crankshaft hole, and has insulating tape wrap around it to match the diameter of the friction plate splined hole.

24 When the friction plate is centralised, tighten the pressure plate bolts evenly and in

a diagonal sequence to the specified torque setting **(see illustration)**. Ensure the pressure plate is drawn squarely onto the flywheel, to prevent the pressure plate being distorted.

25 Refit the transmission as described in Chapter 7A Section 7.

6.23 Clutch friction plate aligning tool

Chapter 7 Part A
Manual gearbox

Contents

Degrees of difficulty

Easy, suitable for novice with little experience	Fairly easy, suitable for beginner with some experience	Fairly difficult, suitable for competent DIY mechanic	Difficult, suitable for experienced DIY mechanic	Very difficult, suitable for expert DIY or professional

Specifications

General

Type	Getrag M66 EH50 6-speed
Ratios:	
First	3.750 : 1
Second	1.905 : 1
Third	1.182 : 1
Fourth	0.838 : 1
Fifth	0.652 : 1
Sixth	0.540 : 1
Reverse	3.436 : 1

Lubrication

Recommended oil	See 'Lubricants and fluids'
Capacity:	
Initial dry fill	1.9 litres

Torque wrench settings

	Nm	lbf ft
Drain plug	30	22
Filler plug	35	25
Front subframe bolts:		
Support bracket bolts	45	33
Subframe mounting bolts* :		
Stage 1	140	103
Stage 2	Angle-tighten a further 240°	
Gearbox-to-engine bolts	65	48
Gearbox mounting bracket bolts:		
M8	24	18
M12	80	59
Gearbox mounting-to-body	175	129
Gearchange selector housing bolts	25	18
Rear, lower engine mounting bolts	110	81
Release bearing sleeve bolt	12	9

*Do not re-use

1 General information

1 The manual gearbox is contained in a cast-aluminium alloy casing bolted to the engine's left-hand end. The same transmission is fitted regardless of whether the vehicle is FWD or 4WD. A transfer case is attached to the right-hand side of the differential casing on 4WD models, and a propeller shaft attached to transmit drive to the rear wheels/final drive unit. See Chapter 7C for details of the transfer case.

2 Drive is transmitted from the crankshaft via the clutch to the input shaft, which has a splined extension to accept the clutch friction plate, and rotates in sealed ball-bearings. From the input shaft, drive is transmitted to the output shaft, which rotates in a roller bearing at its right-hand end, and a sealed ball-bearing at its left-hand end. From the output shaft, the drive is transmitted to the final drive gear, and differential.

3 The input and output shafts are arranged side by side, parallel to the crankshaft and driveshafts, so that their gear pinion teeth are in constant mesh. In the neutral position, the output shaft gear pinions rotate freely, so that drive cannot be transmitted to the final drive gear.

4 Gear selection is via a floor-mounted lever and twin-cable assembly. The cables cause the appropriate selector fork to move its respective synchro-sleeve along the shaft, to lock the gear pinion to the synchro-hub. Since the synchro-hubs are splined to the output shaft, this locks the pinion to the shaft, so that drive can be transmitted. To ensure that gear-changing can be made quickly and quietly, a synchro-mesh system is fitted to all gears, consisting of baulk rings and spring-loaded fingers, as well as the gear

pinions and synchro-hubs. The synchro-mesh cones are formed on the mating faces of the baulk rings and gear pinions.

2 Gearbox oil – draining and refilling

Note: *This is not a routine maintenance requirement. Land Rover state that the transmission is 'filled for life'. However, we consider it prudent to change the oil every 150 000 miles, or 10 years, whichever occurs first.*

1 This operation is much quicker and more efficient if the car is first taken on a journey of sufficient length to warm the engine/gearbox up to normal operating temperature.

2 Park the car on level ground, switch off the ignition and apply the handbrake firmly. For improved access, jack up the front of the car and support it securely on axle stands (see 'Vehicle Jacking and Support'). Note that the car must be lowered to the ground and level, to ensure accuracy, when refilling and checking the oil level. Undo the retaining screws and fasteners then remove the engine/gearbox undershield.

3 Remove all traces of dirt from around the filler/level plug which is located on the left-hand side of the gearbox behind the left-hand driveshaft inner joint **(see illustration)**. Unscrew the plug and recover the sealing washer (where fitted).

4 Position a suitable container under the drain plug which is also situated on the left-hand side of the gearbox housing, but underneath the driveshaft inner joint.

5 Unscrew the drain plug and allow the oil to drain completely into the container. If the oil is hot, take precautions against scalding. Clean both the filler/level and the drain plugs, being especially careful to wipe any metallic particles off the magnetic inserts. Discard the original sealing washers (where fitted); they should be renewed whenever they are disturbed.

6 When the oil has finished draining, clean the drain plug threads and those of the gearbox casing, fit a new sealing washer (where applicable) and refit the drain plug, tightening

it to the specified torque. It the car was raised for the draining operation, now lower it to the ground.

7 Refilling the gearbox is an extremely awkward operation. Above all, allow plenty of time for the oil level to settle properly before checking it. Note that the car must be parked on flat level ground when checking the oil level.

8 Refill the gearbox with the exact amount of the specified type of oil (see 'Lubricants and fluids') then check the oil level as described in Chapter 1. When the level is correct, refit the filler/level plug with a new sealing washer (where applicable) and tighten it to the specified torque. Refit the undercover. If the correct amount was poured into the gearbox and a large amount flows out on checking the level, refit the filler/level plug and take the car on a short journey so that the new oil is distributed fully around the gearbox components, then check the level again on your return.

3 Gearchange cables – removal, refitting and adjustment

Removal

1 Park the vehicle on level ground, switch off the ignition, and apply the handbrake firmly. Jack up the front of the vehicle and support it securely on axle stands (see 'Vehicle Jacking and Support'), release the retaining screws and remove the engine/transmission undershield.

2 On 4WD models, remove the propeller shaft as described in Chapter 8 Section 5.

3 Remove the centre console as described in Chapter 11 Section 25.

4 Remove the air cleaner assembly as described in Chapter 4A Section 2.

5 Undo the fasteners and remove the footwell kick panel each side of the facia centre section **(see illustration)**.

6 Unclip the drivers side footwell air duct, and prise the evaporator drain tube from the floor **(see illustration)**.

7 Undo the 4 retaining bolts and remove the facia support bracket from the drivers footwell.

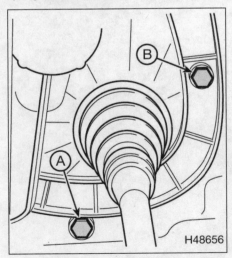
2.3 Oil drain plug (A) and filler plug (B)

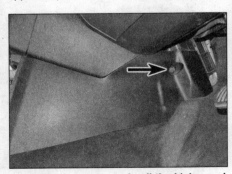
3.5 Undo the screw and pull the kick panel away to release the clips

3.6 Disconnect the evaporator drain tube

3.8a Prise the cable ends from the selector arms

3.8b Slide the locking collar forwards and unclip the cables from the bracket

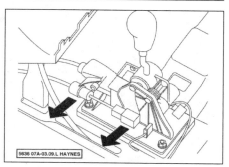

3.9 Prise the ends of the cables from the lever, slide the locking collars forwards and pull the outer cables from the housing brackets

8 Ensure the gear change lever is in the neutral position, then working above the transmission, note their fitted positions, then disconnect the ends of the cables from the selector levers, and pull the outer cables from the support bracket **(see illustrations)**.

9 Disconnect the ends of the cables from the pivot pins on the gearchange lever, and pull the outer cables from the brackets on the lever housing **(see illustration)**.

10 Undo the 2 bolts securing the cable sealing plate in front of the heater housing.

11 Working underneath the vehicle, undo the 6 nuts and remove the heat shield beneath the gearchange lever.

12 Undo the nut securing the outer cables above the front exhaust pipe.

13 Undo the 4 retaining bolts, and remove the gear change lever assembly. Disconnect the wiring plug as the assembly is withdrawn.

14 With the help of an assistant, manoeuvre the cable assembly into the passenger cabin, and out from the vehicle.

15 Thoroughly clean all components and check them for wear or damage, renewing all worn or faulty items.

Refitting

16 Refitting is the reverse of the removal procedure, applying a smear of the specified grease to all linkage pivot points (see *'Lubricants and fluids'*). Ensure all nuts and bolts are securely tightened, and before

refitting the centre console, adjust the gearshift cable as follows.

Adjustment

17 If not already done so, remove the centre console as described in Chapter 11 Section 25.

18 Prise up and release the gearshift (left-hand) cable locking clip **(see illustration)**.

19 Allow the gearchange lever to settle in the central, neutral position, then press the cable locking clip down without moving the gearchange lever.

---

4   Gear lever assembly –
      removal and refitting

Removal

1 Remove the centre console as described in Chapter 11 Section 25.

2 Ensure the gear lever is in the central, neutral position, then detach the cable end fittings and outer cables from the gear lever assembly **(see illustration 3.10)**.

3 Disconnect the wiring plug, undo the 4 retaining bolts and remove the gear lever assembly.

Refitting

4 Refitting is a reversal of removal, but prior to refitting the centre console, adjust the gearshift cable as described in Section 3.

---

5   Oil seals – renewal

Driveshaft oil seals

1 Remove the relevant driveshaft as described in Chapter 8 Section 2.

2 Carefully prise the oil seal out of the gearbox using a large flat-bladed screwdriver, or seal extractor **(see illustration)**.

3 Remove all traces of dirt from the area around the oil seal aperture. Ensure the seal is correctly positioned, with its sealing lip facing inwards, and drive it squarely into position, using a suitable tubular drift (such as a socket) which bears only on the hard outer edge of the seal **(see illustration)**.

4 Ensure the seal is correctly located in the gearbox housing then refit the driveshaft as described in Chapter 8 Section 2.

Input shaft oil seal

5 Remove the gearbox unit from the vehicle and slide off the clutch release bearing/slave cylinder (see Chapter 6).

6 Carefully drill a small hole in the hard, outer part of the seal, screw-in a self-tapping screw, and use a pair of pliers to pull the seal from

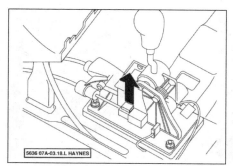

3.18 Prise up the cable locking clip

5.2 Use a piece of wood to protect the casing when levering out the driveshaft oil seal

5.3 Use a socket or tubular spacer to drive in the oil seal

5.6a Drill a small hole in the hard outer edge of the oil seal, then insert a self-tapping screw...

5.6b...and use pliers to pull the seal from place

5.8 Use a suitable tube to drive in the seal

place **(see illustrations)**. Take great care not to damage the input shaft or seal housing.

7 Wrap the splines of the input shaft with self-adhesive tape to prevent damage to the new seal lips.

8 Slide the new seal into place, and using a suitable tubular drift that bears only on the hard, outer part of the seal, drive the new seal into place until it's flush with the seal housing **(see illustration)**.

9 Remove the adhesive tape from the input shaft, and refit the slave cylinder/release bearing as described in Chapter 6.

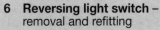

6 Reversing light switch – removal and refitting

Removal

1 The reversing light switch is located on the upper face of the transmission. Remove the air cleaner assembly as described in Chapter 4A Section 2.

2 Disconnect the wiring plug and unscrew the switch from the housing **(see illustration)**.

Refitting

3 Refitting is a reversal of removal.

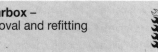

7 Gearbox – removal and refitting

Removal

1 Chock the rear wheels, then firmly apply the handbrake. Jack up the front of the vehicle, and securely support it on axle stands (see *'Vehicle Jacking and Support'*). Remove both front roadwheels then undo the retaining screws and fasteners and remove the undershield from beneath the engine/gearbox unit.

2 Remove the battery, battery tray and starter motor as described in Chapter 5A.

3 Working under the facia, undo the pinch bolt and slide the lower steering column universal joint upwards from the shaft **(see illustration)**. Renew the pinch bolt.

4 Remove the air cleaner assembly as described in Chapter 4A Section 2.

5 Disconnect the selector cables from the transmission as described in Section 3.

6 Drive out the retaining pin and remove the selector lever from the shaft on the transmission.

7 Undo the 5 retaining bolts and pull the gear

change selector housing over the end of the shaft.

8 Attach a lifting hoist or engine crane to the lifting eye on the left-hand end of the engine.

9 Note their fitted positions, and harness routing, then disconnect the various wiring plugs from the transmission.

10 Place a hose clamp on the flexible section of the clutch fluid pressure hose, then prise out the wire retaining clip a little and pull the pipe from the connection on the front of the transmission housing. Be prepared for fluid spillage.

11 Undo the bolt and remove the small cover plate at the front of the transmission bell housing.

12 Undo the 2 bolts accessible from the engine compartment, securing the left-hand engine mounting bracket to the mounting.

13 Detach the earth cable/pipe from the left-hand engine mounting bracket.

14 Drain the gearbox oil as described in Section 2 then refit the drain plug, and tighten it to the specified torque setting.

15 Detach the steering trackrod ends from the hub carrier each side using a balljoint separator tool – see Chapter 10 Section 21.

16 Remove both front driveshafts as described in Chapter 8 Section 2.

6.2 Disconnect the reversing light switch

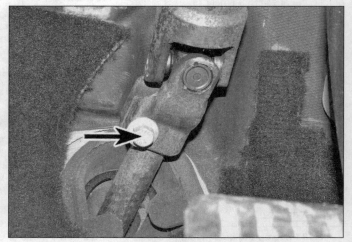

7.3 Remove the steering column pinch bolt

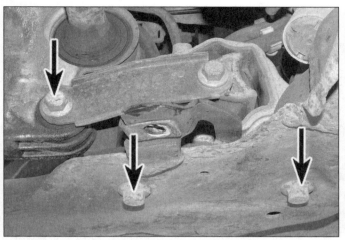

7.20 Remove the front through-bolt and the bracket retaining bolts

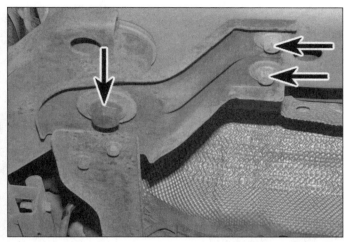

7.24 Undo the 3 bolts each side and remove the support bracket

17 On 4WD models, remove the transfer case as described in Chapter 7C Section 4.

18 Undo the securing bolt and detach the power steering pipes from the steering rack housing. Be prepared for fluid spillage.

19 Unclip the power steering pipes from the front subframe.

20 Remove the front through-bolt, and the 2 bolts securing the rear/lower engine mounting rod and bracket. Manoeuvre the rod and bracket assembly from place **(see illustration)**.

21 Unclip the rubber mountings securing the front exhaust pipes/catalytic converters to the front subframe.

22 Release the clips, undo the retaining bolt and remove the air pipe/hose from the turbocharger to the intercooler under the vehicle.

23 Support the front subframe using a transmission jack or similar. If possible, try to secure the subframe to the jack using ratchets straps, etc.

24 Undo the 6 retaining bolts and remove the support bracket at the rear of the front subframe **(see illustration)**. Discard the bolts, new ones must be fitted.

25 Make alignment marks between the front subframe and vehicle body, then remove the front retaining bolts and, with the help of an assistant, lower the front subframe from place, and manoeuvre it from under the vehicle. Discard the bolts, new ones must be fitted.

26 Undo the bolts and detach the engine mounting bracket from the left-hand end of the transmission.

27 Support the transmission with a transmission jack, then undo the bolts

securing the transmission to the engine. Note the fitted position of the bolts.

28 Using the engine hoist attached, and the transmission jack, slowly lower the left-hand end of the engine, transmission assembly until there is sufficient clearance to slide the transmission from the engine. Do not allow the transmission input shaft to 'hang' in the clutch/flywheel. An assistant will be essential during this procedure.

29 Once the gearbox is free, lower the unit to the floor and manoeuvre it out from under the car. Remove the locating dowels from the gearbox or engine if they are loose, and keep them in a safe place.

Refitting

30 The gearbox is refitted by a reversal of the removal procedure, bearing in mind the following points:

a) *Do not apply any lubricant to the transmission input shaft splines.*

b) *Ensure the locating dowels are correctly positioned prior to installation.*

c) *Tighten all nuts and bolts to the specified torque (where given).*

d) *Renew the driveshaft oil seals (see Section 5) then refit the driveshafts as described in Chapter 8, renewing the inner joint circlips prior to refitting.*

e) *Align the marks made between the subframe and vehicle body. If the marks have been lost, use Land Rover tool no. 502-012 (or equivalent) to align the subframe.*

f) *On completion, refill the gearbox with the specified type and quantity of lubricant (see 'Lubricants and fluids') then check the oil level as described in Section 2.*

8 Gearbox overhaul – general information

1 Overhauling a manual gearbox unit is a difficult and involved job for the DIY home mechanic. In addition to dismantling and reassembling many small parts, clearances must be precisely measured and, if necessary, changed by selecting shims and spacers. Internal gearbox components are also often difficult to obtain, and in many instances, extremely expensive. Because of this, if the gearbox develops a fault or becomes noisy, the best course of action is to have the unit overhauled by a specialist repairer, or to obtain an exchange reconditioned unit.

2 Nevertheless, it is not impossible for the more experienced mechanic to overhaul the gearbox, provided the special tools are available, and the job is done in a deliberate step-by-step manner, so that nothing is overlooked.

3 The tools necessary for an overhaul include internal and external circlip pliers, bearing pullers, a slide hammer, a set of pin punches, a dial test indicator, and possibly a hydraulic press. In addition, a large, sturdy workbench and a vice will be required.

4 During dismantling of the gearbox, make careful notes of how each component is fitted, to make reassembly easier and more accurate.

5 Before dismantling the gearbox, it will help if you have some idea what area is malfunctioning. Certain problems can be closely related to specific areas in the gearbox, which can make component examination and replacement easier. Refer to the *'Fault finding'* Section of this manual for more information.

Chapter 7 Part B
Automatic gearbox

Contents

Degrees of difficulty

Easy, suitable for novice with little experience	**Fairly easy,** suitable for beginner with some experience	**Fairly difficult,** suitable for competent DIY mechanic	**Difficult,** suitable for experienced DIY mechanic	**Very difficult,** suitable for expert DIY or professional

Specifications

General

Type	Aisin AWF21, six forwards speeds and reverse.
Fluid capacity.	7.0 litres (initial dry fill)
Ratios:	
1st.	4.148 : 1
2nd	2.370 : 1
3rd	1.556 : 1
4th.	1.155 : 1
5th.	0.859 : 1
6th.	0.686 : 1
Reverse.	3.394 : 1

Torque wrench settings

	Nm	lbf ft
Gearbox cover plate bolts	24	18
Gearbox housing-to-engine bolts	65	48
Left-hand engine mounting:		
Mounting bracket-to-body:		
M12*	80	59
M8	25	17
Mounting-to-transmission	175	130
Bracket-to-transmission bolts	85	63
Oil drain plug	47	35
Oil filler plug	39	29
Oil level Torx bolt	7	5
Rear, lower engine mounting	110	81
Speed sensor.	5	4
Subframe mounting bolts:		
Support bracket bolts.	45	34
Main retaining bolts*:		
Stage 1	140	103
Stage 2	Angle-tighten a further 240°	
Sump retaining bolts	13	10
TCM bolts.	24	18
Torque converter-to-driveplate bolts*.	60	44

*Do not re-use

2.2 Depress the release button and prise the end of the cable from the joint

2.3 Slide the white collar rearwards and pull the cable from the bracket

2.4 Selector housing rear retaining bolts

1 General information

1 A 6-speed fully-automatic transmission is available as an option on diesel models. The transmission consists of a torque converter, an epicyclic geartrain, and hydraulically-operated clutches and brakes.

2 The torque converter provides a fluid coupling between the engine and transmission, acts as an automatic 'clutch', and also provides a degree of torque multiplication when accelerating.

3 The transmission incorporates various features, including lock-up slip control, 'CommandShift' function, automatic and driver selectable modes, to ensure optimum on and off road performance.

4 The operation of the transmission is controlled by an electronic module, known as the TCM (Transmission Control Module), which is in constant communication with the engine management ECM via a high-speed Controller Area Network (CAN). The transmission is designed to be maintenance-free, and fluid-filled for life.

5 Due to the complexity of the automatic transmission, any repair or overhaul work must be entrusted to a Land Rover dealer, or a suitably-qualified transmission specialist, with the necessary specialist equipment and knowledge for fault diagnosis and repair. Refer to the 'Fault finding' Section at the end of this manual for further information.

2 Selector housing – removal and refitting

Removal

1 Remove the centre console as described in Chapter 11 Section 25.

2 Depress and hold the selector cable balljoint release button, and prise the cable from the joint (see illustration).

3 Slide the collar rearwards, and pull the outer cable from the bracket (see illustration).

4 Disconnect the wiring plug, undo the 4 retaining bolts and remove the selector lever/housing assembly (see illustration).

Refitting

5 Refitting is a reversal of removal.

3 Selector cable – removal, refitting and adjustment

Removal and refitting

1 Park the vehicle on level ground, switch off the ignition, and apply the handbrake firmly.

Jack up the front of the vehicle and support it securely on axle stands (see 'Vehicle Jacking and Support'), release the retaining screws and remove the engine/transmission undershield.

2 Ensure the selector lever is in position 'N', then disconnect the battery negative lead as described in Chapter 5A Section 4.

3 Remove the propeller shaft as described in Chapter 8 Section 5.

4 Remove the centre console as described in Chapter 11 Section 25.

5 Remove the air cleaner assembly as described in Chapter 4A Section 2.

6 Undo the fasteners and remove the footwell kickpanel in front of the centre console each side (see illustration).

7 Slide the rear footwell air duct upwards, and detach the evaporator drain tube from the floor panel (see illustration).

8 Undo the 4 retaining bolts and remove the facia support bracket from the drivers side footwell.

9 Depress the release button, pull the end of the selector cable from the lever on the transmission, then pull forwards the collar and pull the outer cable up from the bracket (see illustration).

10 Undo the 4 retaining bolts and pull the selector lever/housing rearwards a little (see illustration 2.4).

11 Depress and hold the selector cable balljoint release button, and prise the cable from the joint (see illustration 2.2).

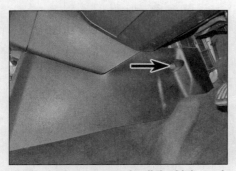

3.6 Undo the screw and pull the kickpanel away to release the clips

3.7 Disconnect the evaporator drain tube

3.9 Slide the collar forwards and pull the outer cable from the bracket

3.13 Cable grommet retaining nuts - facia removed for clarity

3.21 Prise up the yellow cable adjuster

3.22 Align the straight sides of the shaft with the 'P'

12 Slide the collar rearwards, and pull the outer cable from the bracket **(see illustration 2.3)**.
13 Undo the 2 nuts securing the cable sealing plate to the floor **(see illustration)**.
14 Working underneath the vehicle, unto the nuts and remove the heat shield from beneath the selector lever location.
15 Undo the nut securing the cable retaining bracket to the vehicle underside.
16 With the help of an assistant, manoeuvre the cable assembly into the cabin, and out from the vehicle.
17 Refitting is a reversal of removal. However, before refitting centre console and air cleaner assembly, carry out the cable adjustment procedure.

Adjustment

18 Remove the air cleaner assembly as described in Chapter 4A Section 2.
19 Remove the centre console as described in Chapter 11 Section 25.
20 Ensure the selector lever is in position 'P'.
21 Pull up the selector cable adjuster **(see illustration)**.
22 Check the position of the selector shaft on the transmission. It should be aligned with the 'P' mark on the housing **(see illustration)**. If not, rotate the lever until it is.
23 Press down the cable adjuster to lock it in position.
24 Refitting is a reversal of removal.

4 Transmission fluid –
renewal and level check

Renewal

1 To accurately check the fluid level, the temperature of the fluid must be approximately 60°C. The temperature of the fluid can be established by a Land Rover diagnostic tool or generic scan tool connected to the vehicle's diagnostic socket under the drivers side of the facia. If such a tool is not available, check the level with the transmission at normal operating temperature, then have the level checked by a Land Rover dealer or suitably

equipped specialist at the earliest opportunity afterwards.
2 Working in the engine compartment, clean the surrounding area, then remove the fluid filler plug from the top, front face of the transmission casing **(see illustration)**. Renew the seal.
3 Raise the vehicle and support it securely on axle stands (see 'Vehicle jacking and support'). Ensure the vehicle is level, and remove the engine/transmission undershield.
4 Clean the area around the level and drain plugs, then place a container beneath them to catch the fluid.
5 Unscrew the fluid level plug, followed by the drain plug, and allow the fluid to drain into the container **(see illustration)**. Renew the sealing washer.
6 When the fluid has finished draining, refit the drain plug with a new sealing washer, and tighten it to the specified torque.
7 Add the correct specification of fluid through the filler plug, until it begins to run out of the level plug. Refit the level plug and tighten it to the specified torque.
8 Add an additional 0.5 litres of fluid to the transmission, then refit the filler plug with a new seal, and tighten it to the specified torque.
9 Ensure the selector lever is in position 'P', then start the engine and monitor the transmission fluid temperature until it reaches 60°C.
10 While the engine is idling, depress the

brake pedal and move the selector lever through all the positions, pausing in each position for 2-3 seconds, beginning and ending in P. Leave the engine idling until while the fluid level is being checked.
11 Wearing protective gloves, remove the level plug from the centre of the drain plug. A small amount of fluid should drip from the hole. Refit the plug with a new seal, and tighten it to the specified torque.
Caution: Wear suitable gloves as protection against scalding.
12 Refit the engine undershield, and lower the vehicle to the ground.
13 If suitable diagnostic equipment was not used to establish the fluid temperature, it is advisable to have the fluid level finally confirmed by a Land Rover dealer or suitably equipped specialist, at the earliest opportunity.

Level check

14 To accurately check the fluid level, the temperature of the fluid must be approximately 60°C. The temperature of the fluid can be established by a Land Rover diagnostic tool or generic scan tool connected to the vehicle's diagnostic socket under the drivers side of the facia. If such a tool is not available, check the level with the transmission at normal operating temperature, then have the level checked by a Land Rover dealer or suitably equipped specialist at the earliest opportunity afterwards.

4.2 Transmission filler plug

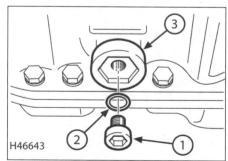

4.5 Transmission level plug (1), drain plug (3) and sealing washer (2)

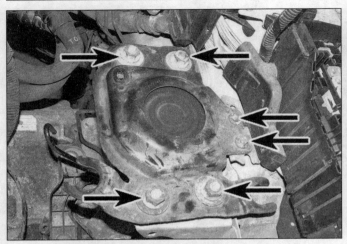

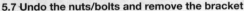

5.7 Undo the nuts/bolts and remove the bracket

5.8 Mounting retaining bolts

15 Working in the engine compartment, clean the surrounding area, then remove the fluid filler plug from the top, front face of the transmission casing (see illustration 4.2). Renew the seal.

16 Raise the vehicle and support it securely on axle stands (see 'Vehicle jacking and support'). Ensure the vehicle is level, and remove the engine/transmission undershield.

17 Clean the area around the level and drain plugs, then place a container beneath them to catch the fluid.

18 Add 0.5 litres of fluid to the transmission, then refit the filler plug with a new seal, and tighten it to the specified torque.

19 Ensure the selector lever is in position 'P', then start the engine and monitor the transmission fluid temperature until it reaches 60°C.

20 While the engine is idling, depress the brake pedal and move the selector lever through all the positions, pausing in each position for 2-3 seconds, beginning and ending in P. Leave the engine idling until while the fluid level is being checked.

21 Wearing protective gloves, remove the level plug from the centre of the drain plug. A small amount of fluid should drip from

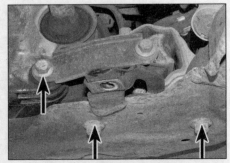

5.18 Remove the through-bolt and the bracket retaining bolts

the hole. Refit the plug with a new seal, and tighten it to the specified torque.

Caution: Wear suitable gloves as protection against scalding.

22 Refit the engine undershield, and lower the vehicle to the ground.

23 If suitable diagnostic equipment was not used to establish the fluid temperature, it is advisable to have the fluid level finally confirmed by a Land Rover dealer or suitably equipped specialist, at the earliest opportunity.

5 Automatic transmission – removal and refitting

Removal

Note: *Although the following procedure is not difficult, the gearbox assembly is heavy, and awkward to handle. Read through the entire procedure before proceeding, to familiarise yourself with the steps. The help of an assistant will prove invaluable during this operation. A suitable engine lifting crane and tackle will be required.*

1 Remove the battery and battery tray as described in Chapter 5A Section 4.

2 Jack up the vehicle, and support securely on axle stand (see 'Vehicle jacking and support'). Remove bolt front roadwheels. Note that the vehicle must be raised sufficiently to give enough clearance for the transmission assembly to be removed from under the vehicle. Release the retaining screws and remove the engine/transmission undershield.

3 Drain the transmission fluid as described in Section 4.

4 Working under the facia, remove the pinch bolt and slide the steering column lower universal joint upwards from the pinion shaft. Discard the bolt, a new one must be fitted.

5 Remove the starter motor as described in Chapter 5A Section 9.

6 Attach a lifting hoist or engine crane to the lifting eye on the left-hand end of the engine.

7 Undo the nuts/bolts, detach the breather pipe and remove the bracket between the mounting and body at the left-hand end of the transmission (see illustration). Detach the vent pipe from the bracket as it's withdrawn.

8 Undo the bolts and remove the mounting assembly from the left-hand end of the transmission (see illustration).

9 Detach the earth strap, then undo the 4 retaining bolts and remove the mounting bracket from the left-hand end of the transmission.

10 Disconnect the selector cable from the transmission as described in Section 3.

11 Remove both front driveshafts as described in Chapter 8 Section 2.

12 Remove the transfer case as described in Chapter 7C Section 4.

13 Detach the steering trackrod ends from the hub carrier each side using a balljoint separator tool – see Chapter 10 Section 21.

14 Undo the securing bolt and detach the power steering pipes from the steering rack housing. Be prepared for fluid spillage.

15 Unclip the power steering pipes from the front subframe.

16 Unclip the rubber mountings securing the front exhaust pipes/catalytic converters to the front subframe.

17 Unclip the fuel pipe from the front subframe.

18 Remove the front through-bolt, and the 2 bolts securing the rear/lower engine mounting rod and bracket. Manoeuvre the rod and bracket assembly from place (see illustration).

19 Support the front subframe using a transmission jack or similar. If possible, try to secure the subframe to the jack using ratchets straps, etc.

20 Undo the 6 retaining bolts and remove

5.21 Remove the subframe front bolts each side

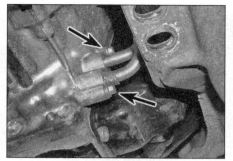

5.23 Disconnect the fluid pipes from the transmission

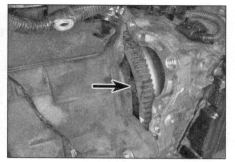

5.26 Torque converter retaining bolts

the support bracket at the rear of the front subframe. Discard the bolts, new ones must be fitted.

21 Make alignment marks between the front subframe and vehicle body, then remove the front retaining bolts and, with the help of an assistant, lower the front subframe from place, and manoeuvre it from under the vehicle (see illustration). Discard the bolts, new ones must be fitted.

22 Release the clips, undo the retaining bolt and remove the air pipe/hose from the turbocharger to the intercooler under the vehicle.

23 Undo the retaining bolts and detach the transmission fluid cooling pipes from the transmission (see illustration). Be prepared for fluid spillage. Plug the openings to prevent contamination. Discard the seals, new ones must be fitted.

24 Note their fitted positions, and harness routing, then disconnect the various wiring plugs from the transmission.

25 Undo the bolt and remove the small cover adjacent to the starter motor aperture.

26 The torque converter is secured to the driveplate by 6 bolts, at 60° intervals around its circumference (see illustration). Working through the starter motor aperture, unscrew and remove the torque converter retaining bolts. It will be necessary to turn the engine, using the crankshaft pulley bolt, so that each of the bolts can be unscrewed through the aperture. Discard the bolts, new ones must be fitted.

27 With the weight of the transmission supported on a trolley jack. Use safety chains or make up a cradle to steady the transmission on the jack.

28 Working your way around the transmission casing, slacken and remove the transmission-to-engine securing bolts. Disconnect any wiring loom brackets, where applicable.

29 With the help of an assistant, withdraw the transmission squarely from the engine, making sure that the torque converter comes away with the transmission, and does not stay in contact with the driveplate. If this precaution is not taken, there is a risk of the torque converter falling out and being damaged (see illustration).

30 Lower the transmission to the ground. Check that the locating dowels are located on the engine mating face, not the transmission.

Refitting

31 Ensure the torque converter is correctly aligned with drive of the oil pump.

32 With the help of an assistant, raise the transmission, and locate it on the rear of the driveplate. Ensure the transmission is correctly aligned with the locating dowels, before pushing it fully into engagement with the engine. Note: *The torque converter must remain in full engagement with the fluid pump at the correct installation depth throughout the fitting procedure.*

33 Working your way around the transmission casing, refit the transmission-to-engine bolts. Do not fully tighten the retaining bolts until all the bolts are in place, then tighten to the specified torque setting.

34 Tighten the new torque converter retaining bolts to the specified torque. Turn the engine as required to bring each of the bolts into view. Note: Insert all of the bolts before fully tightening them to the specified torque.

35 The remainder of the refitting procedure is a reversal of the removal procedure, noting the following special points:

a) *Tighten all retaining bolts to their specified torque wrench setting (where given).*

b) *Align the marks made between the subframe and vehicle body. If the marks have been lost, use Land Rover tool*

5.29 With the transmission removed, secure the torque converter in place with a simple bracket

no. 502-012 (or equivalent) to align the subframe.

c) *Renew the subframe mounting bolts, and engine mounting nuts (see Specifications).*

d) *Reconnect and adjust the selector cable, as described in Section 3.*

e) *Renew the transmission fluid as described in Section 4.*

f) *Bleed the power steering system as described in Chapter 10 Section 22.*

g) *If a new unit has been fitted, depending on the transmission type, it may be necessary to have the transmission TCM 'matched' to the engine management ECM electronically, to ensure correct operation – seek the advice of your Land Rover dealer or automatic transmission specialist.*

h) *Road test the car to check the transmission for correct operation.*

6 Automatic transmission overhaul – general information

1 In the event of a fault occurring on the transmission, it is first necessary to determine whether it is of an electrical, mechanical or hydraulic nature, and to achieve this, special test equipment is required. It is therefore essential to have the work carried out by a Land Rover dealer, or a suitably-equipped specialist if a transmission fault is suspected.

2 Do not remove the transmission from the vehicle for possible repair before professional fault diagnosis has been carried out, since most tests require the transmission to be in the vehicle.

7 Fluid cooler – removal and refitting

Removal

1 Jack up the vehicle, and support securely on axle stands placed under the axle tubes (see 'Vehicle jacking and support'). Release the retaining screws and remove the engine/transmission undershield.

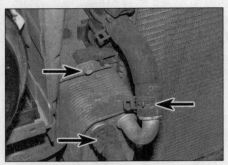

7.4 Fluid cooler hose clamps and retaining bolt

2 Disconnect the battery negative lead as described in Chapter 5A Section 4.

3 Drain the transmission fluid as described in Section 4.

4 Use clamps on the hoses to prevent excessive coolant loss, the release the clips and disconnect the coolant hoses from the fluid cooler at the left-hand end of the radiator **(see illustration)**.

5 The fluid cooler is secured by a single bolt. Undo the bolt and pull the fluid cooler upwards a little to detach it.

6 Position the cooler and tighten the mounting bolt securely.

7 Using new O-rings, reconnect the fluid hoses to the transmission.

8 Reconnect the coolant hoses, and tighten the retaining clips.

9 Refit the engine/transmission undershield, and lower the vehicle to the ground.

10 Reconnect the battery negative lead as described in Chapter 5A Section 4.

11 Check and top up the cooling system as described in 'Weekly checks', and the gearbox fluid as described in Section 4.

8 Torque converter oil seal – renewal

1 Remove the gearbox as described in Section 5, and slide the torque converter from the gearbox input shaft.

2 Using a flat-bladed screwdriver, prise the oil seal from the input shaft housing. Note the fitted depth of the seal.

3 Ensure that the oil seal recess in the gearbox, and the torque converter spigot are clean and dry. Lubricate the new oil seal with clean gearbox fluid, and fit it to the gearbox. Use a tubular drift that bears only on the hard outer edge of the seal. Fit the seal squarely into the housing, with the inner lip facing the gearbox.

4 Position the torque converter over the input shaft, and check that it is fully located.

9 Transmission control module – removal and refitting

Removal

1 With reference to Chapter 5A Section 4, disconnect the battery negative terminal.

2 Remove the air cleaner assembly as described in Chapter 4A Section 2.

3 Depress the release button, and prise the end of the selector cable from the lever on the transmission **(see illustration 3.9)**.

4 Undo the nut and pull the lever upwards from the selector shaft **(see illustration)**.

5 Undo the 3 retaining bolts, disconnect the wiring plug and remove the TCM **(see illustration)**.

Refitting

6 Refitting is a reversal of removal, noting that if a new TCM has been fitted, it must be configured using dedicated diagnostic equipment. Entrust this task to a Land Rover dealer or suitably equipped specialist.

9.4 Undo the nut and pull the lever upwards

9.5 TCM retaining bolts

Chapter 7 Part C
Transfer case

Contents

Degrees of difficulty

Easy, suitable for novice with little experience		**Fairly easy,** suitable for beginner with some experience		**Fairly difficult,** suitable for competent DIY mechanic		**Difficult,** suitable for experienced DIY mechanic		**Very difficult,** suitable for expert DIY or professional	

Specifications

Lubrication

Recommended oil .... See 'Lubricants and fluids'
Capacity .... 0.75 litres

Torque wrench settings

	Nm	lbf ft
Filler plug	35	26
Pinion bolt*	48	35
Transfer case-to-gearbox	65	48
Transfer case support bracket:		
To engine	65	48
To gearbox	65	48

Do not re-use

---

1 General information

The transfer case, is attached to the gearbox, and distributes drive to the rear wheels. Drive is taken from the gearbox differential, through a hollow transfer case primary shaft, via a low-offset hypoid bevel gear set, to the rear drive pinion, where the rear propshaft connects. The right-hand front driveshaft passes through the hollow primary shaft, to take drive directly from the gearbox differential.

2 Transfer case oil – level check

1 The transfer case is intended to be filled for life, there being no requirement for routine checking or renewal of the oil. However, it

may be prudent to check the oil level at least once in the lifetime of the vehicle.

2 Raise the vehicle and support it securely on axle stands (see *Vehicle jacking and support*). Ensure that the vehicle is level. Undo the fasteners and remove the engine undershield.

3 Clean the area around the filler plug at the rear of the transfer case **(see illustration)**.

4 Unscrew the filler plug, then add the correct specification of fluid until the level reaches the bottom of the filler plug hole. **Note:** *The filler plug hole is not a fluid level hole.*

5 Using a syringe, extract exacting 120 ml of fluid from the filler hole. The level should now be correct.

6 Refit the filler plug with a new washer, and tighten it to the specified torque.

7 Refit the engine undershield and lower the vehicle to the ground.

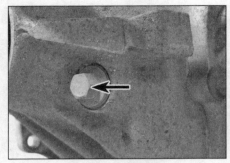
2.3 Transfer case filler plug

3.2 Output flange retaining bolt

3 Output shaft oil seal – renewal

1 Remove the propeller shaft as described in Chapter 8 Section 5.

2 Hold the drive flange stationary by bolting a length of metal bar to it, then unscrew the retaining bolt **(see illustration)**.

3 Slide the flange from place. Be prepared for fluid spillage.

4 Note it's fitted depth, then lever the oil seal from the final drive casing with a screwdriver. Take great care not to damage the transfer case bore. Wipe clean the oil seal seating.

5 Press the new seal squarely into the casing to the depth noted during removal. If necessary the seal can be tapped into position using a metal tube which bears only on its hard outer edge, although a Land Rover special tool (No. 205-871) is available to draw the seal into place.

6 Refit the pinion flange, and tighten the new retaining bolt to the specified torque.

7 Top up the transfer case oil as described in Section 2.

8 Refit the propeller shaft as described in Chapter 8 Section 5.

4 Transfer case – removal and refitting

Removal

1 Remove the propeller shaft and right-hand front driveshaft as described in Chapter 8.

2 Remove the catalytic converter as described in Chapter 4A Section 19.

3 Remove the front through-bolt, and the 2 bolts securing the mounting bracket, then manoeuvre the rear, lower engine mounting link rod assembly from place **(see illustration)**.

4 Release the clamps, undo the retaining bolt, and remove the air duct from between the turbocharger and intercooler.

5 Undo the 8 retaining bolts and remove the support bracket between the transfer case and the engine block **(see illustration)**.

6 Disconnect the vent tube from the top of the transfer case, and unclip it from the transmission housing.

7 Have an assistant support the transfer case, then undo the 7 retaining bolts, slide it from the gearbox, and lower the transfer case from place.

8 If required, undo the bolts and detach the heat shield from the transfer case. No further dismantling is recommended. If faults, consult a Land Rover dealer or specialist.

Refittng

9 If removed, refit the heat shield to the transfer case.

10 Apply a small amount of grease (Land Rover No. 6G92M1C27AA) to the splines of the gearbox output shaft **(see illustration)**.

11 Manoeuvre the transfer case into place, and slide the input shaft into the gearbox differential. Secure it in place with the bolts, and tighten them to the specified torque.

12 The remainder of refitting is a reversal of removal. Top up the transfer case oil as described in Section 2.

5 Transfer case overhaul – general information

1 At the time of writing, only new or exchange transfer cases are available. Consequently, although the unit can be dismantled with common hand tools, no overhaul parts are available.

2 If a fault develops, consult a Land Rover dealer or specialist, on the best course of action.

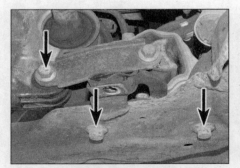
4.3 Rear engine mounting tie-rod front through-bolt and bracket bolts

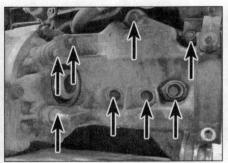
4.5 Transfer case support bracket bolts

4.10 Apply a small amount of grease the output shaft splines

Chapter 8
Driveshafts, propeller shaft and final drive

Contents

Degrees of difficulty

Easy, suitable for novice with little experience	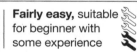	Fairly easy, suitable for beginner with some experience		Fairly difficult, suitable for competent DIY mechanic		Difficult, suitable for experienced DIY mechanic		Very difficult, suitable for expert DIY or professional	

Specifications

General

Final drive capacity	
Final drive...	0.7 litres
Haldex coupling	0.65 litres

Torque wrench settings

	Nm	lbf ft
Anti-roll bar link rod nut*...................................	60	44
Final drive:		
Front mounting bolts	175	129
Rear mounting bolts..................................	110	81
Final drive filler and plug	35	26
Final drive pinion nut*...................................	130	96
Front driveshaft/hub retaining bolt*:		
Stage 1...	45	33
Stage 2...	Angle-tighten a further 80°	
Haldex coupling-to-final drive	24	18
Haldex coupling filler plug	35	26
Intermediate shaft centre bearing bracket-to-block	65	48
Intermediate shaft centre bearing-to-transmission	25	18
Propeller shaft:		
Universal joint bolts*..................................	40	30
Centre support bearing bolts	25	18
Rear driveshaft nut*......................................	395	291
Roadwheel nuts	133	98

*Do not re-use

1 General information

1 On 2WD (front wheel drive only) models, drive is transmitted from the transmission differential to the front wheels by means of two driveshafts, each incorporating two constant velocity (CV) joints. The right-hand driveshaft is in two sections, and incorporates a support bearing.

2 Each front driveshaft consists of three main components: the sliding (tripod type) inner joint, the actual driveshaft, and the outer (fixed ball) joint. The inner (male) end of the left-hand tripod joint is secured in the differential side gear by the engagement of a circlip. The inner (female) end of the right-hand driveshaft is held on the intermediate shaft by the engagement of a circlip. The intermediate shaft is held in the transmission by the support bearing, which in turn is supported by a bracket bolted to the rear of the cylinder block. The outer CV joint on both driveshafts is of fixed ball-bearing type, and is secured in the front hub by the hub bolt.

3 On 4WD (four wheel drive) models, drive is transmitted from the transmission differential to the left-hand front driveshaft in the normal manner. The transfer case takes drive from the right-hand side of the transmission differential, and transfers the drive, via the propeller shaft, to the final drive and rear wheels. The right-hand front driveshaft passes through the hollow transfer case primary shaft, and engages with the transmission differential. The propeller shaft consists of a welded steel tube, with a centre support bearing(s), and universal joints at each end.

4 The rear driveshafts (4WD only) are solid steel bars with a CV joint at each end, protected by rubber boots. The inner end of the shafts locate in the final drive unit, and are retained by circlips. The outer end of the shaft locate in the rear hubs, and are retained by non-reusable nuts.

5 The final drive unit (4WD only), takes the drive from the rear of the propeller shaft and distributes it to the rear wheels through the driveshafts, via its differential unit. On some models, the final drive unit incorporates

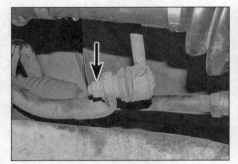

2.3 Anti-roll bar link retaining nut

a Haldex coupling which distributes the drive between the front and rear wheels. Its function is to provide the economic benefits of 2WD when the added traction of rear wheel drive is not required, and make a seamless transition to 4WD when needed. The unit is self-contained, and combines mechanical, hydraulic and electronic functions.

2 Driveshafts – removal and refitting

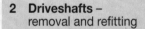

Caution: When removing the driveshafts, the inner CV joint must not be bent by more than 18°, and the outer CV joint must not be bent by more than 45° – in other words, keep the shaft as straight as possible. The outer CV joint must not be dismantled from the driveshaft, as it is a press-fit.

Note: *This procedure includes partially lowering the front suspension subframe.*

Front driveshafts

Removal

1 Loosen the front wheel retaining nuts. Jack up the front of the car and support it on axle stands (see 'Vehicle jacking and support'). Remove both front wheels. Where fitted, remove the engine undershield.

2 Slacken the driveshaft hub bolt. Prevent the hub from rotating by having an assistant apply the foot brakes, or by attaching a metal bar to the hub using the wheel nuts.

3 Undo the nut and detach the lower end of

2.6 Undo the driveshaft hub bolt

the link rod from the front anti-roll bar **(see illustration)**. Note that a new nut will be required.

4 Undo the nut and detach the steering trackrod end from the hub carrier using a joint-separator tool (see Chapter 10 Section 21).

5 Undo the nut and detach the lower balljoint from the hub carrier using a joint-separator tool (see Chapter 10 Section 3).

6 Remove and discard the driveshaft hub bolt **(see illustration)**. A new one must be fitted.

7 Press the outer end of the driveshaft through the front hub and steering knuckle. If necessary, use a universal puller located on the hub flange.

Left-hand driveshaft

8 Insert a lever between the inner driveshaft joint and the transmission case, with a thin piece of wood against the case. Prise free the inner joint from the differential **(see illustration)**. If it proves reluctant to move, strike the lever firmly with the palm of the hand. Be careful not to damage adjacent components, and in particular, make sure that the driveshaft oil seal in the differential is not damaged. Be prepared for some oil spillage from the transmission. Support the inner end of the driveshaft on an axle stand.

9 Withdraw the driveshaft from under the car.

10 Extract the circlip from the groove on the inner end of the driveshaft, and obtain a new one **(see illustration)**.

Right-hand driveshaft

11 Undo the nuts and remove the intermediate bearing support bracket **(see illustration)**.

2.8 Gently lever the driveshaft from the differential

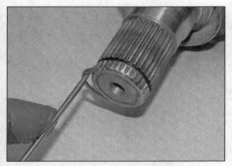

2.10 Renew the circlip on the end of the driveshaft

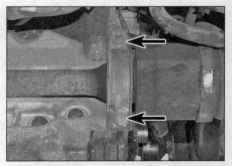

2.11 Intermediate bearing support bracket nuts

2.12 Lever the driveshaft joint housing from place

2.16 'Un-stake' the driveshaft nut with a centre punch

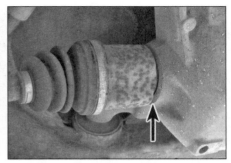

2.22 Lever between the inner joint and the final drive casing

12 Insert a lever between the inner driveshaft joint and the transmission/transfer case, with a thin piece of wood against the case. Prise free the inner joint from the differential **(see illustration)**. If it proves reluctant to move, strike the lever firmly with the palm of the hand. Be careful not to damage adjacent components, and in particular, make sure that the driveshaft oil seal in the differential/transfer case is not damaged. Be prepared for some oil spillage from the transmission/transfer case. Support the inner end of the driveshaft on an axle stand.

Refitting

13 Refitting is a reversal of removal, noting the following points:
a) Renew the circlip at the inner end of the driveshaft (where fitted).
b) Renew the anti-roll bar link rod nut.
c) Renew the driveshaft hub bolt.
d) Tighten all fasteners to their specified torque where given.
e) Replenish the transmission fluid where necessary (see Chapter 7A Section 2 or Chapter 7B Section 4).

Rear driveshafts

Removal

14 Raise the rear of the vehicle and support it securely on axle stands (see 'Vehicle jacking and support'). Remove the road-wheel(s).

15 Drain the final drive fluid as described in Section 7.
16 Slacken the driveshaft hub nut. Prevent the hub from rotating by having an assistant fully apply the foot brake, or attaching a metal bar to the hub using the roadwheel nuts **(see illustration)**.
17 Undo the nut, and detach the lower end of the rear anti-roll bar link rod. Note that a new nut will be required.
18 Unclip the handbrake cable from the subframe.
19 With reference to Chapter 10, detach the front lower arm, rear lower arm, and trailing arm from the hub carrier.
20 Remove and discard the driveshaft hub nut. A new one must be fitted.
21 Press the outer end of the driveshaft through the rear hub. If necessary, use a universal puller located on the hub flange.
22 Insert a lever between the inner driveshaft joint and the final drive casing, with a thin piece of wood against the case. Prise free the inner joint from the differential **(see illustration)**. If it proves reluctant to move, attach Land Rover tool No. 205-928 to the inner joint casing, and lever against this. Be careful not to damage adjacent components, and in particular, make sure that the driveshaft oil seal in the differential is not damaged.
23 Withdraw the driveshaft from under the car.

Refitting

24 Refitting is a reversal of removal, noting the following points:
a) Renew the circlip at the inner end of the driveshaft.
b) Renew the driveshaft hub nut, and 'stake' it using a suitable punch **(see illustration)**.
c) Tighten all fasteners to their specified torque where given.
d) Replenish the final drive fluid, as described in Section 7.

3 CV joint gaiters – renewal

Note: *Read the Caution in Section 2 before proceeding.*
1 Remove the driveshaft as described in Section 2, and mount it in a bench vice.
2 Mark the driveshaft in relation to the joint housing, to ensure correct refitting.
3 Note the fitted location of both of the inner joint gaiter retaining clips, then release the clips from the gaiter, and slide the gaiter back along the driveshaft a little way **(see illustrations)**. Note that new clips will be required – normally supplied in the driveshaft gaiter kit.
4 Withdraw the inner joint housing from the tripod. As the housing is being removed, be prepared for some of the bearing rollers to fall

2.24 'Stake' the new nut to the driveshaft

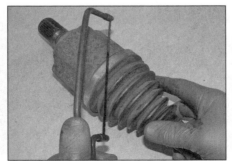

3.3a Cut away the large clip...

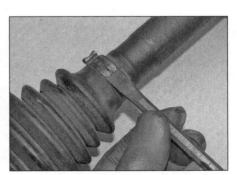

3.3b...and release the small clip

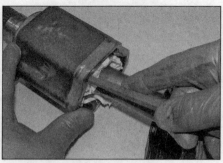

3.4a If necessary, remove the lip from the inner joint housing with a small file

3.4b Withdraw the joint housing from the driveshaft tripod

3.6 Remove the circlip from the driveshaft

out – identify them for position with a dab of paint and tape **(see illustration)**. Scoop out the grease from the joint and gaiter. Note that on some driveshafts, it may be necessary to remove

the lip on the inside of the inner joint housing using a small file. If this is the case, it's absolutely essential that all swarf/filings are washed out of the housing and tripod joint **(see illustration)**.

5 Check that the inner end of the driveshaft is marked in relation to the splined tripod hub. If not, carefully centre-punch the two items, to ensure correct refitting. Alternatively, use dabs of paint on the driveshaft and one end of the tripod.

6 Extract the circlip retaining the tripod on the driveshaft **(see illustration)**.

7 Using a puller, remove the tripod from the end of the driveshaft, and slide off the gaiter **(see illustration)**.

8 Clean the driveshaft and housing.

9 Slide the new gaiters on the driveshaft, together with new clips. Make sure that the gaiter is located at its previously-noted position on the driveshaft, then tighten the small diameter clip **(see illustration)**.

3.7 Use a puller to extract the tripod

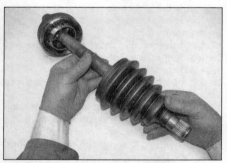

3.9 Slide the new outer gaiter into place

10 Refit the tripod on the driveshaft splines, if necessary using a soft-faced mallet and a suitable metal tube to drive it fully onto the splines. It must be fitted with the chamfered edge leading (towards the driveshaft), and with the previously-made marks aligned. Secure it in position using a new circlip. Ensure that the circlip is fully engaged in its groove **(see illustrations)**.

11 Locate the bearing rollers on the tripod (if removed) in their previously-noted positions, using grease to hold them in place.

12 Pack sufficient CV joint grease into the tripod and joint housings **(see illustrations)**.

13 Guide the joint housing onto the tripod fully, and locate the gaiter in the special groove, ensuring it is not twisted or distorted **(see illustration)**.

3.10a Engage the chamfered edge of the tripod with the driveshaft first

3.10b Align the previously made marks, and fit a new circlip

3.12a Pack the outer joint housing with the grease supplied in the kit...

3.12b...as well as the inner joint housing and tripod rollers

3.13 Located the gaiter in the grooves

3.14 The 'open' end of the clip must point away from the normal direction of rotation

3.15a Use a special tool to secure the large diameter...

3.15b...and small diameter clips on both gaiters

14 Insert a small screwdriver under the lip of the gaiter at the housing end, to allow trapped air to escape, then slide the retaining clips into place, ensuring the 'open' end of the clips point away from the normal direction of rotation **(see illustration)**.
15 Tighten the retaining clips. If possible, use the special tool to tighten the clips, otherwise, use pincers **(see illustrations)**.
16 Refit the driveshaft with reference to Section 2.

4 Driveshaft inspection and joint renewal

Note: *Read the Caution in Section 2 before proceeding.*
1 If any of the checks described in the appropriate part of Chapter 1 Section 14 reveal apparent excessive wear or play in any driveshaft joint, check that the hub nut (driveshaft outer nut) is tightened to the specified torque. Repeat this check on the hub nut on the other side.
2 Road test the car, and listen for a metallic

clicking from the front as the car is driven slowly in a circle on full-lock. If a clicking noise is heard, this indicates wear in the outer constant velocity joint, which means that the driveshaft and outer joint must be renewed; it is not possible to renew the joint separately.
3 If vibration, consistent with roadspeed, is felt through the car when accelerating, there is a possibility of wear in the inner tripod joints. To renew an inner joint, remove the driveshaft as described in Section 2, then separate the joint from the driveshaft with reference to Section 3.
4 Continual noise from the right-hand driveshaft, increasing with roadspeed, may indicate wear in the support bearing. The bearing is not available separately from the intermediate shaft, which prises from the transmission once the driveshaft has been removed.
5 With the exception of the rubber gaiters (outer only on the rear driveshafts) no replacement parts for the shafts are available. If faulty, the complete shaft must be renewed. Consult a Land Rover dealer or parts specialist.

5 Propeller shaft – removal, inspection and refitting

Removal

1 Raise the vehicle and support it securely on axle stands (see *'Vehicle jacking and support'*).
2 Remove the exhaust system as described in Chapter 4A Section 19.
3 Undo the fasteners and remove the heatshield beneath the front section of the propeller shaft.
4 Make alignment marks between the final drive/Haldex coupling flange and the propeller shaft universal joint to aid refitting **(see illustration)**.
5 Make alignment marks between the transfer case output flange and the propeller shaft front universal joint to aid refitting.
6 Working in a diagonal pattern, undo the bolts securing the front universal joint to the transfer case output flange, and recover the reinforcement plates **(see illustration)**. Note that new bolts must be fitted. Support the end of the shaft.

5.4 Make alignment marks at the rear of the propeller shaft

5.6 Undo the bolts, and recover the reinforcement plates

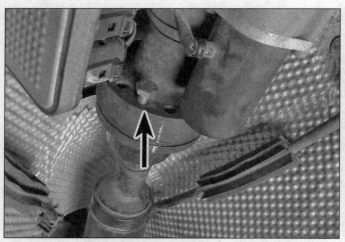

5.11a Insert a 8 x 30 mm bolt into an un-threaded hole...

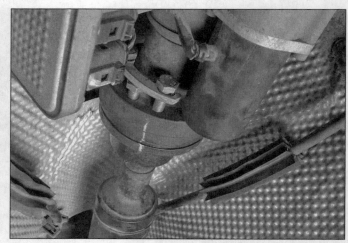

5.11b...then arrange two bolts and reinforcement plates as shown

5.15 Tighten the bolts until the joint detached from the coupling

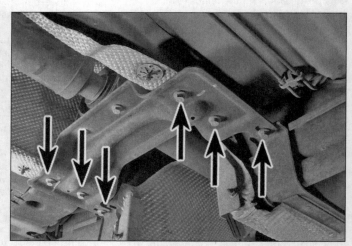

5.16 Undo the centre support bracket bolts

Models without Haldex Active On-demand coupling

7 Working in a diagonal pattern, undo the bolts securing the propeller shaft rear universal joint to the final drive, and recover the reinforcement plates. Note that new bolts must be fitted. Support the end of the propeller shaft.

Models with Haldex Active On-demand coupling

8 Undo the bolts securing the rear of the propeller shaft to the Haldex coupling, and recover the reinforcement plates. Although new bolts must be fitted, do not discard the old ones at this stage.

9 Liberally spray penetrating fluid through the bolt holes in the rear of the Haldex coupling flange.

10 Disconnect the Haldex coupling wiring plug.

11 Insert an 8 x 30 mm bolt into an un-threaded hole in the rear of the Haldex coupling flange, then insert two old propeller shaft rear universal joint bolts and two reinforcement plate as shown **(see illustrations)**.

12 Gradually tighten the old universal joint bolts until movement is detected in the universal joint.

13 Remove the oil universal joint bolts, reinforcement plates and 8 x 30 mm bolt, and rotate the Haldex coupling flange 180°.

14 Insert the 8 x 30 mm bolt into the un-threaded hole now accessible, fit the old bolts and reinforcement flanges, then tighten them until, again, the universal joint shows sign of movement.

15 Repeat the above steps until the propeller joint is detached from the Haldex coupling **(see illustration)**.

All models

16 Have an assistant support the shaft, then undo the bolts securing the centre support bracket(s) to the vehicle body, and manoeuvre the propeller shaft from place **(see illustration)**.

17 If required, undo the bolts and detach the support bracket(s) from the centre bearings.

Inspection

18 Check the front and rear universal joints for roughness, and excessive play.

19 Check the centre bearing(s) for roughness and excessive play.

20 Faulty joints or centre bearing(s) is normally heard/felt as a low frequency vibration through the vehicle floor, relative to road speed.

21 No replacement parts of the propeller shaft are available. If faulty the complete assembly must be renewed. Consult your Land Rover dealer or parts specialist.

Refitting

22 Refitting is a reversal of removal, noting the following points:
a) Renew the front and rear propeller shaft universal joint bolts.
b) Position the shaft and loosely fit the centre bearing support bracket bolts.

6.5 Final drive unit front retaining bolts

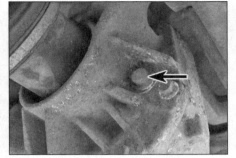

7.3 Final drive filler plug

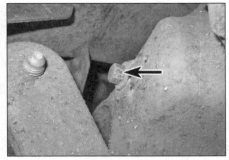

7.8 Haldex coupling filler plug

c) Tighten the universal joint bolts, followed by the centre bearing support bracket bolts.

d) Tighten all fasteners to their specified torque where given.

6 Final drive unit – removal, inspection and refitting

Removal

1 Remove the rear driveshafts as described in Section 2.

2 Undo the retaining bolts and detach the propeller shaft from the final drive/Haldex coupling flange as described in Section 5. Discard the bolts – new ones must be fitted.

3 Disconnect the Haldex coupling/final drive wiring plug(s).

4 Position a transmission/workshop jack and take the weight of the final drive assembly.

5 Remove the final drive front, and rear retaining bolts, then lower the final drive assembly, and disconnect the casing breather pipes **(see illustration)**.

6 Manoeuvre the final drive assembly from under the vehicle.

7 If required, undo the 4 retaining bolts and detach the Haldex coupling assembly from the final drive. Renew the O-ring seal.

Inspection

8 With the exception of the driveshaft oil seals, no replacement parts are available for the final drive unit. If the unit becomes excessively noisy, have the vehicle examined by a Land Rover dealer or suitable repairer. Replacement exchange units may be available.

Refitting

9 Where applicable, refit the Haldex coupling assembly, using a new O-ring seal, and tighten the retaining bolts to the specified torque.

10 Manoeuvre the final drive assembly into position, insert and tighten the retaining bolts to the specified torque.

11 The remainder of refitting is a reversal of removal, noting the following points:

a) Reconnect the propeller shaft as described in Section 5.

b) Refit the rear driveshafts as described in Section 2.

c) Tighten all fasteners to their specified torque where given.

d) If required, top-up the final drive/Haldex coupling fluid as described in Section 7.

7 Final drive and Haldex coupling fluids – renewal

1 Raise the rear of the vehicle and support it securely on axle stands (see 'Vehicle jacking and support').

Final drive fluid

2 No fluid drain plug is fitted to the final drive casing. The following procedure describes checking the fluid level only.

3 Unscrew the final drive casing filler plug and discard the sealing washer **(see illustration)**. A new sealing washer must be fitted.

4 Using a suitable syringe, add the correct specification of clean fluid until is runs from the filler hole.

5 Refit the filler plug with a new sealing washer, and tighten it to the specified torque.

6 Lower the vehicle to the ground.

Haldex coupling fluid

7 No fluid drain plug is fitted to the final drive casing. The following procedure describes checking the fluid level only.

8 Unscrew the Haldex coupling filler plug **(see illustration)**.

9 Using a suitable syringe, add the correct specification of clean fluid until is runs from the filler hole.

10 Temporarily refit the filler plug.

11 Switch the ignition on for approximately 5 minutes, then remove the igntion key.

12 Again, add clean fluid until it runs from the filler hole.

13 Using a syringe, remove exactly 70 ml of fluid.

14 Refit the filler plug, using a new sealing washer, and tighten it to the specified torque.

15 Lower the vehicle to the ground.

8 Final drive oil seals – renewal

Drive pinion oil seal

1 In order to renew the drive pinion oil seal, the Haldex coupling must be removed, as described in Section 6. However, special Land Rover tools are then required to renew the pinion oil seal. Consequently, we recommend that renewal of the seal is entrusted to a Land Rover dealer or specialist.

Driveshaft oil seals

2 Remove the rear driveshafts as described in Section 2.

3 Carefully prise the oil seal out of the final drive casing using a large flat-bladed screwdriver, or seal extractor.

4 Remove all traces of dirt from the area around the oil seal aperture. Ensure the seal is correctly positioned, with its sealing lip facing inwards, and drive it squarely into position, using a suitable tubular drift (such as a socket) which bears only on the hard outer edge of the seal.

5 Ensure the seal is correctly located in the final drive housing then refit the driveshaft as described in Section 2.

Chapter 9
Braking system

Contents

Degrees of difficulty

Easy, suitable for novice with little experience	Fairly easy, suitable for beginner with some experience	Fairly difficult, suitable for competent DIY mechanic	Difficult, suitable for experienced DIY mechanic	Very difficult, suitable for expert DIY or professional

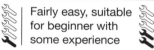

Specifications

Front brakes

Caliper type . . . .   Single piston sliding caliper
Disc:
   TypeVentilated
   Diameter . . . .   300 mm
   Thickness:
     New . . . .   28 mm
     Service limit . . . .   26 mm
     Maximum runout . . . .   0.08 mm
Pad minimum thickness . . . .   2.0 mm

Rear brakes

Caliper type . . . .   Single piston sliding caliper
Disc:
   Type . . . .   Solid
   Diameter . . . .   302 mm
   Thickness:
     New . . . .   12 mm
     Service limit . . . .   10 mm
     Maximum runout . . . .   0.08 mm
Pad minimum thickness . . . .   2.0 mm
Handbrake drum diameter . . . .   185 mm
Handbrake shoe friction material minimum thickness . . . .   1.0 mm

Torque wrench settings

	Nm	lbf ft
Accelerometer bolts	6	5
Bleed screw	10	7
EPB (Electronic Parking Brake) actuator bolts*	10	7
Front caliper bracket-to-hub carrier*	200	148
Front caliper guide pin bolts	28	21
Disc Torx screw	35	26
Master cylinder nuts	26	19
Pedal bracket nuts	25	18
Rear caliper bracket-to-hub carrier bolts*	110	81
Rear caliper guide pin bolts:		
Cable operated handbrake	30	22
EPB (Electronic Parking Brake)	35	26
Roadwheel nuts	133	98
Servo retaining nuts	22	16
Vacuum pump bolts	9	7
Wheel speed sensors	5	4

*Do not re-use

1 General information

1 The braking system is of the servo-assisted, dual-circuit hydraulic type. Under normal circumstances, both circuits operate in unison. However, if there is hydraulic failure in one circuit, full braking force will still be available at two wheels.

2 All models are fitted with front and rear disc brakes. ABS is fitted as standard to all models (refer to Section 21 for further information on ABS operation). On models also equipped with Dynamic Stability Control (DSC), the ABS system also operates the traction control side of the system.

3 All models are also equipped with various other traction-related systems, which rely on the ABS wheel sensors to operate – these being the Hill Descent Control (HDC), traction (anti-wheelspin) control, and Electronic Brake force Distribution (EBD). The speedometer receives its speed signal from the ABS ECU – the signal is derived from the average of the four readings from the wheel sensors.

4 The front disc brakes are actuated by single-piston sliding type calipers, which ensure that equal pressure is applied to each disc pad.

5 All models are fitted with rear disc brakes, actuated by single-piston sliding calipers.

6 On vehicles with a cable-operated hand brake, a separate drum brake arrangement is fitted in the centre of the rear brake disc to provide a separate means of hand brake application.

7 On vehicles with EPB (Electronic Parking Brake) system, a switch on the centre console energizes an electrical actuator on the rear brake caliper. This actuator forces the caliper piston to push the rear brake pads into contact with the disc.

Note: *When servicing any part of the system, work carefully and methodically; also observe scrupulous cleanliness when overhauling any part of the hydraulic system. Always renew*

components (in axle sets, where applicable) if in doubt about their condition, and use only genuine Land Rover replacement parts, or at least those of known good quality. Note the warnings given in "Safety first" and at relevant points in this Chapter concerning the dangers of asbestos dust and hydraulic fluid.

2 Hydraulic system – bleeding

Warning: Hydraulic fluid is poisonous; wash off immediately and thoroughly in the case of skin contact, and seek immediate medical advice if any fluid is swallowed or gets into the eyes. Certain types of hydraulic fluid are flammable, and may ignite when allowed into contact with hot components; when servicing any hydraulic system, it is safest to assume that the fluid is flammable, and to take precautions against the risk of fire as though it is petrol that is being handled. Hydraulic fluid is also an effective paint stripper, and will attack plastics; if any is spilt, it should be washed off immediately, using copious quantities of fresh water. Finally, it is hygroscopic (it absorbs moisture from the air) – old fluid may be contaminated and unfit for further use. When topping-up or renewing the fluid, always use the recommended type, and ensure that it comes from a freshly-opened sealed container.

Warning: If the high-pressure hydraulic system linking the master cylinder and hydraulic control unit (HCU) has been disturbed, then bleeding of the brakes should be entrusted to a Land Rover dealer or specialist. They will have access to the special service tester which is needed to operate the ABS modulator pump and bleed the high-pressure hydraulic system safely.

General

1 The correct operation of any hydraulic

system is only possible after removing all air from the components and circuit; this is achieved by bleeding the system.

2 During the bleeding procedure, add only clean, unused hydraulic fluid of the recommended type; never re-use fluid that has already been bled from the system. Ensure that sufficient fluid is available before starting work.

3 If there is any possibility of incorrect fluid being already in the system, the brake components and circuit must be flushed completely with uncontaminated, correct fluid, and new seals should be fitted to the various components.

4 If hydraulic fluid has been lost from the system, or air has entered because of a leak, ensure that the fault is cured before continuing further.

5 Park the vehicle on level ground, switch off the engine and select first or reverse gear, then chock the wheels and release the handbrake.

6 Check that all pipes and hoses are secure, unions tight and bleed screws closed. Clean any dirt from around the bleed screws.

7 Unscrew the master cylinder reservoir cap, and top the master cylinder reservoir up to the "MAX" level line; refit the cap loosely, and remember to maintain the fluid level at least above the "MIN" level line throughout the procedure, or there is a risk of further air entering the system.

8 There are a number of one-man, do-it-yourself brake bleeding kits currently available from motor accessory shops. It is recommended that one of these kits is used whenever possible, as they greatly simplify the bleeding operation, and reduce the risk of expelled air and fluid being drawn back into the system. If such a kit is not available, the basic (two-man) method must be used, which is described in detail below.

9 If a kit is to be used, prepare the vehicle as described previously, and follow the kit manufacturer's instructions, as the procedure may vary slightly according to the type being used; generally, they are as outlined below

in the relevant sub-section. 10 Whichever method is used, the same sequence must be followed (paragraphs 11 and 12) to ensure the removal of all air from the system.

Bleeding sequence

10 If the system has been only partially disconnected, and suitable precautions were taken to minimise fluid loss, it should be necessary only to bleed that part of the system.

11 If the complete system is to be bled, then the caliper furthest away from the master cylinder should be bled first. Therefore on RHD models, the sequence is:
a) Left-hand rear
b) Right-hand rear
c) Left-hand front
d) Right-hand front

Bleeding – basic (two-man) method

12 Collect a clean glass jar, a suitable length of plastic or rubber tubing which is a tight fit over the bleed screw, and a ring spanner to fit the screw. The help of an assistant will also be required.

13 Remove the dust cap from the first screw in the sequence. Fit the spanner and tube to the screw, place the other end of the tube in the jar, and pour in sufficient fluid to cover the end of the tube.

14 Ensure that the master cylinder reservoir fluid level is maintained at least above the "MIN" level line throughout the procedure.

15 Have the assistant fully depress the brake pedal several times to build up pressure, then maintain it on the final downstroke.

16 While pedal pressure is maintained, unscrew the bleed screw (approximately one turn) and allow the compressed fluid and air to flow into the jar. The assistant should maintain pedal pressure, following it down to the floor if necessary, and should not release it until instructed to do so. When the flow stops, tighten the bleed screw again, have the assistant release the pedal slowly, and recheck the reservoir fluid level.

17 Repeat the steps in paragraphs 16 and 17 until the fluid emerging from the bleed screw is free from air bubbles. If the master cylinder has been drained and refilled, and air is being bled from the first screw in the sequence, allow about 5 seconds between cycles for the master cylinder passages to refill.

18 When no more air bubbles appear, tighten the bleed screw securely, remove the tube and spanner, and refit the dust cap. Do not overtighten the bleed screw.

19 Repeat the procedure on the remaining screws in the sequence, until all air is removed from the system and the brake pedal feels firm again.

Bleeding – using a one-way valve kit

20 As their name implies, these kits consist of a length of tubing with a one-way valve

fitted, to prevent expelled air and fluid being drawn back into the system; some kits include a translucent container, which can be positioned so that the air bubbles can be more easily seen flowing from the end of the tube **(see illustration)**.

21 The kit is connected to the bleed screw, which is then opened. The user returns to the driver's seat, depresses the brake pedal with a smooth, steady stroke, and slowly releases it; this is repeated until the expelled fluid is clear of air bubbles.

22 Note that these kits simplify work so much that it is easy to forget the master cylinder reservoir fluid level; ensure that this is maintained at least above the "MIN" level line at all times.

Bleeding – using a pressure-bleeding kit

23 These kits are usually operated by the reservoir of pressurised air contained in the spare tyre. However, note that it will probably be necessary to reduce the pressure to a lower level than normal; refer to the instructions supplied with the kit.

24 By connecting a pressurised, fluid-filled container to the master cylinder reservoir, bleeding can be carried out simply by opening each screw in turn (in the specified sequence), and allowing the fluid to flow out until no more air bubbles can be seen in the expelled fluid.

25 This method has the advantage that the large reservoir of fluid provides an additional safeguard against air being drawn into the system during bleeding.

26 Pressure-bleeding is particularly effective when bleeding "difficult" systems, or when bleeding the complete system at the time of routine fluid renewal.

All methods

27 When bleeding is complete, and firm pedal feel is restored, wash off any spilt fluid, tighten the bleed screws securely, and refit their dust caps.

28 Check the hydraulic fluid level in the master cylinder reservoir, and top-up if necessary (see *Weekly checks*).

29 Discard any hydraulic fluid that has been bled from the system; it will not be fit for re-use.

30 Check the feel of the brake pedal. If it feels at all spongy, air must still be present in the system, and further bleeding is required. Failure to bleed satisfactorily after a reasonable repetition of the bleeding procedure may be due to worn master cylinder seals.

3 Hydraulic pipes and hoses – renewal

Caution: Under no circumstances should the hydraulic pipes/hoses linking the master cylinder and hydraulic control unit be disturbed. If these unions are disturbed

2.20 Bleeding a rear brake caliper

and air enters the high-pressure hydraulic system, bleeding of the system can only be safely carried out by a Land Rover dealer or suitably equipped specialist using the special service tester.

Note: *Before starting work, refer to the warnings at the beginning of Section 2.*

1 If any pipe or hose is to be renewed, minimise fluid loss by first removing the master cylinder reservoir cap, then tightening it down onto a piece of polythene to obtain an airtight seal. Alternatively, flexible hoses can be sealed, if required, using a proprietary brake hose clamp; metal brake pipe unions can be plugged (if care is taken not to allow dirt into the system) or capped immediately they are disconnected. Place a wad of rag under any union that is to be disconnected, to catch any spilt fluid.

2 If a flexible hose is to be disconnected, unscrew the brake pipe union nut before removing the spring clip which secures the hose to its mounting bracket.

3 To unscrew the union nuts, it is preferable to obtain a brake pipe spanner of the correct size; these are available from most large motor accessory shops. Failing this, a close-fitting open-ended spanner will be required, though if the nuts are tight or corroded, their flats may be rounded-off if the spanner slips. In such a case, using self-locking pliers is often the only way to unscrew a stubborn union, but it follows that the pipe and the damaged nuts must be renewed on reassembly. Always clean a union and surrounding area before disconnecting it. If disconnecting a component with more than one union, make a careful note of the connections before disturbing any of them.

4 If a brake pipe is to be renewed, it can be obtained, cut to length and with the union nuts and end flares in place, from Land Rover dealers or specialists. All that is then necessary is to bend it to shape, following the line of the original, before fitting it to the car. Alternatively, most motor accessory shops can make up brake pipes from kits, but this requires very careful measurement of the original, to ensure that the replacement is of the correct length. The safest answer is usually to take the original to the shop as a pattern.

4.2a If there's a lip on the outside of the disc, insert a screwdriver between the pad and disc, and force the pad away a little

4.2b Remove the spring from the caliper and bracket

4.2c Prise out the guide pin caps...

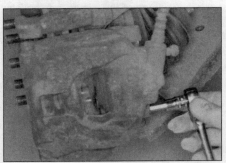

4.2d ...use an Allen key/bit to unscrew...

4.2e ...and remove the guide pins

4.2f Slide the caliper from place...

4.2g ...and suspend it from the suspension strut to prevent straining the rubber hose

4.2h Remove the outer brake pad from the bracket...

4.2i ...and pull the inner pad from the caliper piston

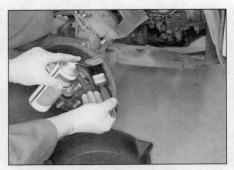

4.2j Clean away the brake dust/debris with a soft brush and aerosol brake cleaner

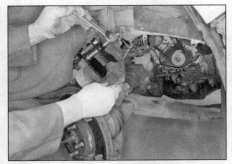

4.2k If new pads are being fitted, push the piston fully into the caliper body with a piston retraction tool. Keep and eye on the brake fluid reservoir level whilst pushing the piston back!

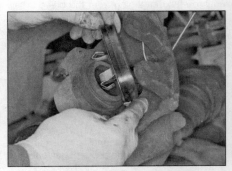

4.2l Press the inner brake pad into the caliper piston

4.2m Fit the outer pad to the caliper bracket, ensuring the friction material is against the disc

4.2n Slide the caliper into place

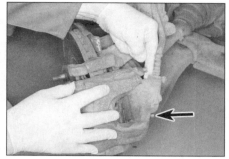

4.2o Insert in the guide pins...

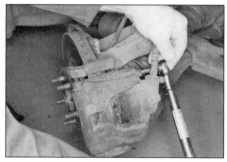

4.2p...tighten them to the specified torque...

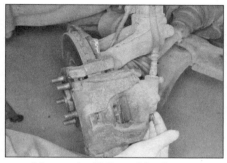

4.2q...and refit the guide pin caps

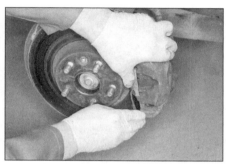

4.2r Press the retaining spring...

5 On refitting, do not overtighten the union nuts. It is not necessary to exercise brute force to obtain a sound joint.

6 Ensure that the pipes and hoses are correctly routed, with no kinks, and that they are secured in the clips or brackets provided. After fitting, remove the polythene from the reservoir, and bleed the hydraulic system as described in Section 2. Wash off any spilt fluid, and check carefully for fluid leaks.

4 Front brake pads – renewal

⚠️ *Warning: Renew both sets of front brake pads at the same time – never renew the pads on only one wheel, as uneven braking may result. Note that the dust created by wear of the pads may contain asbestos, which is a health hazard. Never blow it out with compressed air, and don't inhale any of it. An approved filtering mask should be worn when working on the brakes. DO NOT use petrol or petroleum-based solvents to clean brake parts; use brake cleaner or methylated spirit only.*

1 Apply the handbrake, then slacken the front roadwheel bolts. Jack up the front of the vehicle and support it on axle stands (see *Vehicle jacking and support*). Remove both front roadwheels.

2 Follow the relevant accompanying photos **(illustrations 4.2a to 4.2s)** for the actual pad replacement procedure. Be sure to stay in order and read the caption under each illustration, and note the following points:

a) *New pads may have an adhesive foil on the backplates. Remove this foil prior to installation.*

b) *Land Rover insist that no grease is applied to the pad/caliper contact surfaces.*

c) *When pushing the caliper piston back to accommodate new pads, keep a close eye on the fluid level in the reservoir.*

3 Depress the brake pedal repeatedly, until the pads are pressed into firm contact with the brake disc, and normal (non-assisted) pedal pressure is restored.

4 Repeat the above procedure on the remaining front brake caliper.

5 Apply the little anti-seize grease to the hub-to-wheel mating surface, then refit the roadwheels, lower the vehicle to the ground and tighten the roadwheel nuts to the specified torque.

6 Check the hydraulic fluid level as described in *Weekly checks*.

Caution: New pads will not give full braking efficiency until they have bedded-in. Be prepared for this, and avoid hard braking as far as possible for the first hundred miles or so after pad renewal.

4.2s...into place

5 Rear brake pads – renewal

⚠️ *Warning: Renew both sets of rear brake pads at the same time – never renew the pads on only one wheel, as uneven braking may result. Note that the dust created by wear of the pads may contain asbestos, which is a health hazard. Never blow it out with compressed air, and don't inhale any of it. An approved filtering mask should be worn when working on the brakes. DO NOT use petrol or petroleum-based solvents to clean brake parts; use brake cleaner or methylated spirit only.*

5.2a Hold the guide pin with an open-ended spanner, undo the lower retaining bolt...

5.2b...then pivot the caliper upwards, and tie it to the suspension strut

5.2c Remove the outer brake pad...

5.2d...and the inner brake pad

5.2e Remove the lower shim...

5.2f...and the upper shim

5.2g Clean the pad mounting surfaces of the caliper bracket

5.2h Refit the lower shim, identified by the holes (arrowed)

5.2i Refit the upper shim

5.2j If new pads are to be fitted, push the piston back into the caliper body using a retractor tool. Keep an eye on the reservoir fluid level!

5.2k Fit the inner brake pad...

5.2l...and the outer pad, ensuring the friction material is against the disc surface

5.2m Lower the caliper into place...

5.2n...fit the lower guide pin bolt...

5.2o...and tighten it to the specified torque

1 Apply the handbrake, then slacken the rear roadwheel bolts. Jack up the rear of the vehicle and support it on axle stands (see *Vehicle jacking and support*). Remove both rear roadwheels.

Note: *On vehicles with an EPB (Electronic Parking Brake) system, activate the Service mode as described in Section 18.*

2 Follow the relevant accompanying photos **(illustrations 5.2a to 5.2o)** for the actual pad replacement procedure. Be sure to stay in order and read the caption under each illustration, and note the following points:

a) *New pads may have an adhesive foil on the backplates. Remove this foil prior to installation.*

b) *Land Rover insist that no grease is applied to the pad/caliper contact surfaces.*

c) *When pushing the caliper piston back to accommodate new pads, keep a close eye on the fluid level in the reservoir.*

d) *The gold-coloured pad shim must be fitted in the lower position. The clip with one hole is for petrol models, therefore the clip with two holes must only be fitted to diesel models. The black-coloured shim is fitted in the upper position.*

3 Depress the brake pedal repeatedly, until the pads are pressed into firm contact with the brake disc, and normal (non-assisted) pedal pressure is restored.

4 Repeat the above procedure on the remaining rear brake caliper.

5 Apply the little anti-seize grease to the hub surface, then refit the roadwheels, lower the vehicle to the ground and tighten the roadwheel nuts to the specified torque.

6 Check the hydraulic fluid level as described in *Weekly checks*.

7 On vehicles with EPB system, deactivate the Service mode as described in Section 18. Note that after fitting new brake pads, it may be necessary to calibrate the EPB system using Land Rover diagnostic equipment (or equivalent).

Caution: New pads will not give full braking efficiency until they have bedded-in. Be prepared for this, and avoid hard braking as far as possible for the first hundred miles or so after pad renewal.

6 Front brake disc – inspection, removal and refitting

Note: *Before starting work, refer to the note at the beginning of Section 4 concerning the dangers of asbestos dust.*

Inspection

Note: *If either disc requires renewal, BOTH should be renewed at the same time, to ensure even and consistent braking. New brake pads should also be fitted.*

1 Apply the handbrake, then jack up the front of the car and support it on axle stands (see *Vehicle jacking and support*). Remove the appropriate front roadwheel.

2 Slowly rotate the brake disc so that the full area of both sides can be checked; remove the brake pads if better access is required to the inboard surface. Light scoring is normal in the area swept by the brake pads, but if heavy scoring or cracks are found, the disc must be renewed.

3 It is normal to find a lip of rust and brake dust around the disc's perimeter; this can be scraped off if required. If, however, a lip has formed due to excessive wear of the brake pad swept area, then the disc's thickness must be measured using a micrometer **(see illustration)**. Take measurements at several places around the disc, at the inside and outside of the pad swept area; if the disc has worn at any point to the specified

minimum thickness or less, the disc must be renewed.

4 If the disc is thought to be warped, it can be checked for run-out. Either use a dial gauge mounted on any convenient fixed point, while the disc is slowly rotated, or use feeler blades to measure (at several points all around the disc) the clearance between the disc and a fixed point, such as the caliper mounting bracket. If the measurements obtained are at the specified maximum or beyond, the disc is excessively warped, and must be renewed; however, it is worth checking first that the hub bearing is in good condition (Chapters 1 and/or 10). If the run-out is excessive, the disc must be renewed.

5 Check the disc for cracks, especially around the wheel stud holes, and any other wear or damage, and renew if necessary.

Removal

6 Remove the front brake pads as described in Section 4.

7 Using a piece of wire or string, tie the caliper to the front suspension coil spring, to avoid placing any strain on the hydraulic brake hose.

8 Unscrew the two bolts securing the brake caliper mounting bracket to the hub carrier, then slide the bracket assembly off the disc **(see illustration)**. Discard the bolts – new ones must be fitted.

9 Use chalk or paint to mark the relationship of the disc to the hub, then remove the screw

6.3 Use a micrometer to measure the thickness of the discs

6.8 Caliper mounting bracket bolts

6.9 Disc retaining screw

7.6 Rear caliper mounting bracket bolts

7.8 Rear disc retaining Torx screw

securing the brake disc to the hub, and remove the disc **(see illustration)**. If it is tight, lightly tap its rear face with a hide or plastic mallet.

Refitting

10 Refitting is the reverse of the removal procedure, noting the following points:
a) *Ensure that the mating surfaces of the disc and hub are clean and flat.*
b) *Align (if applicable) the marks made on removal, and tighten the disc retaining screw to the specified torque.*
c) *If a new disc has been fitted, use a suitable solvent to wipe any preservative coating from the disc, before refitting the caliper.*
d) *Tighten the new caliper mounting bolts to the specified torque setting.*
e) *Fit the brake pads as described in Section 4.*
f) *Refit the roadwheel, then lower the vehicle to the ground and tighten the roadwheel nuts to the specified torque. On completion, repeatedly depress the brake pedal until normal (non-assisted) pedal pressure returns.*

7 Rear brake disc – inspection, removal and refitting

Note: *Before starting work, refer to the note at the beginning of Section 5 concerning the dangers of asbestos dust.*

Inspection

Note: *If either disc requires renewal, BOTH should be renewed at the same time, to ensure even and consistent braking. New brake pads should also be fitted.*

1 Firmly chock the front wheels, then jack up the rear of the car and support it on axle stands (see *Vehicle jacking and support*). Remove the appropriate rear roadwheel. Release the handbrake.
2 Inspect the disc as described in Section 6.

Removal

3 Remove the brake pads as described in Section 5.
4 On vehicles with EPB (Electronic Parking Brake), disconnect the actuator wiring plug.

5 Undo the remaining caliper guide bolt, and slide the caliper from place. Using a piece of wire or string, tie the caliper to the rear suspension coil spring/body, to avoid placing any strain on the hydraulic brake hose.
6 Undo the 2 caliper mounting bracket bolts, and slide the bracket from place **(see illustration)**. Discard the bolts – new ones must be fitted.
7 Prise out the rubber plug, insert a screwdriver through the access hole in the brake disc, and rotate the adjuster knurled wheel on the pivot to retract the shoes **(see illustration 14.5 and 14.6)**.
8 Slacken and remove the brake disc retaining screw **(see illustration)**.
9 If the disc is to be refitted, make alignment marks between the disc and hub.
10 It should now be possible to withdraw the brake disc from the rear hub by hand. If it is tight, lightly tap its rear face with a hide or plastic mallet.

Refitting

11 If a new disc is been fitted, use a suitable solvent to wipe any preservative coating from the disc. Ensure the disc mounting surface on the hub is free from dirt and corrosion.
12 Align (if applicable) the marks made on removal, then fit the disc and tighten the retaining screw to the specified torque.
13 Refit the caliper mounting bracket, and tighten the new bolts to the specified torque.
14 Adjust the handbrake shoes and cable as described in Section 14.
15 Fit the brake pads as described in Section 5.

8 Front brake caliper – removal, overhaul and refitting

Note: *Before starting work, refer to the note at the beginning of Section 2 concerning the dangers of hydraulic fluid, and to the warning at the beginning of Section 4 concerning the dangers of asbestos dust.*

Removal

1 Apply the handbrake, then jack up the front of the vehicle and support it on axle stands

(see *Vehicle jacking and support*). Remove the appropriate roadwheel.
2 Minimise fluid loss by using a brake hose clamp, a G-clamp or a similar tool to clamp the flexible hose.
3 Clean the area around the union, then slacken the brake hose union nut.
4 Remove the brake pads Section 4.
5 Unscrew the caliper from the end of the brake hose and remove it from the vehicle.

Overhaul

6 With the exception of the pad retaining spring and guide pin gaiters, it would appear that at the time of writing, no overhaul parts are available for Freelander 2 brake calipers. If the caliper is leaking/seized, consult a Land Rover dealer or specialist – reconditioned/exchange calipers may be available.

Refitting

7 Screw the caliper fully onto the flexible hose union.
8 Refit the brake pads Section 4.
9 Securely tighten the brake pipe union nut.
10 Remove the brake hose clamp, and bleed the hydraulic system as described in Section 4. Note that, providing the precautions described were taken to minimise brake fluid loss, it should only be necessary to bleed the relevant front brake.
11 Refit the roadwheel, then lower the vehicle to the ground and tighten the roadwheel nuts to the specified torque. On completion, check the hydraulic fluid level as described in *Weekly Checks*.

9 Rear brake caliper – removal, overhaul and refitting

Note: *Before starting work, refer to the note at the beginning of Section 2 concerning the dangers of hydraulic fluid, and to the warning at the beginning of Section 5 concerning the dangers of asbestos dust.*

Removal

1 Chock the front wheels, then jack up the rear of the vehicle and support on axle stands

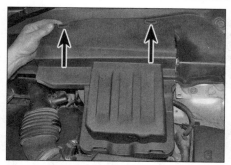

10.2 Release the clips and remove the battery cover

10.3a Undo the centre screws, prise out the plastic expansion rivets at the front edge...

10.3b...and pull the scuttle trim panel upwards from the base of the windscreen

(see *Vehicle jacking and support*). Remove the relevant rear wheel.

2 On vehicles with an EPB (Electronic Parking Brake) system, activate the Service Mode as described in Section 18, then disconnect the EPB actuator wiring plug.

3 Minimise fluid loss by using a brake hose clamp, a G-clamp or a similar tool to clamp the flexible hose.

4 Clean the area around the union, then loosen the brake hose union nut.

5 Remove the brake pads as described in Section 5.

6 Undo the remaining caliper guide pin bolt, and slide the caliper from place.

7 Unscrew the caliper from the end of the flexible hose, and remove it from the vehicle.

Overhaul

8 It would appear that at the time of writing, no overhaul parts are available for Freelander 2 brake calipers. If the caliper is leaking/seized, consult a Land Rover dealer or specialist – reconditioned/exchange calipers may be available.

Refitting

9 Screw the caliper fully onto the flexible hose union.

10 Refit the upper guide pin bolt and tighten it to the specified torque.

11 Refit the brake pads as described in Section 5.

12 Securely tighten the brake pipe union nut.

13 Remove the brake hose clamp, and bleed the hydraulic system as described in Section 2. Note that, providing the precautions described were taken to minimise brake fluid loss, it should only be necessary to bleed the relevant rear brake.

14 On vehicles with an EPB, reconnect the actuator wiring plug.

15 Refit the roadwheel, then lower the vehicle to the ground and tighten the roadwheel nuts to the specified torque. On completion, check the hydraulic fluid level as described in *Weekly Checks*.

16 On vehicles with an EPB system, deactivate the Service mode as described in Section 18.

10 Master cylinder – removal, overhaul and refitting

Note: *Although it is possible for the home mechanic to remove the master cylinder, if the hydraulic unions are disconnected from the master cylinder, air can enter the high-pressure hydraulic system linking the master cylinder and hydraulic control unit. Bleeding of the high-pressure system then may need to be carried out by a Land Rover dealer or specialist who has access to the service tester (see Section 2). Consequently, once the master cylinder has been refitted, the vehicle may need to be taken on a trailer or transporter to a suitably equipped Land Rover dealer or specialist.*

Note: *Before starting work, refer to the warning at the beginning of Section 2 concerning the dangers of hydraulic fluid.*

Removal

1 Remove both front wiper arms as described in Chapter 12 Section 13.

2 Remove the battery cover, and the master cylinder reservoir cover **(see illustration)**.

3 On RHD models, undo the fasteners, and with the help of an assistant, pull the windscreen scuttle trim panel upwards from place **(see illustrations)**. Note the locating pins on the trim panel underside.

4 On LHD models, remove the battery.

5 Using an old syringe/poultry baster (or

similar) try to remove as much fluid as possible from the master cylinder fluid reservoir.

6 Disconnect the wiring plug from the fluid reservoir level sensor, and undo the pin securing the reservoir to the master cylinder body **(see illustration)**.

7 On manual transmission models, squeeze together the release buttons, and disconnect the clutch master cylinder fluid supply pipe from the brake fluid reservoir. Be prepared for fluid spillage. Plug/cover the openings to prevent contamination.

8 Pull the fluid reservoir upwards from the brake master cylinder, and if necessary, renew the sealing grommets. Be prepared for fluid spillage. Plug/cover the openings to prevent contamination.

9 Undo the fasteners and pull the bulkhead panel in front of the master cylinder, forwards a little.

10 Slacken and disconnect the rigid fluid pipes from the side of the master cylinder. Be prepared for fluid spillage. Plug/cover the openings to prevent contamination.

11 Undo the 2 retaining nuts, and pull the master cylinder forwards from place. Examine the seal between the master cylinder and the servo unit – renew if necessary.

Overhaul

12 At the time of writing, it would appear that no overhaul parts for the master cylinder are available. If the unit is faulty, consult a Land Rover dealer or parts specialist – an exchange or reconditioned master cylinder may be available.

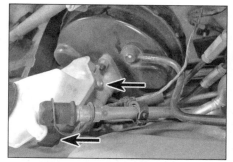

10.6 Disconnect the level sensor wiring plug, and undo the reservoir retaining pin

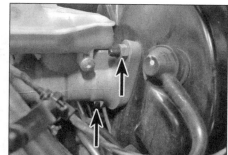

10.11 Master cylinder retaining nuts

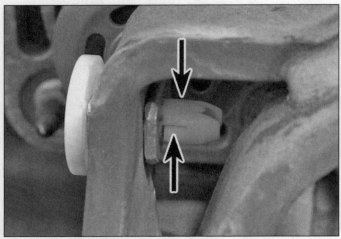

11.4 Squeeze together the tangs and slide the pin from the pushrod/pedal

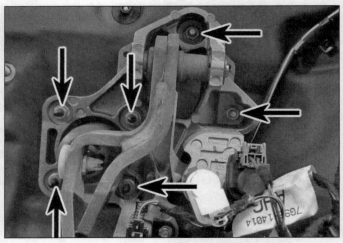

11.5 Pedal bracket assembly retaining nuts

Refitting

13 Remove all traces of dirt from the master cylinder and servo unit mating surfaces, and where necessary, renew the seal.

14 Fit the master cylinder to the servo unit, ensuring that the servo unit pushrod enters the master cylinder bore centrally. Fit the master cylinder retaining nuts, and tighten them to the specified torque.

15 Wipe clean the brake pipe unions, then refit them to the master cylinder/hydraulic unit ports and tighten them securely.

16 Press the new reservoir seals firmly into the master cylinder ports, then ease the reservoir into position. Refit the reservoir locking pin securely. Reconnect the fluid hose(s) to the reservoir, and reconnect the wiring connector(s).

17 The remainder of refitting is a reversal of removal, noting the following points:

a) Tighten all fasteners to their specified torque where given.

b) Refill the master cylinder reservoir with new fluid, and bleed the complete hydraulic system as described in Section 2.

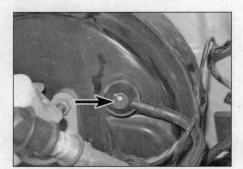

12.1 Servo unit check valve

11 Brake pedal – removal and refitting

Removal

1 Remove the drivers side lower air bag as described in Chapter 12 Section 20.

2 Remove the accelerator pedal assembly as described in Chapter 4A Section 4.

3 Disconnect the wiring plugs from the switch(es) on the pedal bracket, and unclip the wiring from the bracket.

4 Squeeze together the tangs and remove the servo pushrod-to-pedal pin (see illustration).

5 Undo the retaining nuts then manoeuvre the pedal and bracket assembly from under the facia (see illustration). If required, remove the switch(es) from the pedal bracket. No further dismantling is recommended.

Refitting

6 Refitting is a reversal of removal.

12 Vacuum servo unit check valve – removal, testing and refitting

Removal

1 The servo unit check valve is located in the end of the plastic pipe attached to the servo unit on the right-hand side of the engine compartment bulkhead (see illustration).

2 Remove the scuttle trim panel as described in Section 10.

3 Disconnect the hoses from the check valve.

Testing

4 Examine the valve for signs of damage and renew if necessary.

5 Test the valve by blowing through it in both directions; air should only flow through the valve in one direction only – when blown

through from the servo end of the valve. Renew the valve if this is not the case.

Refitting

6 Refitting is a reversal of removal.

13 Vacuum servo unit – testing, removal and refitting

Testing

1 To test the operation of the servo unit, depress the footbrake several times to exhaust the vacuum, then start the engine whilst keeping the pedal firmly depressed. As the engine starts, there should be a noticeable "give" in the brake pedal as the vacuum builds up. Allow the engine to run for at least two minutes, then switch it off. If the brake pedal is now depressed it should feel normal, but further applications should result in the pedal feeling firmer, with the pedal stroke decreasing with each application.

2 If the servo does not operate as described, first inspect the servo unit check valve as described in Section 12.

3 If the servo unit still fails to operate satisfactorily, the fault may lie within the unit itself. Repairs to the unit are not possible – if faulty, the servo unit must be renewed.

Removal

4 Remove the brake master cylinder as described in Section 10.

5 Remove the brake pedal assembly as described in Section 11.

6 Manoeuvre the servo unit from place. Examine the seal between the servo unit and bulkhead – renew if necessary.

Refitting

7 Refitting is a reversal of removal.

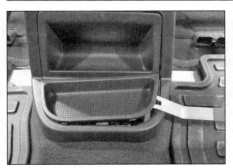
14.2a Prise up the coin tray...

14.2b...and the rear storage tray

14.3 Slacken the handbrake lever adjusting nut

14.5a Prise out the rubber blanking plug...

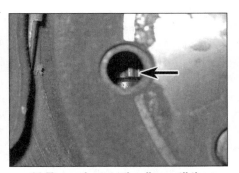
14.5b...and rotate the disc until the adjusting ring is visible

14.6 Use a flat-bladed screwdriver to rotate the adjuster ring

14 Handbrake – adjustment

Note: *Adjustment is only possible on models equipped with a cable-operated handbrake mechanism.*

1 Applying normal moderate pressure, pull the handbrake lever to the fully applied position, counting the number of clicks emitted from the handbrake ratchet mechanism. If adjustment is correct, there should be approximately 3 to 9 clicks before the handbrake is fully applied. If there are more than 9 clicks, adjust as follows.
2 Prise out the coin tray and rear storage tray from the rear section of the centre console **(see illustrations)**.
3 Ensure the handbrake lever is fully released, then undo the adjusting nut several turns so the cable is relaxed **(see illustration)**.
4 Chock the front wheels, raise the rear of the vehicle and support it securely on axle stands (see *Vehicle jacking and support*). Remove both rear roadwheels.
5 Starting on the right-hand rear wheel, prise out the blanking plug, then rotate the disc so the adjuster knurled ring is visible through the hole **(see illustrations)**.
6 Insert a screwdriver in through the bolt hole and fully expand the handbrake shoes by rotating the adjuster knurled ring. When the disc can no longer be turned, back the knurled ring off by 8 notches so that

the disc is free to rotate easily **(see illustration)**.
7 Repeat the procedure on the left-hand rear brake.
8 Tighten the cable adjustment nut until the handbrake is fully applied after 3 to 9 clicks from the ratchet mechanism.
9 With the handbrake adjustment satisfactorily carried out, refit the blanking plugs, and roadwheels, lower the vehicle to the ground and tighten the retaining nuts to the specified torque.
10 Refit the coin tray and rear storage tray.
11 If after replacement of the brake shoes the performance of the handbrake is still inadequate, drive along a deserted road at 25 mph and apply the handbrake until a braking effect can be felt. Pull the lever to the next

15.4 Handbrake lever assembly retaining nuts

notch and drive for approximately 400 m to bed the shoes in. Release the handbrake and allow the brakes to cool.

15 Handbrake lever – removal and refitting

Removal

1 Remove the centre console as described in Chapter 11 Section 25.
2 Undo the cable adjusting nut completely **(see illustration 14.3)**.
3 Disconnect the wiring plug from the handbrake warning switch.
4 Undo the 4 retaining nuts, and manoeuvre the handbrake lever assembly from place **(see illustration)**.
5 Refitting is a reversal of removal. Prior to refitting the centre console, adjust the handbrake as described in Section 14.

16 Handbrake cables – removal and refitting

Removal

Note: *The front cable is integral with the handbrake lever. Removal of the lever is described in Section 15.*

1 Slacken the handbrake adjuster nut as described in Section 15, then disengage the

16.1 Slide the ends of the cables from the balance arm

16.3 Disengage the end of the cable from the expander

17.2 Depress and slide the upper and lower shoe retaining clips to remove them

ends of the cables from the balance arm **(see illustration)**.
2 Remove the handbrake shoes as described in Section 17.
3 Disengage the cable end fitting from the expander **(see illustration)**.
4 Working back along the length of the cable, noting its correct routing, and free it from all the relevant retaining clips.

Refitting

5 Fit the cable into the hub carrier, and engage the end fitting with the expander.
6 Locate the front of the cable at the rear of the centre console.
7 The remainder of refitting is a reversal of removal. Prior to refitting the centre console, adjust the handbrake as described in Section 14.

17 Handbrake shoes – removal and refitting

Removal

1 Remove the rear brake discs as described in Section 7, and make a note of the correct fitted position of all components.
2 Depress the retaining clips and slide them from the shoe retaining pins **(see illustration)**.
3 Lever the ends of the shoe from the expander and adjuster, then disengage the shoe return springs **(see illustrations)**.
4 Remove both handbrake shoes, and recover the shoe adjuster mechanism, noting which way around it is fitted **(see illustrations)**.
5 Inspect the handbrake shoes for wear or contamination, and renew if necessary. It is

recommended that the return springs are renewed as a matter of course. Land Rover state the wear limit for shoe friction material thickness is 1.0 mm.
6 While the shoes are removed, clean and inspect the condition of the shoe adjuster and expander mechanisms, renew them if they show signs of wear or damage **(see illustration)**. If all is well, apply a fresh coat of brake grease to the threads of the adjuster and sliding surfaces of the expander mechanism. Do not allow the grease to contact the shoe friction material.

Refitting

7 Prior to installation, clean the backplate, and apply a thin smear of high-temperature brake grease or anti-seize compound to all those surfaces of the backplate which bear on the shoes **(see illustration)**. Do not allow the lubricant to foul the friction material.

17.3a Lever the end of the shoe from the expander…

17.3b…and the adjuster, then disengage the return springs

17.4a Remove the shoes…

17.4b…and recover the adjuster mechanism

17.6 Check the condition of the adjuster mechanism

17.7 Apply a thin smear of high-temperature grease to the backplate areas indicated

8 Engage the expander mechanism with the end of the handbrake cable, refit the return springs to the shoes, then offer up the handbrake shoes engaging the upper ends with the expander mechanism and adjuster.
9 Push the retaining pins through the shoes and secure them with the clips.
10 Centralise the handbrake shoes, and refit the brake disc as described in Section 7.
11 Prior to refitting the roadwheel, adjust the handbrake as described in Section 14.

18 Electronic parking brake

Service mode

Activation

1 Prior to removing the rear brake pads, or the EPB (Electronic Parking Brake) actuator, the system must be placed in Service mode. This withdraws the pistons into the rear calipers, creating clearance between the brake pads and discs. The procedure for activating the Service mode is as follows:
a) *Turn on the ignition (don't start the engine), then press and hold the parking brake switch in the release position.*
b) *Wait for 2 seconds.*
c) *Fully depress and hold down the throttle pedal.*
d) *Wait for 2 seconds.*
e) *Switch the ignition OFF, then back ON immediately.*
f) *Release the throttle pedal and parking brake switch. A noise will be heard to confirm the EPB in Service mode.*
g) *Switch OFF the ignition.*

Deactivation

2 Upon completion, the EPB system Service mode must be reactivated, and the system returned to normal operation as follows:
a) *With the ignition turned ON (don't start the engine), press and hold the parking brake switch in the 'apply' position.*
b) *Wait 2 seconds.*
c) *Fully depress and hold down the throttle pedal.*
d) *Wait for 2 seconds.*
e) *Turn the ignition OFF, then back ON immediately. A noise will be heard to confirm the Service mode has been deactivated.*
f) *Release the throttle pedal and brake switch.*
g) *Switch OFF the ignition.*

EPB actuator – removal and refitting

Removal

3 Raise the rear of the vehicle and support it securely on axle stands (see *Vehicle jacking and support*). Remove the rear wheels.
4 Activate the EPB Service mode as described earlier in this Seciton.

5 Disconnect the battery negative lead as described in Chapter 5A Section 4.
6 Disconnect the EPM actuator wiring plug.
7 Undo the 2 retaining bolts and withdraw the actuator from the brake caliper. Discard the bolts – new ones must be fitted upon reassembly.
8 Renew the EPB actuator-to-caliper O-ring seal.

Refitting

9 With a new O-ring seal installed on the caliper, fit the EPB actuator, insert the new retaining bolts and tighten them to the specified torque.
10 Reconnect the actuator wiring plug.
11 Reconnect the battery negative lead as described in Chapter 5A Section 4.
12 Deactivate the EPB Service mode as described earlier in this Section.
13 The remainder of refitting is a reversal of removal.
Note: *If a new EPB actuator has been fitted, the system calibration procedure must be carried out using Land Rover diagnostic equipment (or equivalent).*

Emergency EPB release

14 If the vehicle has no electrical power, the EPB can be released manually. As a precaution, disconnect the battery negative lead as described in Chapter 5A Section 4.
15 Raise the rear of the vehicle and support it securely on axle stands (see *Jacking and vehicle support*). Remove the rear wheels.
16 Remove the EPB actuator from the rear caliper as described previously in this Section.
17 Insert a suitable Allen key/bit into the centre of the caliper spindle, then rotate the spindle clockwise to withdraw the piston into the caliper.
18 Upon completion, refit the EPB actuator as described previously in this Section.
Note: *After the EPB has been released in this manner, it may be necessary for the system calibration procedure to the carried out using Land Rover diagnostic equipment (or equivalent).*

EPB module – removal and refitting

19 The EPB module is located behind the

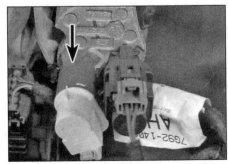

19.4 Rotate the stop-light switch clockwise to remove it

left-hand side luggage compartment side trim panel. Remove the left-hand side trim panel as described in Chapter 11 Section 24.
20 Disconnect the battery negative lead as described in Chapter 5A Section 4.
21 Undo the 2 retaining nuts and remove the upper ECU to access the EPB module.
22 Release the EPB module from place, and disconnect the wiring plug.
23 Refitting is a reversal of removal.
Note: *If a new EPB module has been fitted, the EPB system may need to be calibrated using Land Rover diagnostic equipment (or equivalent).*

19 Braking system switches – removal and refitting

Stop-light switch

Removal

1 The stop-light switch is located on the pedal bracket behind the facia.
2 Remove the drivers side lower facia panel as described in Chapter 11 Section 24.
3 Disconnect the wiring connector from the switch.
4 Rotate the switch clockwise and remove it from the bracket **(see illustration)**.

Refitting

5 Refitting is a reversal of removal.

Handbrake warning switch

Removal

6 Remove the centre console as described in Chapter 11 Section 25.
7 Chock the wheels and release the handbrake.
8 Disconnect the wiring plug, undo the retaining screw and remove the switch **(see illustration)**.

Refitting

9 Refitting is a reversal of removal.

EPB (Electronic Parking Brake) switch

10 Remove the upper section of the centre console as described in Chapter 11 Section 25.

19.8 Undo the handbrake warning switch screw from the base of the lever bracket

11 Undo the 6 screws, release the 5 clips and remove the panel on the underside of the centre console.

12 Undo the 3 retaining screws and detach the EPB switch from the console.

13 Refitting is a reversal of removal.

20 Vacuum pump – removal and refitting

Removal

1 Release the clamps securing the air and breather hoses to the ducting on the top of the engine, then undo the 2 retaining bolts and remove the engine top cover **(see illustration)**.

2 Remove the air cleaner assembly as described in Chapter 4A Section 2.

3 Undo the 2 bolts securing the engine oil filler cap assembly, unclip the fuel hoses and disconnect the hoses from the pump **(see illustrations)**.

4 Undo the 3 retaining bolts, and remove the vacuum pump **(see illustration)**. Examine the seal, and renew if necessary. No further dismantling of the pump is recommended.

Refitting

5 Refitting is a reversal of removal.

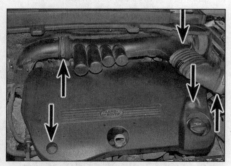

20.1 Release the clamps, disconnect the hoses, undo the bolts and remove the engine cover

21 Anti-lock braking system (ABS) – general information

Note: *On all models the ABS unit is a multi function unit, and works the anti-lock braking system (ABS), traction control function of the Dynamic Stability Control (DSC) system, and the Hill Descent Control (HDC).*

1 ABS is fitted to all models as standard. The system comprises a Hydraulic Control Unit (HCU) block which contains the hydraulic solenoid valves and the electrically-driven return pump, the four roadwheel sensors (one fitted to each wheel), and the electronic control unit (ECU). The purpose of the system is to prevent the wheel(s) locking during heavy braking. This is achieved by automatic release of the brake on the relevant wheel, followed by re-application of the brake.

2 The solenoids are controlled by the ECU, which itself receives signals from the four wheel sensors (one fitted on each hub), which monitor the speed of rotation of each wheel. By comparing these signals, the ECU can determine the speed at which the vehicle is travelling. It can then use this speed to determine when a wheel is decelerating at an abnormal rate, compared to the speed of the vehicle, and therefore predicts when a wheel is about to lock. During normal operation, the system functions in the same way as a non-ABS braking system. In addition to this, the brake pedal position sensor (which is fitted to the vacuum servo unit) also informs the ECU of how hard the brake pedal is being depressed.

3 If the ECU senses that a wheel is about to lock, it operates the relevant solenoid valve in the hydraulic unit, which then isolates the brake caliper on the wheel which is about to lock from the master cylinder, effectively sealing-in the hydraulic pressure.

4 If the speed of rotation of the wheel continues to decrease at an abnormal rate, the ECU switches on the electrically-driven return pump operates, and pumps the hydraulic fluid back into the master cylinder, releasing pressure on the brake caliper so that the brake

is released. Once the speed of rotation of the wheel returns to an acceptable rate, the pump stops; the solenoid valve opens, allowing the hydraulic master cylinder pressure to return to the caliper, which then re-applies the brake. This cycle can be carried out at up to 10 times a second.

5 The action of the solenoid valves and return pump creates pulses in the hydraulic circuit. When the ABS system is functioning, these pulses can be felt through the brake pedal.

6 The operation of the ABS system is entirely dependent on electrical signals. To prevent the system responding to any inaccurate signals, a built-in safety circuit monitors all signals received by the ECU. If an inaccurate signal or low battery voltage is detected, the ABS system is automatically shut down, and the warning light on the instrument panel is illuminated, to inform the driver that the ABS system is not operational. Normal braking should still be available, however.

7 If a fault does develop in the ABS system, the vehicle must be taken to a Land Rover dealer or suitably equipped specialist for fault diagnosis and repair.

8 An accumulator is also incorporated into the hydraulic system. As well as performing the ABS function as described above, the hydraulic unit also works the traction/stability control side of the DSC system. If the ECU senses that the wheels are about to lose traction under acceleration, the hydraulic unit momentarily applies the rear brakes to prevent the wheel(s) spinning. If the system senses that the lateral acceleration/yaw rate of the vehicle is about to exceed a pre-determined threshold – resulting in oversteer or understeer, the system can apply the brake of each individual wheel to maintain stability and prevent/control a skid

9 In addition to detecting when a wheel is locking under braking, the system also detects a wheel that is spinning under acceleration. When this condition is detected, the brake on that wheel is momentarily applied to reduce, or eliminate the wheel spin. When the rotational speed of the spinning wheel is detected to be equal to the other wheels, the brake is released. The ETC system is automatically

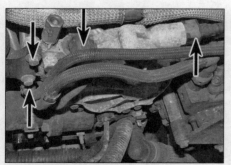

20.3a Undo the filler cap retaining bolts, and disconnect the hoses from the vacuum pump

20.3b Prise up the hose locking clip

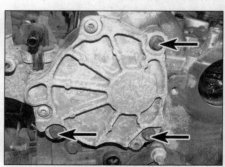

20.4 Vacuum pump retaining bolts

enabled at speeds up to 31 mph, provided the brakes are off. If the brakes are pressed while the ETC is active, the system will revert to ABS mode.

10 The Hill Descent Control is a very specialised system, intended for use when descending slippery slopes off-road. Normal practice here is to select first or reverse gear, and to allow the vehicle to descend the slope using only engine braking – touching the brake pedal would result in locked wheels and no steering control. The HDC uses intermittent application of the brakes to limit descent speeds further, while retaining steering control. When HDC is selected (using the gear lever switch), the descent speed can be controlled by the throttle alone – if the throttle is not pressed, the HDC will select its minimum target speed, which is just a few mph. If a fault occurs with the HDC, or the clutch pedal is pressed, or the brakes overheat through prolonged use, the system will 'fade out' gradually, indicated by the HDC warning light flashing.

11 When the ABS is in operation, the brakes are operated in axle pairs, and the braking force is distributed between the front and rear axles as necessary, to maintain the stability of the vehicle. Distribution of the braking effort is dependent on direction of travel and the amount of braking effort being applied.

12 Should a fault develop with the ABS/DSC/HDC/Terrain reponse system, the vehicle must be taken to a Land Rover dealer or suitably equipped specialist who will be able to interrogate the systems self-diagnosis capacity, and pin-point the fault.

22 Anti-lock braking system (ABS) components – removal and refitting

Hydraulic control unit (HCU) and ECU

Removal

Note: *If the hydraulic circuit between the master cylinder and the ABS hydraulic control unit is disturbed, the system must be bled using Land Rover diagnostic equipment (or equivalent). Bear this in mind before before commencing work.*

Note: *If a new hydraulic control unit is fitted, it must be configured using Land Rover diagnostic equipment (or equivalent).*

1 Remove the battery and battery tray as described in Chapter 5A Section 4.

2 Undo the fasteners and remove the engine compartment bulkhead panel.

3 Remove the ECM as described in Chapter 4A Section 12.

Place a piece of polythene over the master cylinder filler neck, and securely refit the cap. This will minimise brake fluid loss during subsequent operations. As a precaution, place absorbent rags beneath the modulator brake pipe unions.

4 Undo the union nuts at the HCU, and release the rigid fluid pipes between the master cylinder and HCU from the retaining clips. Be prepared for fluid spillage. Plug/seal all openings to prevent contamination.

5 Note their fitted locations, then undo the union nuts and disconnect the various fluid pipes from the HCU. Be prepared for fluid spillage. Plug/seal all openings to prevent contamination.

6 Disconnect the HCU/ECU wiring plug.

7 Undo the nuts and remove the HCU assembly.

8 The ECU is integral with the modulator – check with your Land Rover dealer or specialist for parts availability.

Refitting

9 Refitting is the reversal of removal, noting the following points:

a) *Ensure all pipes are correctly routed, securely connected, and clipped into their original locations.*

b) *Bleed the complete hydraulic circuit as described in Section 2.*

c) *If a new HCU has been fitted, it must be configured using Land Rover diagnostic equipment (or equivalent). Entrust this task to a Land Rover dealer or suitably equipped repairer.*

Front wheel speed sensor

Removal

10 Firmly apply the handbrake, then loosen the relevant front roadwheel nuts. Jack up the front of the vehicle and support on axle stands

(see *Vehicle jacking and support*). Remove the appropriate front roadwheel.

11 Undo the various fasteners and remove the front wheel arch liner.

12 Trace the wheel sensor wiring back to its wiring plug on the inner wing, and release it from the various retaining clips. Disconnect the wiring plug.

13 Slacken and remove the bolt securing the sensor to the hub carrier, and remove the sensor and lead assembly from the vehicle **(see illustration)**.

Refitting

14 Prior to refitting, apply a thin coat of multi-purpose grease to the sensor where it locates in the hub carrier.

15 Ensure that the sensor and hub carrier sealing faces are clean, then fit the sensor to the hub. Refit the retaining bolt and tighten it to the specified torque.

16 Ensure that the sensor wiring is correctly routed and retained by all the necessary clips, and reconnect its wiring plug.

17 The remainder of refitting is a reversal of removal. If a new sensor has been fitted, Land Rover state that the system must be configured using their diagnostic equipment (or equivalent).

Rear wheel speed sensor

Removal

18 Chock the front wheels and loosen the relevant rear wheel nuts, then jack up the rear of the vehicle and support it on axle stands (see *Vehicle jacking and support*). Take off the rear wheel.

19 Undo the various fasteners and remove the front wheel arch liner.

20 Trace the sensor wiring back to the wiring plug on the inner wing, and release it from the various retaining clips. Disconnect the wiring plug **(see illustration)**.

21 Slacken and remove the bolt securing the sensor, and remove the sensor and lead from the vehicle **(see illustration)**.

Refitting

22 Prior to refitting, apply a thin coat of multi-purpose grease to the sensor where it locates in the hub carrier.

22.13 Front wheel speed sensor retaining Torx bolt

22.20 Disconnect the wheel speed sensor wiring plug

22.21 Rear wheel speed sensor retaining Torx bolt

22.28 The accelerometer is located beneath the front of the centre console

23 Ensure the sensor and hub carrier sealing faces are clean, the fit the sensor to the hub carrier. Refit the retaining bolt and tighten it to the specified torque.

24 Ensure the sensor wiring is correctly routed, and retaining by all the necessary clips. Reconnect the wiring plug.

25 The remainder of refitting is a reversal of removal. If a new sensor has been fitted, Land Rover state that it must be configured using their diagnostic equipment (or equivalent).

Accelerometer

Removal

26 Disconnect the battery negative lead as described in Chapter 5A Section 4.

27 Remove the centre console as described in Chapter 11 Section 25.

28 Disconnect the wiring plug, undo the retaining nuts and remove the accelerometer **(see illustration)**.

Refitting

29 Refitting is a reversal of removal, noting the following points:

a) *Tighten the accelerometer retaining nuts to the specified torque.*

b) *If a new accelerometer has been fitted, it must be configured using Land Rover diagnostic equipment (or equivalent).*

Chapter 10
Suspension and steering

Contents

Degrees of difficulty

Easy, suitable for novice with little experience	Fairly easy, suitable for beginner with some experience	Fairly difficult, suitable for competent DIY mechanic	Difficult, suitable for experienced DIY mechanic	Very difficult, suitable for expert DIY or professional

Specifications

Front suspension
Type . . . . Independent MacPherson struts, coil springs, lower suspension arms mounted to the front subframe, with an anti-roll bar.

Rear suspension
Type . . . . Independent MacPherson struts, with high stress anti-roll bar. Two transverse links, and a lower trailing arm.

Ride height
Vehicles with AWD:
 Front . . . . 490.7 ± 12 mm
 Rear . . . . 504.6 ± 12 mm
Vehicles with FWD:
 Front . . . . 495.2 ± 12 mm
 Rear . . . . 511.3 ± 12 mm

Steering system
Type Hydraulic power assisted, with rack and pinion.

Front wheel alignment and steering angles
Camber . . . . 0° ± 0.75° (0° ± 45')
Castor . . . . 0° ± 0.75° (0° ± 45')
Toe-in . . . . 0.20° ± 0.20° (12' ± 12')

Rear wheel alignment angles
Toe-in . . . . 0.33° ± 0.20° (20' ± 12')
Note: *All measurements should be taken with the fuel tank full, no occupants or luggage, correct tyre pressures, and at correct ride height – measured from wheel centre to underside of wheelarch.*

Tyre pressures . . . . See end of 'Weekly checks'

Torque wrench settings

	Nm	lbf ft
Front suspension:		
Anti-roll bar clamp bolts..	175	129
Anti-roll bar link nuts*..	60	44
Damper locknut*..	80	59
Front subframe:		
M10*...	45	33
M16*:		
Stage 1...	140	103
Stage 2...	Angle-tighten a further 240°	
Subframe-to-body bolts*:		
Stage 1...	140	103
Stage 2...	Angle-tighten a further 240°	
Driveshaft/hub bolt*:		
Stage 1...	45	33
Stage 2...	Angle-tighten a further 80°	
Hub carrier-to-strut clamp bolt................................	110	81
Lower control arm front bolt:		
Stage 1...	140	103
Stage 2...	Angle-tighten a further 45°	
Lower control arm rear nut/bolt................................	175	129
Lower control arm balljoint nut*...............................	100	74
Suspension strut upper mounting nuts	30	22
Rear suspension		
Anti-roll bar clamp bolts*.....................................	60	44
Anti-roll bar link nuts*.......................................	60	44
Damper locknut..	80	59
Hub carrier-to-strut clamp bolt................................	110	81
Lower transverse arms nuts/bolts	175	129
Strut upper mounting nuts....................................	32	24
Trailing arm nuts/bolts	270	199
Trailing arm bracket-to-body*.................................	110	81
Steering		
Power steering pump bolts	24	18
Steering column bolts..	25	18
Steering column pinch bolt*...................................	25	18
Steering rack-to-subframe....................................	105	77
Steering wheel bolt..	48	35
Track-rod end nut*..	70	52
Track-rod end lock nut	55	41

Do not re-use

1 General information

1 Unlike traditional Land Rovers, the Freelander 2 has fully-independent front and rear suspension, by conventional coil springs and MacPherson struts, bolted to the wheel hubs. Subframes are fitted front and rear, to provide mounting points for the suspension components.

2 At the front, the hubs are attached to pressed-steel lower arms, which pivot on bushes mounted to the subframe; the bushes are designed to deform progressively under load, to reduce any unwanted suspension 'steering' effects. An anti-roll bar is fitted, attached directly to the front subframe, with the bar ends attached to the struts by ball-jointed drop links.

3 At the rear, the hubs are connected to the subframe and underbody via three link arms – two transverse, one trailing – known as 'trapezoidal' links. The rear of the two transverse links has inboard mounting bolts with eccentric heads, to provide toe adjustment. The links arms feature specially-designed bushes which deform slightly under cornering forces, promoting rear wheel toe-in (passive rear wheel steering), to improve handling response. The trailing link further controls rear suspension movement, and provides another fixed attachment point from the hub to the underside of the vehicle.

4 The steering system comprises an impact-absorbing telescopic steering column, power-assisted steering rack and engine-driven fluid pump, with a fluid reservoir, fluid cooler, and connecting pipes and hoses. The adjustable steering column has upper mountings which are designed to detach or deform in the event of a collision, allowing the column to collapse and reduce the risk of injuring the driver. The upper section of the column is splined to accept the steering wheel; the intermediate shaft is joined to the lower shaft by a universal joint, and a further universal joint at the base of the column joins to the splined adaptor which attaches the column to the rack pinion.

5 The conventional rack-and-pinion rack is mounted on the front subframe. Power for the steering rack is provided by high pressure fluid, supplied by the engine-mounted pump, which is driven by the auxiliary drivebelt.

6 Rotary movement of the steering wheel is transferred via the steering column to the valve unit mounted on the steering rack; depending on direction of rotation, fluid pressure is applied to one side of the valve or the other, to boost the turning force applied to the pinion, which in turn moves the rack left or right.

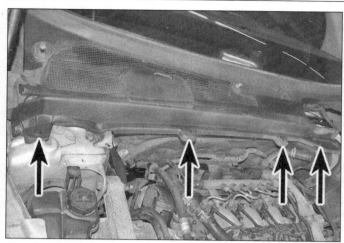

2.3a Undo the centre screws, prise out the plastic expansion rivets...

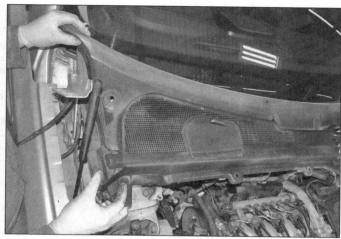

2.3b...and pull the scuttle trim panel upwards from the base of the windscreen

2 Front suspension strut –
removal, overhaul and refitting

Removal

1 Remove both front wiper arms are described in Chapter 12 Section 13.
2 Remove the plastic covers over the battery and the brake fluid reservoir.
3 Unscrew the 5 fasteners and pull the scuttle trim panel upwards from the base of the windscreen. Note the locating lug on the underside of the trim panel **(see illustrations)**.
4 Slacken the roadwheel nuts, raise the front of the vehicle and support it securely on axle stands (see '*Vehicle jacking and support*'). Remove the front roadwheels.
5 Undo the nut securing the anti-roll bar link to the strut. Counterhold the link balljoint shank using an Allen key **(see illustration)**. Discard the nut – a new one must be fitted. Separate the link from the strut, and move it to one side.
6 Unclip the brake hose and wheel speed sensor wiring from the strut/hub.
7 Undo the pinch bolt securing the hub carrier to the base of the strut **(see illustration)**. Note that the bolt is inserted from the front.
8 Undo the lower arm front and rear mounting bolts, and pull the lower arm from the subframe **(see illustrations 5.3a and 5.3b)**. Discard the bolts/nuts – new ones must be fitted.
9 Pull the hub carrier outwards, and disengage the driveshaft. Suspend the driveshaft from the vehicle bodywork to prevent damage to the CV joints etc.
10 Widen the gap at the back of the hub carrier a little, using a screwdriver or chisel, spray releasing fluid around the clamp, and carefully tap the hub carrier downwards from the base of the suspension strut. Support the

hub carrier using a workshop jack (or similar) to prevent any strain on the hose/wiring.
11 Have an assistant support the suspension strut, then undo the 3 upper mounting bolts and lower the strut from place **(see illustration)**.

Overhaul

⚠️ *Warning: Before attempting to dismantle the suspension strut, a suitable tool to hold the coil*

2.5 Use an Allen key to counterhold the anti-roll bar link balljoint

2.11 Front suspension strut upper mounting bolts

spring in compression must be obtained. Adjustable coil spring compressors are readily available, and are recommended for this operation. Any attempt to dismantle the strut without such a tool is likely to result in damage or personal injury.

12 Fit the spring compressors to the coils of the spring **(see illustration)**. Tighten the compressors evenly until the load is taken off the spring seats.
13 Hold the strut piston with an Allen key,

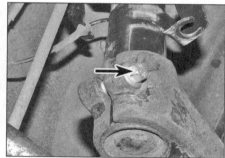

2.7 Remove the hub carrier pinch bolt

2.12 Fit compressors to the coil spring

2.13 Slacken the locknut whilst holding the piston with an Allen key

then use a spanner to loosen the strut locknut. Remove the nut, and discard it – a new nut must be used for reassembly **(see illustration)**.

14 Remove the upper mounting plate, followed by the spring seat, bump stop, gaiter and spring **(see illustrations)**. Take care not to disturb the compressors as the spring is removed.

15 With the strut assembly now completely dismantled, examine all the components for wear, damage or deformation. Renew any of the components as necessary.

16 If any doubt exists about the condition of the coil spring, gradually release the spring compressor, and check the spring for distortion and signs of cracking. Renew the spring if it is damaged or distorted, or if there is any doubt as to its condition. Note that springs should only be replaced with those that have the same colour-coding – mixing them up will result in a difference in ride heights; springs, like shock absorbers, should be replaced in axle pairs.

17 Inspect all other components for signs of damage or deterioration, and renew any that are suspect. The bump stops, for instance, are likely to be in less-than-perfect condition after a high mileage, or prolonged off-road use.

18 Reassembly is a reversal of dismantling, noting the following points:
a) *Compress the spring before fitting it.*
b) *Use a new damper piston locknut, and using a torque wrench adapter, tighten it to the specified torque whilst counterholding the damper piston with an Allen/Torx key.*
c) *Ensure the marks on the spring seat and spring are aligned correctly* **(see illustration)**.

Refitting

19 Refitting is a reversal of the removal procedure, noting the following points:
a) *Use a new anti-roll bar link rod nut.*
b) *Tighten all fixings to the specified torque.*
c) *Suspension nuts and bolts should only be tightened once the weight of the vehicle is back on the wheels (where possible).*

3 Front hub carrier – removal and refitting

Removal

1 Loosen the front wheel retaining nuts. Jack up the front of the car and support it on axle stands (see 'Vehicle jacking and support'). Remove the front wheel.

2 Remove the front driveshaft/hub bolt, and press the driveshaft back through the hub a little as described in Chapter 8 Section 2. Discard the bolt – a new one must be fitted.

2.14a Slide off the upper mounting plate, spring seat, bump stop, gaiter...

2.14b ...and spring

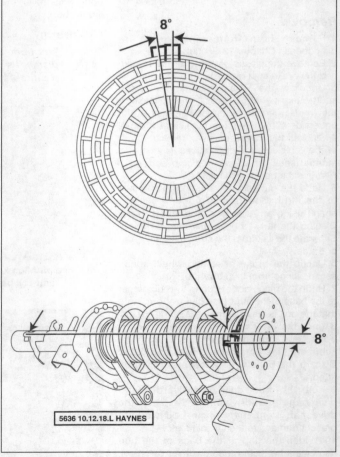

5636 10.12.18.L HAYNES

2.18 The lug on the mounting plate must be in-line with the tab at the base of the strut, and the lug on the spring seat must be within 8° of the lug on the plate

3 Undo the nut securing the anti-roll bar link to the strut. Counterhold the link balljoint shank using an Allen key **(see illustration 2.5)**. Discard the nut – a new one must be fitted. Separate the link from the strut, and move it to one side.
4 Remove the wheel speed sensor from the hub carrier as described in Chapter 9 Section 21.
5 Counterhold the trackrod end balljoint with an Allen key, undo the nut and detach the trackrod end from the hub carrier using a suitable balljoint separator **(see illustration 21.4)**. Discard the nut – a new one must be fitted.
6 Remove the brake disc as described in Chapter 9 Section 6.
7 Undo the 3 retaining bolts and remove the brake disc shield **(see illustration)**.
8 Undo the lower arm front and rear mounting bolts, and pull the lower arm from the subframe **(see illustrations 5.3a and 5.3b)**. Discard the bolts/nuts – new ones must be fitted.
9 Undo the clamp bolt, then lever the hub carrier downwards from the base of the suspension strut. If necessary, insert an Allen key/large flat-bladed screwdriver into the split in the hub carrier clamp, and widen the gap slightly **(see illustration)**.
10 With the hub carrier released from the strut, pull the top edge outwards and detach the driveshaft from the hub.
11 Using an Allen key to counterhold the balljoint, undo the nut then detach the lower arm balljoint from the hub carrier using a universal balljoint separator tool **(see illustration 5.4)**.

Refitting

12 Refitting is a reversal of removal, noting the following points:
a) Ensure the brake hose is correctly routed, and not twisted.
b) Renew the driveshaft/hub bolt, anti-roll bar link nut, trackrod end nut, and the lower arm balljoint nut.
c) Suspension nuts and bolts should only be tightened once the weight of the vehicle is back on the wheels (where possible).
d) Tighten all fasteners to their specified torque where given.

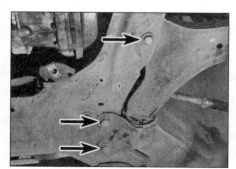
5.3 Front lower arm mounting bolts

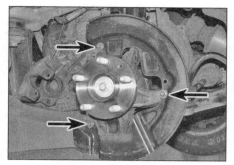
3.7 Disc shield retaining bolts

4.2 The new bearing is supplied complete with hub

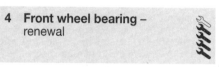
4 Front wheel bearing – renewal

1 Remove the hub carrier as described in Section 3.
2 The new bearing is supplied as an assembly with the hub **(see illustration)**. In order to remove the hub/bearing from the hub carrier, an hydraulic press is required. If necessary, take the hub carrier assembly to a local engineering facility and have them remove the hub/bearing and press the new one into place.
3 Support the hub carrier in a press, and using suitable spacers, press the bearing/hub from place **(see illustration)**.
Note: Land Rover specify special tools Nos. 204-348/1, 204-348/3, 204-528/1,

5.4 Detach the lower arm balljoint from the hub carrier using a separator tool

3.9 Slightly widen the hub carrier clamp gap

4.3 Press the bearing/hub from the carrier

204-536/2, and 205-802/5 for this procedure. This collection of spacers and supports may be available from alternative aftermarket automotive tool manufacturers – check with a Land Rover specialist.
4 Ensure the bore of the hub carrier is clean, and free for debris/burrs etc.
5 Support the new bearing/hub assembly, then using a suitable spacer, press the hub carrier into place.
6 With the new hub/bearing fitted, refit the hub carrier as described in Section 3.

5 Front suspension lower arm – removal and refitting

Removal

1 Loosen the front wheel retaining nuts. Jack up the front of the car and support it on axle stands (see 'Vehicle jacking and support'). Remove the front wheel.
2 Remove the front driveshaft/hub bolt, and press the driveshaft back through the hub a little as described in Chapter 8 Section 2. Discard the bolt – a new one must be fitted.
3 Undo the front and rear bolts and pull the lower arm from the subframe **(see illustration)**. Discard the bolts/nuts – new ones must be fitted.
4 Undo the nut, and detach the lower arm balljoint from the hub carrier using a balljoint separator tool **(see illustration)**.
5 No further dismantling of the lower arm is recommended. If the assembly shows sign of

6.2 Undo the anti-roll bar link rod nut

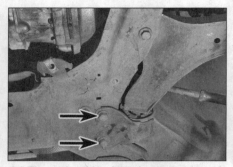

6.3 The anti-roll bar bolts/nuts also secure the rear of the lower arms

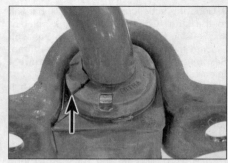

6.6 The split in the bushes should be towards the front

wear or damage, the complete arm must be replaced.

Refitting

6 Refitting is a reversal of removal, noting the following points:
a) *Tighten the lower arm front bush retaining bolt before tightening the rear bush retaining bolts/nuts.*
b) *Tighten all fasteners to their specified torque, where given.*
c) *Ensure the brake hose is not twisted.*
d) *Have the front wheel alignment checked at the earliest opportunity.*

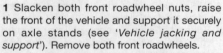

6   Front anti-roll bar bushes – renewal

1 Slacken both front roadwheel nuts, raise the front of the vehicle and support it securely on axle stands (see '*Vehicle jacking and support*'). Remove both front roadwheels.
2 Undo the nut securing the link rod to the anti-roll bar. Counterhold the link balljoint shank using an Allen key **(see illustration)**. Discard the nut – a new one must be fitted. Separate the link from the bar, and move it to one side.
3 Undo and remove the 4 bolts/nuts securing the anti-roll bar to the front subframe **(see illustration)**. Discard the bolts and nuts – new ones must be fitted.
4 Prise the anti-roll bar clamps upwards and

remove the bushes. Note the orientation of the bushes in relation to the bar prior to removal.
5 Inspect the bushes for signs of wear or damage, and replace as necessary.
6 Fit the bushes to the bar, with the split at the front **(see illustration)**.
7 The remainder of refitting is a reversal of removal, remembering to tighten all fasteners to their specified torque where given.

7   Front anti-roll bar link rods – removal and refitting

Removal

1 Slacken the front roadwheel nuts, raise the front of the vehicle and support is securely on axle stands (see '*Vehicle jacking and support*'). Remove the front roadwheels.
2 Unscrew the nut securing the lower end of each link rod to the anti-roll bar. It may be necessary to use an Allen key to prevent the link rod balljoint shank from turning as the nut is unscrewed **(see illustration 6.2)**. Discard the nut – a new one must be fitted.
3 Unscrew the nut securing the upper end of each link rod to the suspension strut. It may be necessary to use an Allen key to prevent the link rod balljoint shank from turning as the nut is unscrewed. Discard the nut – a new one must be fitted.

Refitting

4 Refitting is a reversal of removal. Tighten the fasteners to the specified torque.

8   Front subframe – removal and refitting

Removal

1 Loosen the wheel nuts, apply the handbrake, then jack up the front of the car and support it securely on axle stands (see '*Vehicle jacking and support*'). Do not support under the front subframe, for obvious reasons. Remove the front wheels.
2 Undo the fasteners and remove the engine undershield **(see illustration)**.
3 Note the harness routing, then unclip any wiring harnesses from the front subframe.
4 Disconnect the lower end of the link rods from the front anti-roll bar **(see illustration 6.2)**.
5 Counterhold the trackrod end balljoint with an Allen key, undo the nut and detach the trackrod end from the hub carrier using a suitable balljoint separator **(see illustration 21.4)**. Discard the nut – a new one must be fitted.
6 Undo the bolts securing the fluid pipes to the steering rack pinion housing **(see illustration)**. Be prepared for fluid spillage. Plug/seal the openings to prevent contamination.
7 Release the power steering pipes from the retaining clips on the steering rack.
8 Working under the facia, undo the steering column pinch bolt, and slide the universal joint upwards from the steering rack pinion **(see illustration)**. Discard the bolt – a new one must be fitted.

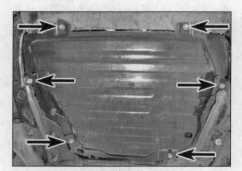

8.2 Engine undershield fasteners

8.6 Undo the bolt securing the fluid pipes to the pinion housing

8.8 Remove the steering column pinch bolt

9 Working underneath the vehicle, release the catalytic converter rubber mountings from the subframe.

10 Undo the bolts/nuts each side securing the lower arms to the subframe **(see illustration 5.3)**. Discard the bolts/nuts – new ones must be fitted.

11 Note their fitted locations/routing, and release any hoses from the subframe.

12 Undo the bolts securing the rear engine mounting link rod to the subframe.

13 Before proceeding further, securely support the weight of the front subframe. It may also be useful to have an assistant on hand, to help with lowering the subframe.

14 Carefully mark the position of the front subframe on the underbody to ensure correct refitting. **Note:** *Land Rover technicians use special alignment pins to locate the subframe accurately when refitting – equivalent pins are available from parts specialists.*

15 Undo the 3 bolts each side, and remove the front subframe cross brace **(see illustration)**. Note that new bolts will be required.

16 Undo the 2 bolts each side securing the subframe at the front **(see illustration)**. Note that new bolts will be required.

17 Carefully lower the subframe, and manoeuvre it from under the vehicle.

Refitting

18 Manoeuvre the subframe into position, ensuring the suspension lower arms are correctly located. Before fully raising the subframe, slide the anti-roll bar into place.

19 Insert the new subframe retaining bolts, but do not tighten them at this stage.

20 Raise the subframe against the underbody, and position it accurately with the marks made during removal. If available, use the special Land Rover alignment pins **(see illustration)**. Tighten all of the subframe bolts to the specified torque. Make sure the subframe does not move when tightening the bolts. If applicable, remove the Land Rover alignment pins.

21 The remainder of refitting is a reversal of removal, noting the following points:

a) *Tighten all fasteners to their specified torque.*
b) *Renew the fasteners where specified.*
c) *Bleed the power steering system as described in Section 22.*

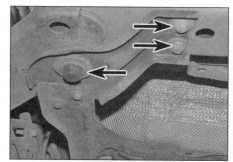

8.15 Undo the bolts each side and remove the crossbrace

8.16 Undo the subframe bolts each side at the front

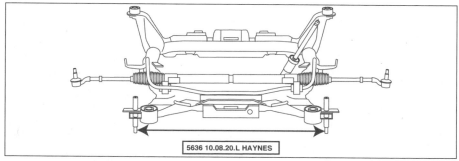

5636 10.08.20.L HAYNES

8.20 If available, use alignment pins (502-012) at the rear of the subframe

d) *Have the front wheel alignment checked at the earliest opportunity.*

9 Rear suspension strut – removal, overhaul and refitting

Removal

1 Loosen the relevant rear wheel nuts, then chock the front wheels and jack up the rear of the car and support on axle stands (see 'Vehicle jacking and support'). Remove the relevant rear wheel.

2 Remove the luggage compartment side trim panel as described in Chapter 11 Section 24.

3 Undo the 2 bolts securing the rear brake caliper, and slide the caliper from the disc **(see illustration)**. Suspend the caliper from a suitable body location to prevent any strain on the flexible brake hose.

4 Undo the nut securing the anti-roll bar link rod to the strut. Use an Allen key to prevent the balljoint shank from rotating whilst the nut is slackened. Release the link rod from the strut and position it to one side.

5 Undo the bolts securing the brake hose and wheel speed sensor wiring harness bracket to the strut.

6 Undo the clamp bolt securing the hub carrier to the base of the strut **(see illustration)**. Note that the bolt is inserted from the front. Discard the bolt – a new one must be fitted.

7 With reference to Section 10, detach the transverse and trailing arms from the hub carrier.

8 Using a large flat-bladed screwdriver, chisel or Allen key, gently widen the gap a little at the hub carrier, and slide it down from the strut **(see illustration)**. Once free from the strut,

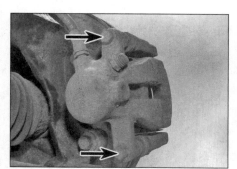

9.3 Remove the caliper retaining bolts (arrowed)

9.6 Remove the bolt (arrowed) securing the hub carrier to the strut

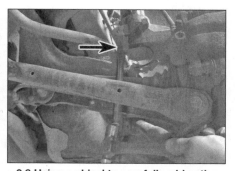

9.8 Using a chisel to carefully widen the gap (arrowed) at the hub carrier clamp

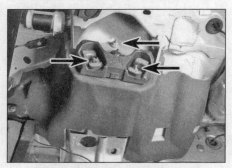

9.9 Rear strut upper mounting nuts (arrowed)

support the hub carrier on an axle stand or similar.

9 Loosen the strut upper mounting nuts, then with an assistant supporting the strut from below, remove the nuts and lower the strut out from under the wheelarch **(see illustration)**.

Overhaul

⚠️ *Warning: Before attempting to dismantle the suspension strut, a suitable tool to hold the coil spring in compression must be obtained. Adjustable coil spring compressors are readily available, and are recommended for this operation. Any attempt to dismantle the strut without such a tool is likely to result in damage or personal injury.*

10 Fit the spring compressors to the springs, and tighten the compressors evenly until the load is taken off the spring seats **(see illustration 2.12)**.

11 Before removing the damper inner locknut, note the alignment of the top mounting plate, spring end and dust boot.

12 Hold the damper piston with an Allen key, then use a spanner to loosen the locknut.

13 Make alignment marks between the spring, seats and mounting plates.

14 Remove the upper mounting plate/spring seat, followed by the spring, gaiter and bump stop. Take care not to disturb the compressors as the spring is removed.

15 With the strut assembly now completely dismantled, examine all the components for

wear, damage or deformation. Renew any of the components as necessary.

16 If any doubt exists about the condition of the coil spring, gradually release the spring compressor, and check the spring for distortion and signs of cracking. Renew the spring if it is damaged or distorted, or if there is any doubt as to its condition. Note that springs should only be replaced with those that have the same colour-coding – mixing them up will result in a difference in ride heights; springs, like shock absorbers, should be replaced in axle pairs.

17 Inspect all other components for signs of damage or deterioration, and renew any that are suspect. The bump stops, for instance, are likely to be in less-than-perfect condition after a high mileage, or prolonged off-road use.

18 Reassembly is a reversal of dismantling, noting the following points:
a) Compress the spring before fitting it.
b) Tighten the damper piston locknut, using an Allen key to counterhold the piston shaft.
c) Align the previously made marks, ensuring the spring and seats are correctly located.

Refitting

19 Refitting is a reversal of removal, noting the following points:
a) Renew the fasteners where specified.
b) Tighten all fasteners to their specified torque where given.
c) All suspension bolts/nuts should be tightened only when the weight of the vehicle is back on its' wheels (where possible).

---

10 Rear suspension link arms – removal and refitting 🔧

Front transverse link

Removal

1 Slacken the roadwheel nuts, raise the rear of the vehicle and support it securely on axle stands (see '*Vehicle jacking and support*'). Remove the rear roadwheel.

2 Undo the bolt securing the handbrake cable retaining bracket to the front link arm. Examine the bolt and renew if necessary.

3 Undo the nut, then withdrawn the link arm outer mounting bolt/washer from place **(see illustration)**.

4 Undo the nut securing the link inner mounting bolt, then partially withdraw the bolt from it's location **(see illustration)**.

5 Using a hacksaw, remove the head of the inner bolt, and drive the bolt out from the front. A new nut and bolt will be required.

6 Manoeuvre the link arm from position. Note that no further dismantling is recommend. If worn/damaged, the link arm must be replaced.

Refitting

7 Manoeuvre the link arm into place, then insert the new inner bolt from the rear, and fit the retaining nut. Do not fully tighten at this stage.

8 Refit the link arm outer bolt/washer and nut. Do not fully tighten the bolt/nut at this stage.

9 Reposition the handbrake cable bracket, and tighten the retaining nut securely.

10 Position a workshop jack under the rear hub and take the weight of the vehicle.

11 Tighten the link arm inner and outer bolts to the specified torque.

12 Refit the roadwheel, lower the vehicle to the ground, and tighten the roadwheel nuts to their specified torque.

13 Have the rear wheel alignment checked, and if necessary, adjusted at the earliest opportunity.

Rear transverse link

Removal

14 Slacken the roadwheel nuts, raise the rear of the vehicle and support it securely on axle stands (see '*Vehicle jacking and support*'). Remove the rear roadwheel.

15 To facilitate rear wheel alignment, the rear transverse link arm inner bolt incorporates an eccentric washer, and an eccentric washer is fitted under the retaining nut. In order to preserve the alignment, mark the eccentric washers in relation to the rear subframe **(see illustration)**.

16 Undo the nuts, recover the washers, then withdraw the link arms inner and outer

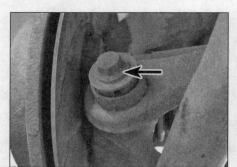

10.3 Remove the front transverse link outer bolt

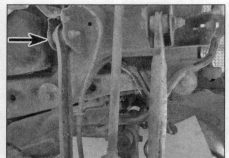

10.4 Partially withdraw the link inner bolt

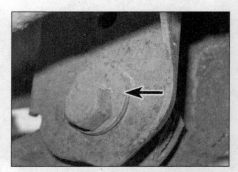

10.15 Make alignment marks between the eccentric washer and the subframe

10.16 Rear transverse link outer mounting bolt

10.19a Remove the trailing arm rear...

10.19b...and front mounting bolts

mounting bolts **(see illustration)**. Note that no further dismantling is recommend. If worn/damaged, the link arm must be replaced.

Refitting

17 Refitting is a reversal of removal, noting the following points:
a) *Examine the condition of the mounting bolts, and renew if necessary.*
b) *Align the eccentric washers with the previously made marks (where applicable).*
c) *Tighten the bolts/nut to the specified torque where given.*
d) *Have the rear wheel alignment checked, and if necessary adjusted at the earliest opportunity.*

Trailing arm

Removal

18 Slacken the roadwheel nuts, raise the rear of the vehicle and support it securely on axle stands (see '*Vehicle jacking and support*'). Remove the rear roadwheel.
19 Undo the nuts, then withdraw the trailing arm front and rear mounting bolts **(see illustrations)**.
20 Manoeuvre the trailing arm from position.

Refitting

21 Manoeuvre the trailing arm into position, insert the bolts and fit the retaining nuts. Do not fully tighten the bolts/nuts at this stage.
22 Position a workshop jack under the rear hub and take the weight of the vehicle.
23 Tighten the trailing arm front, and rear bolts/nuts to the specified torque.
24 Refit the roadwheel, lower the vehicle to the ground, then tighten the roadwheel nuts to the specified torque.
25 Have the rear wheel alignment checked at the earliest opportunity.

11 Rear hub carrier – removal and refitting

Removal

1 Slacken the roadwheel nuts, raise the rear of the vehicle and support it securely on axle

stands (see '*Vehicle jacking and support*'). Remove the rear roadwheel.
2 Have an assistant firmly apply the brakes, then slacken and remove the rear driveshaft/stub axle/hub nut. Discard the nut – a new one must be fitted.
3 Remove the rear handbrake shoes as described in Chapter 9 Section 17.
4 Undo the nut securing the rear anti-roll bar link rod to the suspension strut. Use an Allen key to counterhold the link rod balljoint. Discard the nut – a new one must be fitted.
5 Undo the nuts, then detach the brake hose and wheel speed sensor harness brackets from the hub carrier.
6 Undo the retaining bolt, and remove the wheel speed sensor from the hub carrier.
7 Undo the retaining bolt, and detach the handbrake cable bracket from the front transverse link arm **(see illustration)**.
8 Release the clips and pull the handbrake cable from the hub carrier.
9 With reference to Section 10, detach the transverse link arms, and trailing arm from the hub carrier.
10 Press the outer end of the driveshaft/stub axle through the rear hub. If necessary, use a universal puller located on the hub flange.
11 Undo the clamp bolt securing the hub carrier to the base of the strut **(see illustration 9.6)**. Note that the bolt is inserted from the front. Discard the bolt – a new one must be fitted.
12 Using a large flat-bladed screwdriver or Allen key, gently widen the gap a little at the

11.7 Handbrake cable bracket retaining bolt

hub carrier, and slide it down from the strut **(see illustration 9.8)**. Take care to support the hub carrier – it's heavy!

Refitting

13 Refitting is a reversal of removal, noting the following points:
a) *Tighten all fasteners to their specified torque, where given.*
b) *The transverse link and trailing arm bolts/nuts should only be fully tightened when the weight of the vehicle is supported as described in Section 10.*
c) *Upon completion, have the rear wheel alignment checked, and if necessary, adjusted.*

12 Rear hub carrier bush – renewal

1 The hub carrier is equipped with a replaceable bush where the rear of the trailing arm attaches. If access to the Land Rover special tools is available, the bush can be replaced with the hub carrier in-situ.
2 Remove the rear trailing arm as described in Section 10.

With Land Rover special tool

3 Land Rover special tools No. LR-121 and 204-620 is an pneumatic puller, and some suitable sized spacers. Note the fitted depth of the bush, assemble the tool as per the instructions supplied, and draw the old bush from the hub carrier.
4 Ensure the bore in the hub carrier is clean and free from rust etc.

Without Land Rover special tool

5 Remove the hub carrier as described in Section 11, and hold it securely in a bench vice.
6 Note the fitted depth of the bush.
7 Use a length of threaded bar, nuts and suitable spacers to draw the bush from the hub carrier.
8 Ensure the bore in the hub carrier is free from rust etc.

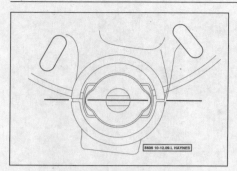
12.9 Hub carrier bush alignment

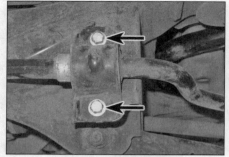
14.2 Rear anti-roll bar clamp bolts

15.3 Insert an Allen key into the balljoint shank to prevent it from rotating

All

9 Align the new bush as shown **(see illustration)**, then draw it into position using the method employed to remove the old one, to the depth previously noted.
10 The remainder of refitting is a reversal of removal.

13 Rear hub bearing – renewal

Note: *The hub assembly should not be removed unless it, or the hub bearing, is to be renewed. The hub is a press fit in the bearing inner race, and removal of the hub will damage the bearings. If the hub is to be removed, be prepared to renew the hub bearing at the same time.*

1 Remove the hub carrier as described in Section 11.
2 The bearing and hub must be pressed from the hub carrier.
3 Use a hydraulic press and suitable sized spacers to force the hub from the centre of the bearing.
4 If the hub is to be reused, remove the bearing inner race using a chisel, or bearing remover. Remove the disc shield if necessary.
5 Remove the circlip, then press the bearing from the hub carrier.
6 Thoroughly clean the hub carrier bore, removing all traces of dirt and grease, and polish away any burrs or raised edges which might hinder reassembly. Renew the circlip if there is any doubt about its condition.

7 One side of the bearing is magnetic – identifiable by the matt black finish. This magnetic surface is the 'signal disc' for the ABS wheel speed sensor. The magnetic side of the bearing must face in towards the final drive housing. Locate the bearing in the hub carrier and press it into position, ensuring that it enters the carrier squarely, using a suitable tubular spacer which bears only on the bearing outer race. Note: The bearing magnetic surface is delicate – handle it carefully.
8 Secure the bearing in position with the new circlip, making sure it is correctly located in the hub carrier groove.
9 Press the hub into place supporting the bearing with a spacer that bears only on the bearing inner race. Note: Do not be tempted to knock the hub into position with a hammer and drift, as this will almost certainly damage the bearing.
10 Refit the hub carrier as described in Section 11.

14 Rear anti-roll bar bushes – renewal

1 Chock the front wheels, raise the rear of the vehicle and support it securely on axle stands (see 'Vehicle jacking and support').
2 Undo the retaining bolts, and prise the clamps from the anti-roll bar **(see illustration)**. Discard the bolts – new ones must be fitted.
3 Note their fitted locations, then remove the bushes from the bar.

4 Ensure the anti-roll bar is clean and free from rust etc.
5 Locate the new bushes on the bar. Do not lubricate the bushes or the bar.
6 Refit the clamps with the new bolts, but don't fully tighten the bolts at this stage.
7 Lower the vehicle to the ground, and tighten the clamp bolts to the specified torque.

15 Rear anti-roll bar link rods – removal and refitting

Removal

1 Chock the front wheels, slacken the rear roadwheel nuts, raise the rear of the vehicle and support it securely on axle stands (see 'Vehicle jacking and support'). Remove the rear roadwheels.
2 Unscrew the nut securing the lower end of each link rod to the anti-roll bar. It may be necessary to use an Allen key to prevent the link rod balljoint shank from turning as the nut is unscrewed. Discard the nut – a new one must be fitted.
3 Unscrew the nut securing the upper end of each link to to the strut. Again, it may be necessary to use an Allen key to prevent the link rod balljoint shaft from turning as the nut is unscrewed **(see illustration)**. Discard the nut – a new one must be fitted.

Refitting

4 Refitting is a reversal of removal. Tighten the new nuts to the specified torque.

16 Steering wheel – removal and refitting

Removal

1 Remove the drivers air bag as described in Chapter 12 Section 20.
2 Disconnect the wiring plug from the rotary contact unit **(see illustration)**.
3 Hold the steering wheel to prevent it turning (don't rely on the steering lock for this, as it may not be strong enough, and damage could result), and undo the steering wheel retaining bolt **(see illustration)**.

16.2 Disconnect the upper wiring plug from the rotary contact unit

16.3 Undo the steering wheel bolt

16.4 Make alignment marks between the top of the column and the steering wheel

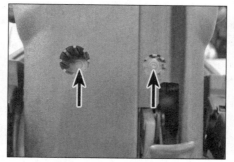

17.3 Undo the bolts on the underside and remove the steering column lower shroud

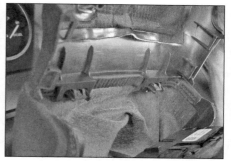

17.4 Unclip the upper shroud

4 Make an alignment mark between the wheel boss and the top of the column, to ensure the wheel goes back on straight. Pull the steering wheel from the splined end of the steering column. This should not require great effort, but if it sticks, put the wheel bolt back on by a few threads (to prevent it flying off), and tap the wheel off from behind the boss **(see illustration)**. Whilst the steering wheel is removed, wrap adhesive tape around the airbag contact unit. This will prevent unnecessary rotation of the contact unit, and will ensure that it remains correctly positioned until the steering wheel is refitted.

Refitting

5 Position the steering wheel on the column shaft, aligning the previously made marks, then refit the bolt and tighten it to the specified torque.
6 Reconnect the wiring plug
7 Refit the drivers air bag as described in Chapter 12 Section 20.

17 Steering column – removal and refitting

Removal

1 Remove the steering wheel as described in Section 16. Although not necessary if the column is being removed to access other components, removal of the wheel will make manoeuvring the column easier.
2 Remove the drivers lower air bag as described in Chapter 12 Section 20.
3 Undo the 2 retaining bolts, pull down the adjusting handle, and remove the steering column lower shroud **(see illustration)**.
4 Release the 2 clips and remove the steering column upper shroud **(see illustration)**.
5 Note the wiring harness routing, release it from the retaining clip, and disconnect the steering column wiring plugs.
6 Undo the pinch bolt, and pull the lower steering column universal joint from the steering rack pinion **(see illustration 8.8)**. Discard the bolt – a new one must be fitted.
7 Undo the 4 retaining bolts and manoeuvre

the steering column from place **(see illustration)**.

Refitting

8 Refitting is a reversal of removal, noting the following points:
a) *When the column is first offered in, only tighten the mounting bolts hand-tight until the column has been engaged correctly with the rack pinion, and the new pinch-bolt tightened to the specified torque.*
b) *Tighten all fasteners to their specified torque where given.*
c) *On completion, check the operation of the steering column lock, indicator self-cancelling before taking the car out on the road.*

18 Steering lock module – removal and refitting

Removal

1 Remove the steering column as described in Section 17.
2 Mark both shear bolts with a centre punch, and drill them out. Alternatively, it may be possible to unscrew the shear bolts with careful use of a sharp chisel.
3 Slide the lock module from the column.

Refitting

4 Refitting is a reversal of removal, noting the following points:

17.7 Steering column retaining bolts

a) *New shear bolts will obviously be needed. Tighten the new bolts until the heads shear off.*
b) *Refit the steering column as described in Section 17.*
c) *Check for correct operation.*
d) *If a new lock module has been fitted, it may need to be configured using Land Rover diagnostic equipment. Entrust this task to a Land Rover dealer or suitably equipped repairer.*

19 Steering rack – removal and refitting

Removal

1 Remove the front subframe as described in Section 8.
2 Undo the 2 retaining bolts, and detach the steering rack from the subframe **(see illustration)**.

Refitting

3 Position the steering rack on the subframe, insert the retaining bolts, and tighten them to the specified torque.
4 Refit the front subframe as described in Section 8.
5 On completion, top-up and bleed the power steering system as described in Section 22. Have the front wheel alignment checked and if necessary adjusted as soon as possible.

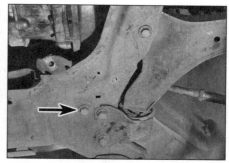

19.2 Undo the steering rack mounting bolt each side

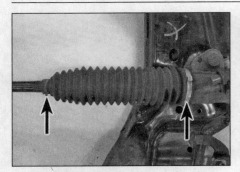

20.4 Release the steering rack gaiter clamps

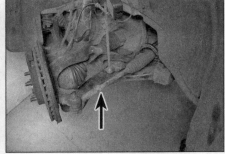

21.3 Slacken the track rod end lock nut

21.4 Detach the balljoint using a separator tool

20 Steering rack gaiter – renewal

1 Slacken the front road wheel nuts, raise the front of the vehicle and support it securely on axle stands (see 'Vehicle jacking and support'). Remove the front roadwheels.
2 Remove the track rod ends as described in Section 21.
3 Unscrew the track rod end lock nuts from the track rods. Count the number of turns required to remove the nuts, in order that they may be fitted to their original positions, to aid preserving the front wheel alignment.
4 Release the inner and outer clamps securing the gaiter to the steering rack housing and track rod (see illustration).
5 Pull the gaiter over the track rod.
6 Thoroughly clean the track rod and the steering rack housing, using fine abrasive paper to polish off any corrosion, burrs or sharp edges, which might damage the new gaiter's sealing lips on installation. Scrape off all the grease from the old gaiter, and apply it to the track rod inner balljoint. (This assumes that grease has not been lost or contaminated as a result of damage to the old gaiter. Use fresh grease if in doubt – consult a Land Rover dealer or parts specialist.)
7 Apply a little grease to the track rod so the gaiter will slide, then carefully slide the new gaiter (with the retaining clips in place) over the track rod, and locate it on the steering

rack housing. Position the outer edge of the gaiter on the track rod.
8 Secure the gaiter to the rack and track rod with the retaining clamps.
9 Refit the lock nut, followed by the track rod end as described in Section 21.

21 Track rod end – removal and refitting

Removal

1 Slacken the front road wheel nuts, raise the front of the vehicle and support it securely on axle stands (see 'Vehicle jacking and support'). Remove the front roadwheels.
2 Slacken the nut on the track rod end stud.
3 Slacken the track rod end lock nut enough to mark the position of the track rod end end in relation to the threads (see illustration).
4 Use a balljoint separator to detach the track rod end from the hub carrier (see illustration). Completely unscrew the nut from the track rod end stud.
5 Unscrew the track rod end from the track rod, counting the number of turns required, to aid refitting (see illustration).

Refitting

6 Thread the track rod end to the marked position on the track rod and insert the track rod end stud into the hub carrier. Count the number of turns required, to confirm the

correct position of the track rod. Tighten the lock nut securely.
7 Fit the new track rod end stud nut, and tighten it to the specified torque.
8 The remainder of refitting is a reversal of removal. Have the front wheel alignment check at the earliest opportunity.

22 Power steering system – bleeding

1 Check and if necessary top up the fluid level in the power steering fluid reservoir. Note: If the fluid appears to be aerated, wait a few minutes for the bubbles to dissipate.
2 Refit the reservoir cap, start the engine, run it for 10 seconds then stop the engine.
3 Check the fluid level again, and if necessary top it up to the MAX level. Note: If the fluid appears to be aerated, wait a few minutes for the bubbles to dissipate.
4 Start the engine, turn the steering lock-to-lock, then stop the engine.
5 Check the fluid level again, and if necessary top it up to the MAX level. Note: If the fluid appears to be aerated, wait a few minutes for the bubbles to dissipate.
6 Start and run the engine for 2 minutes, turning the steering from lock-to-lock.
7 Stop the engine, then check, and if necessary, top up the fluid level in the reservoir.

23 Power steering pump – removal and refitting

Removal

1 Remove the auxiliary drivebelt as described in Chapter 1 Section 28.
2 Using a large syringe or old poultry baster, remove as much fluid out of the power steering fluid reservoir as possible. Place a container under the vehicle to catch any fluid that spills out when the hoses are disconnected. Cap or cover the hoses to prevent entry of dirt or other contaminants.
3 Release the clamp and disconnect the fluid supply hose from the pump (see illustration).

21.5 Count the number of turns as the track rod end is unscrewed

23.3 Fluid supply hose clamp

23.4 Fluid pressure pipe retaining bolt

24.3 Release the clips each side and remove the cowling

4 Undo the retaining bolt and disconnect the fluid pressure pipe from the pump **(see illustration).**
5 Unclip the fuel pipes from above the power steering pump. If greater access is required, disconnect the hoses from the filter.
6 Undo the 3 retaining bolts and manoeuvre the power steering pump from place.

Refittng

7 Refitting is a reversal of removal. Bleed the power steering system as described in Section 22.

24 Power steering cooler – removal and refitting

Removal

1 Remove the front bumper as described in Chapter 11 Section 6.
2 Remove the right-hand headlight as described in Chapter 12 Section 7.
3 Undo the fasteners and remove the cowling covering the power steering cooler **(see illustration).**
4 Slide the power steering fluid reservoir upwards a little, then disconnect the fluid hose at the quick-release connector.
5 Release the clamp and disconnect the fluid return hose in the right-hand headlight aperture.
6 Undo the 2 retaining bolts and manoeuvre the power steering cooler from position.

Refitting

7 Refitting is a reversal of removal. Bleed the power steering system as described in Section 22.

25 Wheel alignment and steering angles – general information

Definitions

1 A car's steering and suspension geometry is defined in four basic settings **(see illustration)** – all angles are usually expressed in degrees; the steering axis is defined as an imaginary line drawn through the axis of the suspension strut, extended where necessary to contact the ground.
2 Camber is the angle between each roadwheel and a vertical line drawn through its centre and tyre contact patch, when viewed from the front or rear of the car. Positive camber is when the roadwheels are tilted outwards from the vertical at the top; negative camber is when they are tilted inwards.
3 The front and rear camber angles are not adjustable, and are given for reference only.
4 Castor is the angle between the steering axis and a vertical line drawn through each roadwheel's centre and tyre contact patch, when viewed from the side of the car. Positive castor is when the steering axis is tilted so that it contacts the ground ahead of the vertical; negative castor is when it contacts the ground behind the vertical.
5 Castor is not adjustable, and is given for reference only; while it can be checked using a castor checking gauge, if the figure obtained is significantly different from that specified, the car must be taken for careful checking by a professional, as the fault can only be caused by wear or damage to the body or suspension components.
6 Toe is the difference, viewed from above, between lines drawn through the roadwheel centres and the car's centre-line. 'Toe-in' is when the roadwheels point inwards, towards each other at the front, while 'toe-out' is when they splay outwards from each other at the front.
7 The front wheel toe setting is adjusted by screwing the track rod in or out of the track rod end, to alter the effective length of the track rod assembly.
8 Rear wheel toe adjustment is provided by an eccentric bolt securing the inner end of each rear transverse link to the rear subframe.
9 Accurate wheel alignment is essential for precise steering and handling, and for even tyre wear. Before carrying out any checking or adjusting operations, make sure that the tyres are correctly inflated, that all steering and suspension joints and linkages are in sound condition, and that the wheels are not buckled or distorted, particularly around the rims.
10 Ideally a four-wheel alignment check

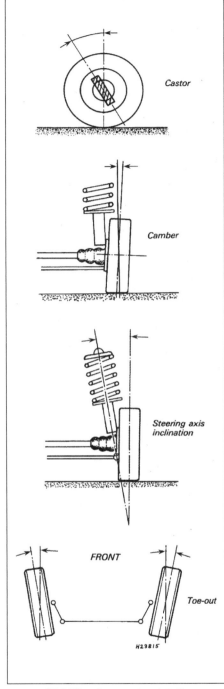

25.1 Wheel geometry details

should be carried out by a Land Rover dealer or suitably equipped specialist. Bear in mind the Freelander 2 models are equipped with a steering angle sensor incorporated into the steering column, and if the steering linkage/ wheel angles are not correctly set, the ESP (Electronic Stability Program) may not function correctly.

Chapter 11
Bodywork and fittings

Contents

Degrees of difficulty

Easy, suitable for novice with little experience 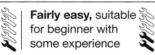	Fairly easy, suitable for beginner with some experience	Fairly difficult, suitable for competent DIY mechanic	Difficult, suitable for experienced DIY mechanic	Very difficult, suitable for expert DIY or professional

Specifications

Torque wrench settings	Nm	lbf ft
Drivers lower air bag.	6	4
Front seat belt inertia reel bolt*	40	30
Front seat belt lower anchorage bolt*	40	30
Front seat belt stalk bolt.	40	30
Front seat belt upper anchorage bolt*	40	30
Front seat Torx bolts*	40	30
Impact sensors.	10	7
Facia crossmember bolts:		
M8	24	18
M12.	40	30
Passengers air bag bracket Torx screws	7	5
Passengers air bag module nuts	10	7
Rear centre belt inertia reel bolt	35	26
Rear centre belt lower anchorage bolt	55	41
Rear centre belt stalk nut	55	41
Rear side belt inertia reel bolt.	40	30
Rear side belt lower anchorage bolt*	40	30
Rear side belt upper anchorage bolt	40	30
Restraint control module (RCM) Torx screws.	10	7
Side air bag module nuts	10	7

*Do not re-use

1 General information

1 Unlike traditional Land Rovers, the Freelander 2 does not have a separate 'ladder-frame' chassis and body, but instead has a car-like 'unitary' bodyshell, made of pressed-steel sections. The Freelander is available is five-door versions only. Most components are welded together, but some use is made of structural adhesives; the front wings are bolted on.

2 Extensive use is made of plastic materials, mainly for the interior but also for exterior components. The front wings are made of a polymer-composite material, designed to be flexible enough to shrug off minor bumps, while the front and rear bumpers are injection-moulded from a synthetic material, which is very strong and yet light. Plastic components such as wheelarch liners are fitted to the underside of the vehicle, to improve the body's resistance to corrosion.

2 Maintenance – bodywork and underframe

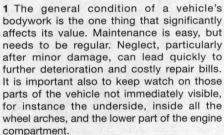

1 The general condition of a vehicle's bodywork is the one thing that significantly affects its value. Maintenance is easy, but needs to be regular. Neglect, particularly after minor damage, can lead quickly to further deterioration and costly repair bills. It is important also to keep watch on those parts of the vehicle not immediately visible, for instance the underside, inside all the wheel arches, and the lower part of the engine compartment.

2 The basic maintenance routine for the bodywork is washing – preferably with a lot of water, from a hose. This will remove all the loose solids which may have stuck to the vehicle. It is important to flush these off in such a way as to prevent grit from scratching the finish. The wheel arches and underframe need washing in the same way, to remove any accumulated mud, which will retain moisture and tend to encourage rust. Paradoxically enough, the best time to clean the underframe and wheel arches is in wet weather, when the mud is thoroughly wet and soft. In very wet weather, the underframe is usually cleaned of large accumulations automatically, and this is a good time for inspection.

3 Periodically, except on vehicles with a wax-based underbody protective coating, it is a good idea to have the whole of the underframe of the vehicle steam-cleaned, engine compartment included, so that a thorough inspection can be carried out to see what minor repairs and renovations are necessary. Steam-cleaning is available at many garages, and is necessary for the removal of the accumulation of oily grime,

which sometimes is allowed to become thick in certain areas. If steam-cleaning facilities are not available, there are some excellent grease solvents available which can be brush-applied; the dirt can then be simply hosed off. Note that these methods should not be used on vehicles with wax-based underbody protective coating, or the coating will be removed. Such vehicles should be inspected annually, preferably just prior to Winter, when the underbody should be washed down, and any damage to the wax coating repaired. Ideally, a completely fresh coat should be applied. It would also be worth considering the use of such wax-based protection for injection into door panels, sills, box sections, etc, as an additional safeguard against rust damage, where such protection is not provided by the vehicle manufacturer.

4 After washing paintwork, wipe off with a chamois leather to give an unspotted clear finish. A coat of clear protective wax polish will give added protection against chemical pollutants in the air. If the paintwork sheen has dulled or oxidised, use a cleaner/polisher combination to restore the brilliance of the shine. This requires a little effort, but such dulling is usually caused because regular washing has been neglected. Care needs to be taken with metallic paintwork, as special non-abrasive cleaner/polisher is required to avoid damage to the finish. Always check that the door and ventilator opening drain holes and pipes are completely clear, so that water can be drained out. Windscreens and windows can be kept clear of the smeary film which often appears, by the use of proprietary glass cleaner. Never use any form of wax or other body polish on glass.

3 Maintenance – upholstery and carpets

1 Mats and carpets should be brushed or vacuum-cleaned regularly, to keep them free of grit. If they are badly stained, remove them from the vehicle for scrubbing or sponging, and make quite sure they are dry before refitting. Seats and interior trim panels can be kept clean by wiping with a damp cloth. If they do become stained (which can be more apparent on light-coloured upholstery), use a little liquid detergent and a soft nail brush to scour the grime out of the grain of the material. Do not forget to keep the headlining clean in the same way as the upholstery. When using liquid cleaners inside the vehicle, do not over-wet the surfaces being cleaned. Excessive damp could get into the seams and padded interior, causing stains, offensive odours or even rot. If the inside of the vehicle gets wet accidentally, it is worthwhile taking some trouble to dry it out properly, particularly where carpets are involved. Do not leave oil or electric heaters inside the vehicle for this purpose.

4 Minor body damage – repair

Repair of minor scratches in the vehicle's bodywork

1 If the scratch is very superficial, and does not penetrate to the metal of the bodywork, repair is very simple. Lightly rub the area of the scratch with a paintwork renovator, or a very fine cutting paste, to remove loose paint from the scratch and to clear the surrounding bodywork of wax polish. Rinse the area with clean water.

2 In the case of metallic paint, the most commonly-found 'scratches' are not in the paint, but in the lacquer top coat, and appear white. If care is taken, these can sometimes be rendered less obvious by very careful use of paintwork renovator (which would otherwise not be used on metallic paintwork); otherwise, repair of these scratches can be achieved by applying lacquer with a fine brush.

3 Apply touch-up paint to the scratch using a thin paintbrush; continue to apply thin layers of paint until the surface of the paint in the scratch is level with the surrounding paintwork. Allow the new paint at least two weeks to harden, then blend it into the surrounding paintwork by rubbing the paintwork in the scratch area with a paintwork renovator or a very fine cutting paste. Finally, apply wax polish.

4 Where the scratch has penetrated right through to the metal of the bodywork, causing the metal to rust, a different repair technique is required. Remove any loose rust from the bottom of the scratch with a penknife, then apply rust-inhibiting paint, to prevent the formation of rust in the future. Using a rubber or nylon applicator fill the scratch with bodystopper paste. If required, this paste can be mixed with cellulose thinners, to provide a very thin paste which is ideal for filling narrow scratches. Before the stopper-paste in the scratch hardens, wrap a piece of smooth cotton rag around the top of a finger. Dip the finger in cellulose thinners, and then quickly sweep it across the surface of the stopper-paste in the scratch; this will ensure that the surface of the stopper-paste is slightly hollowed. The scratch can now be painted over as described earlier in this Section.

Repair of dents in bodywork

5 When deep denting of the vehicle's bodywork has taken place, the first task is to pull the dent out, until the affected bodywork almost attains its original shape. There is little point in trying to restore the original shape completely, as the metal in the damaged area will have stretched on impact, and cannot be reshaped fully to its original contour. It is better to bring the level of the dent up to a point which is about 3 mm below the level of the surrounding bodywork. In cases where

the dent is very shallow anyway, it is not worth trying to pull it out at all. If the underside of the dent is accessible, it can be hammered out gently from behind, using a mallet with a wooden or plastic head. Whilst doing this, hold a suitable block of wood firmly against the outside of the panel to absorb the impact from the hammer blows and thus prevent a large area of the bodywork from being 'belled-out'.

6 Should the dent be in a section of the bodywork which has a double skin or some other factor making it inaccessible from behind, a different technique is called for. Drill several small holes through the metal inside the area – particularly in the deeper section. Then screw long self-tapping screws into the holes just sufficiently for them to gain a good purchase in the metal. Now the dent can be pulled out by pulling on the protruding heads of the screws with a pair of pliers.

7 The next stage of the repair is the removal of the paint from the damaged area, and from an inch or so of the surrounding 'sound' bodywork. This is accomplished most easily by using a wire brush or abrasive pad on a power drill, although it can be done just as effectively by hand using sheets of abrasive paper. To complete the preparation for filling, score the surface of the bare metal with a screwdriver or the tang of a file, or alternatively, drill small holes in the affected area. This will provide a really good 'key' for the filler paste.

8 To complete the repair, see the Section on filling and re-spraying.

Repair of rust holes or gashes in bodywork

9 Remove all paint from the affected area, and from an inch or so of the surrounding 'sound' bodywork, using an abrasive pad or a wire brush on a power drill. If these are not available, a few sheets of abrasive paper will do the job just as effectively. With the paint removed, you will be able to gauge the severity of the corrosion, and therefore decide whether to renew the whole panel (if this is possible) or to repair the affected area. New body panels are not as expensive as most people think, and it is often quicker and more satisfactory to fit a new panel than to attempt to repair large areas of corrosion.

10 Remove all fittings from the affected area, except those which will act as a guide to the original shape of the damaged bodywork. Then, using tin snips or a hacksaw blade, remove all loose metal and any other metal badly affected by corrosion. Hammer the edges of the hole inwards in order to create a slight depression for the filler paste.

11 Wire-brush the affected area to remove the powdery rust from the surface of the remaining metal. Paint the affected area with rust-inhibiting paint; if the back of the rusted area is accessible treat this also.

12 Before filling can take place, it will be necessary to block the hole in some way. This can be achieved by the use of aluminium or plastic mesh, or aluminium tape.

13 Aluminium or plastic mesh or glass fibre matting is probably the best material to use for a large hole. Cut a piece to the approximate size and shape of the hole to be filled, then position it in the hole so that its edges are below the level of the surrounding bodywork. It can be retained in position by several blobs of filler paste around its periphery.

14 Aluminium tape should be used for small or very narrow holes. Pull a piece off the roll and trim it to the approximate size and shape required, then pull off the backing paper (if used) and stick the tape over the hole; it can be overlapped if the thickness of one piece is insufficient. Burnish down the edges of the tape with the handle of a screwdriver or similar, to ensure that the tape is securely attached to the metal underneath.

15 Before using this Section, see the Sections on dent, deep scratch, rust holes and gash repairs.

16 Many types of bodyfiller are available, but generally speaking those proprietary kits which contain a tin of filler paste and a tube of resin hardener are best for this type of repair; some can be used directly from the tube. A wide, flexible plastic or nylon applicator will be found invaluable for imparting a smooth and well contoured finish to the surface of the filler.

17 Mix up a little filler on a clean piece of card or board – measure the hardener carefully (follow the maker's instructions on the pack) otherwise the filler will set too rapidly or too slowly. Using the applicator, apply the filler paste to the prepared area; draw the applicator across the surface of the filler to achieve the correct contour and to level the filler surface. As soon as a contour that approximates to the correct one is achieved, stop working the paste – if you carry on too long the paste will become sticky and begin to 'pick up' on the applicator. Continue to add thin layers of filler paste at twenty-minute intervals until the level of the filler is just proud of the surrounding bodywork.

18 Once the filler has hardened, excess can be removed using a metal plane or file. From then on, progressively finer grades of abrasive paper should be used, starting with a 40-grade production paper and finishing with 400-grade wet-and-dry paper. Always wrap the abrasive paper around a flat rubber, cork, or wooden block – otherwise the surface of the filler will not be completely flat. During the smoothing of the filler surface the wet-and-dry paper should be periodically rinsed in water. This will ensure that a very smooth finish is imparted to the filler at the final stage.

19 At this stage the 'dent' should be surrounded by a ring of bare metal, which in turn should be encircled by the finely 'feathered' edge of the good paintwork. Rinse the repair area with clean water, until all of the dust produced by the rubbing-down operation has gone.

20 Spray the whole repair area with a light coat of primer – this will show up any imperfections in the surface of the filler. Repair these imperfections with fresh filler paste or bodystopper, and once more smooth the surface with abrasive paper. If bodystopper is used, it can be mixed with cellulose thinners to form a really thin paste which is ideal for filling small holes. Repeat this spray and repair procedure until you are satisfied that the surface of the filler, and the feathered edge of the paintwork are perfect. Clean the repair area with clean water and allow to dry fully.

21 The repair area is now ready for final spraying. Paint spraying must be carried out in a warm, dry, windless and dust free atmosphere. This condition can be created artificially if you have access to a large indoor working area, but if you are forced to work in the open, you will have to pick your day very carefully. If you are working indoors, dousing the floor in the work area with water will help to settle the dust which would otherwise be in the atmosphere. If the repair area is confined to one body panel, mask off the surrounding panels; this will help to minimise the effects of a slight mis-match in paint colours. Bodywork fittings (e.g. chrome strips, door handles etc) will also need to be masked off. Use genuine masking tape and several thicknesses of newspaper for the masking operations.

22 Before commencing to spray, agitate the aerosol can thoroughly, then spray a test area (an old tin, or similar) until the technique is mastered. Cover the repair area with a thick coat of primer; the thickness should be built up using several thin layers of paint rather than one thick one. Using 400 grade wet-and-dry paper, rub down the surface of the primer until it is really smooth. While doing this, the work area should be thoroughly doused with water, and the wet-and-dry paper periodically rinsed in water. Allow to dry before spraying on more paint.

23 Spray on the top coat, again building up the thickness by using several thin layers of paint. Start spraying in the centre of the repair area and then, with a single side-to-side motion, work outwards until the whole repair area and about 50 mm of the surrounding original paintwork is covered. Remove all masking material 10 to 15 minutes after spraying on the final coat of paint.

24 Allow the new paint at least two weeks to harden, then, using a paintwork renovator or a very fine cutting paste, blend the edges of the paint into the existing paintwork. Finally, apply wax polish.

Plastic components

25 With the use of more and more plastic body components by the vehicle manufacturers (e.g. bumpers, spoilers, and in some cases major body panels), rectification of more serious damage to such items has become a matter of either entrusting repair work to a specialist in this field, or renewing complete components. Repair of such damage by the DIY owner is not really feasible owing to the cost of the equipment and materials required for effecting such repairs. The basic technique involves making a groove along the line of the crack in the plastic using a rotary burr in a power drill. The damaged part is then welded back together by using a hot-air gun to heat up and fuse a plastic filler rod into the groove. Any excess plastic is then removed and the area rubbed down to a smooth finish. It is important that a filler rod of the correct plastic is used, as body components can be made of a variety of different types (e.g. polycarbonate, ABS, polypropylene).

26 Damage of a less serious nature (abrasions, minor cracks etc) can be repaired by the DIY owner using a two-part epoxy filler repair material. Once mixed in equal proportions, this is used in similar fashion to the bodywork filler used on metal panels. The filler is usually cured in twenty to thirty minutes, ready for sanding and painting.

27 If the owner is renewing a complete component himself, or if he has repaired it with epoxy filler, he will be left with the problem of finding a suitable paint for finishing which is compatible with the type of plastic used. At one time the use of a universal paint was not possible owing to the complex range of plastics encountered in body component applications. Standard paints, generally speaking, will not bond to plastic or rubber satisfactorily. However, it is now possible to obtain a plastic body parts finishing kit which consists of a pre-primer treatment, a primer and coloured top coat. Full instructions are normally supplied with a kit, but basically the method of use is to first apply the pre-primer to the component concerned and allow it to dry for up to 30 minutes. Then the primer is applied and left to dry for about an hour before finally applying the special coloured top coat. The result is a correctly-coloured component where the paint will flex with the plastic or rubber, a property that standard paint does not normally possess.

5 Major body damage – repair

1 Where serious damage has occurred, or large areas need renewal due to neglect, it means that complete new panels will need welding in, and this is best left to professionals. If the damage is due to impact, it will also be necessary to check completely the alignment of the bodyshell, and this can only be carried out accurately by a Land Rover dealer using special jigs. If the body is left misaligned, it is primarily dangerous, as the car will not handle properly. Secondly, uneven stresses will be imposed on the steering, suspension and possibly transmission, causing abnormal wear, or complete failure, particularly to such items as the tyres.

6 Front bumper – removal and refitting

Removal

1 Open the bonnet. It is useful to have an assistant on hand for bumper removal, and almost essential when refitting it.

2 Slacken the front road wheel nuts, raise the front of the vehicle, and support it securely on axle stands (see 'Vehicle jacking and support'). Remove both front roadwheels.

3 Rotate the 2 fasteners anti-clockwise and remove the towing eye cover from the bumper **(see illustration)**.

4 Undo the fasteners, and remove the lower splash shield each side, from the wheel arch liners **(see illustration)**.

5 Undo the fastener each side securing the rear edge of the bumper to the wheelarch liner **(see illustration)**.

6 The bumper is now secured by one bolt each side securing the bumper to the inner wing (pull back the wheelarch liner), 4 bolts along the upper edge, and two bolts at the lower edge **(see illustrations)**. Remove these bolts.

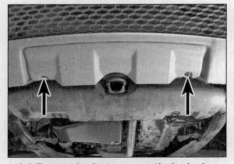

6.3 Rotate the fasteners anti-clockwise and remove the cover

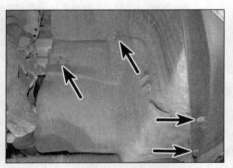

6.4 Lower splash shield fasteners

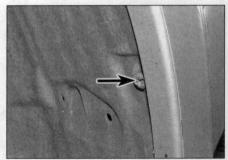

6.5 Bumper-to-wheelarch liner screw

6.6a Undo the bolt each side...

6.6b...the 4 along the upper edge...

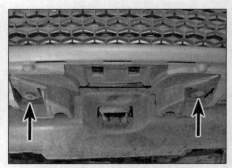

6.6c...and the 2 at the lower edge

6.7 Pull the rear edges of the bumper outwards

7.3a Prise up the step trim...

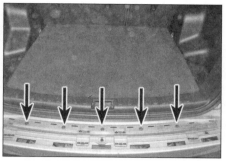

7.3b...undo the centre screws, and prise up the plastic expansion rivets

7 With the help of an assistant, pull the rear edges of the bumper outwards slightly to release the clips, then manoeuvre it forwards a little **(see illustration)**.

8 Disconnect the headlight washer hose (where applicable), and any wiring plugs. Remove the bumper.

Refitting

9 Refitting is a reversal of removal. Have an assistant ready to help with offering the bumper into position, and tighten all fixings securely.

7 Rear bumper –
removal and refitting

Removal

1 Chock the front wheels, slacken the rear road wheel nuts, raise the rear of the vehicle and support it securely on axle stands (see 'Vehicle jacking and support'). Remove the rear road wheels.

2 Remove both rear light assemblies as described in Chapter 12 Section 7.

3 Carefully prise up the rear bumper upper step trim, undo the centre screws and prise out the 5 plastic expansion rivets exposed **(see illustrations)**.

4 Remove the fastener each side adjacent to the rear light apertures **(see illustration)**.

5 Release the 6 fasteners along the lower edge of the bumper **(see illustration)**.

6 Undo the 3 fasteners each side and pull the rear section of the wheelarch liner forwards **(see illustration)**.

7 Undo the 2 bolts each side in the wheelarch aperture securing the bumper to the rear wing **(see illustration)**.

8 Where applicable, disconnect the parking aid sensor wiring plug each side, on the underside of the bumper **(see illustration)**.

9 With the help of an assistant, carefully pull out the front edges of the bumper a little, and manoeuvre it rearwards from place **(see illustration)**.

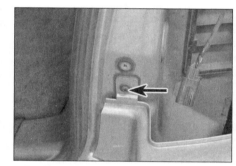

7.4 Remove the screw each side in the light aperture

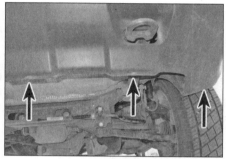

7.5 Undo the 3 fasteners each side underneath the bumper

7.6 Release the fasteners and pull the wheelarch liner forwards

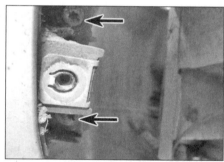

7.7 Undo the bolts securing the bumper to the wing

7.8 The parking aid sensor wiring plug is located under the right-hand side of the bumper

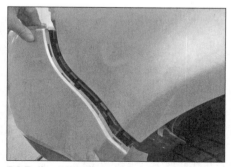

7.9 Pull out the front edge of the bumper to release the clips

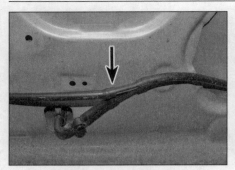

8.3 Disconnect the washer tube

8.4 Bonnet hinge bolts

bulkhead, then pull the cable through into the engine compartment.

Refitting

7 Refitting is a reversal of removal, noting the following points:
a) *Feed the cable back through into the car from the engine compartment, and work the rubber grommet into position using a small screwdriver (it may also be helpful to lubricate the grommet with a little washing-up liquid, prior to fitting).*
b) *Use new cable-ties to secure the cable to the wiring harness.*
c) *Ensure that the cable is routed as noted before removal, with no sharp bends.*
d) *Attach the cable to the string left in the front crosspanel, and use the string to draw the cable into position for refitting to the bonnet lock.*
e) *Refit the bonnet lock as described in Section 10.*

Refitting

10 Refitting is a reversal of removal. Have an assistant ready to help with offering the bumper into position, and tighten all fixings securely.

8 Bonnet – removal, refitting and adjustment

Removal

1 Open the bonnet, and have an assistant support it. Using a pencil or felt tip pen, mark the outline position of each bonnet hinge relative to the bonnet, to use as a guide on refitting.
2 Prise out the clips and remove the bonnet insulation panel.
3 Disconnect the washer tube from the joint before the driver's side washer jet **(see illustration)**. Unclip the hose from the bonnet retaining clips.
4 Undo the bonnet retaining bolts and, with the help of an assistant, carefully lift the bonnet clear **(see illustration)**.

Refitting and adjustment

5 With the aid of an assistant, offer up the bonnet, and loosely fit the retaining bolts. Align the hinges with the marks made on removal, then tighten the retaining bolts securely.
6 Close the bonnet, and check for alignment

with the adjacent panels. If necessary, slacken the bonnet bolts and realign the bonnet to suit, or screw the rubber buffers at the front corners in or out. Once the bonnet is correctly aligned, securely tighten the bolts. Check that the bonnet fastens and releases in a satisfactory manner.

9 Bonnet release cable – removal and refitting

Removal

1 Remove the bonnet lock as described in Section 10.
2 Tie a piece of string to the end of the release cable, and pull the cable out of the front crosspanel. When the cable has been withdrawn, untie the string, and leave it in position for refitting.
3 Work back along the cable, releasing it from the cable-ties securing it to the wiring harness, and noting its correct routing.
4 From inside the vehicle, unscrew the retaining bolt securing the bonnet release lever to its mounting bracket **(see illustration)**.
5 Unhook the cable end fitting from the release lever, and remove the lever **(see illustration)**.
6 Returning to the engine compartment, pull away the sound insulation from the bulkhead where the cable passes through. Prise the release cable rubber grommet out of the

10 Bonnet lock – removal and refitting

Removal

1 Working in the engine compartment, undo the bolts securing the bonnet locks to the crosspanel **(see illustration)**.
2 Disconnect the release cables from the locks.

Refitting

3 Refitting is a reversal of removal. Prior to closing the bonnet, simulate bonnet closure by 'closing' the locks using a screwdriver or similar. Ensure both locks release and lock correctly before closing the bonnet.

11 Door – removal and refitting

Removal

1 Disconnect the battery negative lead as described in Chapter 5A Section 4.

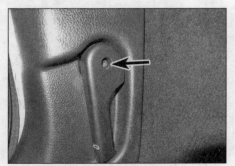

9.4 Bonnet release lever retaining bolt

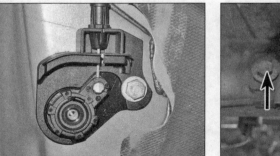

9.5 Unhook the cable from the lever

10.1 Bonnet lock securing bolts

11.2 Remove the check strap Torx bolt

11.3 Remove the door hinge bolts

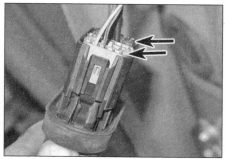

11.4 Disconnect the wiring plugs

2 Undo the bolt securing the door check strap to the pillar **(see illustration)**.
3 Have an assistant support the door, then remove the door hinge bolts **(see illustration)**. Lift the door from the hinges.

Front door

4 Squeeze together the upper, and lower clips, then pull the door wiring harness rubber gaiter and fitting from the pillar **(see illustration)**. Disconnect the wiring plugs.

Rear door

5 Slide the door wiring harness gaiter end fitting downwards, pull it from the pillar, and disconnect the wiring plug.

Refitting

6 Refitting is a reversal of removal.

12 Door inner trim panel – removal and refitting

Removal

Front door

1 Carefully prise the door grab handle cover from the panel **(see illustration)**.
2 The door trim panel is secured by 5 screws and 15 clips around it's circumference **(see illustrations)**. Undo the screws, and use a blunt, flat-bladed tool to release the clips.
3 Disconnect any wiring plugs, and the interior release handle cable as the panel is

> **HAYNES HiNT** *It is a good idea to obtain a few trim panel retaining clips before starting, as they are often broken in the course of removal, or will be found to have broken during previous removal attempts.*

withdrawn **(see illustration)**. Prior to refitting, examine the panel retaining clips for signs of damage – renew any broken clips.

Rear door

4 Carefully prise the door grab handle cover from the panel **(see illustration)**.
5 The door trim panel is secured by 4 screws and 10 clips around its circumference **(see**

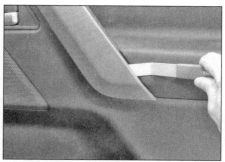

12.1 Prise the grab handle cover from the panel

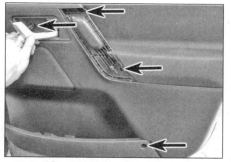

12.2a Prise out the cap, undo the screw in the handle recess, followed by the 2 screws adjacent to the grab handle, the storage pocket screw...

12.2b...and the screw at the rear edge

12.2c Use a blunt, flat tool to release the door trim retaining clips

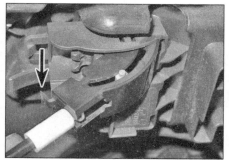

12.3 Release the clip and detach the cable end fitting from the handle

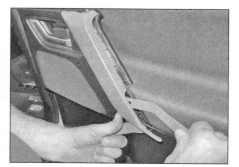

12.4 Prise off the grab handle cover

illustrations). Undo the screws, and using a blunt, flat-bladed tool, release the clips.

6 Pull the panel inwards to release the 4 clips along the upper edge.

7 Disconnect any wiring plugs, and the interior release handle cable as the panel is withdrawn. Prior to refitting, examine the panel retaining clip for signs of damage – renew any broken clips.

Refitting

8 Refitting is a reversal of removal.

---

13 Door handle and lock components – removal and refitting

Removal

Door interior release handle

1 Remove the door inner trim panel as described in Section 12.

2 Release the retaining clips and withdraw the handle assembly from the panel **(see illustration)**.

Door exterior handle

3 Remove the door inner trim panel as described in Section 12.

4 If removing the passengers door exterior handle, remove the door lock cylinder as described later in this Section.

12.5a Prise out the cap, undo the screw in the release handle recess, and the screws adjacent to the grab handle

5 If removing the drivers or rear door exterior handle, carefully squeeze together the retaining clips, pull the front edge of the handle rear trim outwards, and manoeuvre it from the door **(see illustration)**. It's quite likely that the cover clips will break during removal. Renew the cover if necessary.

6 On either door, pull the exterior handle outwards, then rearwards and manoeuvre it from the door **(see illustration)**.

Front lock cylinder

7 Slide the emergency lock release key from the remote control key fob.

8 Insert the lock release key into the slot in

12.5b Use a blunt, flat tool to release the door trim retaining clips

the base of the exterior handle rear trim, and pull the trim outwards **(see illustration)**.

9 Prise out the grommet in the end of the door frame, and slacken the Torx screw just enough (approximately 5.5 turns) to be able to withdraw the lock cylinder from the handle **(see illustrations)**. Note that the lock cylinder and ignition lock cylinders are replaced as a set.

Door lock

10 Remove the door window regulator and motor assembly as described in Section 14.

11 Remove the door exterior handle as described earlier in this Section.

12 Undo the screw securing the exterior

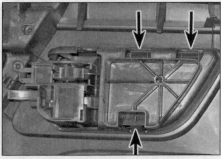

13.2 Interior release handle retaining clips

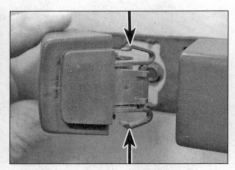

13.5 Using a small screwdriver, squeeze together the retaining clips

13.6 Pull the handle outwards, then rearwards

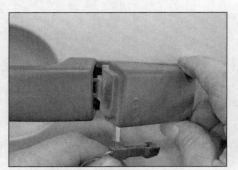

13.8 With the key inserted, pull the trim outwards

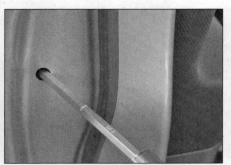

13.9a Slacken the Torx screw approximately 5.5 turns...

13.9b...and withdraw the lock cylinder

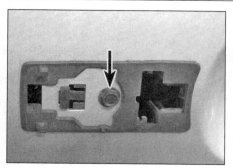

13.12a Undo the screw...

13.12b..pull back the rubber trim, and prise out the plastic clip

13.13 Door lock retaining screws

handle frame to the door, then prise out the clip securing it to the door skin **(see illustrations)**.

13 Undo the 3 screws at the end of the door frame, and reposition the lock assembly to access the wiring plug. Disconnect the lock wiring plug **(see illustrations)**.

14 Manoeuvre the lock and handle frame from the door, complete with cables.

15 If required, detach the cables from the lock.

Refitting

16 Refitting is a reversal of removal, noting the following points:

a) *When refitting the exterior handle, ensure the lock lever engages correctly* **(see illustration)**.

b) *Before closing the door, check for correct operation by 'closing' the lock with a screwdriver, then ensuring that it 'opens' correctly when the exterior and interior handles are operated.*

14 Door window glass and regulator – removal and refitting

Removal

Window glass

1 Lower the window approximately a third of the way down, then open the door, undo the retaining screw at the end of the door, and

pull the rear edge of the external weatherstrip outwards and manoeuvre it from place **(see illustrations)**.

2 Slide Land Rover tool No. 501-114 down between the glass and the door skin, and release the window clamp(s). In the absence of this tool, a thin strip of steel, approximately 500 mm long should suffice **(see illustrations)**. Note that the front window is secured by 2 clamps, whereas the rear window is secured by 1 clamp.

Rear door glass

3 Slide the window glass to the top of the door and secure it there using tape.

4 Remove the window regulator assembly as described later in this Section.

13.16 Ensure the lock lever engages with the handle correctly

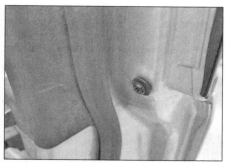

14.1a Undo the screw at the end of the door...

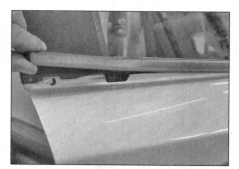

14.1b...and pull up the external weatherstrip

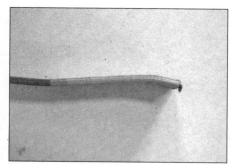

14.2a Shape a strip of steel as shown

14.2b Slide the tool down between the door skin and the window...

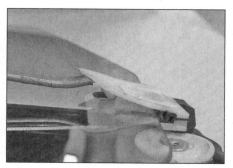

14.2c...and gently push the plastic clamp away from the glass

14.6 Pull the front, and rear rubber guides from the channels

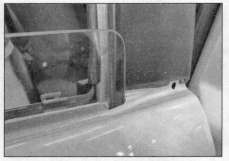

14.7a Position the front edge of the glass outside the front trim...

14.7b...and slide it upwards from place

5 Remove the tape and lower the glass fully into the base of the door.

6 Carefully prise out the front and rear channel rubber guides from the door frame **(see illustration)**.

14.8 Slide up the rear edge and remove the front door glass

7 Manoeuvre the glass from the door **(see illustrations)**.

Front door glass

8 With both clamps released, slide up the rear edge of the glass, and manoeuvre it from the door **(see illustration)**.

Regulator

9 Lower the window glass approximately one third of the way down, then disconnect the battery negative lead as described in Chapter 5A Section 4.

10 Remove the door trim as described in Section 12.

Front door

11 Undo the 3 retaining screws, disconnect the wiring plug and remove the door speaker.

12 Release the door window clamps as described earlier in this Section, then slide the

glass upwards and secure it into the top of the door frame using tape.

13 Undo the bolt securing the lower end of the front window guide channel. Move the channel to one side **(see illustration)**.

14 Undo the 3 screws securing the front door control module **(see illustration)**.

15 Undo the screws and remove the door trim panel support bracket **(see illustration)**.

16 The window regulator and motor assembly is secured by 2 bolts and 4 nuts. Remove the bolts/nuts and manoeuvre the assembly from the door **(see illustrations)**.

Rear door

17 Release the door window clamp as described earlier in this Section, then slide the glass upwards and secure it to the door frame using tape.

18 Undo the 3 screws securing the door control module **(see illustration)**.

14.13 Front window channel retaining bolt

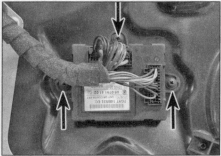

14.14 Door control module retaining screws

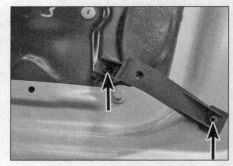

14.15 Door panel support bracket screws

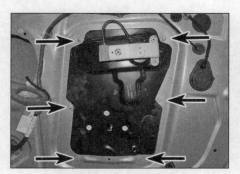

14.16a Undo the nuts/bolts...

14.16b...rotate the window regulator 90°, and manoeuvre it from the door

14.18 Rear door control module retaining screws

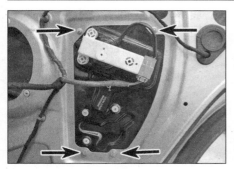

14.19a Undo the nuts/bolts...

14.19b...and manoeuvre the rear window regulator from the door

14.21 Unclip the trim from the door frame

19 The window regulator and motor assembly is secured by 2 bolts and 2 nuts. Remove the nuts/bolts and manoeuvre the assembly from the door **(see illustrations)**.

Rear door fixed quarter window

20 Fully lower the door window glass, then remove the door inner trim panel as described in Section 12.
21 Carefully unclip and remove the door frame trim **(see illustration)**.
22 Pull the door window glass guide rubber forwards from the quarter window frame.
23 Undo the 2 screws, and 2 nuts, then manoeuvre the quarter glass from place **(see illustration)**.

Refitting

24 Refitting is a reversal of removal, noting the following points:
a) *When refitting the door sliding windows, lower the glass squarely until it rests on the clamps, then push the glass downwards until it engages audibly clamps. Check by trying to slide the glass upwards.*
b) *When refitting the glass guide rubbers, lubricate them with silicone spray to aid correct positioning.*
c) *When refitting the rear door fixed quarter glass, tighten the nuts/bolts evenly.*
d) *Check for correct operation of the window/regulator before fully refitting the door inner trim panels.*

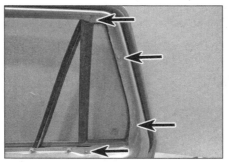

14.23 Quarter glass retaining nuts/screws

3 Disconnect the tailgate wiring plugs, and release the loom from the retaining clips.
4 Prise the wiring loom/hose rubber gaiter/grommet from place, then disconnect the washer hose.
5 Detach the struts from the tailgate as described later in this Section. Have an assistant support the tailgate.
6 Make alignment marks between the tailgate hinges and the vehicle body, then undo the bolts and remove the tailgate.
Warning: The tailgate is extremely heavy!

Struts

7 Using a screwdriver, prise out the retaining clips, and pull the strut from the mounting studs **(see illustration)**.

Refitting

8 Refitting is a reversal of removal.

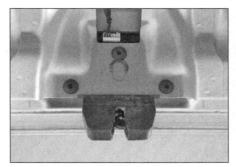

16.3 Tailgate lock retaining bolts

15.7 Prise out the clip a little, and pull the strut from the mounting stud

16 Tailgate lock componets – removal and refitting

Removal

Lock

1 Remove the tailgate inner trim panel as described in Section 24.
2 Disconnect the lock wiring plug.
3 Undo the 3 retaining bolts, and manoeuvre the lock from the tailgate **(see illustration)**.

Release button/handle

4 Remove the tailgate inner trim panel as described in Section 24.
5 Disconnect the release button wiring plug.
6 Undo the 6 retaining nuts, and remove the tailgate handle assembly **(see illustration)**.

15 Tailgate and struts – removal and refitting

Removal

Tailgate

1 Remove the left-hand D-pillar trim as described in Section 24.
2 Pull the weatherstrip from the upper edge of the tailgate aperture, prise out the fasteners and slightly lower the rear section of the headlining. Take great care not to crease the headlining.

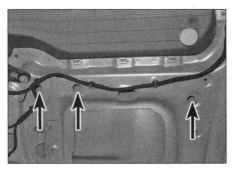

16.6 Tailgate handle retaining nuts locations (left-hand side arrowed)

16.7 Release button clips

Check the condition of the gaskets between the handle and tailgate – renew if necessary.

7 Depress the retaining clips and remove the release button **(see illustration)**. Release the wiring loom as necessary.

Refitting

8 Refitting is a reversal of removal.

17 Central locking system – general information

1 The central locking system fitted to the Freelander 2 is fully integrated with the anti-theft alarm system, and a whole host of other systems on the car. As such, the central locking comes under the control of a multi-function electronic control unit incorporated into the Central Junction box (CJB).

2 The CJU controls the locking and unlocking functions, when triggered by the microswitch in the driver's door lock barrel, by the remote locking keyfob, facia or door switches. The central locking motors are incorporated into the main door lock assemblies, and are not available separately.

3 In conjunction with the anti-theft alarm, the CJB enables the car to be locked as normal, or 'superlocked' (deadlocked) – a state in which the doors cannot be opened even using the interior handles, denying a thief entry even if a window has been smashed.

4 The CJU monitors whether the doors, fuel filler flap and tailgate are open or closed, and uses this information to control a range of other dependent functions, such as interior light delay, door-ajar, and headlights-on.

5 The CJU is located under the drivers side of the facia. Any suspected faults should be referred to a Land Rover dealer or specialist, for testing with the dedicated diagnostic equipment.

18 Windscreen and fixed window glass – general information

These areas of glass are secured by the tight fit of the weatherstrip in the body aperture, and are bonded in position with a special adhesive. The removal and refitting of these areas of fixed glass is difficult, messy and time-consuming task, which is considered beyond the scope of the home mechanic. It is difficult, unless one has plenty of practice, to obtain a secure, waterproof fit. Furthermore, the task carries a high risk of breakage; this applies especially to the laminated glass windscreen. In view of this, owners are strongly advised to have this sort of work carried out by one of the many specialist windscreen fitters.

19 Sunroof – general information

1 A complex tilt and slide sunroof is available as an option on most models.

2 If the electric roof operates slowly, or the motor appears to be struggling, first ensure that this is not down to a lack of maintenance – all the moving parts and slides should be regularly lubricated with light oil (your Land Rover dealer will be able to advise on a suitable product). The sunroof motor draws quite a heavy current – a battery which is low on charge may struggle to open the roof.

3 If the sunroof motor fails to operate, first check the relevant fuse. The motor incorporates an automatic cut-out facility, which cuts the motor if the sunroof encounters an obstruction – the motor may therefore cut out if the mechanism is partially seized. An occasional failure to work could also be due to wear in the sunroof switch. Due to the complexity of the tilt/slide sunroof mechanism, considerable expertise is needed to repair, replace or adjust the sunroof components successfully. Removal of the roof first requires the headlining to be removed, which is a complex and tedious operation in itself, and not a task to be undertaken lightly. Therefore, any problems with the sunroof should be referred to a Land Rover dealer or specialist.

4 If the battery has been disconnected when the sunroof is partially open, it will need to be recalibrated as follows:
a) Switch the ignition on.
b) Press and release the front of the sunroof switch. The sunroof should move to the tilted position.
c) Press and hold the front of the switch for 60 seconds.
d) After 60 seconds, the sunroof will begin to move. Keep the switch pressed until the sunroof has fully opened, then closed.
e) Once the sunroof has stopped moving, the calibration is complete. Release the switch.

20 Mirrors and associated components – removal and refitting

Exterior mirror glass

1 Push the top edge of the mirror glass forwards then downwards, and pull the lower edge rearwards **(see illustration)**.
Caution: We recommend wearing gloves to protect your hands from glass breakage!
2 With the lower edge released, slide the glass upwards from place. Disconnect the wiring plug as the glass is withdrawn.
3 Refitting is a reversal of removal.

Exterior mirror

4 Fully lower the door window glass, then disconnect the battery negative lead as described in Chapter 5A Section 4.
5 Remove the door inner trim panel as described in Section 12.
6 Starting at the front and rear lower edges, carefully prise the door frame trim from place **(see illustration)**. Disconnect the door 'tweeter' speaker wiring plug as the trim is withdrawn.
7 Disconnect the mirror wiring plug(s), undo the nuts and withdraw the mirror from the door **(see illustration)**.
8 Refitting is a reversal of removal.

20.1 Push the top edge downwards, and the lower edge rearwards

20.6 Pull the trim from the door frame

20.7 Door mirror retaining nuts

20.11 Release the 3 clips around the motor

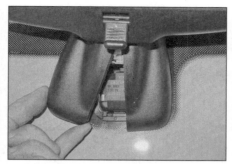

20.13 Prise apart the mirror stem trim

20.14 Rotate the mirror stem clockwise

Exterior mirror motor

9 Remove the mirror glass as described earlier in this Section.
10 Disconnect the mirror motor wiring plug.
11 Undo the central screw, release the 3 retaining clips, and withdraw the motor (see illustration).
12 Refitting is a reversal of removal.

Interior mirror

13 Prise apart the 2 halves of the mirror stem trim (see illustration).
14 Disconnect the wiring plug, then gently twist the mirror stem clockwise (viewed from under the mirror) and detach it from the base (see illustration). No further dismantling of the mirror is recommended – the humidity sensor within the mirror is not available as a separate part.
15 Refitting is a reversal of removal.

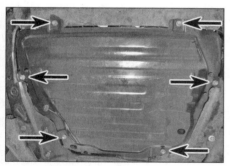

21.6 Remove these fasteners

21 Body exterior fittings – removal and refitting

Rear quarter panel exterior moulding

1 Open the tailgate, and remove the 4 fasteners from the tailgate aperture.
2 Carefully slide the quarter panel mounding rearwards to release the retaining clips.
3 Refitting is a reversal of removal.

Wheelarch liners and body under-panels

4 The various plastic covers fitted to the underside of the vehicle are secured in position by a mixture of screws, nuts and retaining clips. Removal will be fairly obvious on inspection.
5 In order to remove the wheelarch liners, begin by slackening the roadwheel nuts, raising the relevant end of the vehicle and support it securely on axle stands (see 'Vehicle jacking and support'), and removing the roadwheel(s). The liners are retained by a combination of 'scrivets', push-in clips and plastic nuts. Removal will be fairly obvious on inspection.
6 The engine undershield is secured by a total of 6 fasteners (see illustration).

Body trim strips and badges

7 Most of the various body trim strips and badges are held in position with a special

adhesive tape. Removal requires the trim/badge to be heated, to soften the adhesive, and then cut away from the surface. Due to the high risk of damage to the vehicle's paintwork during this operation, it is recommended that this task should be entrusted to a Land Rover dealer.

22 Seats – removal and refitting

Removal

Front seat

1 Slide the front seat fully rearwards, and carefully prise forwards the plastic covers over the seat rail front fixings (see illustration).
2 Undo the retaining bolts at the front of the seat rails.
3 Slide the seat fully forwards, prise up the front edge, then pull the plastic covers rearwards from the ends of the seat rails (see illustration).
4 Undo the retaining bolts at the rear of the seat rails.
5 Disconnect the battery negative lead as described in Chapter 5A Section 4.
6 Carefully prise up the plastic cover from the seat base to access the seat belt anchorage (see illustration).
7 On models with electric seats, remove the

22.1 Pull the covers forwards from the seat rail fixings

22.3 Prise up the front edge, and pull the covers rearwards

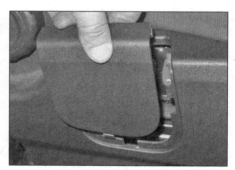

22.6 Slide up the cover from the seat base

22.7a Undo the screw at the inside-front...

22.7b...and rear of the seat base trim

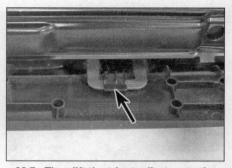

22.7c Then lift the trim to disengage the clip

22.8 Seat belt retaining bolt

22.9 Undo the bolt and disconnect the seat wiring plug

22.11 Remove the rear seat hinge bolts

plastic trim panel from the side of the seat base **(see illustrations)**.

8 Disconnect the wiring plug (where applicable), undo the retaining bolt and detach the seat belt from the seat base **(see illustration)**. Discard the bolt – a new one must be fitted.

9 Working at the front, underside of the seat, undo the retaining bolt and disconnect the seat wiring plug **(see illustration)**.

10 With the help of an assistant, carefully manoeuvre the seat from the cabin.
Caution: The seat is very heavy!

Rear seat

11 Prise off the trims, and undo the hinge fasteners at the front of the cushion **(see illustration)**. Manoeuvre the cushion from the cabin.

12 Pull up the rear of the seat cushion and manoeuvre it from place.

13 To remove the rear seat backrest, remove the cushion, fold down the backrest, and prise the plastic cover inwards over the hinge point **(see illustration)**.

14 Undo the Torx screw at the rear of the hinge bracket **(see illustration)**.

15 Push the hinge fitting inwards, then insert a screwdriver and depress the release mechanism lever to release the fittings **(see illustration)**. Manoeuvre the right-hand backrest from the centre hinge pin.

16 If required, repeat the above procedure on the left-hand backrest, then undo the seat belt stalk bracket retaining nut, and manoeuvre the backrest from place.

Refitting

17 Refitting is a reversal of removal, remembering to tighten the seat/belt retaining

bolts to their specified torque, where given. Note that the rear seat backrest outer hinge brackets will only slot into place once the backrest is in the upright position.

23 Seat belts – removal and refitting

Removal

Front seat belt

1 Disconnect the battery negative lead as described in Chapter 5A Section 4.

2 Remove the B-pillar lower trim panel as described in Section 24.

3 Disconnect the wiring plug, then undo the retaining bolt and manoeuvre seat belt

22.13 Prise the hinge point cover inwards to release the clips

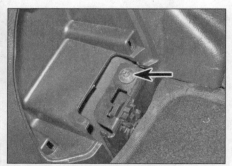

22.14 Remove the screw at the rear of the bracket

22.15 Lever the hinge fitting inwards, and depress the release lever to raise the hinge from the bracket

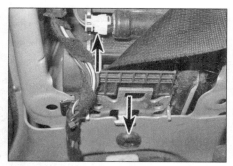

23.3 Front seat belt inertia reel wiring plug and retaining bolt

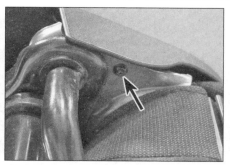

23.5a Undo the screw on the inside of the plastic cover...

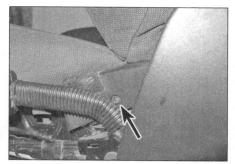

23.5b...and the screw on the outside

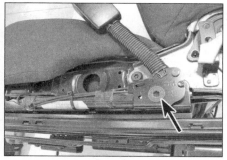

23.6 Seat belt stalk retaining bolt

23.9a Rear outer seat belt inertia reel...

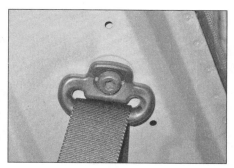

23.9b...and upper anchorage

and inertia reel assembly from place **(see illustration)**. Discard the bolt – a new one must be fitted.

Front seat belt stalk

4 Remove the front seat as described in Section 22.
5 Undo the 2 fasteners and remove the plastic cover over the seat belt stalk mounting **(see illustrations)**.
6 Undo the retaining bolt and detach the seat belt stalk from the seat **(see illustration)**.
7 Unclip the wiring loom and detach the wiring terminals from the seat wiring plug.

Rear outer seat belt

8 Remove the luggage compartment side trim panel and C-pillar trim panel as described in Section 24.

9 Undo the seat belt upper anchorage bolt and the inertia reel bolt **(see illustrations)**.

Rear seat belt stalk

10 Remove the rear seat cushion as described in Section 22.
11 Undo the retaining nuts and remove the seat belt stalks **(see illustration)**.

Rear centre seat belt

12 This is an involved procedure which requires the backrest cover to be partially removed. Begin by removing the backrest as described in Section 22.
13 Unclip the seat belt guide trim **(see illustration)**.
14 Remove both headrests, then using a screwdriver, push-in the clip and pull the right-hand headrest guide tubes upwards from the backrest **(see illustration)**.

15 Unclip the seat cover around the top and right-hand side of the backrest **(see illustration)**.

23.11 Rear seat belt stalk retaining nut

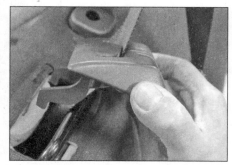

23.13 Prise up the front edge, and manoeuvre the belt guide trim from the backrest

23.14 Push down the upholstery, depress the clip and slide the headrest guide tubes out

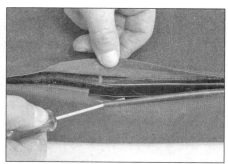

23.15 Unclip the seat cover beading from the backrest

23.16 Prise out the clip and remove the plastic trims

23.17 Cut through the sealant and release the carpet from the backrest

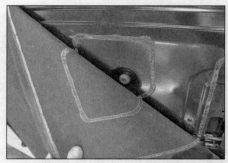

23.18 Rear centre seat belt inertia reel retaining bolt

16 Unclip the plastic trims from around the hooks on the rear of the backrest **(see illustration)**.

17 Using a sharp craft knife, release the carpet from the rear of the backrest to access the inertia reel retaining bolt **(see illustration)**.

18 Undo the retaining bolt and manoeuvre the inertia reel from between the seat backrest and foam **(see illustration)**.

Refitting

19 Refitting is a reversal of removal, noting the following points:

a) *Tighten all fasteners to their specified torque where given.*
b) *Renew the front seat belt inertia reel, upper and lower anchorage bolts*

24 Interior trim – removal and refitting

Interior trim panel – general

1 The interior trim panels are secured using either screws or various types of trim fasteners, usually studs or clips.

2 Check that there are no other panels overlapping the one to be removed; usually there is a sequence to be followed that will become obvious on close inspection.

3 Remove all obvious fasteners, such as screws. If the panel will not come free, it is held by hidden clips or fasteners. These are usually situated around the edge of the panel, and can

be prised up to release them. Note, however, that they can break quite easily, so replacements should be available. The best way of releasing such clips in the absence of the correct type of tool, is to use a large flat-bladed screwdriver. Note in many cases that an adjacent sealing strip (such as the rubber door seal) must be prised back to release a panel.

4 When removing a panel, never use excessive force, or the panel may be damaged. Always check carefully that all fasteners have been removed or released before attempting to withdraw a panel.

5 Refitting is the reverse of the removal procedure; secure the fasteners by pressing them firmly into place, and ensure that all disturbed components are correctly secured, to prevent rattles.

A-pillar trim panel

6 Pull the rubber weatherstrip away from the door pillar in the area adjacent to the pillar trim.

7 Prise out the airbag emblem, and undo the screw revealed **(see illustration)**.

8 Pull the pillar trim panel inwards to release the retaining clips, then lift it from place **(see illustration)**. Note how the lug at the base of the trim panel engages with the facia.

B-pillar trim panel

Lower panel

9 Pull the rubber weatherstrips from the pillar in the area adjacent to the pillar trims.

10 The lower B-pillar trim panel is secured by 4 'push-in' clips. Grasp the panel and pull it into the centre of the vehicle to release the clips **(see illustration)**. If greater access is required, remove the front seat as described in Section 22.

Upper panel

11 Remove the lower B-pillar trim panel as previously described.

12 Slide up the plastic panel from the seat base, undo the retaining bolt and detach the seat belt from the seat **(see illustration 22.6)**. Discard the bolt – a new one must be fitted.

13 Prise out the airbag emblem at the top of the pillar trim, and undo the screw revealed **(see illustration)**.

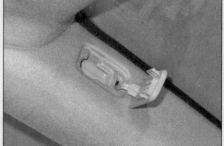

24.7 Remove the screw beneath the emblem

24.8 Note how the A-pillar trim panel engages with the facia lug

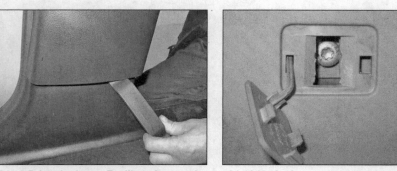

24.10 Prise the lower B-pillar trim panel inwards to release the clips

24.13 Undo the screw beneath the airbag emblem

24.14a Prise out the clips at the lower edge

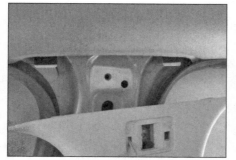

24.14b Pull the B-pillar trim panel downwards to disengage the upper lugs

24.19 Prise out the airbag emblem to reveal the screw

14 Pull the lower edge of the pillar trim inwards to release the clips, and manoeuvre it from place **(see illustrations)**. When refitting, ensure the height adjustment moulding aligns with the lug on the seat belt upper anchorage.

C-pillar trim panel

15 Remove the rear seat cushion as described in Section 22.
16 Undo the rear seat belt lower anchorage bolt. Discard the bolt – a new one must be fitted.
17 Pull away the rubber weatherstrip from the pillar adjacent to the trim panel.
18 Remove the luggage compartment side trim panel as described later in this Section.
19 Prise out the cover at the top of the C-pillar trim panel and remove the screw revealed **(see illustration)**.
20 Pull the trim panel inwards to release the retaining clips **(see illustration)**. Feed the seat belt through the slot as the trim panel is withdrawn.

D-pillar trim panel

21 Remove the spare wheel cover.
22 Remove the luggage compartment side trim panel as described later in this Section.
23 Pull away the rubber weatherstrip from the pillar adjacent to the trim panel.
24 The D-pillar trim panel is secured by 4 'push-in' clips. Pull the trim panel inwards to release the clips **(see illustration)**. Where applicable, disconnect the speaker wiring plug as the panel is withdrawn.

Tailgate trim panel

25 Open the tailgate, and undo the 2 screws in the handle recesses **(see illustration)**.
26 Carefully pull the trim panel away from the lower edge of tailgate to release the retaining clips, then lift the upper edge of the panel towards the top of the tailgate to release the clips **(see illustration)**.

Headlining

27 The rigid headlining is clipped to the roof, and can only be withdrawn once all fittings such as the grab handles, sunvisors, interior light, and related trim panels have been removed, and the door, tailgate and sunroof aperture sealing strips have been prised clear.
28 As with carpet removal, taking out the

headlining is not especially difficult, just time-consuming.

Footwell kick panels

29 Where applicable, undo the screw and remove the bonnet release lever **(see illustration 9.4)**.
30 Pull up the edge of the door sill trim panel.
31 Grasp the upper edge of the kick panel, and pull it rearwards to release the retaining clips, then slide the lower edge forwards to disengage it from the sill trim **(see illustration)**.

Front sill trim panel

32 Remove the lower B-pillar trim panel as described earlier in this Section.
33 Pull away the rubber weatherstrip adjacent to the sill trim panel.

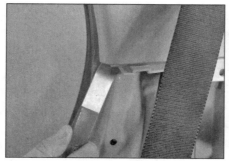

24.20 Pull the C-pillar trim panel inwards to release the clips

24.24 Pull the D-pillar trim panel inwards to release the clips

24.25 Undo the screws in the tailgate panel handle recesses

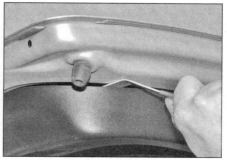

24.26 Carefully ease the panel away from the tailgate

24.31 Pull the upper edge of the panel rearwards

24.37 Prise up the tailgate sill trim panel

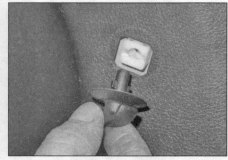

24.39 Rotate the bag hook anti-clockwise

24.44 Pull the luggage compartment side trim panel inwards

34 Pull the front edge of the rear sill trim upwards a little.

35 The front sill trim panel is secured by 4 'push-in' clips. Pull the panel upwards to release the clips, and manoeuvre it from the cabin.

Luggage compartment side trim panel

36 Remove the spare wheel cover
37 Pull the tailgate sill trim panel upwards to release the clips **(see illustration)**.
38 Pull away the rubber weatherstrips from the pillars adjacent to the front, and rear edges of the luggage compartment side trim panel.
39 Rotate the bag hook anti-clockwise and remove it **(see illustration)**.
40 Undo the bolts and remove the loadspace securing rings.

41 Where fitted, remove the luggage compartment extendable cover.
42 Prise out the luggage compartment light lens, and disconnect the wiring plug.
43 Fold the rear seat backrest fully forwards.
44 Carefully pull the luggage compartment side trim panel inwards to release the retaining clips **(see illustration)**.

Glovebox

45 Slide the passengers seat fully rearwards.
46 Release the 'stops' and open the glovebox to the 'service' position **(see illustration)**.
47 Detach the damper from the glovebox **(see illustration)**.
48 Manoeuvre the glovebox from the facia **(see illustration)**.

Overhead console

49 Carefully prise the interior light lens from place.
50 Starting at the rear edge, carefully prise the interior light from the console **(see illustration)**. Disconnect the wiring plugs as the light is withdrawn.
51 Pull the overhead console downwards to release the retaining clips. Disconnect the wiring plugs as the console is withdrawn.

Sunvisors

52 The sunvisor outer mountings are secured by 2 screws **(see illustration)**. Undo the screws and remove the sunvisor.
53 To remove the inner mounting, prise open the cover, and remove the retaining screw revealed **(see illustration)**.

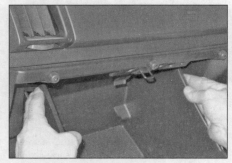

24.46 Squeeze in the sides to release the 'stops'

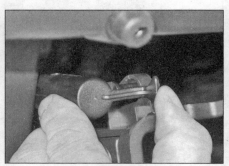

24.47 Unclip the damper...

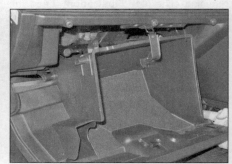

24.48...and pull the glovebox rearwards

24.50 Depress the clips at the rear of the interior light

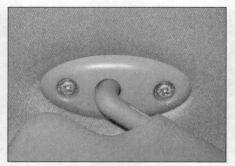

24.52 Undo the screws to release the sunvisor outer mounting

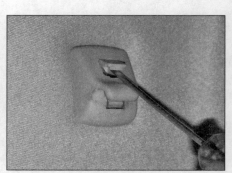

24.53 Prise open the cover and undo the screw

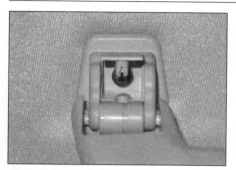

24.54 Prise open the grab handle cover to expose the retaining screw

25.2 Prise out the rear coin tray...

25.3...and the rear storage tray

Grab handles

54 Prise open the covers and undo the retaining screws **(see illustration)**.

Carpet

55 The passenger compartment floor carpet is in one piece (with a separate piece used in the luggage area), and is secured at its edges by screws or clips, usually the same fasteners used to secure the various adjoining trim panels.

56 Carpet removal and refitting is reasonably straightforward, but very time-consuming, due to the fact that all adjoining trim panels must be removed first, as must components such as the seats, the centre console and seat belt lower anchorages.

25 Centre console – removal and refitting

Removal

1 Ensure that the selector lever is in position 'N' (where applicable) then disconnect the battery negative lead as described in Chapter 5A Section 4.

2 Prise up the coin tray from the rear of the console **(see illustration)**.

3 Carefully prise out the rear audio controls (where fitted) and disconnect the wiring plugs.

25.5 Prise up the rear of the lever surround trim panel

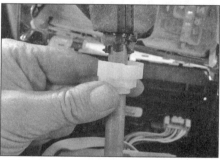

25.6 Rotate the lock ring anti-clockwise

On models without audio controls, prise out the storage tray **(see illustration)**.

4 On manual transmission models, ease the gear change lever gaiter downwards a little, then pull the knob upwards from the lever.

Automatic transmission models

5 Starting at the rear, carefully prise up the selector lever surround trim panel **(see illustration)**.

6 Rotate the lock ring at the base of the lever gaiter anti-clockwise, and slide it down the lever **(see illustration)**. Examine the lock ring for damage or wear – renew if necessary.

7 Cut-away the clip securing the gaiter to the knob **(see illustration)**.

8 Lower the selector lever surround trim panel, then release the 2 retaining clips at the base of the knob, depress the lever position release button, and pull the knob upwards from the lever **(see illustration)**.

All models

9 Carefully prise the Ride and Handling Optimisation switch or storage tray from the front of the gearchange/selector lever surround trim panel **(see illustration)**. Disconnect the wiring plug(s) as the switch is withdrawn (where applicable).

10 Pull up the rear edge of the selector/gearchange lever surround trim panel and

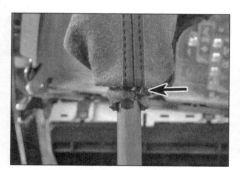

25.7 Cut-way the plastic clip

25.8 Release the clip and the front and rear of the knob

25.9 Prise up the switch to release the clips at the rear edge

25.10 Unclip the printed circuit board from the underside of the selector lever panel

25.11 Remove the handbrake gaiter

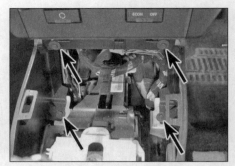

25.12a Remove the 4 screws at the front of the console...

25.12b...and the 4 screws at the rear

26.6 Prise the A-pillar centre trims rearwards

release it from the retaining clip. On automatic transmission models, carefully unclip the printed circuit board from the underside of the panel **(see illustration)**. Do not touch the printed circuit with bare fingers.

11 Carefully prise up the handbrake gaiter, and slide it from the lever grip **(see illustration)**.

12 The console is secured by 4 screws at the front, and 4 screws at the rear. Undo the screws, pull the handbrake lever to its highest position, and with the help of an assistant, lift the console upwards from place **(see illustrations)**. If necessary, slacken the handbrake adjuster nut to allow the handbrake lever to be raised enough. Disconnect any wiring plugs as the console is withdrawn, and unclip the wiring harness.

Refitting

13 Refitting is a reversal of removal, ensuring that all wiring is correctly routed, and does not become trapped as the console is fitted.

---

26 Facia panel assembly – removal and refitting

Removal

1 Have the air conditioning refrigerant circuit evacuated at a dealer service department or suitably equipped repairer.

2 Disconnect the battery negative lead as described in Chapter 5A Section 4.

3 Remove the windscreen wiper motor assembly as described in Chapter 12 Section 13.

4 Remove both front doors as described in Section 11.

5 Remove both A-pillar trim panels as described in Section 24.

6 Pull away the rubber weatherstrips adjacent to the door pillar, then pull the A-pillar centre trim panels rearwards to release the retaining clips **(see illustration)**.

7 Pull up the front edges of the front door sill trim panels each side.

8 Remove both front footwell kick panels as described in Section 24.

9 Remove both front seats as described in Section 22.

10 Remove the selector lever assembly (Chapter 7B Section 2), or gearchange lever assembly (Chapter 7A Section 4).

11 Remove the selector lever/gearchange lever mounting bracket from the floor **(see illustration)**.

12 Undo the fasteners and unclip the footwell centre panels each side **(see illustration)**.

13 Note their fitted positions, and disconnect the wiring pugs from the base of the centre facia controls.

Note: *Cover the fibre optic connectors to prevent dust ingress, and avoid bending them at a radius of less than 30 mm.*

14 Lift the passengers side carpet a little, and disconnect the earth lead attached to the chassis member level with the front edge of the seat **(see illustration)**.

15 Disconnect the wiring plugs as necessary, and release the facia wiring harness from the transmission tunnel.

26.11 Lift the mounting bracket from the floor

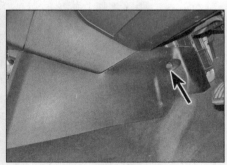

26.12 Undo the screw, and pull the panel inwards to release the clips

26.14 Lift the carpet and disconnect the earth lead

26.16a Release the clips and remove the access cover

26.16b Unclip the cover...

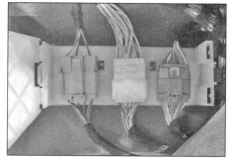

26.16c...and disconnect the wiring plugs revealed

26.16d Depress the clip...

26.16e...fold back the locking catch and disconnect the wiring plug from the base of the fusebox

26.17 Unclip the central, lower air ducts

16 Remove the auxiliary junction box access cover, pull the carpet rearwards, unclip the cover, then disconnect the facia wiring plugs at the passengers end of the facia **(see illustrations)**.
17 Remove the foam insulation beneath the heater controls (where fitted), then unclip and remove the central, lower air ducts from the heater housing **(see illustration)**.
18 Disconnect the wiring plugs from the auxiliary electrical heating element (where applicable) **(see illustration)**.
19 Pull away the drivers side carpet and disconnect the evaporator drain hose from the floor tube **(see illustration)**.
20 Undo the pinch bolt, and pull the steering column lower universal joint upwards from the steering column pinion **(see illustration)**. Discard the bolt – a new one must be fitted.
21 Working in the engine compartment,

disconnect the engine management ECM wiring plugs, then undo the bolts and remove the ECM mounting bracket **(see illustration)**.
22 Undo the retaining nut, and pull the

refrigerant pipes from the expansion valve at the engine compartment bulkhead **(see illustration)**. Note that new pipe seals will be required. Plug the openings to prevent contamination.

26.18 Pull the wiring plugs from the auxiliary heating element

26.19 Disconnect the evaporator drain tube

26.20 Remove the steering column pinch bolt

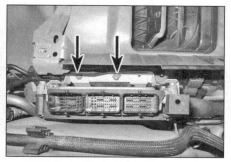

26.21 Undo the nuts and remove the bracket, complete with ECM

26.22 Undo the nut and detach the pipes from the expansion valve

26.23 Rotate the collars anti-clockwise, and disconnect the heater hoses

26.24a Remove the bolt in the centre of the bulkhead...

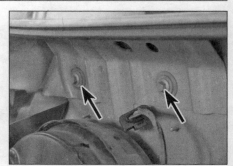

26.24b...and the 2 bolts on the right-hand side

23 Apply clamps to the hoses to minimise coolant loss, then rotate the collars anti-clockwise 90° and disconnect the heater matrix hoses at the engine compartment bulkhead **(see illustration)**.

24 Undo the 3 facia retaining bolts at the engine compartment bulkhead **(see illustrations)**.

25 Prise up the plastic covers at each end of the central facia demister vent, and undo the screws revealed **(see illustration)**.

26 Prise out the caps and undo the bolt each side securing the facia to the door frames **(see illustration)**.

27 The facia is now secured by 2 bolts at each end, and 2 bolts each side of the central transmission tunnel **(see illustration)**. Undo the bolts, and with the help of an assistant, carefully manoeuvre the facia assembly, complete with heater housing, from the cabin. Be prepared for fluid spillage.

Caution: The facia/heater assembly is very heavy!

26.25 Prise up the cover at each end of the demister vent

Refitting

28 Refitting is a reversal of removal, noting the following points:

a) *Tighten the facia fasteners to the specified torque, where given.*

b) *Ensure the various wiring harnesses are correctly routed, and the wiring plugs securely reconnected. Take great care not*

26.26 Remove the bolt in each door frame

to trap any wiring as the facia is installed.

c) *Top up the coolant system as described in Chapter 1 Section 34.*

d) *Have the air conditioning system recharged by a Land Rover dealer or suitably equipped repairer.*

e) *On completion, reconnect the battery and check that all the electrical components and switches function correctly.*

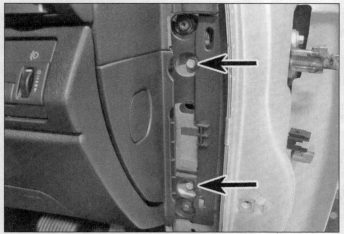

26.27a Undo the bolts at each end of the facia...

26.27b...and the bolts each side of the transmission tunnel

Chapter 12
Body electrical systems

Contents

Degrees of difficulty

Easy, suitable for novice with little experience 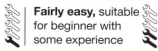	Fairly easy, suitable for beginner with some experience	Fairly difficult, suitable for competent DIY mechanic	Difficult, suitable for experienced DIY mechanic	Very difficult, suitable for expert DIY or professional

Specifications

System type . . . . 12 volt negative earth

Fuses . . . . See inside fusebox lid

Bulbs

	Wattage
Exterior lights:	
Direction indicator	21 PY
Direction indicator side repeater	5 capless
Front foglight	55 H11
Front sidelight	5 capless
Headlight:	
Main beam	55 H7
Dipped beam:	
Halogen	55 H7
Bi-Xenon	35 D1S
High level stop light	16 capless
Number plate light	5 capless
Rear fog light	21 P21
Stop/tail light	21/5 P21/5
Interior lights:	
Door puddle lights	5 capless
Glovebox light	5 capless
Interior lights	5 capless
Luggage compartment lights	5 capless
Vanity lights	5 capless

Torque wrench settings	Nm	lbf ft
Drivers lower air bag	6	4
Impact sensor bolts	10	7
Passengers air bag nuts	10	7
Passengers air bag bracket screws	7	5
Restraint control module screws	10	7

1 General information and precautions

⚠️ *Warning: Before carrying out any work on the electrical system, read through the precautions given in 'Safety First!' at the beginning of this manual and Chapter 5A Section 1.*

1 The electrical system is of the 12 volt negative earth type. Power for the lights and all electrical accessories is supplied by a lead-acid type battery which is charged by the alternator.

2 This Chapter covers repair and service procedures for the various electrical components not associated with engine. Information on the battery, alternator and starter motor can be found in Chapter 5A.

3 It should be noted that prior to working on any component in the electrical system, the battery negative terminal should first be disconnected to prevent the possibility of electrical short circuits and/or fires (see Chapter 5A Section 4).

2 Electrical fault finding – general information

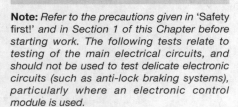

Note: *Refer to the precautions given in 'Safety first!' and in Section 1 of this Chapter before starting work. The following tests relate to testing of the main electrical circuits, and should not be used to test delicate electronic circuits (such as anti-lock braking systems), particularly where an electronic control module is used.*

General

1 A typical electrical circuit consists of an electrical component, any switches, relays, motors, fuses, fusible links or circuit breakers related to that component, and the wiring and connectors which link the component to both the battery and the chassis. To help to pinpoint a problem in an electrical circuit, wiring diagrams are included at the end of this manual.

2 Before attempting to diagnose an electrical fault, first study the appropriate wiring diagram to obtain a complete understanding of the components included in the particular circuit concerned. The possible sources of a fault can be narrowed down by noting if other components related to the circuit are operating properly. If several components or circuits fail at one time, the problem is likely to be related to a shared fuse or earth connection.

3 Electrical problems usually stem from simple causes, such as loose or corroded connections, a faulty earth connection, a blown fuse, a melted fusible link, or a faulty relay (refer to Section 3 for details of testing relays). Visually inspect the condition of all fuses, wires and connections in a problem circuit before testing the components. Use the wiring diagrams to determine which terminal connections will need to be checked in order to pinpoint the trouble-spot.

4 The basic tools required for electrical fault-finding include a circuit tester or voltmeter (a 12-volt bulb with a set of test leads can also be used for certain tests); a self-powered test light (sometimes known as a continuity tester); an ohmmeter (to measure resistance); a battery and set of test leads; and a jumper wire, preferably with a circuit breaker or fuse incorporated, which can be used to bypass suspect wires or electrical components. Before attempting to locate a problem with test instruments, use the wiring diagram to determine where to make the connections.

⚠️ *Warning: Under no circumstances may live measuring instruments such as ohmmeters, voltmeters or a bulb and test leads be used to test any of the airbag circuitry. Any testing of these components must be left to a Land Rover dealer or specialist, as there is a danger of activating the system if the correct procedures are not followed.*

5 To find the source of an intermittent wiring fault (usually due to a poor or dirty connection, or damaged wiring insulation), a 'wiggle' test can be performed on the wiring. This involves wiggling the wiring by hand to see if the fault occurs as the wiring is moved. It should be possible to narrow down the source of the fault to a particular section of wiring. This method of testing can be used in conjunction with any of the tests described in the following sub-Sections.

6 Apart from problems due to poor connections, two basic types of fault can occur in an electrical circuit – open-circuit, or short-circuit.

7 Open-circuit faults are caused by a break somewhere in the circuit, which prevents current from flowing. An open-circuit fault will prevent a component from working, but will not cause the relevant circuit fuse to blow.

8 Short-circuit faults are caused by a 'short' somewhere in the circuit, which allows the current flowing in the circuit to 'escape' along an alternative route, usually to earth. Short-circuit faults are normally caused by a breakdown in wiring insulation, which allows a feed wire to touch either another wire, or an earthed component such as the bodyshell. A short-circuit fault will normally cause the relevant circuit fuse to blow.

Caution: The Freelander electrical system is extremely complex. Many of the ECMs are connected via a 'Databus' system, where they are able to share information from the various sensors, and communicate with each other. For instance, as the automatic gearbox approaches a gear ratio shift point, it signals the engine management ECM via the Databus. As the gearchange is made by the transmission ECM, the engine management ECM retards the injection timing, momentarily reducing engine output, to ensure a smoother transition from one gear ratio to the next. Due to the design of the Databus system, it is not advisable to backprobe the ECMs with a multimeter, in the traditional manner. Instead, the electrical systems are equipped with a sophisticated self-diagnosis system, which can interrogate the various ECMs to reveal stored fault codes, and help pin-point faults. In order to access the self-diagnosis system, specialist test equipment (Land Rover Testbook – or equivalent) is required.

Finding an open-circuit

9 To check for an open-circuit, connect one lead of a circuit tester or voltmeter to either the negative battery terminal or a known good earth.

10 Connect the other lead to a connector in the circuit being tested, preferably nearest to the battery or fuse.

11 Switch on the circuit, bearing in mind that some circuits are live only when the ignition switch is moved to a particular position.

12 If voltage is present (indicated either by the tester bulb lighting or a voltmeter reading, as applicable), this means that the section of the circuit between the relevant connector and the battery is problem-free.

13 Continue to check the remainder of the circuit in the same fashion.

14 When a point is reached at which no voltage is present, the problem must lie between that point and the previous test point with voltage. Most problems can be traced to a broken, corroded or loose connection.

Finding a short-circuit

15 To check for a short-circuit, first disconnect the load(s) from the circuit (loads are the components which draw current from a circuit, such as bulbs, motors, heating elements, etc).

16 Remove the relevant fuse from the circuit, and connect a circuit tester or voltmeter to the fuse connections.

17 Switch on the circuit, bearing in mind that some circuits are live only when the ignition switch is moved to a particular position.

18 If voltage is present (indicated either by the tester bulb lighting or a voltmeter reading, as applicable), this means that there is a short-circuit.

19 If no voltage is present, but the fuse still blows with the load(s) connected, this indicates an internal fault in the load(s).

Finding an earth fault

20 The battery negative terminal is connected to 'earth' – the metal of the engine/transmission and the car body – and most systems are wired so that they only receive a positive feed, the current returning via the

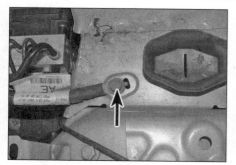

2.20a The main body earth is located at the left-hand rear of the engine compartment

2.20b Other earthing points may be on the tailgate...

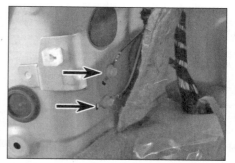

2.20c...left-hand rear quarter panel...

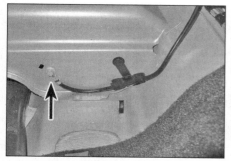

2.20d...beneath the passengers seat...

2.20e...left-hand chassis leg in the engine compartment...

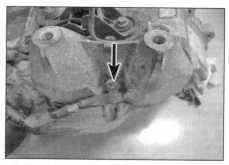

2.20f...left-hand end of the transmission casing

metal of the car body **(see illustrations)**. This means that the component mounting and the body form part of that circuit.

21 Loose or corroded mountings can therefore cause a range of electrical faults, ranging from total failure of a circuit, to a puzzling partial fault. In particular, lights may shine dimly (especially when another circuit sharing the same earth point is in operation), motors (eg, wiper motors or the radiator cooling fan motor) may run slowly, and the operation of one circuit may have an apparently unrelated effect on another. Note that on many vehicles, earth straps are used between certain components, such as the engine/transmission and the body, usually where there is no metal-to-metal contact between components due to flexible rubber mountings, etc.

22 To check whether a component is properly earthed, disconnect the battery and connect one lead of an ohmmeter to a known good earth point. Connect the other lead to the wire or earth connection being tested. The resistance reading should be zero; if not, check the connection as follows.

23 If an earth connection is thought to be faulty, dismantle the connection and clean back to bare metal both the bodyshell and the wire terminal or the component earth connection mating surface. Be careful to remove all traces of dirt and corrosion, then use a knife to trim away any paint, so that a clean metal-to-metal joint is made. On reassembly, tighten the joint fasteners securely; if a wire terminal is being refitted, use serrated washers between the terminal and the bodyshell to ensure a clean and

secure connection. When the connection is remade, prevent the onset of corrosion in the future by applying a coat of petroleum jelly or silicone-based grease or by spraying on (at regular intervals) a proprietary ignition sealer or a water dispersant lubricant.

3   Fuses and relays –
general information

Main fuses

1 The majority of fuses are located on the left-hand side of the engine compartment, whist others are located under the drivers side of the facia, and under the floor covering in the luggage compartment **(see illustrations)**.

3.1a Engine compartment fusebox

3.1b Fusebox under the passengers side of the facia

3.1c Luggage compartment fusebox

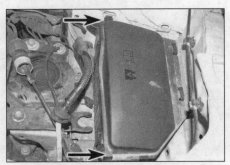

3.2 Engine fusebox cover clips

3.3 Release the clips and remove the fusebox cover

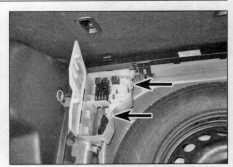

3.4 Luggage compartment fusebox cover clips

2 To gain access to the engine compartment fusebox, release the clips and open the cover (see illustration).

3 To gain access to the passenger cabin fusebox, remove the glovebox as described in Chapter 11 Section 24, and unclip the cover (see illustration).

4 To gain access to the luggage compartment fusebox, lift the loadspace cover, release the clips open the fusebox cover (see illustration).

5 A list of the circuits each fuse protects is given in the Owners Handbook supplied with the vehicle. A pair of tweezers for removing the fuses is also clipped to the engine compartment fusebox. High amperage fuses are located in the main fusebox.

6 To remove a fuse, first switch off the circuit concerned (or the ignition), then pull the fuse out of its terminals. The wire within the fuse should be visible; if the fuse is blown it will be broken or melted.

7 Always renew a fuse with one of an identical rating; never use a fuse with a different rating from the original or substitute anything else. Never renew a fuse more than once without tracing the source of the trouble. The fuse rating is stamped on top of the fuse; note that the fuses are also colour-coded for easy recognition.

8 If a new fuse blows immediately, find the cause before renewing it again; a short to earth as a result of faulty insulation is most likely. Where a fuse protects more than one circuit, try to isolate the defect by switching on each circuit in turn (if possible) until the fuse blows again. Always carry a supply of spare fuses of each relevant rating on the vehicle, a spare of each rating should be clipped into the base of the fusebox.

Relays

9 The majority of relays are located in the engine compartment fusebox.

10 If a circuit or system controlled by a relay develops a fault and the relay is suspect, operate the system; if the relay is functioning it should be possible to hear it click as it is energised. If this is the case the fault lies with the components or wiring of the system. If the relay is not being energised then either the relay is not receiving a main supply or a switching voltage or the relay itself is faulty. Testing is by the substitution of a known good unit but be careful; while some relays are identical in appearance and in operation, others look similar but perform different functions.

11 To renew a relay first ensure that the ignition switch is off. The relay can then simply be pulled out from the socket and the new relay pressed in.

4 Switches – removal and refitting

Note: Disconnect the battery negative lead (see Chapter 5A Section 4) before removing any switch, and reconnect the lead after refitting the switch.

Start control unit

Note: If a new start control unit is to be fitted, use Land Rover diagnostic equipment (or equivalent) to interrogate the unit, and upload the stored data. After refitting the information is used to configure the new control unit.

1 Remove the drivers lower air bag as described in Section 20.

2 Carefully prise the starter control unit trim cover from the facia (see illustration).

3 Undo the 2 retaining screws, and carefully prise the instrument panel surround trim rearwards to release the retaining clips (see illustrations). Disconnect any wiring plugs as the trim is withdrawn.

4 Undo the 2 retaining screws, and remove the steering column lower shroud (see illustration).

4.2 Prise the trim cover from the facia

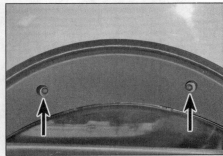

4.3a Undo the 2 screws...

4.3b...and prise the instrument panel surround rearwards

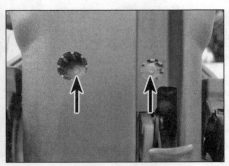

4.4 Lower steering column shroud screws

4.6 Remove the screw at the end of the air bag support bracket

4.7a Undo the lower screws...

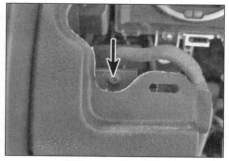

4.7b...upper screw...

5 Set the steering column in its lowest position, then unclip the steering column upper shroud.

6 Remove the Torx bolt securing the left-hand end of the air bag support bracket **(see illustration)**.

7 Undo the 3 retaining screws, disconnect the wiring plug, and remove the start control unit **(see illustrations)**.

8 Refitting is a reversal of removal, but if a new unit has been fitted, it must be configured using Land Rover diagnostic equipment (or equivalent).

Starter inhibitor switch

9 Remove the drivers lower air bag as described in Section 20.

10 Undo the screw and remove the drivers side footwell air duct.

11 Release the retaining clips, and slide the inhibitor switch from the pedal bracket. Disconnect the wiring plug as the switch is withdrawn.

12 Refitting is a reversal of removal. Note that if a new inhibitor switch has been fitted, it must be configured using Land Rover diagnostic equipment (or equivalent).

Headlight switch

13 Using a blunt, flat-bladed tool, carefully prise the switch from the facia **(see illustration)**. Take care not to damage the

4.7c...and manoeuvre the start control unit downwards from place

facia. Disconnect the wiring plug as the switch is withdrawn.

14 Refitting is a reversal of removal.

Stop light switch

15 Renewal of the stop light switch is described in Chapter 9 Section 18.

Central locking/hazard warning light/stop-start switches

16 Remove the heating/air conditioning control panel as described in Chapter 3 Section 9.

17 Undo the 2 retaining screws and detach the switch block from the panel **(see illustration)**.

18 Refitting is a reversal of removal.

4.13 Prise the headlight control switch assembly from the facia

Steering column switches

Complete assembly

19 Remove the steering wheel as described in Chapter 10 Section 16.

20 Disconnect the wiring plugs from the switch assembly.

21 Undo the 2 retaining screws, release the clip, and slide the switch assembly from the steering column **(see illustrations)**.

22 Refitting is a reversal of removal.

Individual switches

23 Undo the 2 retaining screws, and unclip the steering column lower shroud **(see illustration 4.4)**.

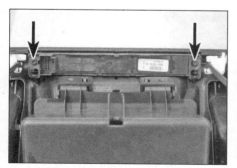

4.17 Hazard warning/central locking/ stop-start switch block retaining screws

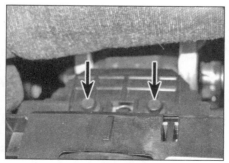

4.21a Undo the 2 screws...

4.21b...lift the clip and slide the switch assembly from the column

4.25 Undo the screws and slide the switch outwards

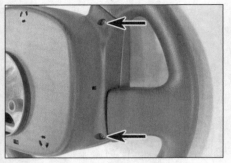

4.28 Steering wheel switch assembly retaining screws

4.30 Prise up the rear of the switch to release the clips

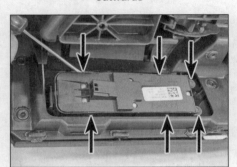

4.35 Undo the screws, release the clips and remove the window switch

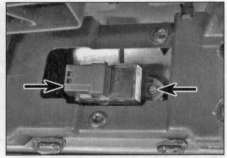

4.36 Passengers/rear door window switch screws

Air conditioning/heating switches

38 These switches are an integral part of the control unit and cannot be renewed. If the switch is faulty seek the advice of a Land Rover dealer.

Courtesy light switches

39 The function of the courtesy light switches is incorporated into the door/boot lid/tailgate lock assembly. To remove the relevant lock, refer to Chapter 11 Section 13.

24 Release the retaining clips and remove the steering column upper shroud.
25 Each switch is retained by 2 screws **(see illustration)**. Undo the screws and remove the relevant switch.
26 Refitting is a reversal of removal.

Steering wheel switches

27 Remove the drivers air bag as described in Section 20.
28 Undo the 2 Torx screws on the front face of the steering wheel, and lift the switch(es) from place **(see illustration)**. Disconnect the wiring plug as the switch is withdrawn.
29 Refitting is a reversal of removal.

Terrain response switch

30 Carefully prise up the switch from the centre console **(see illustration)**. Disconnect the wiring plug(s) as the switch is withdrawn.
31 Refitting is a reversal of removal.

Handbrake-on warning switch

32 Renewal of the switch is described in Chapter 9 Section 18.

Oil pressure warning switch

33 Renewal of the switch is described in Chapter 2A Section 16.

Electric window switches

34 Remove the door inner trim panel as described in Chapter 11 Section 12.

Drivers switch

35 Undo the 2 retaining screws, release the clips and detach the switch from the door trim panel **(see illustration)**.

Passengers switch

36 Undo the 2 retaining screws and remove the switch **(see illustration)**.
37 Refitting is a reversal of removal.

5	Bulbs (exterior lights) – renewal	

General

1 Whenever a bulb is renewed, note the following points.
a) *Remember that if the light has just been in use the bulb may be extremely hot.*
b) *Always check the bulb contacts and holder, ensuring that there is clean metal-to-metal contact between the bulb and its live(s) and earth. Clean off any corrosion or dirt before fitting a new bulb.*
c) *Wherever bayonet-type bulbs are fitted ensure that the live contact(s) bear firmly against the bulb contact.*
d) *Always ensure that the new bulb is of the correct rating and that it is completely clean before fitting it; this applies particularly to headlight/foglight bulbs (see below).*

Headlight

2 Remove the relevant headlight as described in Section 7.
3 Fold down the locking lever, release the 2 clips and remove the plastic cover from the rear of the headlight **(see illustration)**.

Dipped and main beams – Halogen headlights

4 Squeeze and pull the wiring plug/bulbholder from the bulb **(see illustration)**.
5 Manoeuvre the bulb from the headlight.
Note: *When handling the new bulb, use a tissue or clean cloth to avoid touching the glass with the fingers; moisture and grease*

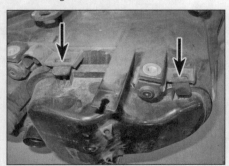

5.3 Fold down the locking lever, and release the clips

5.4 Squeeze top and bottom, then pull the bulbholder from place

5.6 Note how the lug on the bulb engages with the cut-out in the reflector

from the skin can cause blackening and rapid failure of this type of bulb. If the glass is accidentally touched, wipe it clean using methylated spirit.

6 Fit the new bulb, ensuring the cut-outs in the reflector align with the lug on the bulb flange **(see illustration)**.

7 Refitting is a reversal of removal.

Dipped/main beam – Xenon headlights

Note: *On models equipped with Xenon headlights, a Bi-Xenon bulb is fitted, that operates in dipped and main beam modes. This bulb is supplemented by a conventional halogen main beam bulb, which is replaced as described above.*

8 Undo the 2 retaining screws, remove the Xenon bulb unit, and disconnect the wiring plug **(see illustration)**. Note that the bulb is integral with the Xenon unit.

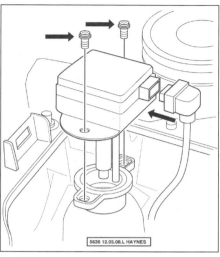

5.8 Undo the 2 screws and remove the Xenon bulb

9 Refitting is a reversal of removal.

Front sidelight

10 Remove the relevant headlight as described in Section 7.

11 Remove the cover from the rear of the headlight assembly **(see illustration)**.

12 Twist the bulbholder clockwise and pull it from the headlight **(see illustration)**.

13 Pull the capless bulb from the holder **(see illustration)**.

14 Refitting is a reversal of removal.

5.11 Pull the rubber cover from the headlight

Front direction indicator

15 Remove the relevant headlight as described in Section 7.

16 Remove the cover from the rear of the headlight assembly **(see illustration 5.11)**.

17 Twist the bulbholder anti-clockwise and pull it from the headlight **(see illustration)**.

18 Push-in the bulb a little, rotate it anti-clockwise and pull it from the bulbholder **(see illustration)**.

19 Refitting is a reversal of removal. Note that the bulb retaining pins are offset – the bulb will only fit in one position.

Side repeater

20 Gently press the side repeater lens forwards, and prise the rear edge from the wing **(see illustration)**. Remove the repeater.

21 Rotate the bulbholder anti-clockwise, and pull it from the repeater **(see illustration)**.

5.12 Twist the sidelight bulbholder and remove it

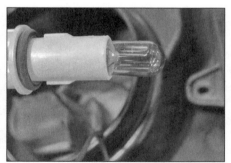

5.13 The bulb simply pulls from the holder

5.17 Direction indicator bulbholder

5.18 Push-in and twist the bulb anti-clockwise to remove it

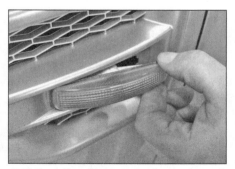

5.20 Push the side repeater forwards, and pull out the rear edge

5.21 Twist and pull the side repeater bulbholder

5.24a Prise the fog light surround from the bumper – pre-facelift models

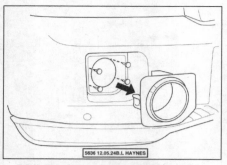

5.24b Fog light surround and screws – post-facelift models

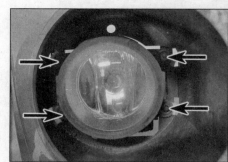

5.25 Front fog light retaining screws

22 Pull the capless bulb from the bulbholder.
23 Refitting is a reversal of removal.

Front fog light

24 Carefully unclip the fog light surround trim from the bumper (see illustrations).
25 Undo the 4 retaining screws, and manoeuvre the fog light from the bumper (see illustration).
26 Disconnect the wiring plug from the bulbholder.
27 Rotate the bulbholder anti-clockwise a little, and detach it from the fog light (see illustration). Note that the bulb is integral with the holder.
28 Refitting is a reversal of removal.

Rear light cluster

29 Remove the relevant rear light unit as described in Section 7.
30 Rotate the relevant bulbholder anti-

5.27 Rotate the bulb/holder anti-clockwise

5.30 Rotate the bulbholder anti-clockwise

clockwise, and pull it from the light unit (see illustration).
31 Push-in the bulb a little, rotate it anti-clockwise and pull it from the bulbholder (see illustration).

32 Refitting is a reversal of removal. If renewing the stop light bulb, the bayonet fitting pins are offset and will only fit in one way.

High-level stop light

33 Carefully unclip the cover from the tailgate to reveal the high-level stop light (see illustration).
34 Using a flat-bladed screwdriver (or similar) press-in the clip at each end of the high-level light unit (see illustration).
35 Close the tailgate, and lift the light unit from place (see illustration).
36 Rotate the bulbholder anti-clockwise and detach it from the light unit (see illustration).
37 Pull the capless bulb from the holder.
38 Refitting is a reversal of removal.

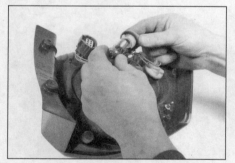

5.31 Push-in the bulb, rotate it anti-clockwise, and pull it from the holder

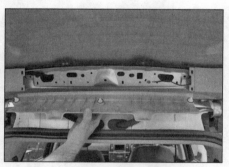

5.33 Prise the cover from the tailgate

5.34 Depress the clip at each end of the light unit

5.35 Lift the light unit from the tailgate

5.36 Twist and pull the bulbholder

5.39 Insert a screwdriver into the slot, compress the clip and prise out the light unit

5.40 Twist and pull the bulbholder

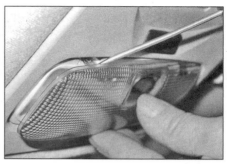

6.2 Prise the interior light lens from the overhead console

Number plate light

39 Compress the retaining clip and prise the light unit from place **(see illustration)**.
40 Rotate the bulbholder anti-clockwise, and detach it from the light unit **(see illustration)**.
41 Pull the capless bulb from the holder.
42 Refitting is a reversal of removal.

6 Bulbs (interior lights) – renewal

General

1 Whenever a bulb is renewed, note the following points:
a) *Remember that if the light has just been in use, the bulb may be extremely hot.*
b) *Always check the bulb contacts and holder, ensuring that there is clean metal-*

to-metal contact between the bulb and its live(s) and earth. Clean off any corrosion or dirt before fitting a new bulb
c) *Always ensure that the new bulb is of the correct rating and that it is completely clean before fitting it.*

Interior lights

2 Carefully prise the light lens from place **(see illustration)**.
3 Pull the bulb from the contacts **(see illustration)**.
4 Refitting is a reversal of removal.

Glovebox light

5 Open the glovebox, and pull the capless bulb from the holder **(see illustration)**.
6 Refitting is a reversal of removal.

Luggage compartment light

7 Squeeze together the clips at each end

and pull the light unit from the side panel **(see illustration)**.
8 Squeeze together the clips and slide the bulbholder from the lens **(see illustration)**.
9 Pull the bulb from the contacts.
10 Refitting is a reversal of removal.

Door 'puddle' lights

11 Carefully prise the light unit from the base of the door trim panel.
12 Pull the bulb from the contacts.
13 Refitting is a reversal of removal.

Footwell lights

14 Reach under the facia and pull the capless bulb from the holder **(see illustration)**.
15 Refitting is a reversal of removal.

Vanity lights

16 Carefully prise the light unit from place **(see illustration)**.
17 Pull the capless bulb from the holder.

6.3 Pull the festoon bulb from the contacts

6.5 Pull the bulb from the holder (shown with the switch removed for clarity)

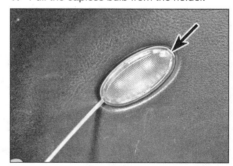

6.7 Squeeze the clip at each end of the luggage compartment light

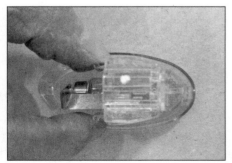

6.8 Squeeze together the clips and slide out the bulbholder

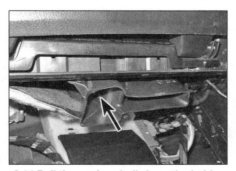

6.14 Pull the capless bulb from the holder

6.16 Prise the vanity light unit from the headlining

7 Exterior light units –
removal and refitting

Headlight

1 Undo the 2 retaining screws along the upper edge of the headlight unit **(see illustration)**.
2 Pull up the locking lever, and manoeuvre the headlight forwards a little **(see illustration)**. Disconnect the wiring plug as the headlight is withdrawn.
3 Refitting is a reversal of removal.

Side repeater light

4 Gently press the light lens forwards, and prise the rear edge from the wing **(see illustration 5.20)**. Twist the bulbholder anti-clockwise, and detach it from the light unit.
5 Refitting is a reversal of removal.

Rear light cluster

6 Open the tailgate, undo the 2 retaining screws, and pull the light cluster rearwards from the vehicle body. Take care not to damage the locating pins **(see illustrations)**. Disconnect the wiring plug as the rear light cluster is withdrawn.
7 Refitting is a reversal of removal.

Front fog light

8 Carefully unclip the fog light surround trim from the bumper **(see illustrations 5.24a and 5.24b)**.
9 Undo the 4 retaining bolts and manoeuvre

the fog light forwards from the bumper **(see illustration 5.25)**. Disconnect the wiring plug as the light is withdrawn.
10 Refitting is a reversal of removal. If required, the aim of the fog light can be adjusted by removing the front section of the wheelarch liner, and rotating the thumb wheel adjuster on the rear of the light unit **(see illustration)**.

High-level stop light

11 Remove the tailgate trim panel as described in Chapter 11 Section 24.
12 Remove the tailgate trim panel as described in Chapter 11 Section 24.
13 Carefully unclip the cover from the tailgate to reveal the high-level stop light **(see illustration 5.33)**.
14 Using a flat-bladed screwdriver (or similar) press-in the clip at each end of the high-level light unit **(see illustration 5.34)**.
15 Close the tailgate, and lift the light unit from place **(see illustration 5.35)**.
16 Disconnect the wiring plug and washer hose from the light unit.
17 Refitting is a reversal of removal.

8 Headlight beam adjustment
– general information

1 Accurate adjustment of the headlight beam is only possible using optical beam setting equipment and this work should therefore be carried out by a Land Rover dealer or suitably-equipped workshop.

2 For reference, the headlights can be adjusted by rotating the adjuster screws on the top of the headlight unit **(see illustration)**.
3 All models have an electrically-operated headlight beam adjustment system which is controlled through the switch in the facia. On these models ensure that the switch is set to the off position before adjusting the headlight aim.

9 Instrument panel –
removal and refitting

Removal

1 Disconnect the battery negative lead as described in Chapter 5A Section 4. **Note:** *If the instrument panel is to be renewed, Land Rover state that their dedicated test equipment must be connected, and data downloaded from the panel prior to disconnecting the battery. Consult your Land Rover dealer or specialist.*
2 Remove the drivers lower air bag as described in Section 20.
3 Carefully prise the starter control unit trim cover from the facia **(see illustration 4.2)**.
4 Release the steering column adjustment handle, then undo the 2 retaining screws and unclip the column lower shroud **(see illustration 4.4)**.
5 Set the column to its lowest position, release the 2 clips and remove the column upper shroud.
6 Undo the 2 retaining screws, and gently prise

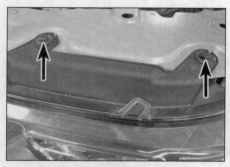

7.1 Headlight retaining screws

7.2 Pull up the locking lever

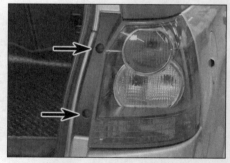

7.6a Undo the rear light retaining screws (arrowed)

7.6b Pull the light unit rearwards, to release the retaining pins (arrowed)

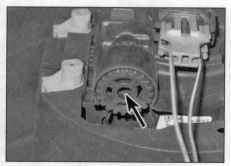

7.10 Insert an Allen key and rotate to adjust the fog light aim

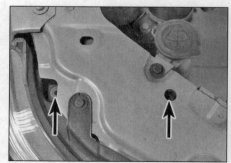

8.2 Headlight aim adjuster screws

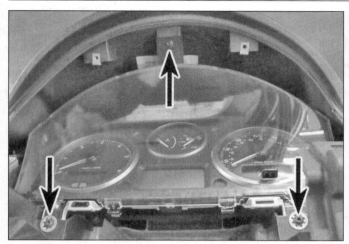

9.7 Instrument panel retaining screws

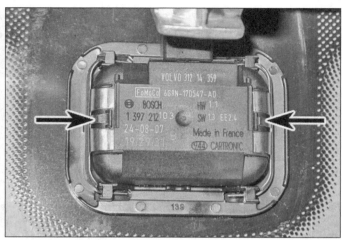

10.2 Pivot the retaining clips outwards

the instrument panel surround trim rearwards to release the clips (see illustrations 4.3a and 4.3b). Disconnect the wiring plug(s) as the surround trim is withdrawn.

7 Undo the 3 retaining screws, and manoeuvre the instrument panel rearwards from the facia (see illustration). Disconnect the wiring plug as the panel is withdrawn.

8 Should a fault occur with the instrument panel, it would appear that the complete assembly must be renewed – consult a Land Rover dealer or specialist.

Refitting

9 Refitting is a reversal of removal. If the panel has been renewed, it will need to be configured using Land Rover diagnostic equipment (or equivalent).

11.3 Release the clips and remove the cover

10 Rain sensor – removal and refitting

1 Remove the interior mirror as described in Chapter 11 Section 20.

2 Pivot the retaining clips outwards and detach the rain sensor from the windscreen (see illustration). Disconnect the wiring plug as the sensor is withdrawn.

3 Refitting is a reversal of removal.

11 Central Junction Box (CJB) – removal and refitting

Removal

1 Disconnect the battery negative lead as described in Chapter 5A Section 4. Note: If the CJB is to be renewed, it must be interrogated using Land Rover diagnostic equipment (or equivalent) prior to battery disconnection. The stored data is used to configure the new unit.

2 Remove the passengers glovebox as described in Chapter 11 Section 24.

3 Undo the 2 fasteners and remove the cover from the CJB (see illustration).

4 Note their fitted positions, then disconnect the wiring plugs from the CJB (see illustrations).

5 Release the retaining clip at the upper edge, and manoeuvre the CJB from the mounting bracket.

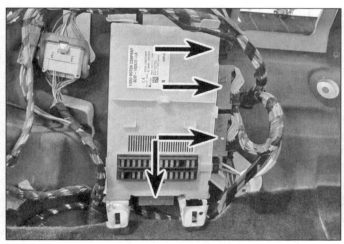

11.4a CJB wiring plugs

11.4b To disconnect the wiring plugs, depress the catch and fold open the lock lever

12.2 Release the clip each side and pull the air cowling forwards

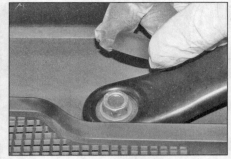

13.2 Prise up the cap and undo the spindle nut

13.3 If necessary, use a puller to remove the wiper arm

Refitting

6 Refitting is a reversal of removal. Note that if a new unit has been fitted, it must be configured using Land Rover diagnostic equipment (or equivalent).

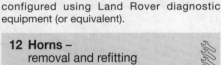
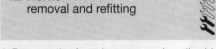

12 Horns – removal and refitting

1 Remove the front bumper as described in Chapter 11 Section 6.
2 Where fitted, carefully prise the condenser air cowling forwards to release the clips **(see illustration)**.
3 Undo the retaining nut and remove the horns assembly. Disconnect the wiring plug as the assembly is withdrawn.
4 Refitting is a reversal of removal.

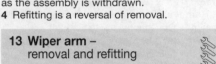

13 Wiper arm – removal and refitting

Removal

1 Operate the wiper motor, then switch it off so that the wiper arm returns to the at-rest ('parked') position.

Front wiper arm

2 Prise up the plastic cap and unscrew the wiper spindle nut **(see illustration)**.
3 Lift the blade off the glass and pull the wiper arm off its spindle. If necessary the arm can be

14.2a Unclip the battery cover...

13.4 Open the cover to reveal the spindle nut

levered off the spindle using a suitable flat-bladed screwdriver or suitable puller **(see illustrations)**.

Rear wiper arm

4 Pivot up the plastic cover, and slacken the wiper arm spindle nut **(see illustration)**.
5 Lift the blade from the glass and pull the wiper arm from the spindle. It is common for the arm to be corroded onto the spindle, in which case a suitable puller will be required to remove it.

Refitting

Front wiper arm

6 Locate the arm on the spindle, setting the end of the blade approximately 35 mm above the end of the scuttle trim panel **(see illustration)**. Tighten the spindle nut securely, and refit the spindle cap.

Rear wiper arm

7 Locate the arm on the spindle, align the

14.2b...and the cover over the fluid reservoir

13.6 Set the end of the wiper blade 35 mm above the end of the scuttle trim panel

inner end of the blade with the mark on the windscreen. Tighten the spindle nut securely, and refit the spindle cover.

14 Windscreen wiper motor and linkage – removal and refitting

Removal

Front windscreen wiper motor

1 Remove the wiper arms as described in Section 13.
2 Release the retaining clips, and remove the battery cover, and the plastic cover over the brake fluid reservoir **(see illustrations)**.
3 Undo the centre screws, prise out the 5 plastic expansion rivets, and with the help of an assistant, pull the scuttle trim panel upwards from the base of the windscreen **(see**

14.3a Remove the plastic expansion rivets at the front edge...

14.3b...then pull the scuttle trim panel upwards from the base of the windscreen

14.4 Windscreen wiper motor/linkage retaining bolts

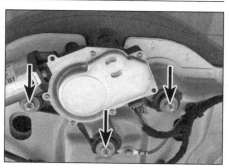

14.7 Rear wiper motor retaining nuts

illustrations). Take care not to damage the locating pins on the underside of the panel.
4 Undo the 2 retaining bolts, and manoeuvre the windscreen wiper motor and linkage assembly from place **(see illustration)**. Disconnect the wiring plug as the assembly is withdrawn. No further dismantling is recommended.

Rear screen wiper motor

5 Remove the rear wiper arm as described in Section 13.
6 Remove the tailgate inner trim panel as described in Chapter 11 Section 24.
7 Disconnect the wiring plug, undo the 3 retaining nuts, and manoeuvre the tailgate wiper motor from place **(see illustration)**. No further dismantling is recommended.

Refitting

8 Refitting is a reversal of removal.

---

15 Windscreen/tailgate washer system components –
removal and refitting

Washer reservoir

Removal

1 One reservoir provides washer fluid for the front windscreen, tailgate, and headlamp washers (where fitted). The reservoir is located behind the right-hand end of the front bumper.
2 Remove the front bumper as described in Chapter 11 Section 6.
3 Note their fitted positions, then disconnect the fluid supply hose from the top of the

15.7 Disconnect the hoses and wiring plugs from the pumps

reservoir, and the hoses from the pump(s). Be prepared for fluid spillage.
4 Undo the 3 retaining bolts, and manoeuvre the reservoir from the wheelarch aperture.

Refitting

5 Refitting is a reversal of removal.

Windscreen and headlight washer pumps – removal and refitting

Removal

6 One pump provides fluid to the front and rear windscreens, and another pump supplies fluid to the headlight washers (where fitted). Begin by removing the right-hand front roadwheel and wheelarch liner as described earlier in this Section.
7 Note their fitted positions, then disconnect the wiring plug and hoses from the relevant pump. The outermost pump is for the

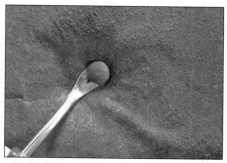

15.10a Prise out the clips and fold up the soundproofing

headlight washers, and the innermost for the windscreens **(see illustration)**.
8 Pull the relevant pump from the fluid reservoir. Be prepared for fluid spillage. Examine the rubber sealing grommet, and renew if necessary.

Refitting

9 Refitting is a reversal of removal.

Jets

10 To remove the front windscreen washer jets, open the bonnet, unclip the soundproofing, disconnect the washer hose, depress the clip and remove the jet **(see illustrations)**.
11 The rear washer jet is integral with the high-level brake light. Removal of the brake light is described in Section 7.
12 To remove a headlight washer jet, remove the front bumper (Chapter 11 Section 6), then disconnect the hose, slide out the clip, and detach the jet from the bumper **(see illustration)**.

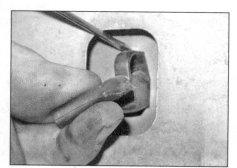

15.10b Depress the clip...

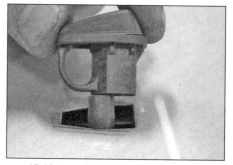

15.10c...and remove the washer jet

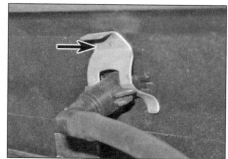

15.12 Headlight washer jet retaining clip

16.2 Starting at the front edge, prise up and remove the speaker grille

16.3a Undo the 6 retaining screws...

16.3b...and prise the central panel rearwards

16 Infotainment units – removal and refitting

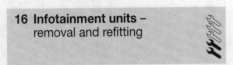

Caution: Do not bend the fibre optic cables at a radius of less than 25 mm.

Audio unit

1 Unclip the rubber mat from the central storage compartment and oddment tray in the facia.
2 Carefully prise up the facia speaker grille **(see illustration)**.
3 Undo the 6 retaining screws, and pull the facia central panel rearwards to release the clips **(see illustrations)**. Disconnect the wiring plugs as the panel is withdrawn.
4 The audio unit is secured by 4 screws **(see illustration)**. Undo the screws, manoeuvre the unit rearwards from the facia, and disconnect the wiring plugs.
5 Refitting is a reversal of removal.

Video display unit

6 Remove the facia central panel as described earlier in this Section.
7 Undo the 2 retaining screws, manoeuvre the video display unit from the facia and disconnect the various wiring plugs.
8 Refitting is a reversal of removal. Note that if a new unit is fitted, it must be configured using Land Rover diagnostic equipment (or equivalent).

16.4 Undo the screws and pull the audio unit rearwards

Bluetooth module

9 Remove the right-hand luggage compartment side trim panel as described in Chapter 11 Section 24.
10 Note their fitted positions, disconnect the wiring plugs, undo the 4 retaining screws, and remove the Bluetooth module.
11 Refitting is a reversal of removal. If a new module has been fitted, it must be configured using Land Rover diagnostic equipment (or equivalent).

Navigation system DVD unit

12 Slide the passengers seat fully rearwards, then undo the 4 retaining bolts, and move the unit rearwards a little to access the wiring plugs.
13 Note their fitted locations, disconnect the wiring plugs, and manoeuvre the unit from place.
14 Refitting is a reversal of removal. If a new unit has been fitted, it must be configured using Land Rover diagnostic equipment (or equivalent).

Subwoofer amplifier

15 Remove the Bluetooth module as described earlier in this Section.
16 Note their fitted positions, disconnect the wiring plugs, unto the 4 retaining bolts, and remove the subwoofer amplifier complete with its mounting bracket.
17 Refitting is a reversal of removal.

Satellite radio tuner

18 Remove the left-hand luggage

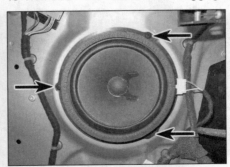

17.2 Door speaker retaining screws

compartment side trim panel as described in Chapter 11 Section 24.
19 Note their fitted positions, disconnect the various wiring plugs, undo the 3 retaining nuts and manoeuvre the tuner from place.
20 Refitting is a reversal of removal. If a new unit has been fitted, it must be configured using Land Rover diagnostic equipment (or equivalent).

AM/FM antenna

21 The AM/FM antenna is integral with the right-hand rear quarter panel window, and cannot be renewed separately.
22 The amplifier for the antenna is located above the right-hand rear quarter panel window, behind the headlining. For this reason, we recommend replacement of the amplifier be entrusted to a Land Rover dealer or experienced specialist.

17 Speakers – removal and refitting

Door speaker

1 Remove the door inner trim panel as described in Chapter 11 Section 12.
2 Disconnect the wiring plug, undo the 3 retaining screws, and remove the speaker **(see illustration)**.
3 Refitting is a reversal of removal.

Subwoofer

4 Remove the right-hand luggage compartment side trim panel as described in Chapter 11 Section 24.
5 Lift out the spare wheel, and the storage tray beneath.
6 Undo the 4 retaining nuts, disconnect the wiring plug, and lift the subwoofer assembly from the luggage compartment floor.
7 Refitting is a reversal of removal.

Facia speaker

8 Carefully prise the speaker grille upwards from the facia **(see illustration 16.2)**.
9 Undo the retaining screws, lift the speaker from place and disconnect the wiring plug.
10 Refitting is a reversal of removal.

18 Anti-theft alarm – general information

The Freelander 2 models are equipped with a sophisticated anti-theft alarm and immobiliser system. Should a fault develop, the system's self-diagnosis facility should be interrogated using dedicated test equipment. Consult your Land Rover dealer or suitably-equipped specialist.

19 Airbag system – general information and precautions

1 The models covered by this manual are equipped with a driver's airbag mounted in the centre of the steering wheel, a drivers lower airbag mounted under the facia, a passenger's airbag located behind the facia, two head airbags located in each A-pillar/headlining, and two airbags located in each front seat. The airbag system comprises of the airbag unit(s) (complete with gas generators), impact sensors, the control unit and a warning light in the instrument panel.
2 The airbag system is triggered in the event of a heavy frontal or side impact above a predetermined force; depending on the point of impact. The airbag(s) is inflated within milliseconds and forms a safety cushion between the cabin occupants and the cabin interior, and therefore greatly reduces the risk of injury. The airbag then deflates almost immediately.
3 Every time the ignition is switched on, the airbag control unit performs a self-test. The self-test takes approximately 2 to 6 seconds and during this time the airbag warning light on the facia is illuminated. After the self-test has been completed the warning light should go out. If the warning light fails to come on,

remains illuminated after the initial period, or comes on at any time when the vehicle is being driven, there is a fault in the airbag system. The vehicle should be taken to a Land Rover dealer for examination at the earliest possible opportunity.

⚠️ *Warning: Before carrying out any operations on the airbag system, disconnect the battery negative terminal, and wait for at least 2 minutes. This will allow the capacitors in the system to discharge. When operations are complete, make sure no one is inside the vehicle when the battery is reconnected. Note that the airbag(s) must not be subjected to temperatures in excess of 90°C (194°F). When the airbag is removed, ensure that it is stored the correct way up to prevent possible inflation (padded surface uppermost).*
• *The airbags and control unit are both sensitive to impact. If either is dropped or damaged they should be renewed.*
• *Disconnect the airbag control unit wiring plug prior to using arc-welding equipment on the vehicle.*
• *Do not allow any solvents or cleaning agents to contact the airbag assemblies.*

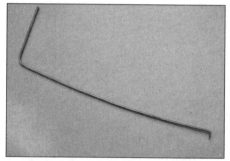

20.2a Shape a length of 2.5 mm diameter weld rod...

They must be cleaned using only a damp cloth.

20 Airbag system components – removal and refitting

Caution: Refer to the warnings in Section 19 before carrying out the following operations.
1 Disconnect the battery negative lead as described in Chapter 5A Section 4.

Drivers airbag

2 Insert Land Rover tool No. 501-106 into the hole in the left-, or right-hand side of the steering wheel boss, and release the airbag retaining clip. Repeat on the other side of the steering wheel boss. In the absence of the tool, use a length of weld rod, 2.5 mm diameter shaped as shown (see illustrations).
3 With the retaining clips released, ease the airbag rearwards from the steering wheel, and disconnect the wiring plugs (see illustrations).
4 Note that the airbag must not be knocked or dropped and should be stored the correct way up with its padded surface uppermost.

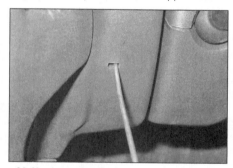

20.2b...insert it into the hole each side of the steering wheel boss...

20.2c...hook it around the spring clip, then pull the rod to release the air bag

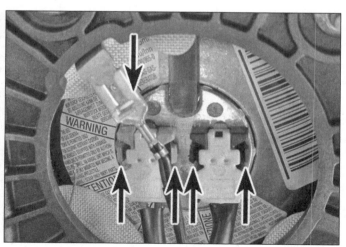

20.3 Squeeze together the clips, disconnect the wiring plugs, and the earth connection

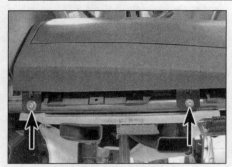

20.7a Undo the 2 screws at the lower edge...

20.7b...and the screw each side of the steering column

20.8 Disconnect the airbag wiring plug

5 On refitting reconnect the wiring connectors and seat the airbag unit in the steering wheel, making sure the wire does not become trapped, then press the airbag into the wheel until the retaining clips 'click' into place. Reconnect the battery as described in Chapter 5A Section 4.

Drivers lower airbag

6 Move the steering wheel to the fully raised position.
7 Undo the 4 retaining screws, then carefully pull the lower airbag assembly rearwards to release the retaining clips (see illustrations).
8 Disconnect the wiring plugs as the airbag is withdrawn (see illustration).
9 If required, release the clips and detach the lighting control switch from the airbag.
10 Note that the airbag must not be knocked

or dropped and should be stored the correct way up with its padded surface uppermost.
11 Refitting is a reversal of removal. Reconnect the battery as described in Chapter 5A Section 4.

Passengers airbag

12 Remove the passengers glovebox as described in Chapter 11 Section 24.
13 Disconnect the wiring plugs from the airbag, and the glovebox light (see illustration).
14 Undo the 2 bolts, 1 nut, and remove the rear airbag support bracket (see illustration).
15 Undo the 6 retaining nuts, and 2 bolts, then manoeuvre the airbag, complete with lower support bracket, from the facia (see illustrations).
16 If required, detach the lower support bracket from the airbag.

17 Note that the airbag must not be knocked or dropped and should be stored the correct way up with its padded surface uppermost.
18 Refitting is a reversal of removal, tightening the fasteners to their specified torque where given.

Seat airbags

19 Removal of the seat airbags requires the seat upholstery to be removed. This is a complex task, requiring patience and experience. Consequently, we recommend this is entrusted to a Land Rover dealer or specialist.

Headlining airbags

20 On each side of the passenger cabin, a Head Protection Airbag (HPS) is fitted. The airbag runs from the lower part of the windscreen pillar to the D-pillar. To remove the airbag, the entire headlining must be removed. This task is outside the scope of the DIY'er, and therefore we recommend that the task be entrusted to a Land Rover dealer or specialist.

Restraint control module (RCM)

21 Remove the centre console as described in Chapter 11 Section 25.
22 Using a sharp craft knife, carefully cut the carpet above the RCM for access. Pull the carpet aside.
23 Disconnect the RCM wiring plugs, undo the 4 retaining nuts, and manoeuvre the RCM from position (see illustration).

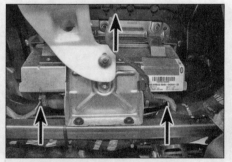

20.13 Disconnect the wiring plug from each end of the airbag, and the glovebox light

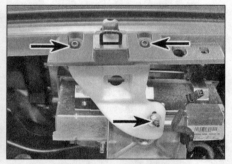

20.14 Undo the bolts, nut, and remove the support bracket

20.15a The passengers airbag is secured by 2 bolts, 3 nuts at the rear edge...

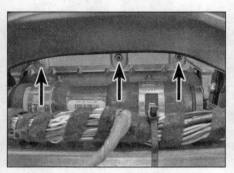

20.15b...and 3 nuts at the front edge

20.23 Disconnect the wiring plugs from the rear of the RCM

20.25 An impact sensor is fitted each side of the bonnet slam panel

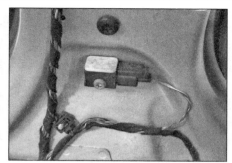

20.29 B-pillar impact sensor

20.35 The yellow marker should be visible through the window in the rotary contact unit

24 Refitting is a reversal of removal, tightening the RCM nuts to the specified torque. Note that if a new RCM has been fitted, it must be configured using Land Rover diagnostic equipment (or equivalent).

Impact sensors

Front sensor

25 Open the bonnet. The sensor is fitted to the rear face of the bonnet slam panel **(see illustration)**.
26 Disconnect the wiring plug, undo the retaining bolt, and remove the sensor.
27 Refitting is a reversal of removal, tightening the sensor bolt to the specified torque.

B-pillar sensor

28 Remove the front door sill trim panel as described in Chapter 11 Section 24.
29 Disconnect the wiring plug, undo the retaining bolt, and remove the sensor **(see illustration)**.
30 Refitting is a reversal of removal, tightening the sensor bolt to the specified torque.

C-pillar sensor

31 Remove the luggage compartment side trim panel as described in Chapter 11 Section 24.
32 Disconnect the wiring plug, undo the retaining bolt, and remove the sensor.
33 Refitting is a reversal of removal, tightening the sensor bolt to the specified torque.

Rotary contact unit (clockspring)

34 The rotary contact unit is integral with the steering column switch assembly. Remove the assembly as described in Section 4.
35 If the central position of the rotary contact unit has been lost, gently turn the clockspring clockwise to the stop, then 3.25 turns anti-clockwise. In this position a yellow marker should be visible through the window on the unit face **(see illustration)**.

21 Parking aid system – general information and component renewal

General information

1 In order to aid parking, all models in the Freelander 2 range can be equipped with a system that informs the driver of the distance between the vehicle, and any vehicle/obstacle behind whilst reversing or manoeuvring forwards. The system consists of several ultrasonic sensors mounted in the bumpers which measure the distance between themselves and the nearest object. The distance is indicated by an audible signal in the passenger cabin. The closer the object, the more frequent the signals, until at less than 30 cm, the signal becomes continuous.

Electronic control module

2 Remove the left-hand side luggage compartment side trim panel as described in Chapter 11 Section 24.
3 Disconnect the wiring plugs, undo the 2 retaining bolts, and remove the control module **(see illustration)**.
4 Refitting is a reversal of removal. Note that if a new control module is fitted, it must

21.3 Parking aid control module

be configured using Land Rover diagnostic equipment (or equivalent).

Ultrasonic sensors

Front sensors

5 To remove the inner sensors, remove the bumper as described in Chapter 11 Section 6.
6 To remove the outer sensors, undo the fasteners and remove the lower, front section of the wheelarch liner.
7 Press apart the retaining clips, and pull the sensor from place **(see illustration)**. Disconnect the wiring plug as the sensor is withdrawn.

Rear sensors

8 To remove the inner sensors, raise the rear of the vehicle and support it securely on axle stands (see 'Vehicle jacking and support').
9 To remove the outer sensors, undo the fasteners and remove the rear section of the wheelarch liner.
10 Press apart the retaining clips, and pull the sensor from place. Disconnect the wiring plug as the sensor is withdrawn.

All sensors

11 If a replacement sensor is to be painted, ensure that only the 3.0 to 5.0 mm of the protruding sensor tip is painted. If more is painted, the sensor may not function correctly.

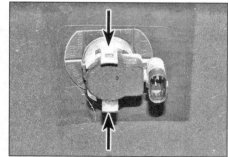

21.7 Pull apart the clips to release the sensor

Exterior lighting 2007 – 2012

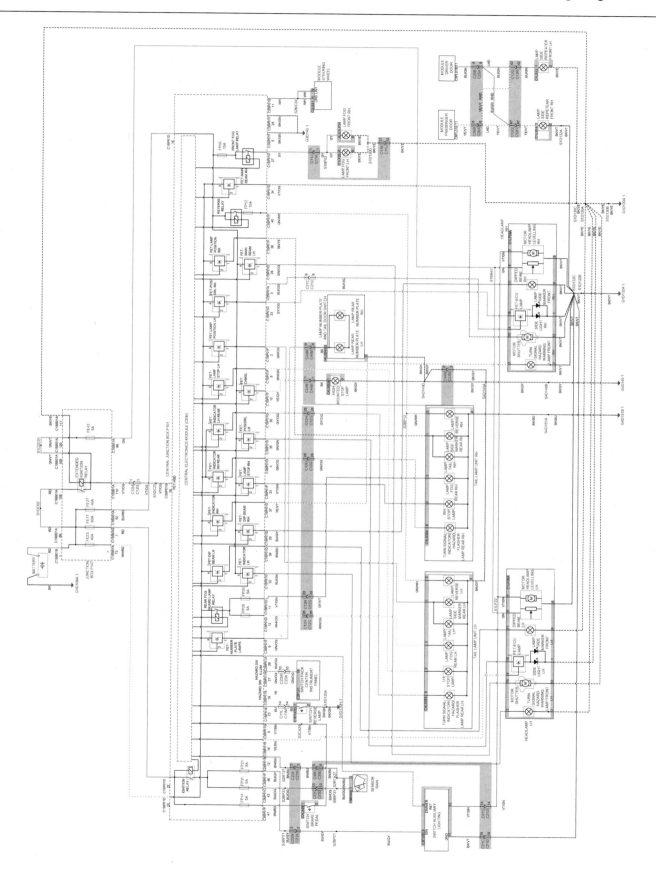

Exterior lighting 2013 – 2014

High intensity discharge lights 2007 – 2012

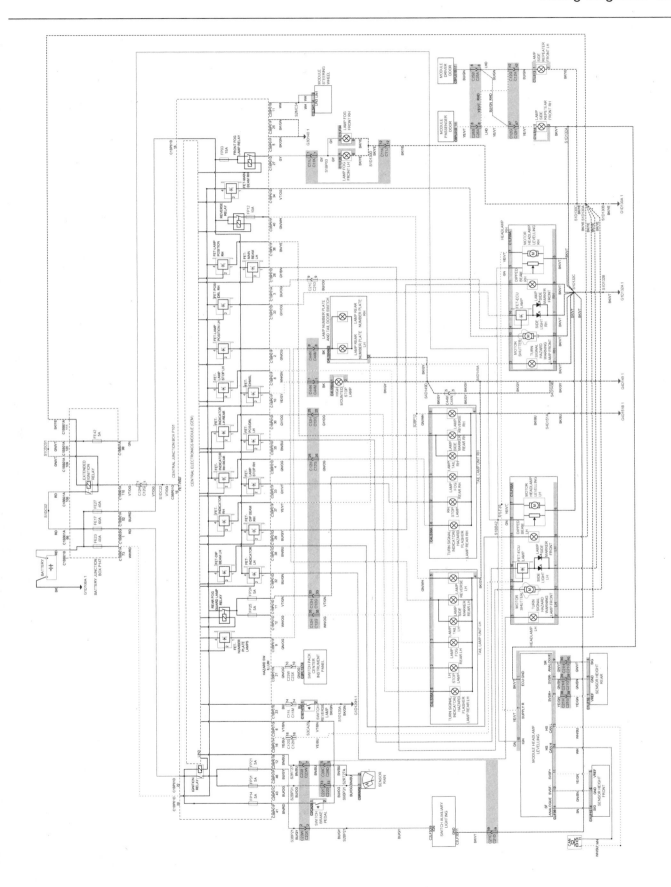

High intensity discharge lights 2013 – 2014

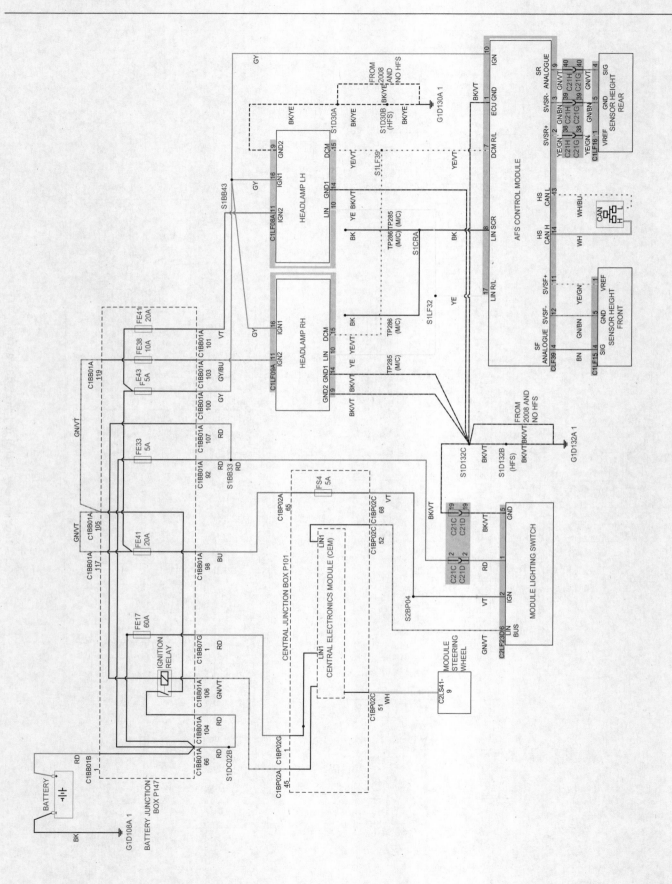

Adaptive lighting system

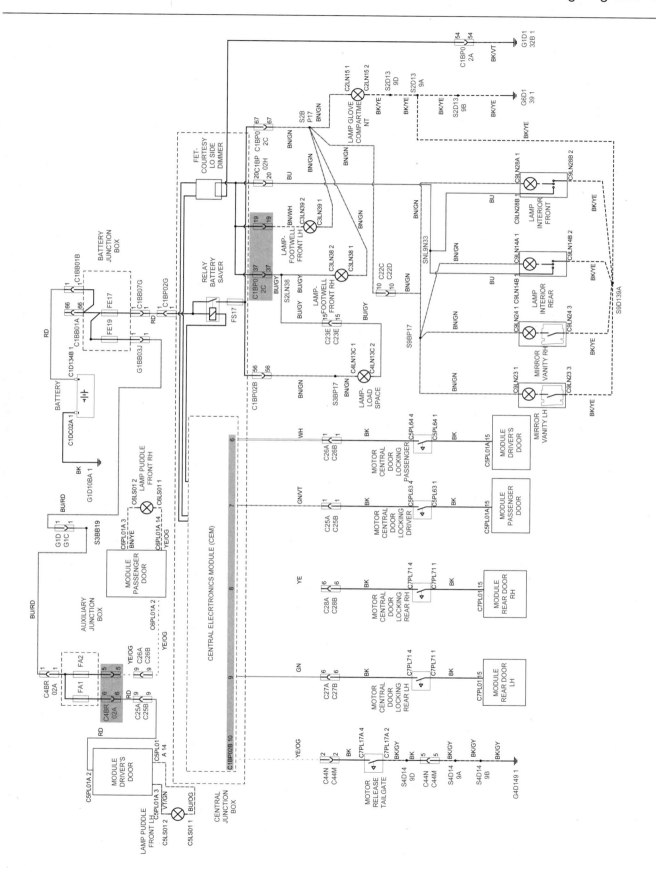

Interior lights upto VIN 321214

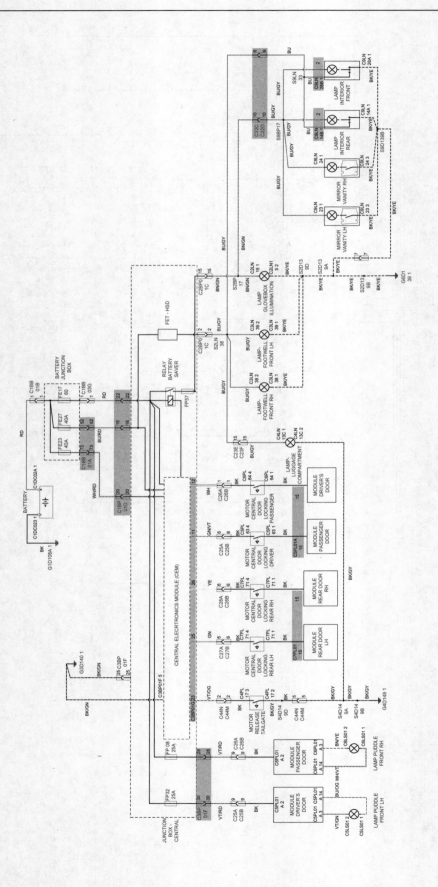

Interior lights from VIN 321215

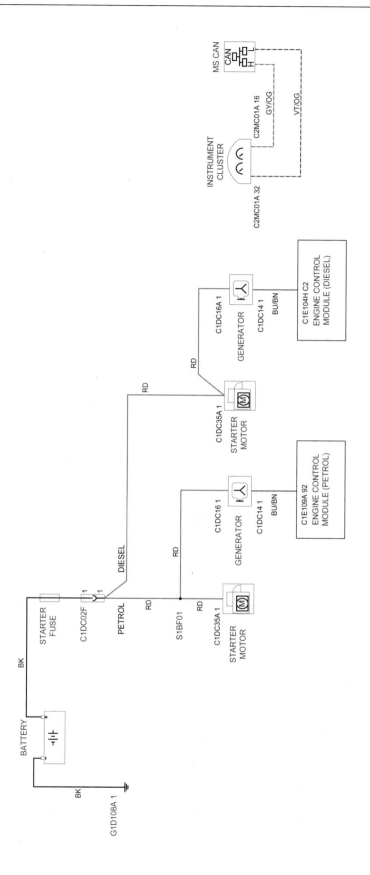

Charging system VIN 000201 - 148519

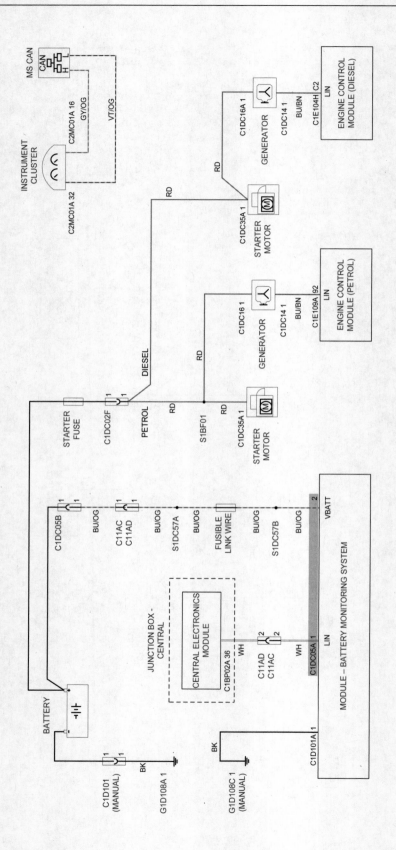

Charging system VIN 148519 - 321214

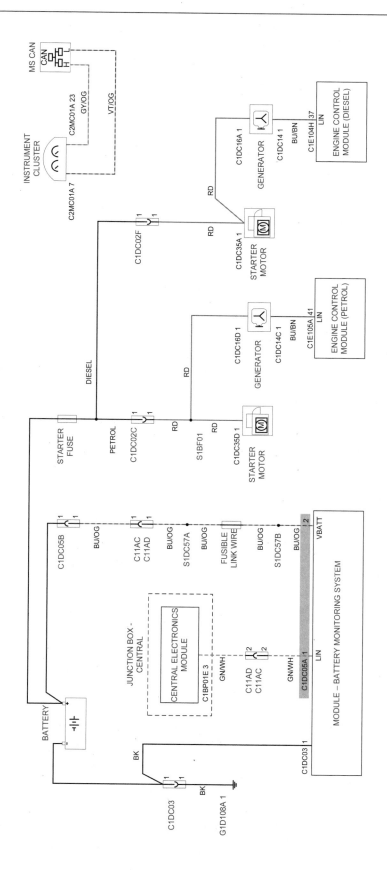

Charging system from VIN 321215

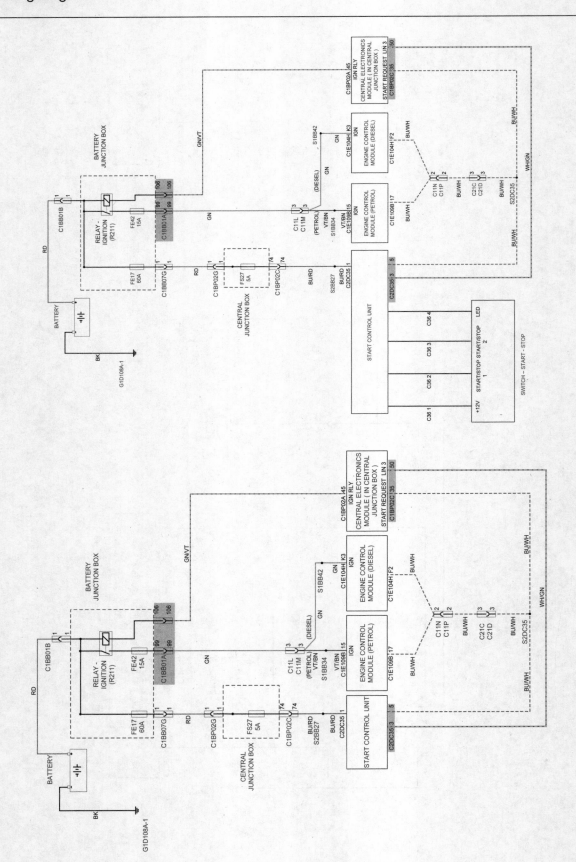

Starting system VIN 057872 – 148519

Starting system VIN 000201 – 057871

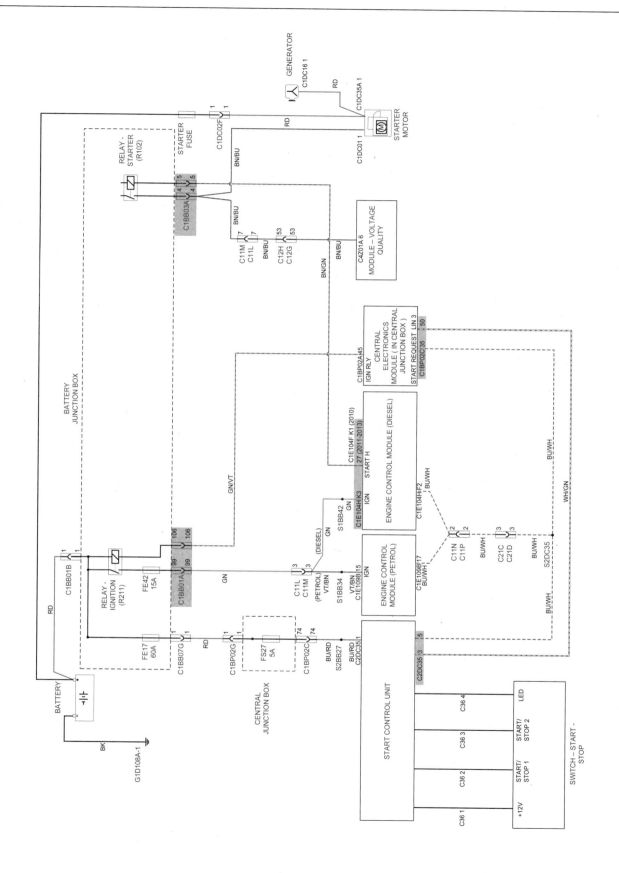

Starting system VIN 148520 – 321214

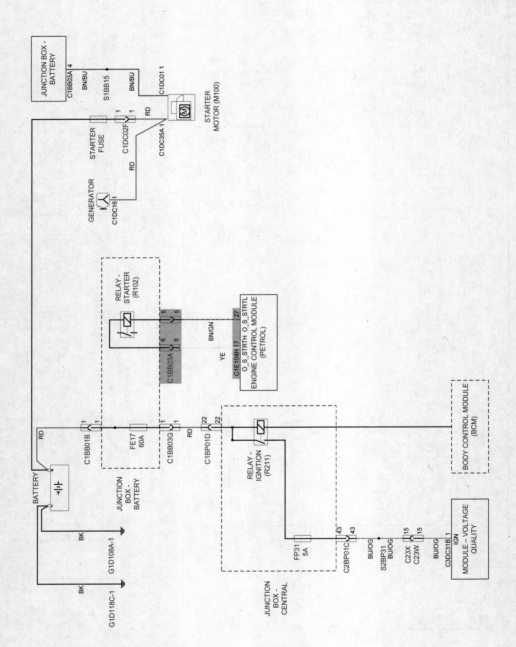

Starting system from VIN 321215

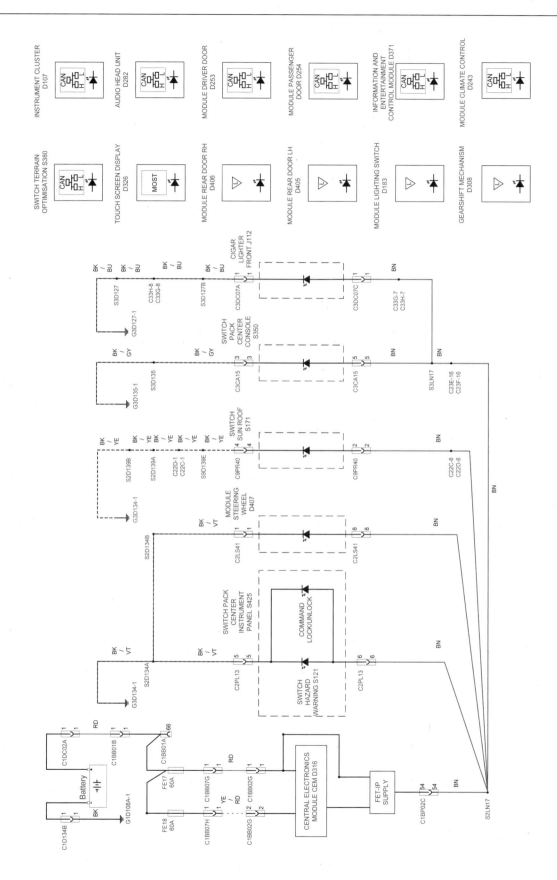

Warning lights

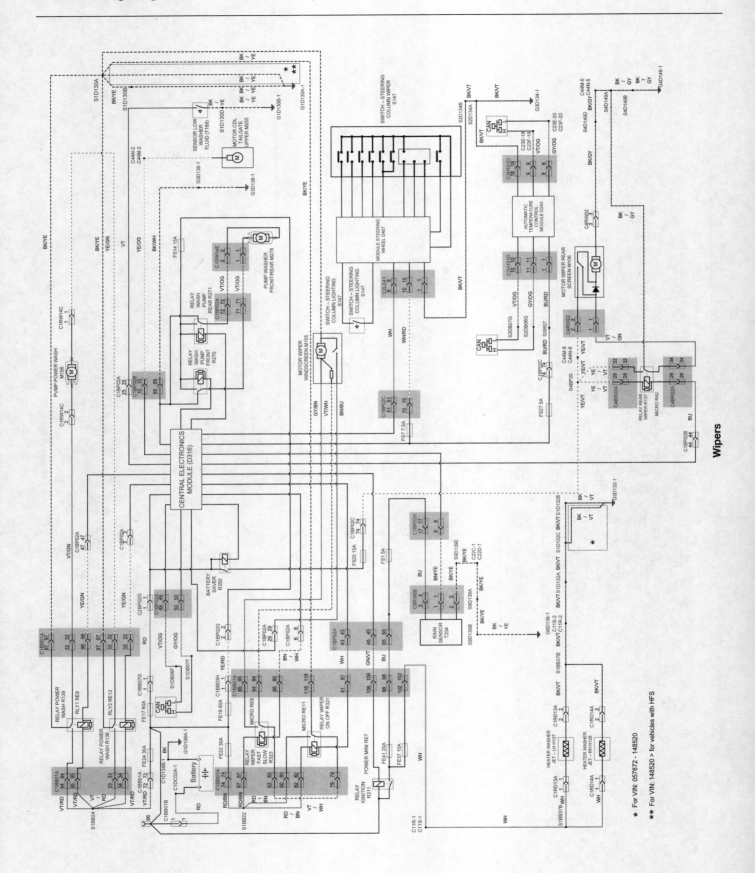

Wipers

* For VIN: 057872 - 148520

** For VIN: 148520 > for vehicles with HFS

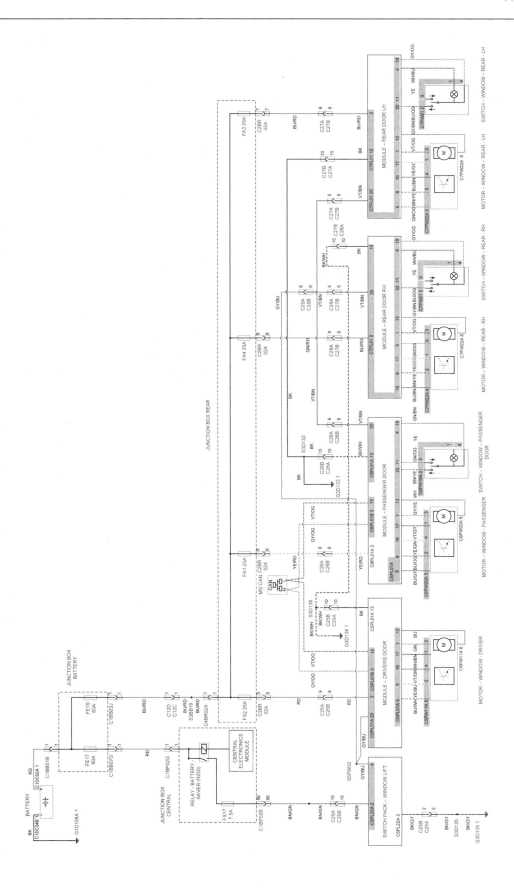

Electric windows RHD VIN 000201 – 321214

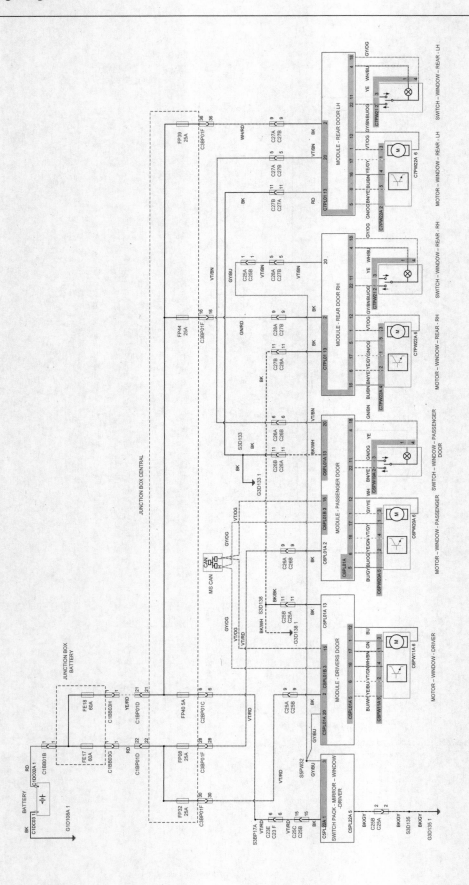

Electric windows RHD from VIN 321215

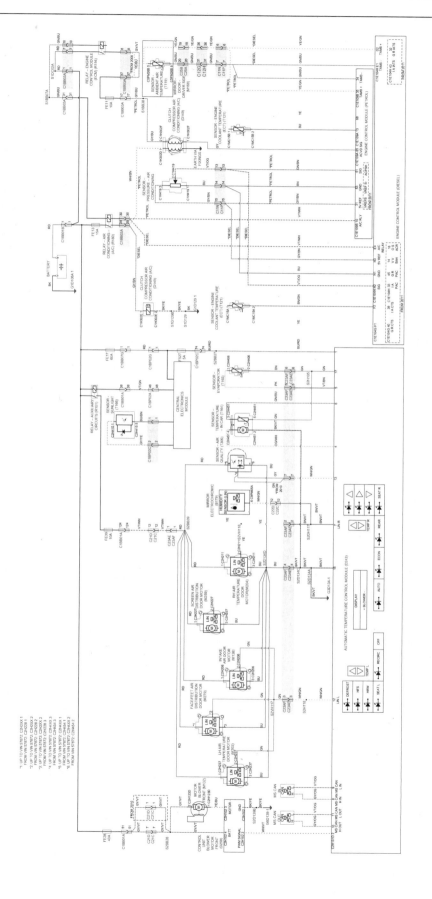

Climate control – Auto air conditioning upto 2013

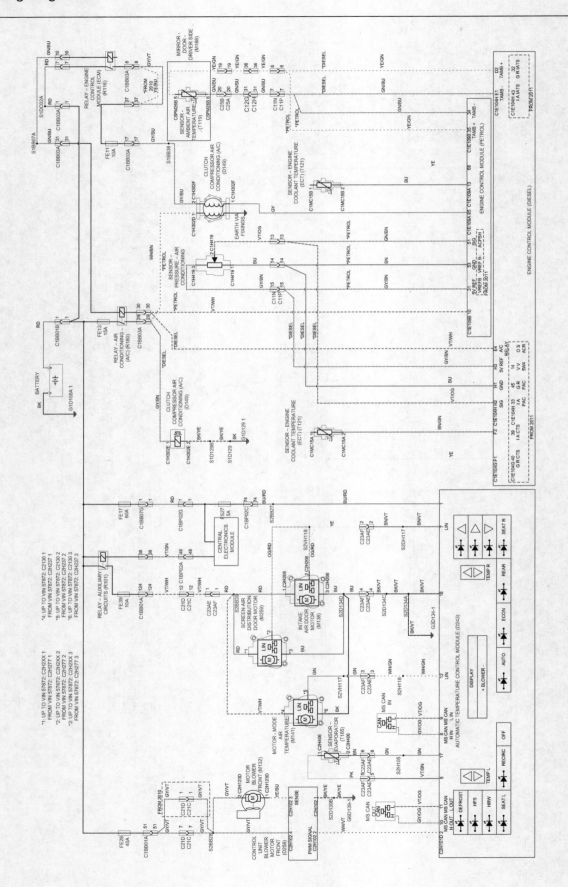

Climate control – Manual air conditioning upto 2013

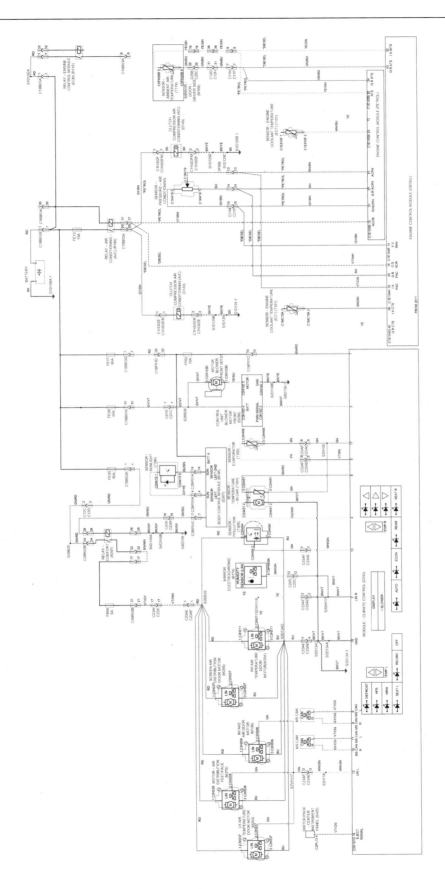

Climate control from 2013

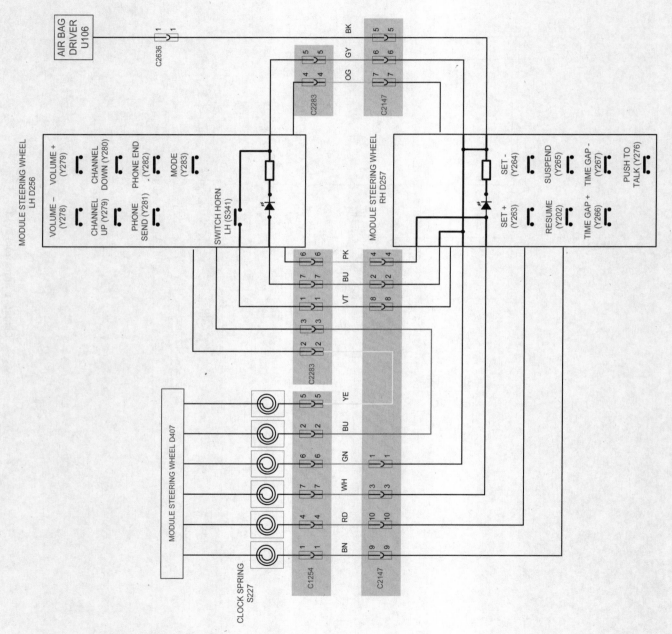

Cruise control

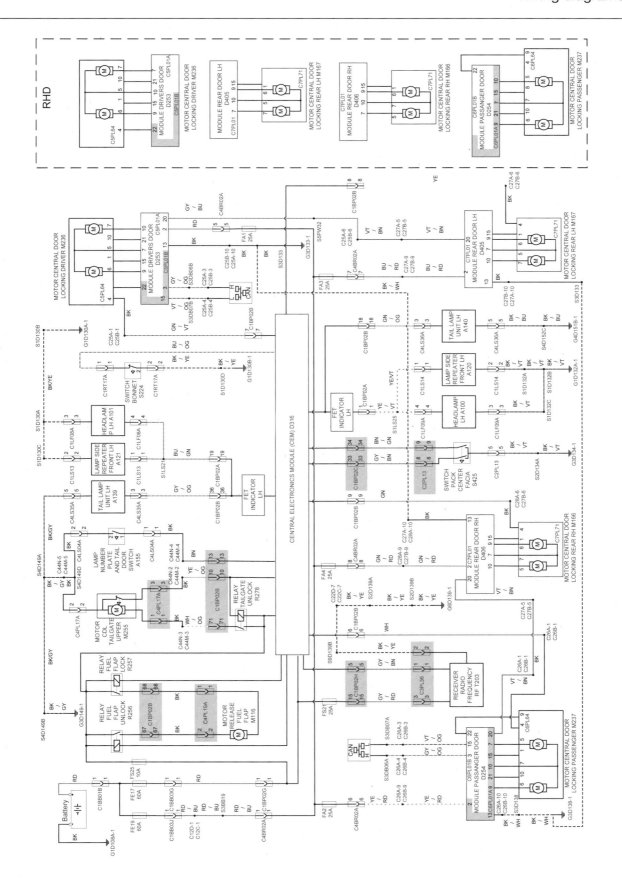

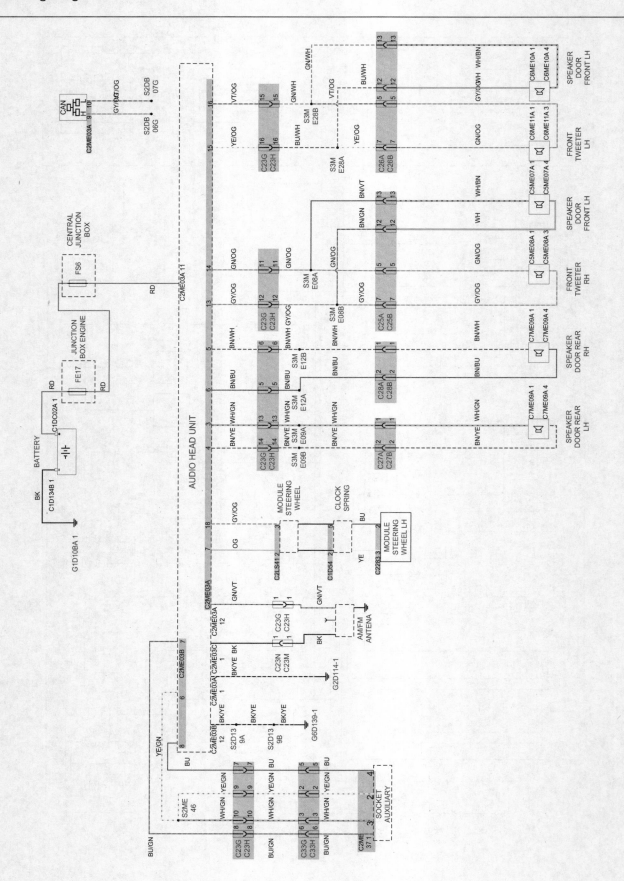

Sound system – Low line 2007 – 2010

Sound system – Low line 2010 – 2013

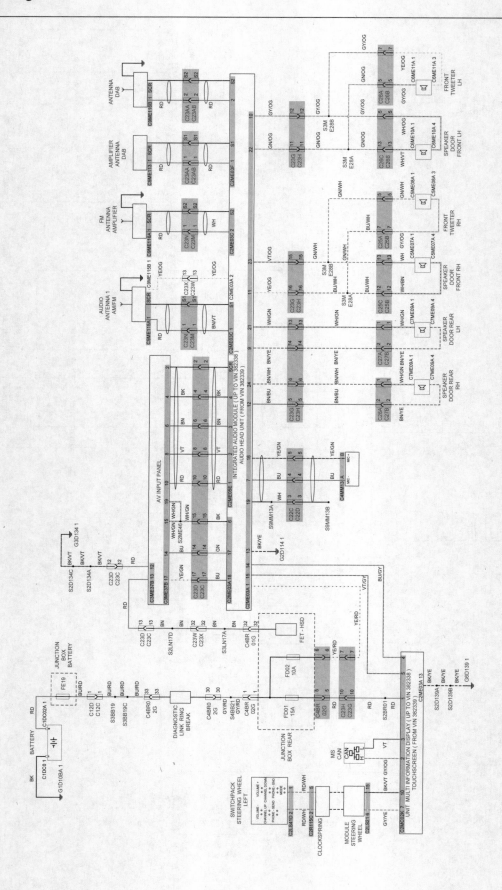

Sound system – Low line from 2013

Reference

Dimensions and weights

Note: *All figures are approximate, and may vary according to model. Refer to manufacturer's data for exact figures.*

Dimensions

Overall length	4500 mm
Overall width (inc. mirrors):	
Vehicles up to 2010 model year	2180 mm
Vehicles 2011 model year-on	2195 mm
Overall height (inc. roof bars):	
Vehicles up to 2008 model year	1820 mm
Vehicles 2009 model year-on	1830 mm
Wheelbase	2660 mm
Turning circle	11.3 m
Maximum wading depth.	500 mm
Track:	
Front	1601 mm
Rear	1614 mm

Weights

Unladen	1820 kg
Gross vehicle weight	2505 kg
Maximum roof rack load	75 kg

Fuel economy

Although depreciation is still the biggest part of the cost of motoring for most car owners, the cost of fuel is more immediately noticeable. These pages give some tips on how to get the best fuel economy.

Working it out

Manufacturer's figures

Car manufacturers are required by law to provide fuel consumption information on all new vehicles sold. These 'official' figures are obtained by simulating various driving conditions on a rolling road or a test track. Real life conditions are different, so the fuel consumption actually achieved may not bear much resemblance to the quoted figures.

How to calculate it

Many cars now have trip computers which will

display fuel consumption, both instantaneous and average. Refer to the owner's handbook for details of how to use these.

To calculate consumption yourself (and maybe to check that the trip computer is accurate), proceed as follows.

1. Fill up with fuel and note the mileage, or zero the trip recorder.
2. Drive as usual until you need to fill up again.
3. Note the amount of fuel required to refill the tank, and the mileage covered since the previous fill-up.
4. Divide the mileage by the amount of fuel used to obtain the consumption figure.

For example:

Mileage at first fill-up (a) = 27,903
Mileage at second fill-up (b) = 28,346
Mileage covered (b - a) = 443
Fuel required at second fill-up = 48.6 litres

The half-completed changeover to metric units in the UK means that we buy our fuel in litres, measure distances in miles and talk about fuel consumption in miles per gallon. There are two ways round this: the first is to convert the litres to gallons before doing the calculation (by dividing by 4.546, or see Table 1). So in the example:

48.6 litres ÷ 4.546 = 10.69 gallons
443 miles ÷ 10.69 gallons = 41.4 mpg

The second way is to calculate the consumption in miles per litre, then multiply that figure by 4.546 (or see Table 2).

So in the example, fuel consumption is:

443 miles ÷ 48.6 litres = 9.1 mpl
9.1 mpl x 4.546 = 41.4 mpg

The rest of Europe expresses fuel consumption in litres of fuel required to travel 100 km (l/100 km). For interest, the conversions are given in Table 3. In practice it doesn't matter what units you use, provided you know what your normal consumption is and can spot if it's getting better or worse.

Table 1: conversion of litres to Imperial gallons

litres	1	2	3	4	5	10	20	30	40	50	60	70
gallons	0.22	0.44	0.66	0.88	1.10	2.24	4.49	6.73	8.98	11.22	13.47	15.71

Table 2: conversion of miles per litre to miles per gallon

miles per litre	5	6	7	8	9	10	11	12	13	14
miles per gallon	23	27	32	36	41	46	50	55	59	64

Table 3: conversion of litres per 100 km to miles per gallon

litres per 100 km	4	4.5	5	5.5	6	6.5	7	8	9	10
miles per gallon	71	63	56	51	47	43	40	35	31	28

Maintenance

A well-maintained car uses less fuel and creates less pollution. In particular:

Filters

Change air and fuel filters at the specified intervals.

Oil

Use a good quality oil of the lowest viscosity specified by the vehicle manufacturer (see *Lubricants and fluids*). Check the level often and be careful not to overfill.

Spark plugs

When applicable, renew at the specified intervals.

Tyres

Check tyre pressures regularly. Under-inflated tyres have an increased rolling resistance. It is generally safe to use the higher pressures specified for full load conditions even when not fully laden, but keep an eye on the centre band of tread for signs of wear due to over-inflation.

When buying new tyres, consider the 'fuel saving' models which most manufacturers include in their ranges.

Driving style

Acceleration

Acceleration uses more fuel than driving at a steady speed. The best technique with modern cars is to accelerate reasonably briskly to the desired speed, changing up through the gears as soon as possible without making the engine labour.

Air conditioning

Air conditioning absorbs quite a bit of energy from the engine – typically 3 kW (4 hp) or so. The effect on fuel consumption is at its worst in slow traffic. Switch it off when not required.

Anticipation

Drive smoothly and try to read the traffic flow so as to avoid unnecessary acceleration and braking.

Automatic transmission

When accelerating in an automatic, avoid depressing the throttle so far as to make the transmission hold onto lower gears at higher speeds. Don't use the 'Sport' setting, if applicable.

When stationary with the engine running, select 'N' or 'P'. When moving, keep your left foot away from the brake.

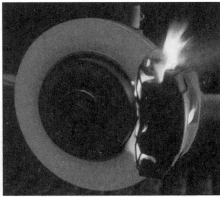

Braking

Braking converts the car's energy of motion into heat – essentially, it is wasted. Obviously some braking is always going to be necessary, but with good anticipation it is surprising how much can be avoided, especially on routes that you know well.

Carshare

Consider sharing lifts to work or to the shops. Even once a week will make a difference.

Electrical loads

Electricity is 'fuel' too; the alternator which charges the battery does so by converting some of the engine's energy of motion into electrical energy. The more electrical accessories are in use, the greater the load on the alternator. Switch off big consumers like the heated rear window when not required.

Freewheeling

Freewheeling (coasting) in neutral with the engine switched off is dangerous. The effort required to operate power-assisted brakes and steering increases when the engine is not running, with a potential lack of control in emergency situations.

In any case, modern fuel injection systems automatically cut off the engine's fuel supply on the overrun (moving and in gear, but with the accelerator pedal released).

Gadgets

Bolt-on devices claiming to save fuel have been around for nearly as long as the motor car itself. Those which worked were rapidly adopted as standard equipment by the vehicle manufacturers. Others worked only in certain situations, or saved fuel only at the expense of unacceptable effects on performance, driveability or the life of engine components.

The most effective fuel saving gadget is the driver's right foot.

Journey planning

Combine (eg) a trip to the supermarket with a visit to the recycling centre and the DIY store, rather than making separate journeys.

When possible choose a travelling time outside rush hours.

Load

The more heavily a car is laden, the greater the energy required to accelerate it to a given speed. Remove heavy items which you don't need to carry.

One load which is often overlooked is the contents of the fuel tank. A tankful of fuel (55 litres / 12 gallons) weighs 45 kg (100 lb) or so. Just half filling it may be worthwhile.

Lost?

At the risk of stating the obvious, if you're going somewhere new, have details of the route to hand. There's not much point in achieving record mpg if you also go miles out of your way.

Parking

If possible, carry out any reversing or turning manoeuvres when you arrive at a parking space so that you can drive straight out when you leave. Manoeuvering when the engine is cold uses a lot more fuel.

Driving around looking for free on-street parking may cost more in fuel than buying a car park ticket.

Premium fuel

Most major oil companies (and some supermarkets) have premium grades of fuel which are several pence a litre dearer than the standard grades. Reports vary, but the consensus seems to be that if these fuels improve economy at all, they do not do so by enough to justify their extra cost.

Roof rack

When loading a roof rack, try to produce a wedge shape with the narrow end at the front. Any cover should be securely fastened – if it flaps it's creating turbulence and absorbing energy.

Remove roof racks and boxes when not in use – they increase air resistance and can create a surprising amount of noise.

Short journeys

The engine is at its least efficient, and wear is highest, during the first few miles after a cold start. Consider walking, cycling or using public transport.

Speed

The engine is at its most efficient when running at a steady speed and load at the rpm where it develops maximum torque. (You can find this figure in the car's handbook.) For most cars this corresponds to between 55 and 65 mph in top gear.

Above the optimum cruising speed, fuel consumption starts to rise quite sharply. A car travelling at 80 mph will typically be using 30% more fuel than at 60 mph.

Supermarket fuel

It may be cheap but is it any good? In the UK all supermarket fuel must meet the relevant British Standard. The major oil companies will say that their branded fuels have better additive packages which may stop carbon and other deposits building up. A reasonable compromise might be to use one tank of branded fuel to three or four from the supermarket.

Switch off when stationary

Switch off the engine if you look like being stationary for more than 30 seconds or so. This is good for the environment as well as for your pocket. Be aware though that frequent restarts are hard on the battery and the starter motor.

Windows

Driving with the windows open increases air turbulence around the vehicle. Closing the windows promotes smooth airflow and

reduced resistance. The faster you go, the more significant this is.

And finally...

Driving techniques associated with good fuel economy tend to involve moderate acceleration and low top speeds. Be considerate to the needs of other road users who may need to make brisker progress; even if you do not agree with them this is not an excuse to be obstructive.

Safety must always take precedence over economy, whether it is a question of accelerating hard to complete an overtaking manoeuvre, killing your speed when confronted with a potential hazard or switching the lights on when it starts to get dark.

Conversion factors

Length (distance)

Inches (in)	x 25.4	= Millimetres (mm)	x 0.0394	= Inches (in)
Feet (ft)	x 0.305	= Metres (m)	x 3.281	= Feet (ft)
Miles	x 1.609	= Kilometres (km)	x 0.621	= Miles

Volume (capacity)

Cubic inches (cu in; in^3)	x 16.387	= Cubic centimetres (cc; cm^3)	x 0.061	= Cubic inches (cu in; in^3)
Imperial pints (Imp pt)	x 0.568	= Litres (l)	x 1.76	= Imperial pints (Imp pt)
Imperial quarts (Imp qt)	x 1.137	= Litres (l)	x 0.88	= Imperial quarts (Imp qt)
Imperial quarts (Imp qt)	x 1.201	= US quarts (US qt)	x 0.833	= Imperial quarts (Imp qt)
US quarts (US qt)	x 0.946	= Litres (l)	x 1.057	= US quarts (US qt)
Imperial gallons (Imp gal)	x 4.546	= Litres (l)	x 0.22	= Imperial gallons (Imp gal)
Imperial gallons (Imp gal)	x 1.201	= US gallons (US gal)	x 0.833	= Imperial gallons (Imp gal)
US gallons (US gal)	x 3.785	= Litres (l)	x 0.264	= US gallons (US gal)

Mass (weight)

Ounces (oz)	x 28.35	= Grams (g)	x 0.035	= Ounces (oz)
Pounds (lb)	x 0.454	= Kilograms (kg)	x 2.205	= Pounds (lb)

Force

Ounces-force (ozf; oz)	x 0.278	= Newtons (N)	x 3.6	= Ounces-force (ozf; oz)
Pounds-force (lbf; lb)	x 4.448	= Newtons (N)	x 0.225	= Pounds-force (lbf; lb)
Newtons (N)	x 0.1	= Kilograms-force (kgf; kg)	x 9.81	= Newtons (N)

Pressure

Pounds-force per square inch (psi; lbf/in^2; lb/in^2)	x 0.070	= Kilograms-force per square centimetre (kgf/cm^2; kg/cm^2)	x 14.223	= Pounds-force per square inch (psi; lbf/in^2; lb/in^2)
Pounds-force per square inch (psi; lbf/in^2; lb/in^2)	x 0.068	= Atmospheres (atm)	x 14.696	= Pounds-force per square inch (psi; lbf/in^2; lb/in^2)
Pounds-force per square inch (psi; lbf/in^2; lb/in^2)	x 0.069	= Bars	x 14.5	= Pounds-force per square inch (psi; lbf/in^2; lb/in^2)
Pounds-force per square inch (psi; lbf/in^2; lb/in^2)	x 6.895	= Kilopascals (kPa)	x 0.145	= Pounds-force per square inch (psi; lbf/in^2; lb/in^2)
Kilopascals (kPa)	x 0.01	= Kilograms-force per square centimetre (kgf/cm^2; kg/cm^2)	x 98.1	= Kilopascals (kPa)
Millibar (mbar)	x 100	= Pascals (Pa)	x 0.01	= Millibar (mbar)
Millibar (mbar)	x 0.0145	= Pounds-force per square inch (psi; lbf/in^2; lb/in^2)	x 68.947	= Millibar (mbar)
Millibar (mbar)	x 0.75	= Millimetres of mercury (mmHg)	x 1.333	= Millibar (mbar)
Millibar (mbar)	x 0.401	= Inches of water (inH$_2$O)	x 2.491	= Millibar (mbar)
Millimetres of mercury (mmHg)	x 0.535	= Inches of water (inH$_2$O)	x 1.868	= Millimetres of mercury (mmHg)
Inches of water (inH$_2$O)	x 0.036	= Pounds-force per square inch (psi; lbf/in^2; lb/in^2)	x 27.68	= Inches of water (inH$_2$O)

Torque (moment of force)

Pounds-force inches (lbf in; lb in)	x 1.152	= Kilograms-force centimetre (kgf cm; kg cm)	x 0.868	= Pounds-force inches (lbf in; lb in)
Pounds-force inches (lbf in; lb in)	x 0.113	= Newton metres (Nm)	x 8.85	= Pounds-force inches (lbf in; lb in)
Pounds-force inches (lbf in; lb in)	x 0.083	= Pounds-force feet (lbf ft; lb ft)	x 12	= Pounds-force inches (lbf in; lb in)
Pounds-force feet (lbf ft; lb ft)	x 0.138	= Kilograms-force metres (kgf m; kg m)	x 7.233	= Pounds-force feet (lbf ft; lb ft)
Pounds-force feet (lbf ft; lb ft)	x 1.356	= Newton metres (Nm)	x 0.738	= Pounds-force feet (lbf ft; lb ft)
Newton metres (Nm)	x 0.102	= Kilograms-force metres (kgf m; kg m)	x 9.804	= Newton metres (Nm)

Power

Horsepower (hp)	x 745.7	= Watts (W)	x 0.0013	= Horsepower (hp)

Velocity (speed)

Miles per hour (miles/hr; mph)	x 1.609	= Kilometres per hour (km/hr; kph)	x 0.621	= Miles per hour (miles/hr; mph)

Fuel consumption*

Miles per gallon, Imperial (mpg)	x 0.354	= Kilometres per litre (km/l)	x 2.825	= Miles per gallon, Imperial (mpg)
Miles per gallon, US (mpg)	x 0.425	= Kilometres per litre (km/l)	x 2.352	= Miles per gallon, US (mpg)

Temperature

Degrees Fahrenheit = (°C x 1.8) + 32   Degrees Celsius (Degrees Centigrade; °C) = (°F - 32) x 0.56

It is common practice to convert from miles per gallon (mpg) to litres/100 kilometres (l/100km), where mpg x l/100 km = 282

The jack supplied with the vehicle tool kit should only be used for changing the roadwheels - see 'Wheel changing' at the front of this manual. When carrying out any other kind of work, raise the vehicle using a hydraulic trolley jack, and always supplement the jack with axle stands positioned under the vehicle jacking points.

When using a trolley jack or axle stands, always position the jack head or axle stand head under, or adjacent to one of the relevant wheel changing jacking points under the sills. Use a block of wood between the jack or axle stand and the sill. It is permissible to raise the front or rear of the vehicle with a trolley jack head under the front body crossmember or rear subframe crossmember, providing axle stands are placed under the sill jacking points **(see illustration).**

Do not attempt to jack the vehicle under the sump, final drive unit, or any of the suspension components.

Never work under, around, or near a raised vehicle, unless it is adequately supported in at least two places.

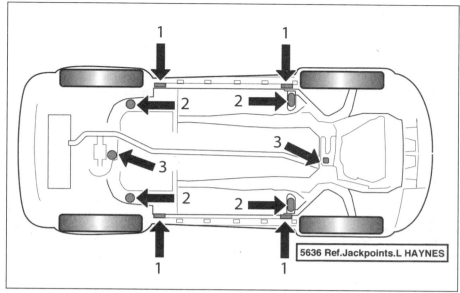

5636 Ref.Jackpoints.L HAYNES

Axle stands should be placed in positions 1 & 2, whilst a workshop hydraulic jack can be placed in positions 1 & 3

Buying spare parts

Spare parts are available from many sources, including maker's appointed garages, accessory shops, and motor factors. To be sure of obtaining the correct parts, it will sometimes be necessary to quote the vehicle identification number. If possible, it can also be useful to take the old parts along for positive identification. Items such as starter motors and alternators may be available under a service exchange scheme - any parts returned should be clean.

Our advice regarding spare parts is as follows.

Officially appointed garages

This is the best source of parts which are peculiar to your car, and which are not otherwise generally available (eg, badges, interior trim, certain body panels, etc). It is also the only place at which you should buy parts if the vehicle is still under warranty.

Accessory shops

These are very good places to buy materials and components needed for the maintenance of your car (oil, air and fuel filters, light bulbs, drivebelts, greases, brake pads, tough-up paint, etc). Components of this nature sold by a reputable shop are of the same standard as those used by the car manufacturer.

Besides components, these shops also sell tools and general accessories, usually have convenient opening hours, charge lower prices, and can often be found close to home. Some accessory shops have parts counters where components needed for almost any repair job can be purchased or ordered.

Motor factors

Good factors will stock all the more important components which wear out comparatively quickly, and can sometimes supply individual components needed for the overhaul of a larger assembly (eg, brake seals and hydraulic parts, bearing shells, pistons, valves). They may also handle work such as cylinder block reboring, crankshaft regrinding, etc.

Tyre and exhaust specialists

These outlets may be independent, or members of a local or national chain. They frequently offer competitive prices when compared with a main dealer or local garage, but it will pay to obtain several quotes before making a decision. When researching prices, also ask what 'extras' may be added - for instance fitting a new valve and balancing the wheel are both commonly charged on top of the price of a new tyre.

Other sources

Beware of parts or materials obtained from market stalls, car boot sales, internet auction sites or similar outlets. Such items are not invariably sub-standard, but there is little chance of compensation if they do prove unsatisfactory. In the case of safety-critical components such as brake pads, there is the risk not only of financial loss, but also of an accident causing injury or death

Second-hand components or assemblies obtained from a car breaker can be a good buy in some circumstances, but this sort of purchase is best made by the experienced DIY mechanic.

Whenever servicing, repair or overhaul work is carried out on the car or its components, observe the following procedures and instructions. This will assist in carrying out the operation efficiently and to a professional standard of workmanship.

Joint mating faces and gaskets

When separating components at their mating faces, never insert screwdrivers or similar implements into the joint between the faces in order to prise them apart. This can cause severe damage which results in oil leaks, coolant leaks, etc upon reassembly. Separation is usually achieved by tapping along the joint with a soft-faced hammer in order to break the seal. However, note that this method may not be suitable where dowels are used for component location.

Where a gasket is used between the mating faces of two components, a new one must be fitted on reassembly; fit it dry unless otherwise stated in the repair procedure. Make sure that the mating faces are clean and dry, with all traces of old gasket removed. When cleaning a joint face, use a tool which is unlikely to score or damage the face, and remove any burrs or nicks with an oilstone or fine file.

Make sure that tapped holes are cleaned with a pipe cleaner, and keep them free of jointing compound, if this is being used, unless specifically instructed otherwise.

Ensure that all orifices, channels or pipes are clear, and blow through them, preferably using compressed air.

Oil seals

Oil seals can be removed by levering them out with a wide flat-bladed screwdriver or similar implement. Alternatively, a number of self-tapping screws may be screwed into the seal, and these used as a purchase for pliers or some similar device in order to pull the seal free.

Whenever an oil seal is removed from its working location, either individually or as part of an assembly, it should be renewed.

The very fine sealing lip of the seal is easily damaged, and will not seal if the surface it contacts is not completely clean and free from scratches, nicks or grooves. If the original sealing surface of the component cannot be restored, and the manufacturer has not made provision for slight relocation of the seal relative to the sealing surface, the component should be renewed.

Protect the lips of the seal from any surface which may damage them in the course of fitting. Use tape or a conical sleeve where possible. Where indicated, lubricate the seal lips with oil before fitting and, on dual-lipped seals, fill the space between the lips with grease.

Unless otherwise stated, oil seals must be fitted with their sealing lips toward the lubricant to be sealed.

Use a tubular drift or block of wood of the appropriate size to install the seal and, if the seal housing is shouldered, drive the seal down to the shoulder. If the seal housing is unshouldered, the seal should be fitted with its face flush with the housing top face (unless otherwise instructed).

Screw threads and fastenings

Seized nuts, bolts and screws are quite a common occurrence where corrosion has set in, and the use of penetrating oil or releasing fluid will often overcome this problem if the offending item is soaked for a while before attempting to release it. The use of an impact driver may also provide a means of releasing such stubborn fastening devices, when used in conjunction with the appropriate screwdriver bit or socket. If none of these methods works, it may be necessary to resort to the careful application of heat, or the use of a hacksaw or nut splitter device. Before resorting to extreme methods, check that you are not dealing with a left-hand thread!

Studs are usually removed by locking two nuts together on the threaded part, and then using a spanner on the lower nut to unscrew the stud. Studs or bolts which have broken off below the surface of the component in which they are mounted can sometimes be removed using a stud extractor.

Always ensure that a blind tapped hole is completely free from oil, grease, water or other fluid before installing the bolt or stud. Failure to do this could cause the housing to crack due to the hydraulic action of the bolt or stud as it is screwed in.

For some screw fastenings, notably cylinder head bolts or nuts, torque wrench settings are no longer specified for the latter stages of tightening, "angle-tightening" being called up instead. Typically, a fairly low torque wrench setting will be applied to the bolts/nuts in the correct sequence, followed by one or more stages of tightening through specified angles.

When checking or retightening a nut or bolt to a specified torque setting, slacken the nut or bolt by a quarter of a turn, and then retighten to the specified setting. However, this should not be attempted where angular tightening has been used.

Locknuts, locktabs and washers

Any fastening which will rotate against a component or housing during tightening should always have a washer between it and the relevant component or housing.

Spring or split washers should always be renewed when they are used to lock a critical component such as a big-end bearing retaining bolt or nut. Locktabs which are folded over to retain a nut or bolt should always be renewed.

Self-locking nuts can be re-used in non-critical areas, providing resistance can be felt when the locking portion passes over the bolt or stud thread. However, it should be noted that self-locking stiffnuts tend to lose their effectiveness after long periods of use, and should then be renewed as a matter of course.

Split pins must always be replaced with new ones of the correct size for the hole.

When thread-locking compound is found on the threads of a fastener which is to be re-used, it should be cleaned off with a wire brush and solvent, and fresh compound applied on reassembly.

Special tools

Some repair procedures in this manual entail the use of special tools such as a press, two or three-legged pullers, spring compressors, etc. Wherever possible, suitable readily-available alternatives to the manufacturer's special tools are described, and are shown in use. In some instances, where no alternative is possible, it has been necessary to resort to the use of a manufacturer's tool, and this has been done for reasons of safety as well as the efficient completion of the repair operation. Unless you are highly-skilled and have a thorough understanding of the procedures described, never attempt to bypass the use of any special tool when the procedure described specifies its use. Not only is there a very great risk of personal injury, but expensive damage could be caused to the components involved.

Environmental considerations

When disposing of used engine oil, brake fluid, antifreeze, etc, give due consideration to any detrimental environmental effects. Do not, for instance, pour any of the above liquids down drains into the general sewage system, or onto the ground to soak away. Many local council refuse tips provide a facility for waste oil disposal, as do some garages. You can find your nearest disposal point by calling the Environment Agency on 08708 506 506 or by visiting www.oilbankline.org.uk.

Note: It is illegal and anti-social to dump oil down the drain. To find the location of your local oil recycling bank, call 08708 506 506 or visit www.oilbankline.org.uk.

Modifications are a continuing and unpublicised process in vehicle manufacture, quite apart from major model changes. Spare parts manuals and lists are compiled upon a numerical basis, the individual vehicle identification numbers being essential to correct identification of the component concerned.

When ordering spare parts, always give as much information as possible. Quote the car model, year of manufacture, body and engine numbers as appropriate.

The vehicle identification plate is situated at the bottom of the left-hand door B-pillar. It gives the VIN (vehicle identification number), vehicle weight information and paint and trim colour codes. The vehicle identification number is visible on a plate visible through the lower left-hand corner of the windscreen **(see illustrations)**.

The engine number is stamped on the front of the cylinder block adjacent to the gearbox.

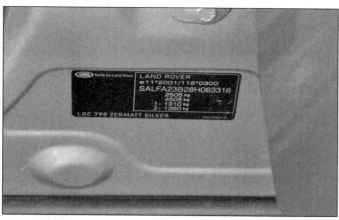

The VIN is located on a plate at the base of the left-hand door B-pillar...

...and at the base of the windscreen

Introduction

A selection of good tools is a fundamental requirement for anyone contemplating the maintenance and repair of a motor vehicle. For the owner who does not possess any, their purchase will prove a considerable expense, offsetting some of the savings made by doing-it-yourself. However, provided that the tools purchased meet the relevant national safety standards and are of good quality, they will last for many years and prove an extremely worthwhile investment.

To help the average owner to decide which tools are needed to carry out the various tasks detailed in this manual, we have compiled three lists of tools under the following headings: *Maintenance and minor repair*, *Repair and overhaul*, and *Special*. Newcomers to practical mechanics should start off with the *Maintenance and minor repair* tool kit, and confine themselves to the simpler jobs around the vehicle. Then, as confidence and experience grow, more difficult tasks can be undertaken, with extra tools being purchased as, and when, they are needed. In this way, a *Maintenance and minor repair* tool kit can be built up into a *Repair and overhaul* tool kit over a considerable period of time, without any major cash outlays. The experienced do-it-yourselfer will have a tool kit good enough for most repair and overhaul procedures, and will add tools from the *Special* category when it is felt that the expense is justified by the amount of use to which these tools will be put.

Maintenance and minor repair tool kit

The tools given in this list should be considered as a minimum requirement if routine maintenance, servicing and minor repair operations are to be undertaken. We recommend the purchase of combination spanners (ring one end, open-ended the other); although more expensive than open-ended ones, they do give the advantages of both types of spanner.

☐ *Combination spanners:*
Metric - 8 to 19 mm inclusive
☐ *Adjustable spanner - 35 mm jaw (approx.)*
☐ *Spark plug spanner (with rubber insert) - petrol models*
☐ *Spark plug gap adjustment tool - petrol models*
☐ *Set of feeler gauges*
☐ *Brake bleed nipple spanner*
☐ *Screwdrivers:*
Flat blade - 100 mm long x 6 mm dia
Cross blade - 100 mm long x 6 mm dia
Torx - various sizes (not all vehicles)
☐ *Combination pliers*
☐ *Hacksaw (junior)*
☐ *Tyre pump*
☐ *Tyre pressure gauge*
☐ *Oil can*
☐ *Oil filter removal tool (if applicable)*
☐ *Fine emery cloth*
☐ *Wire brush (small)*
☐ *Funnel (medium size)*
☐ *Sump drain plug key (not all vehicles)*

Repair and overhaul tool kit

These tools are virtually essential for anyone undertaking any major repairs to a motor vehicle, and are additional to those given in the *Maintenance and minor repair* list. Included in this list is a comprehensive set of sockets. Although these are expensive, they will be found invaluable as they are so versatile - particularly if various drives are included in the set. We recommend the half-inch square-drive type, as this can be used with most proprietary torque wrenches.

The tools in this list will sometimes need to be supplemented by tools from the *Special* list:

☐ *Sockets to cover range in previous list (including Torx sockets)*
☐ *Reversible ratchet drive (for use with sockets)*
☐ *Extension piece, 250 mm (for use with sockets)*
☐ *Universal joint (for use with sockets)*
☐ *Flexible handle or sliding T "breaker bar" (for use with sockets)*
☐ *Torque wrench (for use with sockets)*
☐ *Self-locking grips*
☐ *Ball pein hammer*
☐ *Soft-faced mallet (plastic or rubber)*
☐ *Screwdrivers:*
Flat blade - long & sturdy, short (chubby), and narrow (electrician's) types
Cross blade - long & sturdy, and short (chubby) types
☐ *Pliers:*
Long-nosed
Side cutters (electrician's)
Circlip (internal and external)
☐ *Cold chisel - 25 mm*
☐ *Scriber*
☐ *Scraper*
☐ *Centre-punch*
☐ *Pin punch*
☐ *Hacksaw*
☐ *Brake hose clamp*
☐ *Brake/clutch bleeding kit*
☐ *Selection of twist drills*
☐ *Steel rule/straight-edge*
☐ *Allen keys (inc. splined/Torx type)*
☐ *Selection of files*
☐ *Wire brush*
☐ *Axle stands*
☐ *Jack (strong trolley or hydraulic type)*
☐ *Light with extension lead*
☐ *Universal electrical multi-meter*

Sockets and reversible ratchet drive

Brake bleeding kit

Torx key, socket and bit

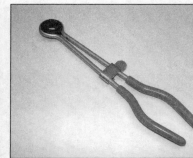
Hose clamp

Angular-tightening gauge

Special tools

The tools in this list are those which are not used regularly, are expensive to buy, or which need to be used in accordance with their manufacturers' instructions. Unless relatively difficult mechanical jobs are undertaken frequently, it will not be economic to buy many of these tools. Where this is the case, you could consider clubbing together with friends (or joining a motorists' club) to make a joint purchase, or borrowing the tools against a deposit from a local garage or tool hire specialist.

The following list contains only those tools and instruments freely available to the public, and not those special tools produced by the vehicle manufacturer specifically for its dealer network. You will find occasional references to these manufacturers' special tools in the text of this manual. Generally, an alternative method of doing the job without the vehicle manufacturers' special tool is given. However, sometimes there is no alternative to using them. Where this is the case and the relevant tool cannot be bought or borrowed, you will have to entrust the work to a dealer.

- ☐ Angular-tightening gauge
- ☐ Valve spring compressor
- ☐ Valve grinding tool
- ☐ Piston ring compressor
- ☐ Piston ring removal/installation tool
- ☐ Cylinder bore hone
- ☐ Balljoint separator
- ☐ Coil spring compressors (where applicable)
- ☐ Two/three-legged hub and bearing puller
- ☐ Impact screwdriver
- ☐ Micrometer and/or vernier calipers
- ☐ Dial gauge
- ☐ Tachometer
- ☐ Fault code reader
- ☐ Cylinder compression gauge
- ☐ Hand-operated vacuum pump and gauge
- ☐ Clutch plate alignment set
- ☐ Brake shoe steady spring cup removal tool
- ☐ Bush and bearing removal/installation set
- ☐ Stud extractors
- ☐ Tap and die set
- ☐ Lifting tackle

Buying tools

Reputable motor accessory shops and superstores often offer excellent quality tools at discount prices, so it pays to shop around.

Remember, you don't have to buy the most expensive items on the shelf, but it is always advisable to steer clear of the very cheap tools. Beware of 'bargains' offered on market stalls, on-line or at car boot sales. There are plenty of good tools around at reasonable prices, but always aim to purchase items which meet the relevant national safety standards. If in doubt, ask the proprietor or manager of the shop for advice before making a purchase.

Care and maintenance of tools

Having purchased a reasonable tool kit, it is necessary to keep the tools in a clean and serviceable condition. After use, always wipe off any dirt, grease and metal particles using a clean, dry cloth, before putting the tools away. Never leave them lying around after they have been used. A simple tool rack on the garage or workshop wall for items such as screwdrivers and pliers is a good idea. Store all normal spanners and sockets in a metal box. Any measuring instruments, gauges, meters, etc, must be carefully stored where they cannot be damaged or become rusty.

Take a little care when tools are used. Hammer heads inevitably become marked, and screwdrivers lose the keen edge on their blades from time to time. A little timely attention with emery cloth or a file will soon restore items like this to a good finish.

Working facilities

Not to be forgotten when discussing tools is the workshop itself. If anything more than routine maintenance is to be carried out, a suitable working area becomes essential.

It is appreciated that many an owner-mechanic is forced by circumstances to remove an engine or similar item without the benefit of a garage or workshop. Having done this, any repairs should always be done under the cover of a roof.

Wherever possible, any dismantling should be done on a clean, flat workbench or table at a suitable working height.

Any workbench needs a vice; one with a jaw opening of 100 mm is suitable for most jobs. As mentioned previously, some clean dry storage space is also required for tools, as well as for any lubricants, cleaning fluids, touch-up paints etc, which become necessary.

Another item which may be required, and which has a much more general usage, is an electric drill with a chuck capacity of at least 8 mm. This, together with a good range of twist drills, is virtually essential for fitting accessories.

Last, but not least, always keep a supply of old newspapers and clean, lint-free rags available, and try to keep any working area as clean as possible.

Micrometers

Dial test indicator ("dial gauge")

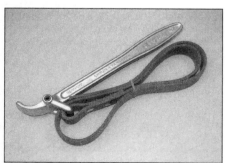

Oil filter removal tool (strap wrench type)

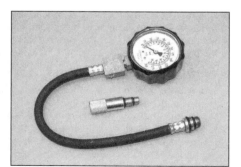

Compression tester

Bearing puller

This is a guide to getting your vehicle through the MOT test. Obviously it will not be possible to examine the vehicle to the same standard as the professional MOT tester. However, working through the following checks will enable you to identify any problem areas before submitting the vehicle for the test.

It has only been possible to summarise the test requirements here, based on the regulations in force at the time of printing. Test standards are becoming increasingly stringent, although there are some exemptions for older vehicles.

An assistant will be needed to help carry out some of these checks.

The checks have been sub-divided into four categories, as follows:

1 Checks carried out **FROM THE DRIVER'S SEAT**

2 Checks carried out **WITH THE VEHICLE ON THE GROUND**

3 Checks carried out **WITH THE VEHICLE RAISED AND THE WHEELS FREE TO TURN**

4 Checks carried out on **YOUR VEHICLE'S EXHAUST EMISSION SYSTEM**

---

1 Checks carried out **FROM THE DRIVER'S SEAT**

Handbrake (parking brake)

☐ Test the operation of the handbrake. Excessive travel (too many clicks) indicates incorrect brake or cable adjustment.
☐ Check that the handbrake cannot be released by tapping the lever sideways. Check the security of the lever mountings.

☐ If the parking brake is foot-operated, check that the pedal is secure and without excessive travel, and that the release mechanism operates correctly.
☐ Where applicable, test the operation of the electronic handbrake. The brake should engage and disengage without excessive delay. If the warning light does not extinguish when the brake is disengaged, this could indicate a fault which will need further investigation.

Footbrake

☐ Depress the brake pedal and check that it does not creep down to the floor, indicating a master cylinder fault. Release the pedal,

wait a few seconds, then depress it again. If the pedal travels nearly to the floor before firm resistance is felt, brake adjustment or repair is necessary. If the pedal feels spongy, there is air in the hydraulic system which must be removed by bleeding.

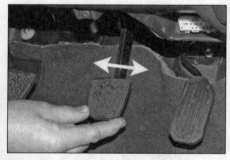

☐ Check that the brake pedal is secure and in good condition. Check also for signs of fluid leaks on the pedal, floor or carpets, which would indicate failed seals in the brake master cylinder.
☐ Check the servo unit (when applicable) by operating the brake pedal several times, then keeping the pedal depressed and starting the engine. As the engine starts, the pedal will move down slightly. If not, the vacuum hose or the servo itself may be faulty.

Steering wheel and column

☐ Examine the steering wheel for fractures or looseness of the hub, spokes or rim.
☐ Move the steering wheel from side to side and then up and down. Check that the steering wheel is not loose on the column, indicating wear or a loose retaining nut. Continue moving the steering wheel as before, but also turn it slightly from left to right.

☐ Check that the steering wheel is not loose on the column, and that there is no abnormal movement of the steering wheel, indicating wear in the column support bearings or couplings.
☐ Check that the ignition lock (where fitted) engages and disengages correctly.
☐ Steering column adjustment mechanisms (where fitted) must be able to lock the column securely in place with no play evident.

Windscreen, mirrors and sunvisor

☐ The windscreen must be free of cracks or other significant damage within the driver's field of view. (Small stone chips are acceptable.) Rear view mirrors must be secure, intact, and capable of being adjusted.

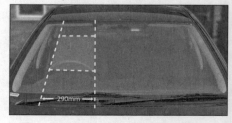

☐ The driver's sunvisor must be capable of being stored in the "up" position.

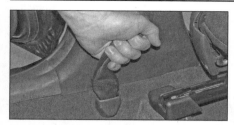

Seat belts and seats

Note: *The following checks are applicable to all seat belts, front and rear.*

☐ Examine the webbing of all the belts (including rear belts if fitted) for cuts, serious fraying or deterioration. Fasten and unfasten each belt to check the buckles. If applicable, check the retracting mechanism. Check the security of all seat belt mountings accessible from inside the vehicle, ensuring any height adjustable mountings lock securely in place.

☐ Seat belts with pre-tensioners, once activated, have a "flag" or similar showing on the seat belt stalk. This, in itself, is not a reason for test failure.

☐ The front seats themselves must be securely attached and the backrests must lock in the upright position.

Doors

☐ Both front doors must be able to be opened and closed from outside and inside, and must latch securely when closed.

Bonnet and boot/tailgate

☐ The bonnet and boot/tailgate must latch securely when closed.

2 Checks carried out WITH THE VEHICLE ON THE GROUND

Vehicle identification

☐ Number plates must be in good condition, secure and legible, with letters and numbers correctly spaced – spacing at (A) should be 33 mm and at (B) 11 mm. At the front, digits must be black on a white background and at the rear black on a yellow background. Other background designs (such as honeycomb) are not permitted.

☐ The VIN plate and/or homologation plate must be permanently displayed and legible.

Electrical equipment

☐ Switch on the ignition and check the operation of the horn.

☐ Check the windscreen washers and wipers, examining the wiper blades; renew damaged or perished blades. Also check the operation of the stop-lights.

☐ Check the operation of the sidelights and number plate lights. The lenses and reflectors must be secure, clean and undamaged.

☐ Check the operation and alignment of the headlights. The headlight reflectors must not be tarnished and the lenses must be undamaged.

☐ Switch on the ignition and check the operation of the direction indicators (including the instrument panel tell-tale) and the hazard warning lights. Operation of the sidelights and stop-lights must not affect the indicators - if it does, the cause is usually a bad earth at the rear light cluster. Indicators should flash at a rate of between 60 and 120 times per minute – faster or slower than this could indicate a fault with the flasher unit or a bad earth at one of the light units.

☐ Check the operation of the rear foglight(s), including the warning light on the instrument panel or in the switch.

☐ The warning lights must illuminate in accordance with the manufacturer's design. For most vehicles, the ABS and other warning lights should illuminate when the ignition is switched on, and (if the system is operating properly) extinguish after a few seconds. Refer to the owner's handbook.

Footbrake

☐ Examine the master cylinder, brake pipes and servo unit for leaks, loose mountings, corrosion or other damage. If ABS is fitted, this unit should also be examined for signs of leaks or corrosion.

☐ The fluid reservoir must be secure and the fluid level must be between the upper (A) and lower (B) markings.

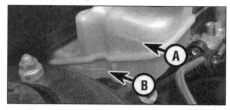

☐ Inspect both front brake flexible hoses for cracks or deterioration of the rubber. Turn the steering from lock to lock, and ensure that the hoses do not contact the wheel, tyre, or any part of the steering or suspension mechanism. With the brake pedal firmly depressed, check the hoses for bulges or leaks under pressure.

Steering and suspension

☐ Have your assistant turn the steering wheel from side to side slightly, up to the point where the steering gear just begins to transmit this movement to the roadwheels. Check for excessive free play between the steering wheel and the steering gear, indicating wear or insecurity of the steering column joints, the column-to-steering gear coupling, or the steering gear itself.

☐ Have your assistant turn the steering wheel more vigorously in each direction, so that the roadwheels just begin to turn. As this is done, examine all the steering joints, linkages, fittings and attachments. Renew any component that shows signs of wear or damage. On vehicles with power steering, check the security and condition of the steering pump, drivebelt and hoses.

☐ Check that the vehicle is standing level, and at approximately the correct ride height.

Shock absorbers

☐ Depress each corner of the vehicle in turn, then release it. The vehicle should rise and then settle in its normal position. If the vehicle continues to rise and fall, the shock absorber is defective. A shock absorber which has seized will also cause the vehicle to fail.

Exhaust system

☐ Start the engine. With your assistant holding a rag over the tailpipe, check the entire system for leaks. Repair or renew leaking sections.

3 Checks carried out **WITH THE VEHICLE RAISED AND THE WHEELS FREE TO TURN**

Jack up the front and rear of the vehicle, and securely support it on axle stands. Position the stands clear of the suspension assemblies. Ensure that the wheels are clear of the ground and that the steering can be turned from lock to lock.

Steering mechanism

☐ Have your assistant turn the steering from lock to lock. Check that the steering turns smoothly, and that no part of the steering mechanism, including a wheel or tyre, fouls any brake hose or pipe or any part of the body structure.
☐ Examine the steering rack rubber gaiters for damage or insecurity of the retaining clips. If power steering is fitted, check for signs of damage or leakage of the fluid hoses, pipes or connections. Also check for excessive stiffness or binding of the steering, a missing split pin or locking device, or severe corrosion of the body structure within 30 cm of any steering component attachment point.

Front and rear suspension and wheel bearings

☐ Starting at the front right-hand side, grasp the roadwheel at the 3 o'clock and 9 o'clock positions and rock gently but firmly. Check for free play or insecurity at the wheel bearings, suspension balljoints, or suspension mount-ings, pivots and attachments.
☐ Now grasp the wheel at the 12 o'clock and 6 o'clock positions and repeat the previous inspection. Spin the wheel, and check for roughness or tightness of the front wheel bearing.

☐ If excess free play is suspected at a component pivot point, this can be confirmed by using a large screwdriver or similar tool and levering between the mounting and the component attachment. This will confirm whether the wear is in the pivot bush, its retaining bolt, or in the mounting itself (the bolt holes can often become elongated).

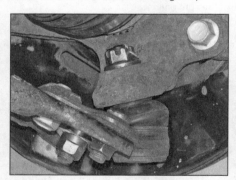

☐ Carry out all the above checks at the other front wheel, and then at both rear wheels.

Springs and shock absorbers

☐ Examine the suspension struts (when applicable) for serious fluid leakage, corrosion, or damage to the casing. Also check the security of the mounting points.
☐ If coil springs are fitted, check that the spring ends locate in their seats, and that the spring is not corroded, cracked or broken.
☐ If leaf springs are fitted, check that all leaves are intact, that the axle is securely attached to each spring, and that there is no deterioration of the spring eye mountings, bushes, and shackles.

☐ The same general checks apply to vehicles fitted with other suspension types, such as torsion bars, hydraulic displacer units, etc. Ensure that all mountings and attachments are secure, that there are no signs of excessive wear, corrosion or damage, and (on hydraulic types) that there are no fluid leaks or damaged pipes.
☐ Inspect the shock absorbers for signs of serious fluid leakage. Check for wear of the mounting bushes or attachments, or damage to the body of the unit.

Driveshafts (fwd vehicles only)

☐ Rotate each front wheel in turn and inspect the constant velocity joint gaiters for splits or damage. Also check that each driveshaft is straight and undamaged.

Braking system

☐ If possible without dismantling, check brake pad wear and disc condition. Ensure that the friction lining material has not worn excessively, (A) and that the discs are not fractured, pitted, scored or badly worn (B).

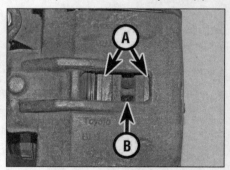

☐ Examine all the rigid brake pipes underneath the vehicle, and the flexible hose(s) at the rear. Look for corrosion, chafing or insecurity of the pipes, and for signs of bulging under pressure, chafing, splits or deterioration of the flexible hoses.
☐ Look for signs of fluid leaks at the brake calipers or on the brake backplates. Repair or renew leaking components.
☐ Slowly spin each wheel, while your assistant depresses and releases the footbrake. Ensure that each brake is operating and does not bind when the pedal is released.

Examine the handbrake mechanism, checking for frayed or broken cables, excessive corrosion, or wear or insecurity of the linkage. Check that the mechanism works on each relevant wheel, and releases fully, without binding.

It is not possible to test brake efficiency without special equipment, but a road test can be carried out later to check that the vehicle pulls up in a straight line.

Fuel and exhaust systems

Inspect the fuel tank (including the filler cap), fuel pipes, hoses and unions. All components must be secure and free from leaks. Locking fuel caps must lock securely and the key must be provided for the MOT test.

Examine the exhaust system over its entire length, checking for any damaged, broken or missing mountings, security of the retaining clamps and rust or corrosion.

Wheels and tyres

Examine the sidewalls and tread area of each tyre in turn. Check for cuts, tears, lumps, bulges, separation of the tread, and exposure of the ply or cord due to wear or damage. Check that the tyre bead is correctly seated on the wheel rim, that the valve is sound and properly seated, and that the wheel is not distorted or damaged.

Check that the tyres are of the correct size for the vehicle, that they are of the same size and type on each axle, and that the pressures are correct.

Check the tyre tread depth. The legal minimum at the time of writing is 1.6 mm over the central three-quarters of the tread width. Abnormal tread wear may indicate incorrect front wheel alignment or wear in steering or suspension components.

If the spare wheel is fitted externally or in a separate carrier beneath the vehicle, check that mountings are secure and free of excessive corrosion.

Body corrosion

Check the condition of the entire vehicle structure for signs of corrosion in load-bearing areas. (These include chassis box sections, side sills, cross-members, pillars, and all suspension, steering, braking system and seat belt mountings and anchorages.) Any corrosion which has seriously reduced the thickness of a load-bearing area (or is within 30 cm of safety-related components such as steering or suspension) is likely to cause the vehicle to fail. In this case professional repairs are likely to be needed.

Damage or corrosion which causes sharp or otherwise dangerous edges to be exposed will also cause the vehicle to fail.

Towbars

Check the condition of mounting points (both beneath the vehicle and within boot/hatchback areas) for signs of corrosion, ensuring that all fixings are secure and not worn or damaged. There must be no excessive play in detachable tow ball arms or quick-release mechanisms.

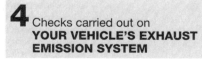

4 Checks carried out on YOUR VEHICLE'S EXHAUST EMISSION SYSTEM

Petrol models

The engine should be warmed up, and running well (ignition system in good order, air filter element clean, etc).

Before testing, run the engine at around 2500 rpm for 20 seconds. Let the engine drop to idle, and watch for smoke from the exhaust. If the idle speed is too high, or if dense blue or black smoke emerges for more than 5 seconds, the vehicle will fail. Typically, blue smoke signifies oil burning (engine wear);

black smoke means unburnt fuel (dirty air cleaner element, or other fuel system fault).

An exhaust gas analyser for measuring carbon monoxide (CO) and hydrocarbons (HC) is now needed. If one cannot be hired or borrowed, have a local garage perform the check.

CO emissions (mixture)

The MOT tester has access to the CO limits for all vehicles. The CO level is measured at idle speed, and at 'fast idle' (2500 to 3000 rpm). The following limits are given as a general guide:

At idle speed – Less than 0.5% CO
At 'fast idle' – Less than 0.3% CO
Lambda reading – 0.97 to 1.03

If the CO level is too high, this may point to poor maintenance, a fuel injection system problem, faulty lambda (oxygen) sensor or catalytic converter. Try an injector cleaning treatment, and check the vehicle's ECU for fault codes.

HC emissions

The MOT tester has access to HC limits for all vehicles. The HC level is measured at 'fast idle' (2500 to 3000 rpm). The following limits are given as a general guide:

At 'fast idle' – Less then 200 ppm

Excessive HC emissions are typically caused by oil being burnt (worn engine), or by a blocked crankcase ventilation system ('breather'). If the engine oil is old and thin, an oil change may help. If the engine is running badly, check the vehicle's ECU for fault codes.

Diesel models

The only emission test for diesel engines is measuring exhaust smoke density, using a calibrated smoke meter. The test involves accelerating the engine at least 3 times to its maximum unloaded speed.

Note: *On engines with a timing belt, it is VITAL that the belt is in good condition before the test is carried out.*

With the engine warmed up, it is first purged by running at around 2500 rpm for 20 seconds. A governor check is then carried out, by slowly accelerating the engine to its maximum speed. After this, the smoke meter is connected, and the engine is accelerated quickly to maximum speed three times. If the smoke density is less than the limits given below, the vehicle will pass:

Non-turbo vehicles: 2.5m-1
Turbocharged vehicles: 3.0m-1

If excess smoke is produced, try fitting a new air cleaner element, or using an injector cleaning treatment. If the engine is running badly, where applicable, check the vehicle's ECU for fault codes. Also check the vehicle's EGR system, where applicable. At high mileages, the injectors may require professional attention.

Engine

- ☐ Engine fails to rotate when attempting to start
- ☐ Engine rotates, but will not start
- ☐ Engine difficult to start when cold
- ☐ Engine difficult to start when hot
- ☐ Starter motor noisy or excessively rough in engagement
- ☐ Engine starts, but stops immediately
- ☐ Engine idles erratically
- ☐ Engine misfires at idle speed
- ☐ Engine misfires throughout the driving speed range
- ☐ Engine lacks power
- ☐ Engine backfires
- ☐ Oil pressure warning light illuminated with engine running
- ☐ Engine runs-on after switching off
- ☐ Whistling or wheezing noises
- ☐ Tapping or rattling noises
- ☐ Knocking or thumping noises

Cooling system

- ☐ Overheating
- ☐ Overcooling
- ☐ External coolant leakage
- ☐ Internal coolant leakage
- ☐ Corrosion

Fuel and exhaust systems

- ☐ Excessive fuel consumption
- ☐ Fuel leakage and/or fuel odour
- ☐ Excessive noise or fumes from the exhaust system

Clutch

- ☐ Pedal travels to the floor – no pressure or very little resistance
- ☐ Clutch fails to disengage (unable to select gears)
- ☐ Clutch slips (engine speed increases, with no increase in vehicle speed)
- ☐ Judder as clutch is engaged
- ☐ Noise when depressing or releasing clutch pedal

Manual transmission

- ☐ Noisy in neutral with the engine running
- ☐ Noisy in one particular gear
- ☐ Difficulty in engaging gears
- ☐ Jumps out of gear
- ☐ Vibration
- ☐ Lubricant leaks

Automatic transmission

- ☐ Fluid leakage
- ☐ General gear selection problems
- ☐ Engine will not start in any gear, or starts in gears other than Park or Neutral
- ☐ Transmission slips, shifts roughly, is noisy, or has no drive in forward or reverse gears

Transfer case

- ☐ Fluid leakage
- ☐ Noisy operation

Final drive

- ☐ Fluid leakage
- ☐ Noisy operation

Driveshafts/Propeller shaft

- ☐ Vibration when accelerating or decelerating
- ☐ Clicking or knocking noise on turns (at low speed on full lock)
- ☐ Knock or clunk when taking up drive
- ☐ Metallic grating sound, consistent with vehicle speed
- ☐ Vibration consistent with vehicle speed

Braking system

- ☐ Vehicle pull to one side under braking
- ☐ Noise (grinding or high-pitched squeal) when brakes applied
- ☐ Excessive brake pedal travel
- ☐ Brake pedal feels spongy when depressed
- ☐ Excessive brake pedal effort required to stop vehicle
- ☐ Judder felt through brake pedal or steering wheel when braking
- ☐ Pedal pulsates when braking hard
- ☐ Brakes binding

Steering and suspension

- ☐ Vehicle pulls to one side
- ☐ Wheel wobble and vibration
- ☐ Excessive pitching and/or rolling around corners, or during braking
- ☐ Wandering or general instablity
- ☐ Excessively stiff steering
- ☐ Excessive play in steering
- ☐ Lack of power assistance
- ☐ Tyre wear excessive

Electrical system

- ☐ Battery will not hold charge for more than a few days
- ☐ Ignition/no-charge warning light remains illuminated with the engine running
- ☐ Lights inoperative
- ☐ Fuel or temperature gauge inaccurate
- ☐ Horn operates continuously
- ☐ Horn inoperative
- ☐ Wipers fail to operate, or operate very slowly
- ☐ Wiper blades sweep over too large, or too small an area of glass
- ☐ Wiper blades fail to clean the glass effectively
- ☐ Screen or headlight washers inoperative, or unsatisfactory in operation
- ☐ Window glass moves only in one direction
- ☐ Window glass slow to move
- ☐ Window glass fails to move
- ☐ Central locking system inoperative, or unsatisfactory in operation.

Introduction

The vehicle owner who does his or her own maintenance according to the recommended service schedules should not have to use this section of the manual very often. Modern component reliability is such that, provided those items subject to wear or deterioration are inspected or renewed at the specified intervals, sudden failure is comparatively rare. Faults do not usually just happen as a result of sudden failure, but develop over a period of time. Major mechanical failures in particular are usually preceded by characteristic symptoms over hundreds or even thousands of miles. Those components which do occasionally fail without warning are often small and easily carried in the vehicle.

With any fault-finding, the first step is to decide where to begin investigations. Sometimes this is obvious, but on other occasions, a little detective work will be necessary. The owner who makes half a dozen haphazard adjustments or replacements may be successful in curing a fault (or its symptoms), but will be none the wiser if the fault recurs, and ultimately may have spent more time and money than was necessary.

A calm and logical approach will be found to be more satisfactory in the long run. Always take into account any warning signs or abnormalities that may have been noticed in the period preceding the fault – power loss, high or low gauge readings, unusual smells, etc – and remember that failure of components such as fuses or spark plugs may only be pointers to some underlying fault.

The pages which follow provide an easy-reference guide to the more common problems which may occur during the operation of the vehicle. These problems and their possible causes are grouped under headings denoting various components or systems, such as Engine, Cooling system, etc. The Chapter and/or Section which deals with the problem is also shown in brackets. Whatever the fault, certain basic principles apply. These are as follows:

Verify the fault. This is simply a matter of being sure that you know what the symptoms are before starting work. This is particularly important if you are investigating a fault for someone else, who may not have described it very accurately.

Don't overlook the obvious. For example, if the vehicle won't start, is there fuel in the tank? (Don't take anyone else's word on this particular point, and don't trust the fuel gauge either!) If an electrical fault is indicated, look for loose or broken wires before digging out the test gear.

Cure the disease, not the symptom. Substituting a flat battery with a fully-charged one will get you off the hard shoulder, but if the underlying cause is not attended to, the new battery will go the same way. Similarly, changing oil-fouled spark plugs for a new set will get you moving again, but remember that the reason for the fouling (if it wasn't simply an incorrect grade of plug) will have to be established and corrected.

Don't take anything for granted. Particularly, don't forget that a 'new' component may itself be defective (especially if it's been rattling around in the boot for months), and don't leave components out of a fault diagnosis sequence just because they are new or recently-fitted. When you do finally diagnose a difficult fault, you'll probably realise that all the evidence was there from the start.

Engine

Engine fails to rotate when attempting to start

☐ Battery terminal connections loose or corroded (see *"Weekly checks"*).
☐ Battery discharged or faulty (Chapter 5A Section 3).
☐ Broken, loose or disconnected wiring in the starting circuit (Chapter 5A Section 8).
☐ Defective starter solenoid or switch (Chapter 5A Section 8).
☐ Defective starter motor (Chapter 5A Section 10).
☐ Starter pinion or flywheel ring gear teeth loose or broken (Chapter 2A Section 14 and Chapter 5A Section 9).
☐ Engine earth strap broken or disconnected (Chapter 12 Section 2).

Engine rotates, but will not start

☐ Fuel tank empty.
☐ Battery discharged (engine rotates slowly) (Chapter 5A).
☐ Battery terminals loose or corroded (see *"Weekly checks"*).
☐ Pre-heating system faulty (Chapter 5B).
☐ Fuel injection system faulty (Chapter 4A Section 9).
☐ Air in the fuel system (Chapter 4A Section 6).
☐ Major mechanical failure (Chapter 2A).

Engine difficult to start when cold

☐ Battery discharged (Chapter 5A Section 3).
☐ Battery terminal connections loose or corroded (see *"Weekly checks"*).
☐ Pre-heating system faulty (Chapter 5B Section 2).
☐ Fuel injection system faulty (Chapter 4A Section 9).
☐ Low cylinder compressions (Chapter 2A Section 2).

Engine difficult to start when hot

☐ Air filter element dirty or clogged (Chapter 1 Section 24).
☐ Fuel injection system faulty (Chapter 4A Section 9).
☐ Low cylinder compressions (Chapter 2A Section 2).

Starter motor noisy or excessively rough in engagement

☐ Starter pinion or flywheel ring gear teeth loose or broken (Chapter 5A Section 8 and Chapter 2A Section 14).
☐ Starter motor mounting bolts loose or mission (Chapter 5A Section 9).
☐ Starter motor internal components worn or damaged (Chapter 5A Section 10).

Engine (continued)

Engine starts, but stops immediately

- ☐ Blocked injector/fuel injection system fault (Chapter 4A Section 9).
- ☐ Air in the fuel system (Chapter 4A Section 6).
- ☐ Immobiliser fault – refer to a Land Rover dealer or specialist.

Engine idles erratically

- ☐ Air filter element clogged (Chapter 1 Section 24).
- ☐ Uneven or low compressions (Chapter 2A Section 2).
- ☐ Camshaft lobes worn (Chapter 2A Section 7).
- ☐ Timing belt incorrectly fitted (Chapter 2A Section 6).
- ☐ Blocked injector/fuel injection system fault (Chapter 4A Section 9).

Engine misfires at idle speed

- ☐ Faulty injectors/fuel injection system fault (Chapter 4A Section 9).
- ☐ Uneven or low compressions (Chapter 2A Section 2).

Engine misfires throughout the driving speed range

- ☐ Fuel filter choked (Chapter 1 Section 25).
- ☐ Fuel tank vent blocked, or fuel pipes restricted (Chapter 4A).
- ☐ Fault injector/fuel injection system fault (Chapter 4A Section 9).
- ☐ Uneven or low compressions (Chapter 2A Section 2).

Engine lacks power

- ☐ Timing belt incorrectly fitted (Chapter 2A Section 6).
- ☐ Fuel filter choked (Chapter 1 Section 25).
- ☐ Air filter blocked (Chapter 1 Section 24).
- ☐ Uneven or low compressions (Chapter 2A Section 2).
- ☐ Faulty injectors/injection system fault (Chapter 4A Section 9).
- ☐ Brakes binding (Chapter 9).
- ☐ Clutch slipping (Chapter 6).
- ☐ Turbocharger fault (Chapter 4A Section 14)Turbocharger air ducts leaking.

Engine backfires

- ☐ Timing belt incorrectly fitted or tensioned (Chapter 2A Section 6).
- ☐ Blocked injector/fuel injection system fault (Chapter 4A Section 9).

Oil pressure warning light illuminated with engine running

- ☐ Low oil level, or incorrect oil grade (see *"Weekly checks"*).
- ☐ Faulty oil pressure sensor (Chapter 2A Section 16).
- ☐ Worn engine bearings and/or oil pump (Chapter 2B).
- ☐ High engine operating temperature (Chapter 3).
- ☐ Oil pressure relief valve defective (Chapter 2A Section 11).
- ☐ Oil pick up strainer clogged (Chapter 2A Section 9).

Engine runs-on after switching off

- ☐ Excessive carbon build-up in engine (Chapter 2B Section 7).
- ☐ High engine operating temperature (Chapter 3).
- ☐ Fuel injection system fault (Chapter 4A Section 9).
- ☐ Incorrect oil level (see *"Weekly checks"*).

Whistling or wheezing noises

- ☐ Leaking exhaust manifold or turbocharger gaskets (Chapter 4A).
- ☐ Leaking vacuum hose (Chapter 4A).
- ☐ Leaking air intake hose//intercooler ducts (Chapter 4A).

Tapping or rattling noises

- ☐ Worn valve gear or camshaft (Chapter 2A Section 7).
- ☐ Ancillary component fault (coolant pump, alternator etc.) (Chapter 3 and Chapter 5A).

Knocking or thumping noises

- ☐ Worn big-end bearings (regular heavy knocking, perhaps more under load) (Chapter 2B).
- ☐ Worn main bearings (rumbling and knocking, perhaps less under load) (Chapter 2B).
- ☐ Piston slap (bmost noticeable when cold) (Chapter 2B).
- ☐ Ancillary component fault (coolant pump, alternator, etc.) (Chapter 3 and Chapter 5A).

Cooling system

Overheating

☐ Insufficient coolant in the system (see "*Weekly checks*").
☐ Thermostat faulty (Chapter 3 Section 4).
☐ Radiator core blocked, or grille restricted (Chapter 3 Section 3).
☐ Electric cooling fan faulty (Chapter 3 Section 6).
☐ Air lock in cooling system (Chapter 1 Section 34).
☐ Expansion tank pressure cap faulty (Chapter 1 Section 34).
☐ Engine coolant temperature sensor faulty (Chapter 3 Section 7).

Overcooling

☐ Thermostat faulty (Chapter 3 Section 4).
☐ Engine coolant temperature sensor faulty (Chapter 3 Section 7).

External coolant leakage

☐ Deteriorated or damaged hoses or hose clips (Chapter 1 Section 8).

☐ Radiator core or heater matrix leaking (Chapter 3).
☐ Pressure cap faulty (Chapter 1 Section 34).
☐ Coolant pump leaking (Chapter 3 Section 5).
☐ Boiling due to overheating (Chapter 3).
☐ Core plug leaking (Chapter 2B Section 2).

Internal coolant leakage

☐ Leaking cylinder head gasket (Chapter 2A Section 8).
☐ Cracked cylinder head or cylinder block (Chapter 2B).

Corrosion

☐ Infrequent draining and flushing (Chapter 1 Section 34).
☐ Incorrect coolant mixture or inappropriate coolant type (Chapter 1 Section 34).

Fuel and exhaust systems

Excessive fuel consumption

☐ Air filter dirty or clogged (Chapter 4A).
☐ Faulty injector/fuel injection system fault (Chapter 4A).
☐ Brakes binding (Chapter 9).
☐ Tyres under-inflated (see "*Weekly checks*").

Fuel leakage and/or fuel odour

☐ Damaged or corroded fuel tank, pipes or connections (Chapter 1 Section 8).

Excessive noise or fumes from the exhaust system

☐ Leaking exhaust system or manifold leaks (Chapter 1 Section 15 and Chapter 4A Section 19).
☐ Leaking or corroded silencers or pipe (Chapter 1 Section 15).
☐ Broken mountings causing body or suspension contact (Chapter 1 Section 15).

Clutch

Pedal travels to the floor – no pressure or very little resistance

☐ Faulty master or slave cylinder (Chapter 6).
☐ Faulty hydraulic release system (Chapter 6 Section 5).
☐ Broken clutch release bearing (Chapter 6 Section 4).
☐ Broken diaphragm spring in clutch pressure plate (Chapter 6 Section 6).

Clutch fails to disengage (unable to select gears)

☐ Faulty master or slave cylinder (Chapter 6).
☐ Faulty hydraulic hose (Chapter 6).
☐ Clutch disc sticking on the gearbox input shaft splines (Chapter 6 Section 6).
☐ Clutch disc sticking on the flywheel or pressure plate (Chapter 6 Section 6).
☐ Faulty pressure plate assembly (Chapter 6 Section 6).

Clutch slips (engine speed increases, with no increase in vehicle speed)

☐ Faulty hydraulic release system (Chapter 6).

☐ Clutch disc linings excessively worn (Chapter 6 Section 6).
☐ Clutch disc lining contaminated with oil or grease (Chapter 6 Section 6).
☐ Faulty pressure plate or weak diaphragm spring (Chapter 6 Section 6).

Judder as clutch is engaged

☐ Clutch disc linings contaminated with oil or grease (Chapter 6 Section 6).
☐ Clutch disc linings excessively worn (Chapter 6 Section 6).
☐ Faulty or distorted pressure plate or diaphragm spring (Chapter 6 Section 6).
☐ Worn or loose engine or gearbox mountings (Chapter 2A Section 15).
☐ Clutch disc or gearbox input shaft splines worn (Chapter 6).

Noise when depressing or releasing clutch pedal

☐ Worn clutch release bearing (Chapter 6 Section 4).
☐ Worn or dry clutch pedal pivot (Chapter 6 Section 2).
☐ Faulty pressure plate assembly (Chapter 6 Section 6).
☐ Pressure plate diaphragm spring broken (Chapter 6 Section 6).

Manual transmission

Noisy in neutral with the engine running

☐ Input shaft bearings worn (noise apparent with clutch pedal released, but not when depressed) (Chapter 7A).

☐ *Clutch release bearings worn (noise apparent with clutch pedal depressed, possibly less when released (Chapter 6 Section 4).

Noisy in one particular gear

☐ Worn, damaged or chipped gear teeth (Chapter 7A).*

Difficulty in engaging gears

☐ Clutch faulty (Chapter 6).
☐ Clutch hydraulic hose faulty (Chapter 6).
☐ Worn or damaged gearchange cables (Chapter 7A Section 3).
☐ Worn synchroniser units (Chapter 7A).*

Jumps out of gear

☐ Worn or damaged gearchange cables (Chapter 7A Section 3).

☐ Worn synchroniser units (Chapter 7A).
☐ *Worn selector forks (Chapter 7A).*

Vibration

☐ Lack of oil (Chapter 1 Section 30).
☐ Worn bearings (Chapter 7A).*

Lubricant leaks

☐ Leaking oil seal (Chapter 7A Section 5).
☐ Leaking housing joint (Chapter 7A).
☐ *Leaking input shaft oil seal (Chapter 7A Section 5).

Note: *Although the corrective action necessary to remedy the symptoms described in beyond the scope of the home mechanic, then above information should be helpful in isolating the cause of the condition, so that the owner can communicate clearly with a professional mechanic.*

Automatic transmission

Fluid leakage

☐ Automatic transmission fluid is usually dark in colour. Fluid leaks should not be confused with engine oil, which can easily be blown onto the transmission by airflow. To determine the source of a leak, first remove all built-up dirt and grime from the transmission housing and surrounding areas using a degreasing agent, or by steam-cleaning. Drive the vehicle at low speed, so airflow will not blow the leak far from its source. Raise and support the vehicle, and determine where the leak is coming from.

General gear selection problems

☐ Chapter 7B deals with checking and adjusting the selector cable on automatic transmissions. The following are common problems which may be caused by a poorly-adjusted cable:
  a) Engine starting in gears other than Park or Neutral.
  b) Indicator panel indicating a gear other than the one actually being used.
  c) Vehicle moves in Park or Neutral.
  d) Poor shift quality or erratic gear changes.
☐ Refer to Chapter 7B Section 3 for the selector cable adjustment procedure.

Engine will not start in any gear, or starts in gears other than Park or Neutral

☐ Incorrect selector cable adjustment (Chapter 7B Section 3).
☐ Transmission control module problem (Chapter 7B Section 9).

Transmission slips, shifts roughly, is noisy, or has no drive in forward or reverse gears

☐ There are many probable causes for the above problems, but unless there is a very obvious reason (such as a loose or corroded wiring plug connection on or near the transmission), the car should be taken to a franchise dealer or specialist for the fault to be diagnosed. The transmission control module incorporates a self-diagnosis facility, and any fault codes can quickly be read and interpreted by a dealer or specialist with the proper diagnostic equipment.

Note: Due to the complexity of the automatic transmission, it is difficult for the home mechanic to properly diagnose and service this unit. For problems other then the following, the vehicle should be taken to a dealer service department or automatic transmission specialist. Do not be too hasty in removing the transmission if a fault is suspected, as most of the testing is carried out with the unit still fitted.

Transfer case

Fluid leakage

☐ Oil seal/O-ring leakage (Chapter 7C).

Noisy operation

☐ Low oil level (Chapter 7C Section 2).
☐ Worn bearings/gears (Chapter 7C).

Final drive

Fluid leakage

☐ Oil seal leaking (Chapter 8 Section 8).

Noisy operation

☐ Low oil level (Chapter 8 Section 7).
☐ Worn bearings/differential gears (Chapter 8).

Driveshafts/Propeller shaft

Vibration when accelerating or decelerating

☐ Worn inner constant velocity joint (Chapter 8 Section 4).
☐ Bent or distorted driveshaft (Chapter 8 Section 4).

Clicking or knocking noise on turns (at low speed on full lock)

☐ Worn outer constant velocity joint (Chapter 8 Section 4).
☐ Lock of constant velocity joint lubricant, possibly due to damaged gaiter (Chapter 8 Section 3).

Knock or clunk when taking up drive

☐ Worn propeller shaft universal joint bearings (Chapter 8 Section 5).
☐ Loose propeller shaft flange bolts (Chapter 8 Section 5).

Metallic grating sound, consistent with vehicle speed

☐ Severe wear in the propeller shaft universal joint bearings (Chapter 8 Section 5).
☐ Worn propeller shaft centre support bearing (Chapter 8 Section 5).

Vibration consistent with vehicle speed

☐ Propeller shaft out of balance (Chapter 8).
☐ Wheels out of balance.Propeller shaft or driveshaft joints worn (Chapter 8).

Braking system

Vehicle pull to one side under braking

☐ Worn, defective, damaged or contaminated brake pads on one side (Chapter 9).
☐ Seized or partially seized front or rear brake caliper (Chapter 9).
☐ A mixture of brake pad lining materials fitted between sides (Chapter 9).
☐ Brake caliper mounting bolts loose (Chapter 9).
☐ Worn or damaged steering or suspension components (Chapter 1 Section 13).

Noise (grinding or high-pitched squeal) when brakes applied

☐ Brake pad friction material worn down to metal backing (Chapter 1 Section 17).
☐ Excessive corrosion of brake disc – may be apparent after the vehicle has been standing for some time (Chapter 1 Section 17).
☐ Foreign object (stone chipping, etc.) trapped between the brake disc and shield (Chapter 1 Section 17).

Excessive brake pedal travel

☐ Faulty master cylinder (Chapter 9 Section 10).
☐ Air in hydraulic system (Chapter 9 Section 2).
☐ Faulty vacuum servo unit (Chapter 9 Section 13).
☐ Faulty vacuum pump (Chapter 9 Section 19).

Brake pedal feels spongy when depressed

☐ Air in hydraulic system (Chapter 9 Section 2).
☐ Deteriorated flexible rubber brake hoses (Chapter 1 Section 16).
☐ Master cylinder mountings loose (Chapter 9 Section 10).
☐ Faulty master cylinder (Chapter 9 Section 10).

Excessive brake pedal effort required to stop vehicle

☐ Faulty vacuum servo unit (Chapter 9 Section 13).
☐ Faulty servo unit check valve (Chapter 9 Section 12).
☐ Disconnected, damaged or insecure brake servo vacuum hose (Chapter 1 Section 8).
☐ Faulty vacuum pump (Chapter 9 Section 19).
☐ Faulty brake pipe or hose (Chapter 1 Section 16).
☐ Seized brake caliper (Chapter 9).
☐ Brake pads incorrectly fitted (Chapter 9 Section 4, 5).
☐ Incorrect grade of brake pads fitted (Chapter 9).
☐ Brake pads contaminated (Chapter 9).

Judder felt through brake pedal or steering wheel when braking

☐ Excessive run-out or distortion of brake disc (Chapter 9).
☐ Brake pad linings worn (Chapter 1 Section 17).
☐ Brake caliper mountings loose (Chapter 9).
☐ Wear in suspension or steering components or mountings (Chapter 1 Section 13).

Pedal pulsates when braking hard

☐ Normal feature of ABS – no fault.

Brakes binding

☐ Seized brake caliper (Chapter 9).
☐ Incorrectly adjusted handbrake (Chapter 9 Section 14).
☐ Faulty master cylinder (Chapter 9 Section 10).

Note: *Before assuming that a brake problem exists, make sure that the tyres are in good condition and correctly inflated, that the front wheel alignment is correct, and that the vehicle is not loaded with weight in an unequal manner. Apart from checking the condition of all pipe and hose connections, any faults occurring on the anti-lock braking system should be referred to a Land Rover dealer or specialist for diagnosis.*

Steering and suspension

Vehicle pulls to one side

☐ Defective tyre (see *"Weekly checks"*).
☐ Excessive wear in suspension or steering components (Chapter 1 Section 13).
☐ Incorrect front wheel alignment (Chapter 10 Section 25).
☐ Accident damage to steering or suspension components.

Wheel wobble and vibration

☐ Front roadwheels out of balance (vibration felt mainly through the steering wheel).
☐ Rear roadwheels out of balance (vibration felt mainly throughout the vehicle).
☐ Roadwheels damaged or distorted (Chapter 1 Section 13).
☐ Faulty or damaged tyre (see *"Weekly checks"*).
☐ Worn steering or suspension joints, bushes or components (Chapter 1 Section 13).
☐ Wheel nuts loose (Chapter 1 Section 13).

Excessive pitching and/or rolling around corners, or during braking

☐ Defective shock absorbers (Chapter 10).
☐ Broken or weak coil spring and/or suspension components (Chapter 1 Section 13).
☐ Worn or damaged anti-roll bar or mountings (Chapter 10).

Wandering or general instablity

☐ Incorrect wheel alignment (Chapter 10 Section 25).
☐ Worn steering or suspension components (Chapter 1 Section 13).
☐ Roadwheels out of balance.Faulty or damaged tyre (see *"Weekly checks"*).
☐ Wheel nuts loose (Chapter 1 Section 13).
☐ Defective shock absorbers (Chapter 10).

Excessively stiff steering

☐ Seized track rod end balljoint or suspension balljoint (Chapters 1 Section 13).
☐ Broken or incorrectly adjusted auxiliary drivebelt (Chapter 1 Section 6).
☐ Incorrect front wheel alignment (Chapter 10 Section 25).
☐ Steering gear damaged (Chapter 10).

Excessive play in steering

☐ Worn steering column universal joints (Chapter 10 Section 17).
☐ Worn steering track rod end balljoints (Chapter).
☐ Worn steering gear (Chapter 10 Section 19).
☐ Worn steering or suspension joints, bushes or components (Chapter 1 Section 13).

Lack of power assistance

☐ Broken or incorrectly adjusted auxiliary drivebelt (Chapter 1 Section 6).
☐ Incorrect power steering fluid level (see *"Weekly checks"*).
☐ Restriction in power steering hoses.Faulty power steering pump (Chapter 10 Section 23).
☐ Faulty steering gear (Chapter 10 Section 19).
☐ Air in hydraulic system (Chapter 10 Section 22).

Tyre wear excessive

☐ Tyres under inflated (wear on both edges) (see *"Weekly checks"*).
☐ Incorrect camber or castor angles (wear on one edge) (Chapter 10 Section 25).
☐ Worn steering or suspension joints, bushes or components (Chapter 1 Section 13).
☐ Accident damage.Incorrect wheel alignment (feathered edges) (Chapter 10 Section 25).
☐ Tyres over-inflated (worn in centre of tread) (see *"Weekly checks"*
☐ Worn shock absorbers (Chapter 10).
☐ Tyres/wheel out of balance (tyres worn unevenly).
☐ Tyre/wheel damage (see *"Weekly checks"*).

Electrical system

Battery will not hold charge for more than a few days

- [ ] Battery defective internally (Chapter 5A).
- [ ] Battery electrolyte level low (Chapter 5A Section 3).
- [ ] Battery terminal connections loose or corroded (see *"Weekly checks"*).
- [ ] Auxiliary drivebelt worn or incorrectly tensioned (Chapter 1 Section 6).
- [ ] Alternator not charging at correct output (Chapter 5A Section 5).
- [ ] Short circuit causing continual current drain (Chapter 12 Section 2).

Ignition/no-charge warning light remains illuminated with the engine running

- [ ] Auxiliary drivebelt broken, worn, or incorrectly adjusted (Chapter 1 Section 6).
- [ ] Internal fault in alternator or voltage regulator (Chapter 5A Section 7).
- [ ] Broken, disconnected, or loose wiring in charging circuit (Chapter 5A Section 2).

Lights inoperative

- [ ] Blown bulb (Chapter 12).
- [ ] Corrosion of bulbholder contacts (Chapter 12 Section 2).
- [ ] Blown fuse (Chapter 12 Section 3).
- [ ] Faulty relay (Chapter 12 Section 3).
- [ ] Broken, loose or disconnected wiring (Chapter 12 Section 2).
- [ ] Faulty switch (Chapter 12 Section 4).

Fuel or temperature gauge inaccurate

- [ ] Faulty fuel level sensor(s) (Chapter 4A Section 7).
- [ ] Faulty engine coolant temperature sensor (Chapter 3 Section 7).
- [ ] Faulty instrument cluster (Chapter 12 Section 9).

Horn operates continuously

- [ ] Horn contacts faulty (Chapter 12 Section 4).

Horn inoperative

- [ ] Horn switch contact faulty (Chapter 12 Section 4).
- [ ] Horn faulty (Chapter 12 Section 12).
- [ ] Fuse blown (Chapter 12 Section 3).

Wipers fail to operate, or operate very slowly

- [ ] Wiper blades stuck to screen, or seized linkage (Chapter 12 Section 14).
- [ ] Blown fuse (Chapter 12 Section 3).
- [ ] Faulty relay (Chapter 12 Section 3).
- [ ] Faulty wiper motor (Chapter 12 Section 14).

Wiper blades sweep over too large, or too small an area of glass

- [ ] Wiper arms incorrectly positioned on spindles (Chapter 12 Section 13).
- [ ] Excessive wear of wiper linkage (Chapter 12 Section 14).
- [ ] Wiper motor or linkage mountings loose (Chapter 12 Section 14).

Wiper blades fail to clean the glass effectively

- [ ] Wiper blade rubbers worn or perished (see *"Weekly checks"*).
- [ ] Wiper arms defective (Chapter 12 Section 13).
- [ ] Insufficient windscreen washer additive to adequately remove road film (see *"Weekly checks"*).

Screen or headlight washers inoperative, or unsatisfactory in operation

- [ ] Blocked washer jet (Chapter 12 Section 15).
- [ ] Disconnected, kinked or restricted fluid hose (Chapter 12 Section 15).
- [ ] Insufficient fluid in washer reservoir (see *"Weekly checks"*).
- [ ] Blown fuse (Chapter 12 Section 3).
- [ ] Faulty washer pump (Chapter 12 Section 15).
- [ ] Faulty switch (Chapter 12 Section 4).

Window glass moves only in one direction

- [ ] Faulty switch (Chapter 12 Section 4).

Window glass slow to move

- [ ] Regulator seized or damaged, or in need of lubrication (Chapter 11 Section 14).
- [ ] Door internal components or trim fouling regulator (Chapter 11 Section 14).
- [ ] Window guide rubber dirty or in need of lubrication (Silicone spray).
- [ ] Faulty motor (Chapter 11 Section 14).

Window glass fails to move

- [ ] Blown fuse (Chapter 12 Section 3).
- [ ] Faulty CJB (Chapter 12 Section 11).
- [ ] Broken or disconnected wiring or connections (Chapter 12 Section 2).
- [ ] Faulty motor (Chapter 11 Section 14).

Central locking system inoperative, or unsatisfactory in operation.

- [ ] Blown fuse (Chapter 12 Section 3).
- [ ] Faulty CJB (Chapter 12 Section 11).
- [ ] Broken or disconnected wiring or connectors (Chapter 12 Section 2).
- [ ] Faulty door/tailgate lock (Chapter 11 Section 13).
- [ ] Faulty relay (Chapter 12 Section 3).
- [ ] Broken or disconnected latch operating cables (Chapter 11 Section 11).

A

ABS (Anti-lock brake system) A system, usually electronically controlled, that senses incipient wheel lockup during braking and relieves hydraulic pressure at wheels that are about to skid.

Air bag An inflatable bag hidden in the steering wheel (driver's side) or the dash or glovebox (passenger side). In a head-on collision, the bags inflate, preventing the driver and front passenger from being thrown forward into the steering wheel or windscreen.

Air cleaner A metal or plastic housing, containing a filter element, which removes dust and dirt from the air being drawn into the engine.

Air filter element The actual filter in an air cleaner system, usually manufactured from pleated paper and requiring renewal at regular intervals.

Air filter

Allen key A hexagonal wrench which fits into a recessed hexagonal hole.

Alligator clip A long-nosed spring-loaded metal clip with meshing teeth. Used to make temporary electrical connections.

Alternator A component in the electrical system which converts mechanical energy from a drivebelt into electrical energy to charge the battery and to operate the starting system, ignition system and electrical accessories.

Ampere (amp) A unit of measurement for the flow of electric current. One amp is the amount of current produced by one volt acting through a resistance of one ohm.

Anaerobic sealer A substance used to prevent bolts and screws from loosening. Anaerobic means that it does not require oxygen for activation. The Loctite brand is widely used.

Antifreeze A substance (usually ethylene glycol) mixed with water, and added to a vehicle's cooling system, to prevent freezing of the coolant in winter. Antifreeze also contains chemicals to inhibit corrosion and the formation of rust and other deposits that would tend to clog the radiator and coolant passages and reduce cooling efficiency.

Anti-seize compound A coating that reduces the risk of seizing on fasteners that are subjected to high temperatures, such as exhaust manifold bolts and nuts.

Asbestos A natural fibrous mineral with great heat resistance, commonly used in the composition of brake friction materials. Asbestos is a health hazard and the dust created by brake systems should never be inhaled or ingested.

Axle A shaft on which a wheel revolves, or which revolves with a wheel. Also, a solid beam that connects the two wheels at one end of the vehicle. An axle which also transmits power to the wheels is known as a live axle.

Axleshaft A single rotating shaft, on either side of the differential, which delivers power from the final drive assembly to the drive wheels. Also called a driveshaft or a halfshaft.

B

Ball bearing An anti-friction bearing consisting of a hardened inner and outer race with hardened steel balls between two races.

Bearing The curved surface on a shaft or in a bore, or the part assembled into either, that permits relative motion between them with minimum wear and friction.

Bearing

Big-end bearing The bearing in the end of the connecting rod that's attached to the crankshaft.

Bleed nipple A valve on a brake wheel cylinder, caliper or other hydraulic component that is opened to purge the hydraulic system of air. Also called a bleed screw.

Brake bleeding Procedure for removing air from lines of a hydraulic brake system.

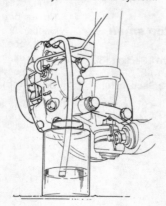

Brake bleeding

Brake disc The component of a disc brake that rotates with the wheels.

Brake drum The component of a drum brake that rotates with the wheels.

Brake linings The friction material which contacts the brake disc or drum to retard the vehicle's speed. The linings are bonded or riveted to the brake pads or shoes.

Brake pads The replaceable friction pads that pinch the brake disc when the brakes are applied. Brake pads consist of a friction material bonded or riveted to a rigid backing plate.

Brake shoe The crescent-shaped carrier to which the brake linings are mounted and which forces the lining against the rotating drum during braking.

Braking systems For more information on braking systems, consult the Haynes Automotive Brake Manual.

Breaker bar A long socket wrench handle providing greater leverage.

Bulkhead The insulated partition between the engine and the passenger compartment.

C

Caliper The non-rotating part of a disc-brake assembly that straddles the disc and carries the brake pads. The caliper also contains the hydraulic components that cause the pads to pinch the disc when the brakes are applied. A caliper is also a measuring tool that can be set to measure inside or outside dimensions of an object.

Camshaft A rotating shaft on which a series of cam lobes operate the valve mechanisms. The camshaft may be driven by gears, by sprockets and chain or by sprockets and a belt.

Canister A container in an evaporative emission control system; contains activated charcoal granules to trap vapours from the fuel system.

Canister

Carburettor A device which mixes fuel with air in the proper proportions to provide a desired power output from a spark ignition internal combustion engine.

Castellated Resembling the parapets along the top of a castle wall. For example, a castellated balljoint stud nut.

Castor In wheel alignment, the backward or forward tilt of the steering axis. Castor is positive when the steering axis is inclined rearward at the top.

Catalytic converter A silencer-like device in the exhaust system which converts certain pollutants in the exhaust gases into less harmful substances.

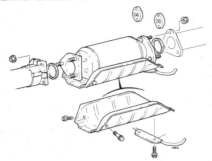

Catalytic converter

Circlip A ring-shaped clip used to prevent endwise movement of cylindrical parts and shafts. An internal circlip is installed in a groove in a housing; an external circlip fits into a groove on the outside of a cylindrical piece such as a shaft.

Clearance The amount of space between two parts. For example, between a piston and a cylinder, between a bearing and a journal, etc.

Coil spring A spiral of elastic steel found in various sizes throughout a vehicle, for example as a springing medium in the suspension and in the valve train.

Compression Reduction in volume, and increase in pressure and temperature, of a gas, caused by squeezing it into a smaller space.

Compression ratio The relationship between cylinder volume when the piston is at top dead centre and cylinder volume when the piston is at bottom dead centre.

Constant velocity (CV) joint A type of universal joint that cancels out vibrations caused by driving power being transmitted through an angle.

Core plug A disc or cup-shaped metal device inserted in a hole in a casting through which core was removed when the casting was formed. Also known as a freeze plug or expansion plug.

Crankcase The lower part of the engine block in which the crankshaft rotates.

Crankshaft The main rotating member, or shaft, running the length of the crankcase, with offset "throws" to which the connecting rods are attached.

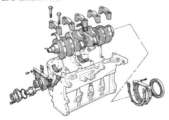

Crankshaft assembly

Crocodile clip See Alligator clip

D

Diagnostic code Code numbers obtained by accessing the diagnostic mode of an engine management computer. This code can be used to determine the area in the system where a malfunction may be located.

Disc brake A brake design incorporating a rotating disc onto which brake pads are squeezed. The resulting friction converts the energy of a moving vehicle into heat.

Double-overhead cam (DOHC) An engine that uses two overhead camshafts, usually one for the intake valves and one for the exhaust valves.

Drivebelt(s) The belt(s) used to drive accessories such as the alternator, water pump, power steering pump, air conditioning compressor, etc. off the crankshaft pulley.

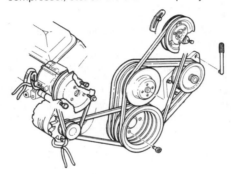

Accessory drivebelts

Driveshaft Any shaft used to transmit motion. Commonly used when referring to the axleshafts on a front wheel drive vehicle.

Drum brake A type of brake using a drum-shaped metal cylinder attached to the inner surface of the wheel. When the brake pedal is pressed, curved brake shoes with friction linings press against the inside of the drum to slow or stop the vehicle.

E

EGR valve A valve used to introduce exhaust gases into the intake air stream.

Electronic control unit (ECU) A computer which controls (for instance) ignition and fuel injection systems, or an anti-lock braking system. For more information refer to the Haynes Automotive Electrical and Electronic Systems Manual.

Electronic Fuel Injection (EFI) A computer controlled fuel system that distributes fuel through an injector located in each intake port of the engine.

Emergency brake A braking system, independent of the main hydraulic system, that can be used to slow or stop the vehicle if the primary brakes fail, or to hold the vehicle stationary even though the brake pedal isn't depressed. It usually consists of a hand lever that actuates either front or rear brakes mechanically through a series of cables and linkages. Also known as a handbrake or parking brake.

Endfloat The amount of lengthwise movement between two parts. As applied to a crankshaft, the distance that the crankshaft can move forward and back in the cylinder block.

Engine management system (EMS) A computer controlled system which manages the fuel injection and the ignition systems in an integrated fashion.

Exhaust manifold A part with several passages through which exhaust gases leave the engine combustion chambers and enter the exhaust pipe.

F

Fan clutch A viscous (fluid) drive coupling device which permits variable engine fan speeds in relation to engine speeds.

Feeler blade A thin strip or blade of hardened steel, ground to an exact thickness, used to check or measure clearances between parts.

Feeler blade

Firing order The order in which the engine cylinders fire, or deliver their power strokes, beginning with the number one cylinder.

Flywheel A heavy spinning wheel in which energy is absorbed and stored by means of momentum. On cars, the flywheel is attached to the crankshaft to smooth out firing impulses.

Free play The amount of travel before any action takes place. The "looseness" in a linkage, or an assembly of parts, between the initial application of force and actual movement. For example, the distance the brake pedal moves before the pistons in the master cylinder are actuated.

Fuse An electrical device which protects a circuit against accidental overload. The typical fuse contains a soft piece of metal which is calibrated to melt at a predetermined current flow (expressed as amps) and break the circuit.

Fusible link A circuit protection device consisting of a conductor surrounded by heat-resistant insulation. The conductor is smaller than the wire it protects, so it acts as the weakest link in the circuit. Unlike a blown fuse, a failed fusible link must frequently be cut from the wire for replacement.

G

Gap The distance the spark must travel in jumping from the centre electrode to the side electrode in a spark plug. Also refers to the spacing between the points in a contact breaker assembly in a conventional points-type ignition, or to the distance between the reluctor or rotor and the pickup coil in an electronic ignition.

Adjusting spark plug gap

Gasket Any thin, soft material - usually cork, cardboard, asbestos or soft metal - installed between two metal surfaces to ensure a good seal. For instance, the cylinder head gasket seals the joint between the block and the cylinder head.

Gasket

Gauge An instrument panel display used to monitor engine conditions. A gauge with a movable pointer on a dial or a fixed scale is an analogue gauge. A gauge with a numerical readout is called a digital gauge.

H

Halfshaft A rotating shaft that transmits power from the final drive unit to a drive wheel, usually when referring to a live rear axle.

Harmonic balancer A device designed to reduce torsion or twisting vibration in the crankshaft. May be incorporated in the crankshaft pulley. Also known as a vibration damper.

Hone An abrasive tool for correcting small irregularities or differences in diameter in an engine cylinder, brake cylinder, etc.

Hydraulic tappet A tappet that utilises hydraulic pressure from the engine's lubrication system to maintain zero clearance (constant contact with both camshaft and valve stem). Automatically adjusts to variation in valve stem length. Hydraulic tappets also reduce valve noise.

I

Ignition timing The moment at which the spark plug fires, usually expressed in the number of crankshaft degrees before the piston reaches the top of its stroke.

Inlet manifold A tube or housing with passages through which flows the air-fuel mixture (carburettor vehicles and vehicles with throttle body injection) or air only (port fuel-injected vehicles) to the port openings in the cylinder head.

J

Jump start Starting the engine of a vehicle with a discharged or weak battery by attaching jump leads from the weak battery to a charged or helper battery.

L

Load Sensing Proportioning Valve (LSPV) A brake hydraulic system control valve that works like a proportioning valve, but also takes into consideration the amount of weight carried by the rear axle.

Locknut A nut used to lock an adjustment nut, or other threaded component, in place. For example, a locknut is employed to keep the adjusting nut on the rocker arm in position.

Lockwasher A form of washer designed to prevent an attaching nut from working loose.

M

MacPherson strut A type of front suspension system devised by Earle MacPherson at Ford of England. In its original form, a simple lateral link with the anti-roll bar creates the lower control arm. A long strut - an integral coil spring and shock absorber - is mounted between the body and the steering knuckle. Many modern so-called MacPherson strut systems use a conventional lower A-arm and don't rely on the anti-roll bar for location.

Multimeter An electrical test instrument with the capability to measure voltage, current and resistance.

N

NOx Oxides of Nitrogen. A common toxic pollutant emitted by petrol and diesel engines at higher temperatures.

O

Ohm The unit of electrical resistance. One volt applied to a resistance of one ohm will produce a current of one amp.

Ohmmeter An instrument for measuring electrical resistance.

O-ring A type of sealing ring made of a special rubber-like material; in use, the O-ring is compressed into a groove to provide the sealing action.

Overhead cam (ohc) engine An engine with the camshaft(s) located on top of the cylinder head(s).

Overhead valve (ohv) engine An engine with the valves located in the cylinder head, but with the camshaft located in the engine block.

Oxygen sensor A device installed in the engine exhaust manifold, which senses the oxygen content in the exhaust and converts this information into an electric current. Also called a Lambda sensor.

P

Phillips screw A type of screw head having a cross instead of a slot for a corresponding type of screwdriver.

Plastigage A thin strip of plastic thread, available in different sizes, used for measuring clearances. For example, a strip of Plastigage is laid across a bearing journal. The parts are assembled and dismantled; the width of the crushed strip indicates the clearance between journal and bearing.

Plastigage

Propeller shaft The long hollow tube with universal joints at both ends that carries power from the transmission to the differential on front-engined rear wheel drive vehicles.

Proportioning valve A hydraulic control valve which limits the amount of pressure to the rear brakes during panic stops to prevent wheel lock-up.

R

Rack-and-pinion steering A steering system with a pinion gear on the end of the steering shaft that mates with a rack (think of a geared wheel opened up and laid flat). When the steering wheel is turned, the pinion turns, moving the rack to the left or right. This movement is transmitted through the track rods to the steering arms at the wheels.

Radiator A liquid-to-air heat transfer device designed to reduce the temperature of the coolant in an internal combustion engine cooling system.

Refrigerant Any substance used as a heat transfer agent in an air-conditioning system. R-12 has been the principle refrigerant for many years; recently, however, manufacturers have begun using R-134a, a non-CFC substance that is considered less harmful to the ozone in the upper atmosphere.

Rocker arm A lever arm that rocks on a shaft or pivots on a stud. In an overhead valve engine, the rocker arm converts the upward movement of the pushrod into a downward movement to open a valve.

Glossary of technical terms REF•27

Rotor In a distributor, the rotating device inside the cap that connects the centre electrode and the outer terminals as it turns, distributing the high voltage from the coil secondary winding to the proper spark plug. Also, that part of an alternator which rotates inside the stator. Also, the rotating assembly of a turbocharger, including the compressor wheel, shaft and turbine wheel.

Runout The amount of wobble (in-and-out movement) of a gear or wheel as it's rotated. The amount a shaft rotates "out-of-true." The out-of-round condition of a rotating part.

S

Sealant A liquid or paste used to prevent leakage at a joint. Sometimes used in conjunction with a gasket.

Sealed beam lamp An older headlight design which integrates the reflector, lens and filaments into a hermetically-sealed one-piece unit. When a filament burns out or the lens cracks, the entire unit is simply replaced.

Serpentine drivebelt A single, long, wide accessory drivebelt that's used on some newer vehicles to drive all the accessories, instead of a series of smaller, shorter belts. Serpentine drivebelts are usually tensioned by an automatic tensioner.

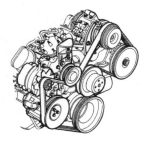

Serpentine drivebelt

Shim Thin spacer, commonly used to adjust the clearance or relative positions between two parts. For example, shims inserted into or under bucket tappets control valve clearances. Clearance is adjusted by changing the thickness of the shim.

Slide hammer A special puller that screws into or hooks onto a component such as a shaft or bearing; a heavy sliding handle on the shaft bottoms against the end of the shaft to knock the component free.

Sprocket A tooth or projection on the periphery of a wheel, shaped to engage with a chain or drivebelt. Commonly used to refer to the sprocket wheel itself.

Starter inhibitor switch On vehicles with an automatic transmission, a switch that prevents starting if the vehicle is not in Neutral or Park.

Strut See MacPherson strut.

T

Tappet A cylindrical component which transmits motion from the cam to the valve stem, either directly or via a pushrod and rocker arm. Also called a cam follower.

Thermostat A heat-controlled valve that regulates the flow of coolant between the cylinder block and the radiator, so maintaining optimum engine operating temperature. A thermostat is also used in some air cleaners in which the temperature is regulated.

Thrust bearing The bearing in the clutch assembly that is moved in to the release levers by clutch pedal action to disengage the clutch. Also referred to as a release bearing.

Timing belt A toothed belt which drives the camshaft. Serious engine damage may result if it breaks in service.

Timing chain A chain which drives the camshaft.

Toe-in The amount the front wheels are closer together at the front than at the rear. On rear wheel drive vehicles, a slight amount of toe-in is usually specified to keep the front wheels running parallel on the road by offsetting other forces that tend to spread the wheels apart.

Toe-out The amount the front wheels are closer together at the rear than at the front. On front wheel drive vehicles, a slight amount of toe-out is usually specified.

Tools For full information on choosing and using tools, refer to the Haynes Automotive Tools Manual.

Tracer A stripe of a second colour applied to a wire insulator to distinguish that wire from another one with the same colour insulator.

Tune-up A process of accurate and careful adjustments and parts replacement to obtain the best possible engine performance.

Turbocharger A centrifugal device, driven by exhaust gases, that pressurises the intake air. Normally used to increase the power output from a given engine displacement, but can also be used primarily to reduce exhaust emissions (as on VW's "Umwelt" Diesel engine).

U

Universal joint or U-joint A double-pivoted connection for transmitting power from a driving to a driven shaft through an angle. A U-joint consists of two Y-shaped yokes and a cross-shaped member called the spider.

V

Valve A device through which the flow of liquid, gas, vacuum, or loose material in bulk may be started, stopped, or regulated by a movable part that opens, shuts, or partially obstructs one or more ports or passageways. A valve is also the movable part of such a device.

Valve clearance The clearance between the valve tip (the end of the valve stem) and the rocker arm or tappet. The valve clearance is measured when the valve is closed.

Vernier caliper A precision measuring instrument that measures inside and outside dimensions. Not quite as accurate as a micrometer, but more convenient.

Viscosity The thickness of a liquid or its resistance to flow.

Volt A unit for expressing electrical "pressure" in a circuit. One volt that will produce a current of one ampere through a resistance of one ohm.

W

Welding Various processes used to join metal items by heating the areas to be joined to a molten state and fusing them together. For more information refer to the Haynes Automotive Welding Manual.

Wiring diagram A drawing portraying the components and wires in a vehicle's electrical system, using standardised symbols. For more information refer to the Haynes Automotive Electrical and Electronic Systems Manual.

Note: *References throughout this index are in the form "Chapter number" • "Page number". So, for example, 2C•15 refers to page 15 of Chapter 2C.*

Note: *References throughout this index are in the form "Chapter number" • "Page number". So, for example, 2C•15 refers to page 15 of Chapter 2C.*

Note: *References throughout this index are in the form "Chapter number" • "Page number". So, for example, 2C•15 refers to page 15 of Chapter 2C.*